TESTBANK

FOR

Cole & Cole's

The Development of Children

Third Edition

MELVYN B. KING

State University of New York at Cortland

DEBRA E. CLARK

W. H. Freeman and Company
New York

ISBN: 0-7167-2796-X

Printed in the United States of America

First printing 1997, RRD

Contents

The Study of Human Development

Multiple-Choice Questions

1.   By studying the Wild Boy of Aveyron, Itard hoped to learn something about the
     a.   behavior of the mentally ill
     b.   causes of mental retardation
     c.   behavior of animals in their natural habitats
     d.   role of the environment in shaping development
Answer: d, Reference: Chapter 1, P. 2, Difficulty: E

2.   The Wild Boy of Aveyron
     a.   eventually learned to speak fluent French
     b.   displayed strong sexual and aggressive instincts
     c.   learned to communicate simple needs, but never mastered speech
     d.   never progressed beyond walking on all fours and making animal-like sounds
Answer: c, Reference: Chapter 1, P. 3, Difficulty: M

3.   Itard's work with the Wild Boy of Aveyron demonstrated that
     a.   science could be applied to human behavior
     b.   human behavior is largely biologically determined
     c.   science and politics should remain separate domains
     d.   not much could be done to improve the lot of retarded children
Answer: a, Reference: Chapter 1, P. 3, Difficulty: E

4.   Itard's work with the Wild Boy of Aveyron demonstrated that
       a.   "nature" is more powerful than "nurture"
       b.   proper training can overcome even extreme early deprivation
       c.   children like Victor were more the responsibility of society than scientists
       d.   scientific research on human behavior can bear on philosophical questions
Answer: d, Reference: Chapter 1, P. 3, Difficulty: E

5.   The work of Itard with the Wild Boy of Aveyron
       a.   predated scientific interest in children
       b.   definitively determined that Victor had been mentally deficient
       c.   lacked diagnostic methods needed to measure mental and linguistic abilities
       d.   failed to show that science can provide practical suggestions about raising
              children
Answer: a, Reference: Chapter 1, P. 3, Difficulty: D

6.   The industrial revolution resulted in
       a.   more children living on farms in rural areas
       b.   children being put to work in mines and factories
       c.   a marked improvement in housing for most families
       d.   children having more time to play and study
Answer: b, Reference: Chapter 1, P 4, Difficulty: E

7.   Why did the publication of Darwin's *The Origin of Species* stimulate interest in
       development?
       a.   people hoped to influence the direction of future human evolution
       b.   Darwin pointed out that humans have little in common with other animals
       c.   people came to view children as imperfect adults who, without intervention
              would behave like lower animals
       d.   people thought that in studying children, they would see how human beings
              might have evolved from lower animals
Answer: d, Reference: Chapter 1, P. 5, Difficulty: M

8.   The individual who founded the Child-Study Association was
       a.   Jerome Kagan
       b.   Albert Bandura
       c.   G. Stanley Hall
       d.   Charles Darwin
Answer: c, Reference: Chapter 1, P. 6, Difficulty: E

9.   The two goals of the U.S. Children's Bureau were to
    a.   provide a universal education for children and to support the scientific study of child behavior
    b.   monitor working conditions of children and to spread information about child-rearing practices
    c.   develop child care programs for working mothers and to establish a research institute for the study of child development
    d.   articulate the philosophical views on child development and to identify ways of determining the relative effects of nature and nurture on development
Answer: b, Reference: Chapter 1, P. 6, Difficulty: M

10.   Human development can be defined as
    a.   a psychological rather than a physical process
    b.   the preprogrammed unfolding of the body's genetic blueprint
    c.   the growth process that commences at birth and continues until adulthood
    d.   a sequence of changes that begins at conception and continues throughout life
Answer: d, Reference: Chapter 1, P. 6, Difficulty: M

11.   Which of the following statements regarding developmental psychologists is true?
    a.   They are active in applying their knowledge to promote healthy development
    b.   They assess developmental status but do not prescribe measures for assisting those in trouble
    c.   They have accumulated little knowledge about the behavior of human beings in the last century
    d.   They have made little or no effort to explain the developmental processes underpinning age-related changes
Answer: a, Reference: Chapter 1, P. 6, Difficulty: M

12.   Phylogeny is studied in order to answer questions about
    a.   how individual human beings develop
    b.   whether there are critical periods in development
    c.   how humans are similar to and different from other animals
    d.   whether the development of children is stage-like or continuous
Answer: c, Reference: Chapter 1, P. 8, Difficulty: D

13.   The evolutionary history of a species is called
    a.   genesis
    b.   ontogeny
    c.   continuity
    d.   phylogeny
Answer: d, Reference: Chapter 1, P. 8, Difficulty: M

14.   Phylogeny refers to
    a.   a stage of development
    b.   the evolutionary history of a species
    c.   the course of development during an individual's lifetime
    d.   the use of language to represent objects and ideas
Answer: b, Reference: Chapter 1, P. 8, Difficulty: M

15.   Darwin, unlike some contemporary evolutionary theorists, believed
    a.   there is a continuity among species
    b.   evolution is guided by an outside force
    c.   related species actually share little genetic material
    d.   new species evolve suddenly and in relative isolation
Answer: a, Reference: Chapter 1, P. 8, Difficulty: M

16.   It has been established that the percentage of genetic material we share with chimpanzees is as much as
    a.   40 %
    b.   60 %
    c.   85 %
    d.   99 %
Answer: d, Reference: Chapter 1, P. 9, Difficulty: D

17.   A society's culture is the accumulation of all of the following except
    a.   wealth
    b.   artifacts
    c.   knowledge
    d.   beliefs and values
Answer: a, Reference: Chapter 1, P. 9, Difficulty: M

18.   Culture is primarily transmitted through
    a.   DNA
    b.   language
    c.   evolution
    d.   maturation
Answer: b, Reference: Chapter 1, P. 9, Difficulty: M

19.   All of the following are characteristic of "culture" *except*
    a.   it is transmitted through language
    b.   it is a man-made part of the environment
    c.   children have innate knowledge of much of the culture
    d.   rudiments of culture have been found in other animals such as chimpanzees
Answer: c, Reference: Chapter 1, P. 9, Difficulty: M

20. Which of the following best defines ontogeny?
    a. a stage of development
    b. the evolutionary history of a species
    c. the use of language to represent objects and ideas
    d. the course of development during an individual's lifetime
Answer: d, Reference: Chapter 1, P. 10, Difficulty: M

21. When we consider what Alma is like at 1, 2, 3, and 4 years of age, we are considering her
    a. culture
    b. ontogeny
    c. phylogeny
    d. maturation
Answer: b, Reference: Chapter 1, P. 10, Difficulty: M

22. The course of development during one individual's lifetime is called
    a. genetics
    b. ontogeny
    c. phylogeny
    d. biological maturation
Answer: b, Reference: Chapter 1, P. 10, Difficulty: E

23. Qualitatively new patterns of behavior during development such as the change from crawling to walking are often referred to as
    a. stages
    b. phases
    c. passages
    d. differences
Answer: a, Reference: Chapter 1, P. 10, Difficulty: E

24. The concept of stages is used inappropriately when it is used
    a. to classify behavior
    b. to examine behavior
    c. as an explanation of behavior
    d. to compare different children's behavior
Answer: c, Reference: Chapter 1, P. 10, Difficulty: M

25. According to John Flavell, a new stage of development in children has been reached when
    a. new skills or behaviors are acquired
    b. a gradual change in behavior appears
    c. qualitatively new patterns of behavior emerge
    d. previously acquired skills are applied to a new problem/situation
Answer: c, Reference: Chapter 1, P. 11, Difficulty: D

26. Stages of development involve changes that are
     a. slow
     b. small
     c. qualitative
     d. quantitative
Answer: c, Reference: Chapter 1, P. 11, Difficulty: M

27. When Albert Bandura asserts that the processes by which we learn things are the
     same for people of all ages, he is arguing *against* the
     a. usefulness of stage theories
     b. .idea of psychological continuity
     c. importance of studying children's learning
     d. idea that children's behavior is different from that of adults
Answer: a, Reference: Chapter 1, P. 12, Difficulty: D

28. One acute problem facing modern stage theories is
     a. an over-reliance on abstract thought
     b. they are too heavily tied to the information-processing approach
     c. the stage a child appears to be in often varies from one situation to another
     d. the focus of the theories is so new that knowledge of the variables is not
         available
Answer: c, Reference: Chapter 1, P. 12, Difficulty: M

29. "Critical periods" in development
     a. occur in some animals but not in humans
     b. are thought to regulate bonding in human infants
     c. are times during which particular events must occur for development to
         proceed normally
     d. have been observed in humans for physical development but not for
         psychological development
Answer: c, Reference: Chapter 1, P. 12, Difficulty: M

30. To begin the development of male genitalia in the embryo, sex hormones must be
     produced by
     a. 4 weeks post conception
     b. 7 weeks post conception
     c. the start of the third trimester
     d. puberty
Answer: b, Reference: Chapter 1, P. 12, Difficulty: M

31. Which area of psychological functioning has the strongest evidence for a critical period in humans?
    a. language
    b. pretend play
    c. peer interaction
    d. mother-infant bonding
Answer: a, Reference: Chapter 1, P. 13, Difficulty: E

32. John Locke described the mind of the child as a "tabula rasa." What did he mean?
    a. children's innate tendencies express themselves only gradually, over many years
    b. children come into the world with innate ideas upon which all later knowledge is built
    c. children know nothing when they are born, and must learn everything through experience
    d. there is no point in beginning children's education in early childhood because they are not yet capable of learning
Answer: c, Reference: Chapter 1, P. 14, (Box 1.1), Difficulty: M

33. John Locke, the seventeenth-century English philosopher, believed that the most important influences in people's lives were those which occurred
    a. before birth
    b. during early childhood
    c. in early adulthood
    d. in middle age
Answer: b, Reference: Chapter 1, P. 14, (Box 1.1), Difficulty: E

34. Jean-Jacques Rousseau, the eighteenth-century French philosopher, viewed children as
    a. miniature adults
    b. natural and unspoiled with capabilities suited to their age
    c. incomplete adults who needed more knowledge about the world
    d. basically evil in their tendencies, and needing guidance to learn right from wrong
Answer: b, Reference: Chapter 1, P. 14, (Box 1.1), Difficulty: M

35. Which of the following characteristics is the most stable over time and related to later behaviors?
    a. shyness
    b. memory
    c. attention
    d. vocabulary
Answer: a, Reference: Chapter 1, P. 16, Difficulty: M

36.   The more a piece of psychological research concentrates on individual children, the
       a.   less the results can be generalized to all children
       b.   more will be revealed about the behavior of all children
       c.   less will be revealed about the behavior of those children
       d.   more likely it is that the information obtained is not accurate
Answer: a, Reference: Chapter 1, P. 16, Difficulty: E

37.   An observation which is free from bias is
       a.   valid
       b.   reliable
       c.   objective
       d.   impossible
Answer: d, Reference: Chapter 1, P. 17, Difficulty: D

38.   When observations made by two or more researchers on the same occasion or by
       one researcher on two different occasions are in agreement we say that the
       observations are
       a.   valid
       b.   reliable
       c.   objective
       d.   replicable
Answer: b, Reference: Chapter 1, P. 17, Difficulty: M

39.   Psychologists want their observations of human behavior to
       a.   be unique
       b.   support their beliefs
       c.   be consistent across different situations
       d.   be carried out on any sample of subjects they can obtain
Answer: c, Reference: Chapter 1, P. 17, Difficulty: M

40.   When a behavior exhibited and measured at one time can be used to predict later
       behavior the criteria of scientific description with which we are concerned is
       a.   validity
       b.   reliability
       c.   replication
       d.   objectivity
Answer: a, Reference: Chapter 1, P. 17, Difficulty: M

41. Which statement best represents psychologists' current attitudes towards replication of studies?
    a. it is a waste of time and money to replicate research that has already been carried out
    b. to be accepted as true, a study should yield the same results more than once, even when different procedures are used
    c. a study with conclusive findings is generally accepted as accurate, even if other investigators are unable to obtain the same results
    d. the findings of a study are more likely to be accepted when other investigators obtain the same results using the same procedures

Answer: d, Reference: Chapter 1, P. 17, Difficulty: E

42. To be able to generalize the results to other groups, researchers need to conduct their work using
    a. naturalistic observation
    b. both children and adults as subjects
    c. identical questions for all age groups
    d. as representative a sample as possible

Answer: d, Reference: Chapter 1, P. 17, Difficulty: E

43. When the sample used in a study is not representative
    a. conclusions are not valid
    b. replication is not possible
    c. conclusions cannot be generalized
    d. it is impossible to draw conclusions

Answer: c, Reference: Chapter 1, P. 17, Difficulty: E

44. A behavior therapist has asked Mrs. Jones to keep a record of what, where, and when she eats for a 1-week period. This is an example of
    a. a self-report
    b. an experiment
    c. the clinical method
    d. naturalistic observation

Answer: a, Reference: Chapter 1, P. 18, Difficulty: E

45. Which of the following is an example of self-report?
    a. a call to a police department to report a disabled car
    b. an observation of a child's behavior conducted as a course assignment
    c. a questionnaire about health habits filled out as part of a visit to a physician
    d. a list of a two-year-old's vocabulary provided to the child's pediatrician by the parents

Answer: c, Reference: Chapter 1, P. 18, Difficulty: E

46.   Research using the self-report technique has indicated that
    a.   teenagers are the most reliable reporters
    b.   no agreement was found between a person's report and their actual behavior
    c.   a very high agreement has been found between a person's report and their actual behavior
    d.   enough disagreement between a person's report and actual behavior exists to cast doubt on validity
Answer: d, Reference: Chapter 1, P. 18, Difficulty: M

47.   When asked about the child-rearing practices they used several years earlier, parents tend to remember
    a.   their child-rearing practices very accurately
    b.   little of their previous child-rearing practices
    c.   their children as being more poorly behaved than they were
    d.   their child-rearing practices as consistent with expert opinion
Answer: d, Reference: Chapter 1, P. 18, Difficulty: M

48.   Who provided one of the first systematic descriptions of infant development by recording observations of his son in a baby biography?
    a.   Jean Piaget
    b.   W. F. Leopold
    c.   Charles Darwin
    d.   Jean-Marc Itard
Answer: c, Reference: Chapter 1, P. 19, Difficulty: M

49.   Which of the following is true of the role of "Baby Biographies" in research?
    a.   information about one child's development is not valuable
    b.   parents rarely keep any records of their children's development
    c.   parents usually are not objective in describing their own children's behavior
    d.   parents' memories for early events in their children's development are just as reliable as written records
Answer: c, Reference: Chapter 1, P. 19, Difficulty: M

50.   Which is an example of naturalistic observation?
    a.   A 3-year-old listens to her sister play a song on the piano, then walks up and plays the keys
    b.   A teacher keeps count of how many children use each piece of playground equipment at recess
    c.   An experimenter brings children into the laboratory to test their language comprehension
    d.   A teacher examines children's test scores to see whether they have learned the multiplication tables
Answer: b, Reference: Chapter 1, P. 19, Difficulty: E

51. A trained observer makes a chart to record the amount of time a teenager spends studying and the amount of time he spends watching television. Which research strategy does this represent?
   a. self-report
   b. experiment
   c. clinical method
   d. naturalistic observation
Answer: d, Reference: Chapter 1, P. 19, Difficulty: E

52. In psychology, the range of situations in which children are actors, the roles they play, the predicaments they encounter, and the consequences of those encounters is referred to as the _____ of the child.
   a. context
   b. ecology
   c. perspective
   d. correlation
Answer: b, Reference: Chapter 1, P. 19, Difficulty: M

53. Which of the following is true of ecological descriptions?
   a. they describe a specific situation in detail
   b. they are inexpensive and quickly obtained
   c. they provide an overall picture of a child in her community
   d. they are rarely conducted outside the United States and Great Britain
Answer: c, Reference: Chapter 1, P. 19, Difficulty: M

54. When people know they are being observed as part of a research project they
   a. often change the way they behave
   b. usually will not allow themselves to be observed
   c. learn to ignore the observer and behave as they ordinarily would
   d. tend to purposely behave in ways that contradict what they think is the experimental hypothesis
Answer: a, Reference: Chapter 1, P. 22, Difficulty: M

55. Professor Jones finds that in his sample of elementary school children, the taller a child, the higher their score on a vocabulary test. The relationship between height and vocabulary is an example of
   a. no relationship
   b. a causal connection
   c. a positive correlation
   d. a negative correlation
Answer: c, Reference: Chapter 1, P. 22, Box 1.2, Difficulty: E

56.   If an investigator found a +.50 correlation between parents' vocabularies and their children's vocabularies, it would mean that
    a.   children know about half as many words as their parents
    b.   the more words parents know, the more words their children know
    c.   by talking to their children, parents increase their children's vocabularies
    d.   the relationship between parents' and children's vocabularies is too small to be of significance

Answer: b, Reference: Chapter 1, P. 22, (Box 1.2), Difficulty: M

57.   A psychology instructor analyzing her students' exam scores notices that the better the students performed on the lecture-based questions, the more poorly they performed on the textbook-based questions, and vice versa. She has discovered
    a.   a zero correlation between scores on the two parts of the exam
    b.   a positive correlation between scores on the two parts of the exam
    c.   a negative correlation between scores on the two parts of the exam
    d.   definite evidence that the students who read the textbook do not attend the lectures and those attending the lectures do not read the text

Answer: c, Reference: Chapter 1, P. 22, (Box 1.2), Difficulty: M

58.   When event A and event B are positively correlated
    a.   it is almost certain that one causes the other
    b.   it is almost certain that they are not causally related
    c.   little can be said about the relationship of A to B or B to A
    d.   A may cause B, B may cause A, or A and B may be causally unrelated

Answer: d, Reference: Chapter 1, P. 23, (Box 1.2), Difficulty: M

59.   A study in which an investigator measures the effect of an introduced change in children's environments upon their behavior is
    a.   a clinical study
    b.   a correlation study
    c.   an experimental study
    d.   an observational study

Answer: c, Reference: Chapter 1, P. 24, Difficulty: M

60.   Which kind of statement in an experiment can be falsified?
    a.   theory
    b.   hypothesis
    c.   conclusion
    d.   description

Answer: b, Reference: Chapter 1, P. 24, Difficulty: E

61.   To be useful a hypothesis must
   a.   be falsifiable
   b.   have good predictive validity
   c.   demonstrate a strong correlation
   d.   be based within a theoretical framework

Answer: a, Reference: Chapter 1, P. 24, Difficulty: E

62.   The type of study that compares the behavior of subjects exposed to an environmental change with the behavior of a control group not exposed to the change is
   a.   an experiment
   b.   a clinical study
   c.   a correlational study
   d.   naturalistic observation

Answer: a, Reference: Chapter 1, P. 24, Difficulty: E

63.   A control group is a group that
   a.   prevents autonomy
   b.   is randomly assigned
   c.   is standard for the level of the independent variable
   d.   is like other groups but does not participate in experimental manipulation

Answer: d, Reference: Chapter 1, P. 24, Difficulty: E

64.   The group in an experimental study which is treated as much like the other subjects as possible, except for not being exposed to the experimental treatment is called the
   a.   control group
   b.   hypothetical group
   c.   experimental group
   d.   observational group

Answer: a, Reference: Chapter 1, P. 24, Difficulty: M

65.   Campos and his colleagues demonstrated experimentally with the visual cliff that a major contributor to the development of children's fear of heights is
   a.   maturation of the brain
   b.   falling from a high place
   c.   experience with locomotion
   d.   experience crossing the visual cliff

Answer: c, Reference: Chapter 1, P. 24, Difficulty: M

66.   When conducting an experiment, researchers usually compare the performance of the experimental group with that of a control group that
   a.   undergoes no experience at all
   b.   is assigned to a different experimental treatment
   c.   consists of people who did not volunteer to be in the experimental group
   d.   is treated like the experimental group except for not receiving the experimental treatment

Answer: d, Reference: Chapter 1, P. 24, Difficulty: E

67.   A series of experiments is often necessary to
   a.   meet ethical restrictions
   b.   isolate specific causal factors
   c.   show relationships between variables
   d.   uncover the details of subjects' behavior

Answer: b, Reference: Chapter 1, P. 25, Difficulty: M

68.   The greatest strength of the experimental method is its ability to
   a.   isolate causal factors
   b.   show relationships between variables
   c.   uncover the details of subjects' behavior
   d.   distinguish important from unimportant variables

Answer: a, Reference: Chapter 1, P. 25, Difficulty: E

69.   The best way to determine whether a particular factor is the cause of an event or a behavior is to
   a.   conduct an experiment
   b.   observe subjects in a naturalistic setting
   c.   tailor study techniques to the individual subject
   d.   determine whether the event is correlated with environmental factors

Answer: a, Reference: Chapter 1, P. 25, Difficulty: M

70.   Research by Watson and Raynor demonstrated that fear
   a.   can be removed
   b.   can be conditioned
   c.   cannot be conditioned unless the stimulus is acutely painful
   d.   can both be conditioned and removed under the proper circumstances

Answer: b, Reference: Chapter 1, P. 25, Difficulty: M

71.   A problem with testing children's reactions to an unfamiliar experimental situation is
       that
       a.   it is not ethical to experiment with children
       b.   children do not enjoy participating in experiments
       c.   children's behavior in experimental situations is probably no different than it
             would be in any other setting
       d.   the situation being studied is artificial, possibly leading children to react
             differently from the way they would in ordinary life
Answer: d, Reference: Chapter 1, P. 26, Difficulty: M

72.   The description of many laboratory experiments as "the strange behavior of children
       in strange situations with strange adults for the briefest periods of time" was made
       by
       a.   Jonathan Cobb
       b.   Albert Bandura
       c.   John B. Watson
       d.   Urie Bronfenbrenner
Answer: d, Reference: Chapter 1, P. 26, Difficulty: M

73.   Psychological investigations in which questions are tailored to the individual subject
       are using
       a.   self-reports
       b.   experiments
       c.   clinical methods
       d.   standardized interviews
Answer: c, Reference: Chapter 1, P. 26, Difficulty: M

74.   Which type of study tailors questions to the individual subjects
       a.   clinical
       b.   educational
       c.   experimental
       d.   observational
Answer: a, Reference: Chapter 1, P. 26, Difficulty: M

75.   Which is not an ethical guideline for research with young children?
       a.   the rights of the child are always more important than those of the
             experimenter
       b.   research that causes physical or psychological harm to children should not be
             carried out
       c.   all information obtained about children participating in research should be
             open to public scrutiny
       d.   children should, if possible, be informed about experimental procedures in
             language they can understand
Answer: c, Reference: Chapter 1, P. 27, Box 1.3, Difficulty: E

76.   Piaget's "clinical method"
       a.   is mainly used to uncover psychopathology
       b.   uses no concrete objects, but only verbal questions and responses
       c.   involves investigators trying to elicit correct answers from the children
       d.   uses interviews to try to uncover the reasoning behind children's answers to
             particular questions
Answer: d, Reference: Chapter 1, P. 27, Difficulty: M

77.   It is most difficult to generalize the findings of
       a.   clinical studies
       b.   longitudinal studies
       c.   experimental studies
       d.   cross-sectional studies
Answer: a, Reference: Chapter 1, P. 27, Difficulty: M

78.   Both longitudinal and cross-sectional research designs reveal how which of the
       following relate to the development of the behavior being studied?
       a.   socioeconomic trends
       b.   individual differences
       c.   increases in intelligence
       d.   changes that occur with time
Answer: d, Reference: Chapter 1, P. 29, Difficulty: M

79.   If the language development of a group of children was measured at monthly
       intervals from the age of 6 months until their fifth birthdays, what type of study
       would this be?
       a.   longitudinal
       b.   experimental
       c.   cross-sectional
       d.   cohort sequential
Answer: a, Reference: Chapter 1, P. 29, Difficulty: M

80.   Which of the following can be answered using a longitudinal research design?
       a.   Do toddlers understand gender as well as five-year-olds?
       b.   What is the sequence of a child's concept of gender development?
       c.   At what age do most children fully understand the concept of gender?
       d.   Is there a greater gender understanding among adolescents than among
             elementary school children?
Answer: b, Reference: Chapter 1, P. 29, Difficulty: D

81.   Subjects may drop out over the course of a study thereby weakening conclusions researchers can draw. This is most likely to be a weakness of which of the following designs?
        a.   longitudinal
        b.   experimental
        c.   observational
        d.   cross-sectional
Answer: a, Reference: Chapter 1, P. 30, Difficulty: M

82.   In longitudinal studies, it is sometimes difficult to tell whether changes in behavior are due to development or simply due to
        a.   experimental bias
        b.   biological maturation
        c.   an experimental manipulation
        d.   familiarity with the testing procedures
Answer: d, Reference: Chapter 1, P. 30, Difficulty: M

83.   Cohort differences present the most difficulties in which research design?
        a.   quasi experiments
        b.   experimental studies
        c.   cross-sectional studies
        d.   cohort sequential studies
Answer: c, Reference: Chapter 1, P. 31, Difficulty: D

84.   A study that compares 2-year-olds, 4-year-olds, and 6-year- olds on the same task is
        a.   longitudinal
        b.   experimental
        c.   cross-sectional
        d.   cohort sequential
Answer: c, Reference: Chapter 1, P. 31, Difficulty: E

85.   Compared to longitudinal studies, cross-sectional research designs are
        a.   less expensive
        b.   more informative
        c.   more difficult to carry out
        d.   more difficult to recruit subjects for
Answer: a, Reference: Chapter 1, P. 31, Difficulty: M

86.   Which is a problem associated with cross-sectional research studies?
        a.   subjects are likely to drop out before the study is over
        b.   subjects may become accustomed to the testing procedures being used
        c.   they require a long-term time commitment by both subjects and researchers
        d.   changes due to age may be confused with characteristics due to growing up in a particular time and place
Answer: d, Reference: Chapter 1, P. 31, Difficulty: M

87.   Which would be most difficult to study using a cross-sectional design?
       a.   the process of memory development in individual subjects
       b.   differences in memory strategies used by subjects of different ages
       c.   differences in the number of words remembered by subjects of different ages
       d.   the effect of teaching a particular memory strategy to subjects of different
             ages
Answer: a, Reference: Chapter 1, P. 32, Difficulty: M

88.   Facts gathered through various research designs help us to understand development
       only if
       a.   they are imbedded in theory
       b.   a clear description of the cognitive structure exists
       c.   there is a significant and very large correlation efficient
       d.   the currently accepted theory loses its ability to direct and organize scientific
             activity
Answer: a, Reference: Chapter 1, P. 33, Difficulty: M

89.   A theory
       a.   consists of a collection of facts
       b.   should not go beyond established facts
       c.   is developed before any facts are collected
       d.   provides a framework for investigating facts
Answer: d, Reference: Chapter 1, P. 33, Difficulty: M

90.   Which of the following represents a consensus of opinion of modern psychologists
       about human development?
       a.   Piaget's theory
       b.   Erikson's stages of development
       c.   no adequate general theoretical framework exists
       d.   the biological-maturation approach with aspects of the environmental-
             learning approach
Answer: c, Reference: Chapter 1, P. 33, Difficulty: M

91.   Psychologists who adopt the theoretical framework that proposes that the driving
       force of development is "endogenous" believe that
       a.   maturation is the major cause of development
       b.   culture is an important source of development
       c.   the environment is the major cause of development
       d.   the interaction of nature and nurture is the major contributor to development
Answer: a, Reference: Chapter 1, P. 33, Difficulty: M

92.   Who was a major biological-maturational theorist?
        a.   Donald Baer
        b.   Erik Erikson
        c.   Arnold Gesell
        d.   Albert Bandura
Answer: c, Reference: Chapter 1, P. 34, Difficulty: D

93.   Whose viewpoint emphasizes sexual urges as the central unconscious motivation?
        a.   Freud
        b.   Piaget
        c.   Erikson
        d.   Bandura
Answer: a, Reference: Chapter 1, P. 34, Difficulty: E

94.   Which of the following suggests that the most important factors in development are "exogenous" factors?
        a.   cultural-context framework
        b.   biological-maturation framework
        c.   environmental-learning framework
        d.   universal-constructivist framework
Answer: c, Reference: Chapter 1, P. 34, Difficulty: D

95.   Which of the following psychologists subscribed to an environmental-learning framework?
        a.   Jean Piaget
        b.   John Watson
        c.   Arnold Gesell
        d.   Sigmund Freud
Answer: b, Reference: Chapter 1, P. 36, Difficulty: M

96.   The theoretical framework which places the greatest importance on the interaction of nature and nurture is
        a.   behaviorist framework
        b.   constructivist framework
        c.   biological-maturation framework
        d.   environmental-learning framework
Answer: b, Reference: Chapter 1, P. 37, Difficulty: M

97.   Emphasis upon children as individuals who are active constructors of their own development is a major contribution of
        a.   Freud
        b.   Piaget
        c.   Erikson
        d.   Bandura
Answer: b, Reference: Chapter 1, P. 37, Difficulty: D

98.	Psychologists who adopt the cultural-context framework differ from adopters of the other frameworks of development in
	a.	identifying the child as an active contributor to her development
	b.	assuming that biological and experiential factors influence each other
	c.	including the history of the child's social group as a factor in development
	d.	concerning themselves with the relative contributions of biological and experiential factors to development
Answer: c, Reference: Chapter 1, P. 38, Difficulty: D

99.	A psychologist working within the cultural context framework would be most likely to agree with one working from the constructivist framework on which of the following?
	a.	The sequence of changes depends on one's cultural-historical circumstances
	b.	Both children and their caretakers are active agents in the process of development
	c.	The developing individual passes through distinct stage-like changes in the course of development
	d.	Wide variability in performance can be anticipated as people move from one kind of activity to another
Answer: c, Reference: Chapter 1, P. 40, Difficulty: D

100.	Which of the following is the "conventional" breakdown of the periods of development?
	a.	oral, anal, phallic latency, genital
	b.	affiliation, play, learning, peer activity, work, theorizing
	c.	sensorimotor, preoperational, concrete operational, and formal operational
	d.	infancy, early childhood, middle childhood, adolescence, adulthood, old age
Answer: d, Reference: Chapter 1, P. 41, Difficulty: D

101.	Youth could be considered as a stage of development in
	a.	early adulthood
	b.	late adolescence
	c.	middle childhood
	d.	early adolescence
Answer: d, Reference: Chapter 1, P. 41, Difficulty: E

102.	When biological, behavioral, and social changes converge to lead to a new level of development, which of the following has occurred?
	a.	critical period
	b.	quantitative leap
	c.	change of status
	d.	bio-social-behavioral shift
Answer: d, Reference: Chapter 1, P. 41, Difficulty: M

Essay Questions

1. What philosophical questions about human development did Itard hope to answer by studying and working with Victor, the Wild Boy of Aveyron?

2. Scientific, philosophical, and public policy goals are often the driving force behind research conducted in the modern field of developmental psychology. Explain this relationship. Give examples to support your answer.

3. How did the growth of industrialization during the nineteenth century change the lives of children?

4. Briefly discuss the three major questions addressed in the text with which modern developmental psychology concerns itself. What additional questions do they suggest?

5. Of what significance for developmental psychologists is the study of the similarities and differences between human beings and animals?

6. What are the three major areas of study that address the continuity/discontinuity issue? How does each area shed light on this issue?

7. What is culture? How does culture help shape the development of human beings as a qualitatively distinct species?

8. What is a developmental stage? Why do some psychologists describe behavior in terms of stages? What problems have they encountered in applying the concept of stage to human development?

9. What is a critical period? Give an example. What evidence (if any) is there for critical periods in the development of human behavior?

10. Why is the "nature/nurture question" important for understanding human development? Give an example of how our perspectives about this can affect children's lives.

11. In what ways did philosophers John Locke and Jean-Jacques Rousseau agree and disagree about sources of individual differences and the role of adults in children's education?

12. Explain the meaning of each of the following criteria with regard to the observations of children's behavior: objectivity, reliability, validity, replicability. Give an example of each.

13. What are self-reports? What are the advantages and disadvantages of using self-reports in psychological research?

14. Give two examples of naturalistic observations in psychological research. What are the limitations of this approach? According to research what special concerns apply to parents' recollection of their children's behavior?

15. What does it mean to say that events are correlated? Give an example of a positive correlation, negative correlation, and zero correlation.

16. What is the relationship between correlation and causation? Explain.

17. Differentiate between naturalistic observations and experiments. What are the advantages and disadvantages of each research method?

18. Describe the basic principles followed when conducting a psychological experiment. What kinds of treatment groups are used?

19. Discuss three or more ethical guidelines that must be followed by investigators when working with children.

20. What is the clinical method? What are the strengths and weaknesses of collecting data in this way?

21. Compare and contrast experiments and clinical observations as far as generalizing to the population at large is concerned.

22. Explain how longitudinal and cross-sectional designs differ. What are the advantages and disadvantages of each? Which design would be more appropriate to assess the stability of traits?

23. What is a cohort sequential design? What limitation of other designs does it seek to overcome? How is this accomplished?

24. What do psychologists mean by cohort? How can cohort effects alter the interpretation of results of longitudinal and cross-sectional studies? Give examples.

25. What is the role of theory in psychological research? How do theories aid us in understanding development?

26. Briefly describe how each of the following theoretical frameworks explains development: biological-maturation; environmental-learning; constructivist; and cultural-context.

27. What is a bio-social-behavioral shift? Give an example of such a shift.

The Human Heritage: Genes and Environment

Multiple-Choice Questions

1. The specialized structures that contain the blueprints for biological development are called
    a. genes
    b. germs
    c. zygotes
    d. chromosomes
Answer: a, Reference: Chapter 2, P. 52, Difficulty: M

2. Each person inherits a unique combination of genetic traits because of
    a. mitosis
    b. osmosis
    c. genetic imitation
    d. sexual reproduction
Answer: d, Reference: Chapter 2, P. 52, Difficulty: D

3. Which number refers to the number of sperm a man ejaculates during intercourse?
    a. 20.000
    b. 200,000
    c. 200 million
    d. 350 million
Answer: d, Reference: Chapter 2, P. 53, Difficulty: D

4.   Sperm cells and ova each contain
       a.   23 chromosomes
       b.   26 chromosomes
       c.   23 pairs of chromosomes
       d.   46 pairs chromosomes
Answer: a, Reference: Chapter 2, P. 53, Difficulty: M

5.   Which number refers to the number of genes contained within a chromosome?
       a.   20.000
       b.   200,000
       c.   200 million
       d.   350 million
Answer: a, Reference: Chapter 2, P. 53, Difficulty: D

6.   The thread-like structures which provide half the genetic information necessary for
       the development of a new individual, and in which individual genes are contained
       are called
       a.   alleles
       b.   zygotes
       c.   somatic cells
       d.   chromosomes
Answer: d, Reference: Chapter 2, P. 53, Difficulty: M

7.   The structure that develops into an egg in a woman is the
       a.   ovum
       b.   uterus
       c.   oocyte
       d.   zygote
Answer: c, Reference: Chapter 2, P. 53, Difficulty: D

8.   Which number refers to the number of oocytes contained within a woman's ovaries?
       a.   20.000
       b.   200,000
       c.   200 million
       d.   350 million
Answer: b, Reference: Chapter 2, P. 53, Difficulty: D

9.   When an ovum is fertilized, both the mother's and the father's genetic material are
       contained in the
       a.   ova
       b.   genes
       c.   zygote
       d.   sperm cells
Answer: c, Reference: Chapter 2, P. 53, Difficulty: E

10.   The process by which the zygote creates new cells is called
   a.   mitosis
   b.   meiosis
   c.   twinning
   d.   crossing over
Answer: a, Reference: Chapter 2, P. 53, Difficulty: M

11.   Mitosis is the process by which
   a.   an ovum is fertilized
   b.   body cells are formed
   c.   generic mutations occur
   d.   sperm cells and ova are formed
Answer: b, Reference: Chapter 2, P. 53, Difficulty: M

12.   The complex molecules on which genes are located are called
   a.   oocytes
   b.   sperm cells
   c.   chromosomes
   d.   deoxyribonucleic acid
Answer: d, Reference: Chapter 2, P. 53, Difficulty: M

13.   The number of chromosomes contained within a somatic cell is
   a.   23 chromosomes
   b.   26 chromosomes
   c.   23 pairs of chromosomes
   d.   46 pairs chromosomes
Answer: c, Reference: Chapter 2, P. 53, Difficulty: M

14.   The process of meiosis produces
   a.   the zygote
   b.   germ cells
   c.   conception
   d.   somatic cells
Answer: b, Reference: Chapter 2, P. 53, Difficulty: M

15.   Meiosis is the
   a.   process by which the body's cells duplicate themselves
   b.   type of cell division that results in two genetically identical individuals
   c.   process of division that results in cells with half the usual number of
          chromosomes
   d.   process of division resulting in cells with twice the normal number of
          chromosomes
Answer: c, Reference: Chapter 2, P. 55, Difficulty: D

16.   Crossing over occurs during the process of
    a.   mitosis
    b.   meiosis
    c.   mutation
    d.   conception
Answer: b, Reference: Chapter 2, P. 55, Difficulty: M

17.   Genetic material is exchanged between members of a pair of chromosomes during
    a.   mitosis
    b.   conception
    c.   codominance
    d.   crossing over
Answer: d, Reference: Chapter 2, P. 55, Difficulty: M

18.   Crossing over
    a.   causes birth defects
    b.   is a source of genetic diversity
    c.   occurs shortly after conception
    d.   occurs during mitosis but not during meiosis
Answer: b, Reference: Chapter 2, P. 55, Difficulty: E

19.   Monozygotic twins
    a.   can be same-sex or opposite-sex
    b.   develop from a single fertilized ovum
    c.   are often joined at one area of the body
    d.   are genetically no more alike than any siblings
Answer: b, Reference: Chapter 2, P. 56, Box 2.1, Difficulty: M

20.   "Identical" twins are also called
    a.   dizygotic twin
    b.   fraternal twins
    c.   monozygotic twins
    d.   heterozygous twins
Answer: c, Reference: Chapter 2, P. 56, Box 2.1, Difficulty: E

21.   Dizygotic twins
    a.   are also called "identical" twins
    b.   develop from the same fertilized egg
    c.   are as genetically similar as other siblings
    d.   are genetically more similar than other siblings
Answer: c, Reference: Chapter 2, P. 57, Box 2.1, Difficulty: M

22. "Fraternal" twins
    a. come from the same fertilized egg
    b. are highly similar in physical appearance
    c. are sometimes same-sex and sometimes opposite-sex
    d. are born only to mothers who have taken fertility drugs
Answer: c, Reference: Chapter 2, P. 57, Box 2.1, Difficulty: E

23. Who of the following is most likely to have dizygotic twins?
    a. woman 25-30 years old
    b. woman in first pregnancy
    c. African American woman
    d. woman who is an identical twin
Answer: c, Reference: Chapter 2, P. 57, Box 2.1, Difficulty: D

24. For an attribute strongly affected by heredity, the greatest degree of similarity should be shown by
    a. dizygotic twins
    b. a mother and child
    c. monozygotic twins
    d. a brother and sister
Answer: c, Reference: Chapter 2, P. 55, Difficulty: M

25. According to the laws of probability, about how many genetic combinations are possible when a sperm and ovum unite?
    a. 1 million
    b. 5 million
    c. 8 million
    d. 13 million
Answer: c, Reference: Chapter 2, P. 55, Difficulty: D

26. When possibilities from crossovers are added, the chance of a particular genetic combination repeating is estimated to be
    a. 1 in 64 million
    b. 1 in 64 billion
    c. 1 in 64 trillion
    d. impossible to estimate
Answer: c, Reference: Chapter 2, P. 56, Difficulty: D

27. Which genotype represents the genetic sex of females?
    a. XY
    b. XO
    c. XX
    d. YY
Answer: c, Reference: Chapter 2, P. 56, Difficulty: E

28.   A person who is genetically female has received
   a.   a Y chromosome from her mother and X chromosome from her father
   b.   an X chromosome from her mother and X chromosome from her father
   c.   an X chromosome from her mother and no sex chromosome from her father
   d.   no sex chromosome from her mother and an X chromosome from her father
Answer: b, Reference: Chapter 2, P. 56, Difficulty: E

29.   Which represents the genetic sex of males?
   a.   XY
   b.   XO
   c.   XX
   d.   YY
Answer: a, Reference: Chapter 2, P. 56, Difficulty: E

30.   A person who is genetically male has received
   a.   a Y chromosome from his mother and a Y chromosome from his father
   b.   a Y chromosome from his mother and an X chromosome from his father
   c.   an X chromosome from his mother and a Y chromosome from his father
   d.   an X chromosome from his mother and an X chromosome from his father
Answer: c, Reference: Chapter 2, P. 56, Difficulty: E

31.   Which are more often conceived, males or females?
   a.   it depends on the hormones present
   b.   more females than males are conceived
   c.   more males than females are conceived
   d.   equal numbers of males and females are conceived
Answer: c, Reference: Chapter 2, P. 56, Difficulty: M

32.   Which of the following statements is true?
   a.   more males than females are conceived and born
   b.   equal numbers of males and females are conceived
   c.   more males are conceived, but more females are born
   d.   more females are conceived, but equal numbers of males and females are
          born
Answer: a, Reference: Chapter 2, P. 58, Difficulty: D

33.   That fewer males are born than conceived and that the ratio of males to females
        declines over the life-span appears to reflect the
   a.   declining quality of the male sex
   b.   declining role of males in the survival of the species
   c.   greater vulnerability of males to genetic diseases and other problems leading
          to death
   d.   greater vulnerability of females to genetic diseases coupled with the greater
          vulnerability of males to other causes of death
Answer: c, Reference: Chapter 2, P. 58, Difficulty: E

34. Alternative forms of genes such as those for type A or type B blood, are called
    a. alleles
    b. germ cells
    c. chromosomes
    d. recessive genes
Answer: a, Reference: Chapter 2, P. 58, Difficulty: M

35. If a person has inherited the same allelic form from both parents, she is _____ for a trait
    a. ontogenetic
    b. homozygous
    c. monozygotic
    d. heterozygous
Answer: b, Reference: Chapter 2, P. 58, Difficulty: E

36. A person is heterozygous for a trait if she has
    a. not inherited the trait from either parent
    b. developed the trait due to environmental factors
    c. inherited the same allelic form from both parents
    d. inherited a different allelic form from each parent
Answer: d, Reference: Chapter 2, P. 58, Difficulty: E

37. A dominant allele is
    a. one that expresses itself in heterozygous individuals
    b. one that is never expressed in heterozygous individuals
    c. the result of interaction among several recessive alleles
    d. one whose phenotypic expression is not affected by the environment
Answer: a, Reference: Chapter 2, P. 58, Difficulty: M

38. A recessive allele is
    a. one that expresses itself in heterozygous individuals
    b. one that is never expressed in heterozygous individuals
    c. the result of interaction among several recessive alleles
    d. one whose phenotypic expression is not affected by the environment
Answer: b, Reference: Chapter 2, P. 58, Difficulty: M

39. When two different alleles both express themselves in a heterozygous individual in a way that is different from either allele alone, the alleles are said to be
    a. recessive
    b. dominant
    c. polygenic
    d. codominant
Answer: d, Reference: Chapter 2, P. 58, Difficulty: M

40.   In blood type, a person whose blood type is 0 must be
        a.   polygenic
        b.   codominant
        c.   homozygous
        d.   heterozygous
Answer: c, Reference: Chapter 2, P. 58, Difficulty: D

41.   Compared to type 0 blood, type A blood is
        a.   recessive
        b.   healthier
        c.   dominant
        d.   extremely rare
Answer: c, Reference: Chapter 2, P. 59, Difficulty: D

42.   Type AB blood is an example of
        a.   codominance
        b.   a recessive trait
        c.   a homozygous genotype
        d.   the effect of the environment on development
Answer: a, Reference: Chapter 2, P. 59, Difficulty: M

43.   When children inherit different alleles for skin color from each parent
        a.   the darker skin tone will be dominant
        b.   the lighter skin tone will be dominant
        c.   the result will often be skin tone intermediate to that of the parents
        d.   a blotchy skin color which combines the skin colors of both parents will
                result
Answer: c, Reference: Chapter 2, P. 59, Difficulty: M

44.   The particular alleles that an individual has inherited is referred to as the individual's
        a.   zygosity
        b.   genotype
        c.   karyotype
        d.   phenotype
Answer: b, Reference: Chapter 2, P. 59, Difficulty: E

45.   Observed characteristics are represented by a person's
        a.   zygosity
        b.   genotype
        c.   karyotype
        d.   phenotype
Answer: d, Reference: Chapter 2, P. 59, Difficulty: E

46.   A person's phenotype develops through
        a.   unfolding of the genetic program
        b.   the action of modifier genes on the genotype
        c.   interaction between genotype and environment
        d.   interplay of dominant and recessive characteristics
Answer: c, Reference: Chapter 2, P. 59, Difficulty: D

47.   When studying the effects of genetic influences on people's behavior, psychologists usually
        a.   directly study their genotypes
        b.   make inferences based on study of phenotypes
        c.   study only individuals with identical genotypes
        d.   closely control the effects of environment on the people being studied
Answer: b, Reference: Chapter 2, P. 59, Difficulty: D

48.   That most human traits are not caused by a single gene, but by the interaction of several different genes is to say the traits are
        a.   polygenic
        b.   polymyotic
        c.   polyzygotic
        d.   polychromosomal
Answer: a, Reference: Chapter 2, P. 59, Difficulty: E

49.   Futuyama's studies have determined that most phenotypical characteristics determined by the interaction of a number of genes are also subject to considerable influence by
        a.   germ cells
        b.   crossing over
        c.   genetic imitation
        d.   environmental influences
Answer: d, Reference: Chapter 2, P. 60, Difficulty: D

50.   Our eyes can have colors other than brown or blue because of
        a.   mutations
        b.   sex-linked characteristics
        c.   the action of modifier genes
        d.   the effects of the environment
Answer: c, Reference: Chapter 2, P. 60, Difficulty: M

51.   If two genes are necessary for a characteristic to be expressed, the genes are said to be
      a.   mutated
      b.   masking
      c.   recessive
      d.   complementary
Answer: d, Reference: Chapter 2, P. 60, Difficulty: D

52.   Which gene type may prevent other genes from being expressed?
      a.   mutated
      b.   masking
      c.   recessive
      d.   complementary
Answer: b, Reference: Chapter 2, P. 60, Difficulty: D

53.   The coat color in the guinea pig is an example of the potential action of
      a.   masking genes
      b.   modifier genes
      c.   codominant genes
      d.   complementary genes
Answer: a, Reference: Chapter 2, P. 60, Difficulty: D

54.   Most sex-linked characteristics are carried on
      a.   the Y chromosome
      b.   the X chromosome
      c.   an extra chromosome
      d.   both X and Y chromosomes
Answer: b, Reference: Chapter 2, P. 60, Difficulty: M

55.   Sex-linked characteristics are commonly expressed in
      a.   females more often than males
      b.   males more often than females
      c.   males and females equally often
      d.   only people with extra sex chromosomes
Answer: b, Reference: Chapter 2, P. 60, Difficulty: E

56.   Which is a sex-linked characteristic?
      a.   Down's syndrome
      b.   Sickle-cell anemia
      c.   some forms of cancer
      d.   red-green color blindness
Answer: d, Reference: Chapter 2, P. 60, Difficulty: E

57.   If the mother carries the gene for hemophilia but the father does not, what is the probability that their daughter will be a hemophiliac?
a.   0%
b.   25%
c.   50%
d.   75%
Answer: a, Reference: Chapter 2, P. 60, Difficulty: D

58.   If the mother carries the gene for hemophilia but the father does not, what is the probability that their son will be a hemophiliac?
a.   0%
b.   25%
c.   50%
d.   75%
Answer: c, Reference: Chapter 2, P. 60, Difficulty: D

59.   Hemophilia, red-green color blindness, and Duchenne muscular dystrophy are all
a.   sex-linked genetic disorders
b.   caused by extra chromosomes
c.   more common in females than males
d.   caused by exposure to environmental pollutants
Answer: a, Reference: Chapter 2, P. 61, Difficulty: E

60.   The total genetic information possessed by a sexually reproducing population is called
a.   genotype
b.   phenotype
c.   the gene pool
d.   a sex-linked characteristic
Answer: c, Reference: Chapter 2, P. 61, Difficulty: M

61.   Futuyama's research indicated that the conditions of individual cells and, hence, the immediate environment of the genes, is determined by outcomes of interactions between
a.   genes and modifiers
b.   genes and cell material
c.   cell material and alleles
d.   chromosomes and genes
Answer: b, Reference: Chapter 2, P. 61, Difficulty: D

62.   The pattern of black fur on a Himalayan rabbit is affected by the temperature the
        rabbit's skin is exposed to. This is an example of
        a.   learning
        b.   a mutation
        c.   gene-environment interaction
        d.   a highly canalized characteristic
Answer: c, Reference: Chapter 2, P. 61, Difficulty: M

63.   To study the variation in phenotype that can be attributed to variations in genes,
        experimenters
        a.   vary both genotype and environment
        b.   keep both genotype and environment constant
        c.   vary genotype and keep the environment constant
        d.   vary environment and keep the genotype constant
Answer: c, Reference: Chapter 2, P. 62, Difficulty: M

64.   To study the variation in phenotype that can be attributed to variations in the
        environment, experimenters
        a.   vary both genotype and environment
        b.   keep both genotype and environment constant
        c.   vary genotype and keep the environment constant
        d.vary environment and keep the genotype constant
Answer: d, Reference: Chapter 2, P. 62, Difficulty: M

65.   For a characteristic, all developmental outcomes compatible with life that result
        from varying the environment from one extreme to the other is called the
        a.   genotype
        b.   phenotype
        c.   range of reaction
        d.   range of mutation
Answer: c, Reference: Chapter 2, P. 62, Difficulty: M

66.   A canalized characteristic is
        a.   carried on the X chromosome
        b.   not easily affected by variations in environment
        c.   one dependent on particular environmental characteristics
        d.   one that is strongly affected by variations in the environment
Answer: b, Reference: Chapter 2, P. 62, Difficulty: M

67.   Which of the following characteristics are not easily affected by environmental variations? Those that are
   a.   recessive
   b.   canalized
   c.   acquired by learning
   d.   generically influenced
Answer: b, Reference: Chapter 2, P. 62, Difficulty: M

68.   In Waddington's view of gene-environment interactions the environment has
   a.   no effect on development
   b.   the same effect at all points in development
   c.   little effect on some species typical behaviors
   d.   progressively greater influence during development
Answer: c, Reference: Chapter 2, P. 62, Difficulty: D

69.   An experimenter who is studying the extent to which a specific behavior is attributed to hereditary influences is studying
   a.   genotypes
   b.   heritability
   c.   canalization
   d.   recessive genes
Answer: b, Reference: Chapter 2, P. 63, Difficulty: D

70.   To assess their similarity, with respect to a particular trait, members with varying degrees of relationship are compared using this type of study
   a.   family
   b.   clinical
   c.   chromosomal
   d.   range of reaction
Answer: a, Reference: Chapter 2, P. 63, Difficulty: E

71.   Adoption studies have shown that
   a.   conditions necessary for establishing a range of reaction are usually met in these studies
   b.   adopted children strongly resemble their biological parents and show little resemblance to their adoptive parents
   c.   the extent to which children are like their biological parents can be attributed entirely to the similarity of their genes
   d.   environmental factors may influence the extent to which children are like their biological parents due to adoption agencies' policies
Answer: d, Reference: Chapter 2, P. 67, Difficulty: D

72.   According to the model proposed by Scarr and McCartney, the particular
        environment to which children are exposed
        a.   is completely determined by the children's parents
        b.   is completely determined by the children themselves
        c.   may be experienced differently by different children
        d.   will be experienced in nearly the same way by all children
Answer: c, Reference: Chapter 2, P. 68, Difficulty: E

73.   An error in gene replication which results in a change in the structure of genetic
        material is called
        a.   meiosis
        b.   a mutation
        c.   crossing over
        d.   a sex-linked disorder
Answer: b, Reference: Chapter 2, P. 68, Difficulty: E

74.   A change in the genetic material may be passed on to a new generation when the
        following is present in sperm or ovum
        a.   mutation
        b.   recessive allele
        c.   dominant allele
        d.   sex-linked disorder
Answer: a, Reference: Chapter 2, P. 68, Difficulty: E

75.   What percentage of all human conceptions may have a genetic or chromosomal
        abnormality of some kind present ?
        a.   10 %
        b.   25 %
        c.   50 %
        d.   100 %
Answer: c, Reference: Chapter 2, P. 69, Difficulty: D

76.   Most genetic or chromosomal abnormalities present at conception
        a.   are corrected by the time of birth
        b.   lead to early spontaneous abortions
        c.   do not express themselves until late in life
        d.   cause the offspring to have severe birth defects
Answer: b, Reference: Chapter 2, P. 69, Difficulty: M

77.   In sickle-cell anemia, the red blood cells are sickle shaped
        a.   at all times
        b.   when the supply of dietary iron is low
        c.   when their supply of oxygen is reduced
        d.   when the sufferer does not get enough exercise
Answer: c, Reference: Chapter 2, P. 69, Difficulty: M

78. Recessive genes provide the mode of transmission for
    a. juvenile diabetes
    b. Down Syndrome
    c. Tay Sachs disease
    d. Klinefelter's syndrome
Answer: c, Reference: Chapter 2, P. 70, Difficulty: M

79. Phenylketonuria, Tay-Sachs disease, and sickle-cell anemia are all caused by
    a. mutations
    b. recessive genes
    c. dominant genes
    d. extra chromosomes
Answer: b, Reference: Chapter 2, P. 70, Table 2.2, Difficulty: E

80. People who are heterozygous for the sickle-cell gene have
    a. not inherited the gene at all
    b. no phenotypic sign of sickle cells
    c. sickle-cell anemia, in which abnormal blood cells clog the blood vessels
    d. the sickle-cell trait, in which some of their blood cells are occasionally affected
Answer: d, Reference: Chapter 2, P. 71, Difficulty: D

81. Which of the following is a disorder more common among black Americans than among other segments of the population?
    a. Thalassemia
    b. juvenile diabetes
    c. sickle-cell anemia
    d. Tay-Sachs disease
Answer: c, Reference: Chapter 2, P. 71, Difficulty: E

82. Heterozygous carriers of the sickle-cell gene
    a. are unlikely to live long enough to reproduce
    b. have greater than normal resistance to malaria
    c. are also more likely than noncarriers to die from malaria
    d. do not usually die of sickle-cell disease, but are considerably handicapped
Answer: b, Reference: Chapter 2, P. 71, Difficulty: D

83. People who do not carry the sickle-cell gene are more likely to suffer from
    a. PKU
    b. malaria
    c. flu viruses
    d. hemophilia
Answer: b, Reference: Chapter 2, P. 71, Difficulty: M

84.   Hydroxyurea is a medication used to treat
       a.   Thalassemia
       b.   juvenile diabetes
       c.   sickle-cell anemia
       d.   Tay-Sachs disease
Answer: c, Reference: Chapter 2, P. 71, Difficulty: M

85.   Which of the following is linked with having an extra 21st chromosome?
       a.   phenylketonuria
       b.   Down's syndrome
       c.   Turner's syndrome
       d.   red-green color blindness
Answer: b, Reference: Chapter 2, P. 71, Difficulty: E

86.   According to findings of studies by Plomin, DeFries, and McClearn (1990), what
       percentage of people in institutions because of mental retardation suffer from
       Down's syndrome?
       a.   less than 2%
       b.   somewhat over 10 %
       c.   at least 50%
       d.   almost 70%
Answer: b, Reference: Chapter 2, P. 71, Difficulty: D

87.   Children with Down's syndrome
       a.   nearly always need to be institutionalized
       b.   are successfully treated with dietary therapy
       c.   are usually not noticeably affected by the disorder
       d.   function at a level determined both by the severity of the disorder and the
             environments arranged for them
Answer: d, Reference: Chapter 2, P. 71, Difficulty: E

88.   Down's syndrome is more likely to occur among children of women who conceive in
       the age range
       a.   12-19
       b.   20-29
       c.   30-39
       d.   40-49
Answer: d, Reference: Chapter 2, P. 72, Difficulty: E

89.   A male is born with an extra X chromosome if he has
       a.   phenylketonuria
       b.   Down's syndrome
       c.   Turner's syndrome
       d.   Klinefelter's syndrome
Answer: d, Reference: Chapter 2, P. 72, Difficulty: D

90. Fragile X Syndrome accounts for approximately what percent of the nation's mental retardation?
    a. 1-2
    b. 5-10
    c. 15-18
    d. Fragile X is not associated with mental retardation
Answer: b, Reference: Chapter 2, P. 72, Difficulty: D

91. Klinefelter's syndrome, Fragile X Syndrome, and Turner's Syndrome are all caused by
    a. mutations
    b. dominant genes
    c. extra chromosomes
    d. sex-linked chromosomal abnormalities
Answer: d, Reference: Chapter 2, P. 72, Difficulty: D

92. Children with Turner's syndrome have the sex chromosome configuration
    a. XX
    b. XY
    c. XO
    d. XXY
Answer: c, Reference: Chapter 2, P. 72, Difficulty: D

93. Which of the following disorders affects only females?
    a. Down's syndrome
    b. Turner's syndrome
    c. fragile X syndrome
    d. Klinefelter's syndrome
Answer: b, Reference: Chapter 2, P. 72, Difficulty: M

94. If not treated with a special diet, which of the following leads to mental retardation?
    a. hemophilia
    b. phenylketonuria
    c. sickle-cell anemia
    d. Down's syndrome
Answer: b, Reference: Chapter 2, P. 73, Difficulty: M

95. Parents of children with PKU need to control the amount of which of the following in their children's diets
    a. sugar
    b. Vitamin A
    c. saturated fats
    d. phenylalanine
Answer: d, Reference: Chapter 2, P. 73, Difficulty: M

96. Genetic counseling
    a. can only advise prospective parents of the population frequencies of particular genetic disorders
    b. can determine the relative likelihood that parents will conceive a child with particular genetic disorders
    c. can determine with a great deal of certainty whether particular parents will have a child affected by a genetic disorder
    d. is of no value in predicting whether the children of a particular couple is likely to inherit a genetic disorder

Answer: b, Reference: Chapter 2, P. 74, Box 2.2, Difficulty: D

97. Genetic population screening programs are possible for which disorders?
    a. Cerebral palsy and Tay-Sachs
    b. Huntington's Disease and PKU
    c. Tay-Sachs and sickle-cell anemia
    d. fetal alcohol syndrome and cystic fibrosis

Answer: c, Reference: Chapter 2, P. 74, Box 2.2, Difficulty: D

98. The alpha-fetoprotein test
    a. screens for defects of the neural tube
    b. is used to reveal the sex of an unborn child
    c. involves collecting and analyzing amniotic fluid
    d. determines whether a fetus is affected by Down's syndrome

Answer: a, Reference: Chapter 2, P. 75, Box 2.2, Difficulty: D

99. According to the text, which of the following disorders can be detected by prenatal testing?
    a. cleft palate
    b. hemophilia
    c. juvenile diabetes
    d. Down's syndrome

Answer: d, Reference: Chapter 2, P. 75, Box 2.2, Difficulty: E

100. A hollow needle collects some of the fluid surrounding the fetus when performing which of the following?
    a. sonogram
    b. amniocentesis
    c. the alpha-fetoprotein test
    d. chorionic villus sampling

Answer: b, Reference: Chapter 2, P. 75, Box 2.2, Difficulty: M

101. Of the following, which yields the result of genetic testing as early as the ninth week of pregnancy?
    a.   sonogram
    b.   amniocentesis
    c.   the alpha-fetoprotein test
    d.   chorionic villus sampling
Answer: d, Reference: Chapter 2, P. 75, Box 2.2, Difficulty: D

102. Which procedure involves the direct observation of the fetus and placenta?
    a.   fetoscopy
    b.   amniocentesis
    c.   the alpha-fetoprotein test
    d.   chorionic villus sampling
Answer: a, Reference: Chapter 2, P. 75, Box 2.2, Difficulty: D

103. Early theorizing about evolution tended to confuse the mechanisms of biological change with those that produce
    a.   historical change
    b.   genetic mutations
    c.   changes in DNA
    d.   natural selection
Answer: a, Reference: Chapter 2, P. 73, Difficulty: D

104. Jean Baptiste Lamarck theorized that
    a.   species differentiated through natural selection
    b.   evolution mainly proceeded by means of genetic mutations
    c.   cultural evolution was more important than biological evolution
    d.   acquired characteristics could be biologically passed to the next generation
Answer: d, Reference: Chapter 2, P. 74, Difficulty: D

105. The knowledge of a generation is passed on to the next through
    a.   cultural evolution
    b.   genetic inheritance
    c.   biological evolution
    d.   changes in brain structure
Answer: a, Reference: Chapter 2, P. 74, Difficulty: M

106. Cultural evolution occurs when
    a.   a mutated gene is passed from one generation to the next
    b.   an acquired biological adaptation is passed from one generation to another
    c.   one generation passes on newly acquired knowledge to the next generation
    d.   each generation learns something for itself, not from the previous generation
Answer: c, Reference: Chapter 2, P. 75, Difficulty: M

107.   Cultural evolution is found almost exclusively among
       a.   human beings
       b.   nonhuman primates
       c.   industrialized cultures
       d.   nonindustrialized cultures
Answer: a, Reference: Chapter 2, P. 75, Difficulty: E

108.   When cultural objects appeared during human evolutionary history
       a.   human biological evolution had already come to an end
       b.   cultural evolution replaced biological evolution as a force in producing
             change
       c.   biological and cultural evolution began a process of interaction that continues
             today
       d.   biological evolution continued to be more important than cultural evolution
             in producing changes, and continues to be today
Answer: c, Reference: Chapter 2, P. 76, Difficulty: D

109.   Pinpointing the cause of differences among people of different cultures is difficult
       because of biological and cultural
       a.   mutation
       b.   evolution
       c.   knowledge
       d.   coevolution
Answer: d, Reference: Chapter 2, P. 76, Difficulty: E

110.   The extent of a child's capacity for a particular type of behavior (for example,
       calculating mathematics problems) is
       a.   expressed in her genotype
       b.   expressed in the context of her physical and cultural environment
       c.   influenced by physical environment, but not generally affected by culture
       d.   most likely the same for all children, given the same exposure to formal
             education
Answer: b, Reference: Chapter 2, P. 76, Difficulty: D

Essay Questions

1.   What are mitosis and meiosis? Describe each process. Under what circumstances
       does each occur?

2.   Describe the factors that contribute to the unique genetic make up of every
       individual.

3. What factors determine the genetic and somatic sex of a fetus?

4. What does it mean if you are homozygous or heterozygous for a particular allele? If two different alleles are present, which will be phenotypically expressed? Give an example.

5. Describe the relationship between genotype and phenotype. How does this bear on the nature/nurture controversy? How does this relate to the concept of heritability?

6. How can genes influence how other genes are expressed?

7. What are sex-linked genetic effects, and whom do they primarily affect? Give an example of a sex-linked effect.

8. How is it possible to determine the range of reaction for a particular characteristic? What are some problems involved in determining ranges of reaction for human characteristics?

9. What are family studies? How do they help us to determine the role of heredity in the development of certain characteristics? What are the limitations of these studies?

10. Describe the role of feedback in gene-environment interactions. Give examples.

11. Describe the model of gene-environment interactions proposed by Scarr and McCartney. What role does feedback play in this model?

12. What is a mutation? What makes mutations more likely to occur? Describe the likely effects.

13. Why are psychologists interested in studying mutations and genetic abnormalities?

14. Why hasn't the genetic trait for sickle-cell anemia disappeared from the gene pool?

15. What is PKU? How does it originate, and how is it treated?

16. What is Down's syndrome? What are the distinctive physical characteristics that accompany this disease?

17. Explain Lamarck's idea of acquired characteristics. How do humans acquire characteristics from past generations?

18. What is coevolution? How does it complicate attempts to explain sources of differences between groups of people?

19. What causes twinning? What are the two kinds of twins? How are they similar and different in both physical and behavioral characteristics?

20. What is the relationship between maternal age and chromosomal abnormalities? Give an example.

21. What is the purpose of genetic counseling? Who should obtain this service? What kind of information can it provide?

22. What is Klinefelter's syndrome? Describe its effects.

23. What is Fragile X syndrome? Which sex is more likely to be affected by this defect?

24. What methods are available for testing unborn babies for genetic defects? Name some defects that can be tested for and others that cannot.

25. Imagine that a friend has just learned that one of his or her parents has been diagnosed as having Huntington's chorea, a genetic disease that emerges in middle age. Your friend has no children, and does not yet know whether he or she carries the defective gene. What steps, if any, would you advise your friend to take in making decisions about his or her future life? Explain.

26. What is Turner's syndrome? What effect does it have on those who have it?

Prenatal Development and Birth

Multiple-Choice Questions

1.   The fertilized egg, which is about 1/175 of an inch at conception is called the
   a.   ovum
   b.   zygote
   c.   gamete
   d.   embryo
Answer: b, Reference: Chapter 3, P. 82, Difficulty: E

2.   The zygote consists of
   a.   a single cell
   b.   three layers of cells
   c.   an interdependent group of cells
   d.   a ball of about one hundred identical cells
Answer: a, Reference: Chapter 3, P. 82, Difficulty: M

3.   According to Gesell, the changes that occur between conception and birth illustrate the influence of primarily what factor on development?
   a.   learning
   b.   maturation
   c.   environment
   d.   nutritional factors
Answer: b, Reference: Chapter 3, P. 82, Difficulty: M

4.   The period of prenatal development is called
        a.   epigenesis
        b.   maturation
        c.   embryology
        d.   embryogenesis
Answer: d, Reference: Chapter 3, P. 82, Difficulty: M

5.   The zygote is surrounded by
        a.   the nucleus
        b.   the placenta
        c.   amniotic fluid
        d.   the zona pellucida
Answer: d, Reference: Chapter 3, P. 83, Difficulty: M

6.   The periods of prenatal development occur in which order?
        a.   embryonic, germinal, fetal
        b.   germinal, embryonic, fetal
        c.   fetal, embryonic, germinal
        d.   germinal, fetal, embryonic
Answer: b, Reference: Chapter 3, P. 83, Difficulty: M

7.   Which period of prenatal development begins at conception?
        a.   fetal
        b.   germinal
        c.   embryonic
        d.   chromosomal
Answer: b, Reference: Chapter 3, P. 83, Difficulty: E

8.   The first week after conception is called the
        a.   germinal period
        b.   menstrual period
        c.   embryonic period
        d.   conceptual period
Answer: a, Reference: Chapter 3, P. 83, Difficulty: E

9.   The germinal period of prenatal development ends with
        a.   birth
        b.   the first cell division
        c.   implantation in the uterine wall
        d.   formation of the major organ systems
Answer: c, Reference: Chapter 3, P. 83, Difficulty: M

10.   The period of prenatal development that ends with the appearance of bone cells is
       the
       a.   fetal period
       b.   germinal period
       c.   menstrual period
       d.   embryonic period
Answer: d, Reference: Chapter 3, P. 83, Difficulty: M

11.   The period of prenatal development that concludes at the end of the eighth week is
       called
       a.   the fetal period
       b.   the zygote period
       c.   the germinal period
       d.   the embryonic period
Answer: d, Reference: Chapter 3, P. 83, Difficulty: E

12.   The major organs of the body develop during which period of prenatal
       development?
       a.   fetal
       b.   amniotic
       c.   germinal
       d.   embryonic
Answer: d, Reference: Chapter 3, P. 83, Difficulty: M

13.   When the bones of the developing organism begin to harder, this marks the
       beginning of which period?
       a.   fetal
       b.   amniotic
       c.   germinal
       d.   embryonic
Answer: a, Reference: Chapter 3, P. 83, Difficulty: M

14.   The period of prenatal development that last the longest, about 30 weeks, is called
       the
       a.   fetal period
       b.   germinal period
       c.   menstrual period
       d.   embryonic period
Answer: a, Reference: Chapter 3, P. 83, Difficulty: E

15.   The genetic material that comes together at conception is incompatible with life
       a.   in most cases
       b.   only occasionally
       c.   in about thirty percent of cases
       d.   in only about one in a thousand conceptions
Answer: c, Reference: Chapter 3, P. 83, Difficulty: D

16.   What is the location of the initial cell divisions of the zygote?
       a.   in the ovary
       b.   in the uterus
       c.   in the vagina
       d.   in the fallopian tube
Answer: d, Reference: Chapter 3, P. 84, Difficulty: D

17.   The first divisions of the zygote into daughter cells are called
       a.   meiosis
       b.   cleavage
       c.   ovulation
       d.   epigenesis
Answer: b, Reference: Chapter 3, P. 84, Difficulty: M

18.   The division of the zygote into daughter cells takes place through the process of
       a.   mitosis
       b.   meiosis
       c.   epigenesis
       d.   conception
Answer: a, Reference: Chapter 3, P. 84, Difficulty: M

19.   During cleavage the
       a.   blastocyst differentiates into two parts
       b.   first cell divisions of the zygote occur
       c.   placenta separates from the uterine wall
       d.   ovum breaks away from the ovary in preparation for fertilization
Answer: b, Reference: Chapter 3, P. 84, Difficulty: D

20.   Cells do not divide simultaneously during cleavage. This characteristic is called
       a.   mitosis
       b.   trophoblasty
       c.   heterochrony
       d.   heterogeneity
Answer: c, Reference: Chapter 3, P. 84, Difficulty: M

21. The term heterochrony refers to the observation that
    a. a cluster of cells takes shape in the zona pellucida
    b. cells do not divide simultaneously during cleavage
    c. the zygote divides into several cells through mitosis
    d. there is variability in the levels of development of different parts of the organism

Answer: b, Reference: Chapter 3, P. 84, Difficulty: M

22. The observation that there is variability in the degree of development of different parts of the organism is called
    a. mitosis
    b. trophoblasty
    c. heterochrony
    d. heterogeneity

Answer: d, Reference: Chapter 3, P. 84, Difficulty: M

23. Heterogeneity is a product of the process of
    a. mitosis
    b. epigenesis
    c. trophoblasty
    d. heterochrony

Answer: d, Reference: Chapter 3, P. 84, Difficulty: M

24. After the first several cleavages occur the cluster of cells inside the zona pellucida is called the
    a. morula
    b. embryo
    c. trophoblast
    d. inner cell mass

Answer: a, Reference: Chapter 3, P. 84, Difficulty: D

25. Which of the following contains two distinctly different kinds of cells?
    a. zygote
    b. morula
    c. blastocyst
    d. inner cell mass

Answer: c, Reference: Chapter 3, P. 85, Difficulty: D

26. The cells that will develop into the embryo come from the part of the blastocyst called the
    a. zygote
    b. trophoblast
    c. zona pellucida
    d. inner cell mass

Answer: d, Reference: Chapter 3, P. 85, Difficulty: D

27.   Membranes that protect the developing embryo develop from the
       a.   cervix
       b.   mesoderm
       c.   trophoblast
       d.   inner cell mass
Answer: c, Reference: Chapter 3, P. 85, Difficulty: D

28.   Which hypothesis envisions all the forms of the body as existing in some way at
       conception?
       a.   the epigenetic hypothesis
       b.   the structuralist hypothesis
       c.   the preformationist hypothesis
       d.   the biological-maturation hypothesis
Answer: c, Reference: Chapter 3, P. 85, Difficulty: M

29.   Which hypothesis stresses the role of interaction with the environment in explaining
       the emergence of new forms during prenatal development?
       a.   genetic
       b.   epigenetic
       c.   preformationist
       d.   biological-maturation
Answer: b, Reference: Chapter 3, P. 85, Difficulty: M

30.   Which of the following was not true?
       a.   The preformationist hypothesis was widely believed by leading scientists in
             the eighteenth century
       b.   The preformationist hypothesis was largely dismissed by 1900 as a mystical
             substitute for science
       c.   The preformationist hypothesis was largely supplanted among embryologist
             by the epigenesis explanation
       d.   The preformationist hypothesis was further discredited by the recent
             discovery of coded instructions in the genes
Answer: d, Reference: Chapter 3, P. 85, Difficulty: M

31.   The epigenetic explanation of development says that the emergence of new forms
       during development results from
       a.   maturation of already present forms
       b.   automatic execution of genetically coded instructions
       c.   different kinds of interactions of cells with the environment
       d.   the presence in the fertilized ovum of a microscopic adult, which gets larger
             and better developed
Answer: c, Reference: Chapter 3, P. 85, Difficulty: M

32. Implantation marks the transition between the
    a. germinal and fetal periods
    b. embryonic and fetal periods
    c. germinal and embryonic periods
    d. conceptual and germinal periods
Answer: c, Reference: Chapter 3, P. 87, Difficulty: E

33. The structure that surrounds the developing organism, and holds in the fluid in which it floats is the
    a. amnion
    b. ectoderm
    c. umbilicus
    d. uterine lining
Answer: a, Reference: Chapter 3, P. 87, Difficulty: M

34. The structure that provides the fetal contribution to the placenta is the
    a. chorion
    b. amnion
    c. umbilicus
    d. uterine lining
Answer: a, Reference: Chapter 3, P. 87, Difficulty: M

35. The umbilical cord
    a. connects the embryo or fetus to the placenta
    b. carries the mother's blood to the embryo or fetus
    c. is formed from the layer of cells called the endoderm
    d. protects the embryo or fetus from being knocked as the mother moves
Answer: a, Reference: Chapter 3, P. 87, Difficulty: D

36. Which of the following structures develop from the layer of the inner cell mass known as the ectoderm?
    a. the bones and muscles
    b. the heart and blood vessels
    c. the digestive system and lungs
    d. the nervous system and outer surface of skin
Answer: d, Reference: Chapter 3, P. 87, Difficulty: E

37. Which does not develop from the layer of cells called the ectoderm?
    a. the nails and teeth
    b. the digestive system
    c. the central nervous system
    d. the outer surface of the skin
Answer: b, Reference: Chapter 3, P. 87, Difficulty: D

38.   During gestation, the digestive system develops from the layer of cells called
        a.   ectoderm
        b.   endoderm
        c.   mesoderm
        d.   trophoblast
Answer: b, Reference: Chapter 3, P. 87, Difficulty: D

39.   Which of the following structures is the last one to appear?
        a.   ectoderm
        b.   endoderm
        c.   mesoderm
        d.   trophoblast
Answer: c, Reference: Chapter 3, P. 88, Difficulty: D

40.   Which of following develop from the part of the inner cell mass called the mesoderm?
        a.   digestive organs
        b.   bones and muscles
        c.   brain and spinal cord
        d.   inner and outer layers of skin
Answer: b, Reference: Chapter 3, P. 88, Difficulty: D

41.   Development proceeding from the head down is characteristic of which developmental pattern?
        a.   proximodistal
        b.   cephalocaudal
        c.   embryonic-fetal
        d.   differentiation and reintegration
Answer: b, Reference: Chapter 3, P. 88, Difficulty: D

42.   Which illustrates the cephalocaudal pattern of prenatal development?
        a.   The arms develop earlier than the legs
        b.   The arms develop earlier than the hands
        c.   The sex organs are among the first to be formed
        d.   The spinal cord is formed earlier than the shoulders
Answer: a, Reference: Chapter 3, P. 88, Difficulty: D

43.   During gestation, the arm forming earlier than the hand illustrates the which pattern of development?
        a.   epigenetic
        b.   proximodistal
        c.   cephalocaudal
        d.   preformationist
Answer: b, Reference: Chapter 3, P. 88, Difficulty: M

44. According to the proximodistal pattern of prenatal development, which should develop first?
    a. hand
    b. upper arm
    c. lower arm
    d. spinal cord

Answer: d, Reference: Chapter 3, P. 88, Difficulty: E

45. The X and Y chromosomes determine
    a. the gender identity of the child
    b. the rhythmic activity of the pituitary gland
    c. whether the fetal gonads will become testes or ovaries
    d. whether external genitalia will be male or female in appearance

Answer: c, Reference: Chapter 3, P. 90, Box 3.1, Difficulty: M

46. Male gonads are prenatally differentiated
    a. several weeks later than female gonads
    b. at about the same time as female gonads
    c. several weeks earlier than female gonads
    d. during the first three weeks of prenatal development

Answer: c, Reference: Chapter 3, P. 90, Box 3.1, Difficulty: D

47. Prenatal sexual differentiation is
    a. controlled entirely by the Y chromosome
    b. controlled entirely by the X and Y chromosomes
    c. principally controlled by the presence or absence of male hormones
    d. principally controlled by the presence or absence of female hormones

Answer: c, Reference: Chapter 3, P. 90, Box 3.1, Difficulty: D

48. In the absence of hormonal stimulation, the embryo will have which of the following genitalia?
    a. male
    b. female
    c. both male nor female
    d. neither male and female

Answer: b, Reference: Chapter 3, P. 90, Box 3.1, Difficulty: M

49. When pregnant monkeys were given testosterone, their female offspring
    a. were not at all affected
    b. developed male genitalia
    c. developed masculine behavior patterns
    d. grew as large as genetically male monkeys

Answer: c, Reference: Chapter 3, P. 90, Box 3.1, Difficulty: M

50.   The skeleton of the developing organism begins to harden, or ossify, marking the beginning of which period?
       a.   fetal
       b.   germinal
       c.   postnatal
       d.   embryonic
Answer: a, Reference: Chapter 3, P. 90, Difficulty: M

51.   Beginning at about the sixth month of gestation, the lungs of the fetus produce a substance which prevents the lungs from collapsing after birth. This substance is called
       a.   lymph
       b.   vernix
       c.   surfactin
       d.   amniotic fluid
Answer: c, Reference: Chapter 3, P. 92, Table 3.2, Difficulty: M

52.   During which time period does the fetus put on most of its subcutaneous fat and therefore weight?
       a.   before the twelfth week of gestation
       b.   before the sixth month of gestation
       c.   during the last month of gestation
       d.   it does so equally throughout the fetal period
Answer: c, Reference: Chapter 3, P. 92, Table 3.2, Difficulty: M

53.   At about what point of gestation is the human fetus large enough so that its mother can feel it moving?
       a.   the eighth week
       b.   the fourth month
       c.   the sixth month
       d.   the eighth month
Answer: b, Reference: Chapter 3, P. 91, Difficulty: M

54.   When, at between 17 and 18 weeks after conception, higher brain regions begin to mature
       a.   fetal activity comes under cortical control
       b.   there is a marked increase in fetal activity
       c.   fetal activity comes under voluntary control
       d.   there is a temporary decrease in fetal activity
Answer: d, Reference: Chapter 3, P. 91, Difficulty: D

55.   Fetal activity that arises from the maturation of the organism's tissues is said to be
    a.   rare
    b.   genetic
    c.   exogenous
    d.   endogenous
Answer: d, Reference: Chapter 3, P. 92, Difficulty: E

56.   Fetal activity that arises in response to stimulation from the environment is
    a.   harmful
    b.   exogenous
    c.   impossible
    d.   endogenous
Answer: b, Reference: Chapter 3, P. 92, Difficulty: E

57.   The view that fetal activity serves to further development during the prenatal period
has been supported by experiments with
    a.   frog embryos
    b.   chick embryos
    c.   one-celled organisms
    d.   Amblystoma (salamanders)
Answer: b, Reference: Chapter 3, P. 93, Difficulty: D

58.   Activity during the embryonic and fetal periods appear important in
    a.   killing off excess neurons
    b.   causing neurons to multiply
    c.   slowing neuronal multiplication
    d.   affecting the migration of neurons to the correct attachment
Answer: a, Reference: Chapter 3, P. 93, Difficulty: D

59.   When paralyzing drugs are used to prevent chick embryos from moving
    a.   their joints fuse, causing them to lose their mobility
    b.   they remain delayed in motor development after hatching
    c.   they are developmentally delayed in moving but soon catch up
    d.   they begin moving appropriately for their age immediately after the drug is
        removed
Answer: a, Reference: Chapter 3, P. 93, Difficulty: D

60.   Through the placenta, the fetus comes in contact with
    a.   oxygen
    b.   nutrients
    c.   disease-causing organisms
    d.   all of these
Answer: d, Reference: Chapter 3, P. 93, Difficulty: E

61.   The ability to sense changes in position
        a.   is fully mature at the time of birth
        b.   begins to develop quite early in gestation
        c.   does not begin to develop until after birth
        d.   is already developed by the beginning of the fetal period
Answer: a, Reference: Chapter 3, P. 94, Difficulty: D

62.   Fetuses presented with light have been found to
        a.   show no response
        b.   change their heart rate
        c.   decrease their movement
        d.   increase their sucking rate
Answer: b, Reference: Chapter 3, P. 94, Difficulty: D

63.   Toward the end of gestation, the fetus can hear
        a.   very little, since the uterus is a quiet place
        b.   only the sound of the mother's heart and digestive system
        c.   very little, since the sense of hearing is poorly developed until after birth
        d.   the sounds of the mother's body and some sounds from the outside world
Answer: d, Reference: Chapter 3, P. 94, Difficulty: M

64.   When they hear sounds from outside their mother's bodies, fetuses
        a.   do not react
        b.   increase activity
        c.   increase sucking
        d.   show a change in heart rate
Answer: d, Reference: Chapter 3, P. 94, Difficulty: E

65.   In an experiment performed by Lee Salk, newborns who were exposed to the sounds
        of a human heart beating at the rate of 80 times a minute
        a.   became too upset for the experiment to be continued
        b.   cried less than newborns who heard no special sounds
        c.   cried more than newborns who heard no special sounds
        d.   were not different from newborns who heard no special sounds
Answer: b, Reference: Chapter 3, P. 95, Difficulty: D

66.   Babies who heard their mothers read The Cat in the Hat while in the womb
        a.   cried when they heard the story after birth
        b.   showed no signs of recognizing the story after birth
        c.   learned, after birth, to modify their rate of sucking to be able to hear the
                story
        d.   preferred, after birth, to change their sucking rate in order to hear a new
                story
Answer: c, Reference: Chapter 3, P. 95, Difficulty: E

67. The study by DeCasper and Spence that asks expectant mothers to read aloud a passage from The Cat in the Hat and later measured their two-day-old infant's sucking rate provided evidence for
    a. prenatal learning
    b. self-soothing behavior
    c. soothing of newborns with rhyming sounds
    d. the role of reading in parent-infant bonding

Answer: a, Reference: Chapter 3, P. 95, Difficulty: E

68. Research by DeCasper and colleagues observed that when a fetus who had been read a rhyme heard a tape of that rhyme, there was
    a. a decrease in heart rate for a new but not the old rhyme
    b. a decrease in heart rate for the old but not a new rhyme
    c. an increase in heart rate for a new but not the old rhyme
    d. an increase in heart rate for the old but not a new rhyme

Answer: b, Reference: Chapter 3, P. 95, Difficulty: E

69. The prospects for a healthy baby appear to be positively influenced by
    a. adequate housing
    b. steady employment
    c. having a sympathetic mate and supportive family members
    d. all of these

Answer: d, Reference: Chapter 3, P. 96, Difficulty: E

70. Husbands who experience the "couvade syndrome"
    a. are not psychologically ready for fatherhood
    b. are usually unaware that their wives are pregnant
    c. may experience such symptoms as nausea, backache, and fatigue
    d. develop symptoms associated with pregnancy after their wives have given birth

Answer: c, Reference: Chapter 3, P. 97, Box 3.2, Difficulty: M

71. Children whose mothers did not want them were _____ compared to control children.
    a. less likely to be breast-fed
    b. more likely to be overweight at birth
    c. less likely to have school related problems later
    d. less likely to be referred for psychiatric help as teenagers

Answer: a, Reference: Chapter 3, P. 97, Difficulty: M

72.   According to research by Van Den Bergh (1992) an expectant mother under stress or
        emotionally upset
        a.   is more likely to have a long and painful labor
        b.   is at increased risk for a miscarriage and premature delivery
        c.   secretes hormones which have a measurable effect on the motor activity of
                the fetus
        d.   is less apt to bear a child that is irritable hyperactive, and has eating, sleeping,
                and digestive problems
Answer: a, Reference: Chapter 3, P. 98, Difficulty: D

73.   Labor complications and prematurity are more common among women who
        a.   continue working while pregnant
        b.   are of upper socioeconomic status
        c.   do not produce sufficient stress hormones
        d.   are under extreme stress during their pregnancy
Answer: d, Reference: Chapter 3, P. 98, Difficulty: E

74.   Research conducted by Friedman and Sigman (1980) found that when a woman is
        under extreme stress for a significant amount of time during her pregnancy, she is
        more likely to give birth to a child who suffers from all of the following except
        a.   irritability
        b.   hyperactivity
        c.   mental retardation
        d.   sleeping problems
Answer: c, Reference: Chapter 3, P. 98, Difficulty: M

75.   About how. many calories per day must pregnant women consume for their unborn
        babies to grow properly?
        a.   1200-2000
        b.   2000-2800
        c.   2800-3600
        d.   more than 3600
Answer: b, Reference: Chapter 3, P. 98, Difficulty: M

76.   Extreme nutritional deprivation during which period of pregnancy is the most likely
        to lead to prematurity or death of the fetus?
        a.   the last three months
        b.   the middle three months
        c.   the first three months
        d.   the first two weeks
Answer: c, Reference: Chapter 3, P. 98, Difficulty: M

77. Which of the following has not been identified as a factor in the impoverished environments of malnourished mothers?
    a. housing
    b. education
    c. medical care
    d. unemployment

Answer: d, Reference: Chapter 3, P. 99, Difficulty: M

78. The WIC program is designed to provide food staples for
    a. infants
    b. pregnant women
    c. mothers and their infants
    d. children in school lunch programs in low income areas

Answer: c, Reference: Chapter 3, P. 100, Difficulty: D

79. When a comparison was made between infants born to mothers in the WIC program, infants born to women not in the WIC program, but otherwise matched to the WIC mothers with respect to age, race, education, and other factors,
    a. no significant differences were observed
    b. the non-WIC infants performed better in school
    c. the non-WIC infants had significantly fewer health problems
    d. the WIC program infants had significantly fewer health problems

Answer: d, Reference: Chapter 3, P. 101, Difficulty: E

80. The Super, Herrera, and Mora(1990) study of infants in Colombia supports the conclusion that food supplements enhance the development of children from families where malnutrition is prevalent, if the supplements are begun in mid-pregnancy and continue for
    a. 6 months
    b. 1 and 1/2 years
    c. 2 years
    d. 3 and 1/2 years

Answer: d, Reference: Chapter 3, P. 101, Difficulty: D

81. What are the effects of prenatal food supplementation on the development of low-income children?
    a. no effect on children's later physical health or their intellectual development
    b. helps prevent low birth weight, but does not otherwise affect children's physical condition
    c. improves children's physical condition but has no effect on their intellectual development
    d. improves children's physical condition and is associated with higher levels of intelligence

Answer: d, Reference: Chapter 3, P. 101, Difficulty: E

82.   Children who are born malnourished, are often all of the following except
    a.   alert
    b.   irritable
    c.   apathetic
    d.   unresponsive
Answer: a, Reference: Chapter 3, P. 101, Difficulty: E

83.   Compared to babies adequately nourished prenatally, babies born malnourished
    often
    a.   are no different
    b.   are more lively and alert
    c.   are unresponsive and apathetic
    d.   respond more positively to stimulation
Answer: c, Reference: Chapter 3, P. 101, Difficulty: E

84.   Which causes deviations from normal prenatal development?
    a.   cleavage
    b.   teratogens
    c.   sonograms
    d.   ossification
Answer: b, Reference: Chapter 3, P. 101, Difficulty: E

85.   Which of the following is not a drug that is thought to adversely affect the fetus?
    a.   aspirin
    b.   alcohol
    c.   caffeine
    d.   tetracycline
Answer: c, Reference: Chapter 3, P. 102, Difficulty: E

86.   What advice about medications is usually given to pregnant women?
    a.   Any drug that is safe for the mother is also likely to be safe for the fetus
    b.   No prescription or "over the counter" drug should be taken without checking
        with their obstetricians
    c.   Prescription drugs are safe to take, but over the counter" drugs should be
        checked with their obstetricians
    d.   "Over the counter" drugs are safe to take, but prescription drugs should be
        checked with their obstetricians.
Answer: b, Reference: Chapter 3, P. 102, Difficulty: E

87.   Smoking during pregnancy is associated with
    a.   birth defects
    b.   overweight babies
    c.   lower birth weights
    d.   a lower rate of stillbirths
Answer: c, Reference: Chapter 3, P. 102, Difficulty: E

88.   What is fetal alcohol syndrome?
    a.   an inherited tendency to become alcoholic
    b.   a set of malformations caused by excessive exposure to alcohol in utero
    c.   an inability to metabolize alcohol caused by prenatal exposure to alcohol
    d.   a set of malformations common among children of female alcoholics, even if no alcohol was consumed during pregnancy
Answer: b, Reference: Chapter 3, P. 102, Difficulty: M

89.   A study by Richardson, Day, and Taylor (1989) on the effects of prenatal alcohol consumption found
    a.   non-drinkers experience fewer complications during childbirth than do 1 or 2 per day drinkers
    b.   the infants of non-drinkers to be in better health than infants of those who had 1 or 2 drinks per day
    c.   no difference in newborn well-being between babies of non-drinkers and those who had 1 or 2 drinks per day
    d.   newborn infants of non-drinkers tended to be more irritable and startled more easily than those of women who had one or more drinks per day
Answer: c, Reference: Chapter 3, P. 103, Difficulty: D

90.   In order to minimize the risk of having a child with fetal alcohol syndrome, health professional advise women to
    a.   cut down on heavy drinking before the baby is born
    b.   abstain from alcohol consumption throughout pregnancy
    c.   cut down on heavy drinking by the sixth month of pregnancy
    d.   limit alcohol consumption to two drinks a day throughout pregnancy
Answer: b, Reference: Chapter 3, P. 103, Difficulty: E

91.   Cocaine-dependent expectant mothers put the fetus at risk of suffering all of the following except
    a.   stroke
    b.   spontaneous abortion
    c.   impaired motor coordination
    d.   decreased response to stimulation
Answer: d, Reference: Chapter 3, P. 103, Difficulty: M

92.   Which is true of babies born to mothers who are addicted to heroin or methadone?
        a.   Babies born addicted to methadone experience withdrawal symptoms but
                those whose mothers are addicted to heroin do not
        b.   Babies whose mothers are addicted to either heroin or methadone are born
                addicted but experience only mild withdrawal symptoms
        c.   Babies whose mothers are addicted to either heroin or methadone experience
                life-threatening withdrawal symptoms if not given small doses of the drugs
                after birth
        d.   Babies whose mothers are addicted to heroin undergo withdrawal symptoms;
                however, those whose mothers are on methadone maintenance do not
                experience withdrawal
Answer: c, Reference: Chapter 3, P. 103, Difficulty: M

93.   While heroin and methadone addicted babies are being weaned from the drug, they
        do not
        a.   cry normally
        b.   become irritable
        c.   have impaired motor skills
        d.   experience sleep disturbances
Answer: a, Reference: Chapter 3, P. 103, Difficulty: E

94.   Babies who are born addicted to drugs
        a.   experience much milder withdrawal symptoms than adults
        b.   are twice as likely to die following birth than nonaddicted babies, but if they
                live, suffer no additional effects
        c.   may experience severe withdrawal symptoms, but are no more likely to die
                following birth than are nonaddicted babies
        d.   are twice as likely to die after birth than nonaddicted babies and show
                behavioral effects of their addiction at one year of age
Answer: d, Reference: Chapter 3, P. 103, Difficulty: M

95.   If treated before the 21st week of pregnancy, which of the following will not affect
        unborn babies?
        a.   Rubella
        b.   Syphilis
        c.   diabetes
        d.   Herpes simplex
Answer: b, Reference: Chapter 3, P. 104, Table 3.5 Difficulty: M

96.   Larger than normal babies are often born to women who
        a.   smoke
        b.   drink heavily
        c.   have diabetes
        d.   are addicted to opiates
Answer: c, Reference: Chapter 3, P. 104, Table 3.5 Difficulty: M

97. Rubella causes developmental defects in what percentage of babies born to mothers who suffered from the disease during the first few months of pregnancy?
   a. 10 - 20 %
   b. 25 - 30 %
   c. over 50 %
   d. over 75 %
Answer: c, Reference: Chapter 3, P. 104, Difficulty: M

98. A rubella infection during the first 3 months of pregnancy may result in birth defects including
   a. congenital heart disease
   b. cataracts
   c. deafness
   d. all of these
Answer: d, Reference: Chapter 3, P. 104, Difficulty: E

99. A rubella infection during the second 3 months of pregnancy
   a. has no effect
   b. results in a spontaneous abortion
   c. may lead to mental and motor retardation
   d. may cause deafness but not mental retardation
Answer: c, Reference: Chapter 3, P. 104, Difficulty: M

100. What percentage of babies born to mothers who test positive for the AIDS virus will acquire the disease?
   a. 25 %
   b. 50 %
   c. 75 %
   d. 100 %
Answer: b, Reference: Chapter 3, P. 105, Difficulty: M

101. The AIDS virus may be passed from mother to baby through
   a. the placental barrier
   b. exposure of the baby to the mother's blood during delivery
   c. both of these
   d. neither of these
Answer: c, Reference: Chapter 3, P. 105, Difficulty: E

102. Rh incompatibility occurs when an
   a. Rh-positive woman is carrying an Rh-negative fetus
   b. Rh-negative woman is carrying an Rh-positive fetus
   c. Rh-positive woman is carrying a fetus, regardless of its Rh status.
   d. Rh-negative woman is carrying a fetus, regardless of its Rh status
Answer: b, Reference: Chapter 3, P. 105, Difficulty: M

103.   In Rh disease
     a.   the fetus fails to develop the normal coating of Rh substance on its red blood cells
     b.   antibodies from the bloodstream of a mother attack the red blood cells of her fetus
     c.   antibodies from the blood stream of the fetus attack the red blood cells of the mother
     d.   exposure to a heavy dose of radiation causes abnormalities in red blood cell formation
Answer: b, Reference: Chapter 3, P. 105, Difficulty: M

104.   Large doses of radiation during gestation has been shown to result in
     a.   deafness
     b.   blindness
     c.   mental retardation
     d.   characteristic facial abnormalities
Answer: c, Reference: Chapter 3, P. 105, Difficulty: E

105.   Pollutants, such as mercury, that result from industrial production
     a.   have not been shown to be causes of birth defects
     b.   cause greater harm to pregnant women who are exposed than to their fetuses
     c.   can cause birth defects when fetuses are exposed to them in high enough concentrations
     d.   can cause stillbirths and spontaneous abortions, but have no lasting effects on surviving babies
Answer: c, Reference: Chapter 3, P. 105, Difficulty: M

106.   Reducing the air pollution in the Brazilian industrial city of Cubata
     a.   did not effect the death rate of infants
     b.   markedly reduced the death rate of infants
     c.   caused birth defects in which the brain failed to develop
     d.   improved the health of pregnant women but did not affect infant death rates
Answer: b, Reference: Chapter 3, P. 105, Difficulty: E

107.   Exposure to teratogenic agents is most likely to result in spontaneous abortion when the exposure occurs
     a.   during the first 2 weeks after conception
     b.   between 2 and 8 weeks after conception
     c.   between 8 and 12 weeks after conception
     d.   at any time during gestation-all periods are equally dangerous for exposure
Answer: a, Reference: Chapter 3, P. 107, Difficulty: D

108.   The risk of fetal malformations is greater in women from which age group(s)?
    a.   teenage mothers
    b.   mothers in their 20s
    c.   mothers in their 30s
    d.   both very young and very old mothers
Answer: d, Reference: Chapter 3, P. 108, Difficulty: M

109.   Which of the following is a general principle of prenatal development?
    a.   continuous rather than stage like
    b.   proceeds forward without regression
    c.   proceeds evenly, with all systems developing at basically the same rate
    d.   effects of environmental influences on development depends on their timing
Answer: d, Reference: Chapter 3, P. 109, Difficulty: D

110.   The first stages of labor lasts until the
    a.   cervix is fully dilated
    b.   baby emerges from the mother's body
    c.   placenta becomes detached from the uterine wall
    d.   baby's head becomes visible at the outside opening of the birth canal
Answer: a, Reference: Chapter 3, P. 110, Difficulty: M

111.   Which stage of labor may last 14 hours or longer?
    a.   first
    b.   second
    c.   third
    d.   all stages last equally long
Answer: a, Reference: Chapter 3, P. 110, Difficulty: M

112.   Contractions push the baby out of the mother's body during which stage of labor?
    a.   first
    b.   second
    c.   third
    d.   fourth
Answer: b, Reference: Chapter 3, P. 110, Difficulty: M

113.   During the second stage of labor
    a.   the cervix dilates to 10 cm
    b.   contractions are 15 to 20 minutes apart
    c.   the placenta separates from the uterine wall
    d.   contractions push the baby out of the mother's body
Answer: d, Reference: Chapter 3, P. 110, Difficulty: M

114.   When a baby is born in a "breech" position the
        a.   arms emerge first
        b.   head emerges first
        c.   placenta emerges first
        d.   feet or buttocks emerge first
Answer: d, Reference: Chapter 3, P. 110, Difficulty: E

115.   During the third stage of labor the
        a.   cervix completes its dilation
        b.   baby passes into the mother's vagina
        c.   placenta and membranes are expelled
        d.   baby emerges from the mother's body
Answer: c, Reference: Chapter 3, P. 110, Difficulty: M

116.   The word "afterbirth" refers to
        a.   rituals practiced in some cultures after birth takes place
        b.   the period during the first few hours after a baby is born
        c.   the placenta and fetal membranes that are expelled shortly after a baby is
              born
        d.   the time after birth during which a baby and mother become emotionally
              bonded
Answer: c, Reference: Chapter 3, P. 110, Difficulty: E

117.   Customs relating to childbirth
        a.   vary widely between cultures
        b.   are basically the same in all cultures
        c.   involve, in most cultures, women giving birth in hospitals
        d.   involve, in most cultures, women giving birth without assistance
Answer: a, Reference: Chapter 3, P. 111, Difficulty: E

118.   Which is not a reason why most U.S. births take place in hospitals?
        a.   hospital births take place in antiseptic conditions, preventing infections that
              can threaten mothers and newborns
        b.   physicians have found that Caesarean sections are the safest kinds of birth,
              and these must take place in a hospital
        c.   medication to relieve pain of labor and delivery can only be given by
              physicians, and they deliver infants mainly in hospitals
        d.   newborns with breathing difficulties or other life-threatening problems can
              be immediately helped by equipment available in hospitals
Answer: b, Reference: Chapter 3, P. 112, Difficulty: M

119.   During childbirth, analgesics
  a.   serve as muscle relaxants
  b.   reduce the perception of pain
  c.   put the mother to sleep during the delivery
  d.   reduce all feeling in the lower part of the body
Answer: b, Reference: Chapter 3, P. 112, Difficulty: M

120.   Drugs administered to the mother during labor and delivery
  a.   increase the mother's oxygen intake and are therefore beneficial to the fetus
  b.   have been definitely proved to cause later learning disabilities in otherwise
         healthy children
  c.   have no effect on the fetus, because they cannot cross the placental barrier
         into the fetus's bloodstream
  d.   accumulate in the fetus's body because the fetus's liver and kidneys cannot
         process and excrete them efficiently
Answer: d, Reference: Chapter 3, P. 113, Difficulty: M

121.   In prepared childbirth classes
  a.   pregnant women learn techniques for reducing feelings of pain during labor
  b.   prospective mothers and fathers learn how to feed, bathe, and diaper babies
  c.   fathers-to-be learn how to deliver babies in case they cannot get to the
         hospital in time
  d.   pregnant women are taught that labor is necessarily painful and prepare
         themselves to put up with this
Answer: a, Reference: Chapter 3, P. 113, Difficulty: E

122.   Methods of prepared childbirth emphasize the importance of
  a.   the use of medication to reduce the pain of labor
  b.   letting the laboring woman be alone as much as possible
  c.   the presence of a supportive person at the laboring woman's side
  d.   distracting the laboring woman from pain stimuli by playing music or telling
         humorous stories
Answer: c, Reference: Chapter 3, P. 113, Difficulty: E

123.   Which of the following is not a reason for delivering a baby by Cesarean section?
  a.   baby is in distress during delivery
  b.   baby is not in a head-first position
  c.   delivery is difficult or complicated
  d.   birth can be more conveniently scheduled
Answer: d, Reference: Chapter 3, P. 113, Difficulty: E

124. Although typically called for in cases of difficult labor, the use of cesarean sections grew in popularity during the decade starting in 1970. By 1993, about what percentage of all births in the United States were by cesarean section?
    a.   5%
    b.   11%
    c.   22%
    d.   32%
Answer: c, Reference: Chapter 3, P. 113, Difficulty: M

125. It is thought that hormones produced by the fetus in response to the stress of the birth process
    a.   are physically dangerous and psychologically traumatic
    b.   have no particular beneficial or harmful effects on the fetus
    c.   are physically harmful to the fetus, though the effects are not long-lasting
    d.   are helpful in adjusting the fetus's respiration and circulation to life outside the womb
Answer: d, Reference: Chapter 3, P. 114, Box 3.3, Difficulty: D

126. According to recent estimates, what percentage of U.S. women choose to have their babies at home?
    a.   1 %
    b.   5 %
    c.   10 %
    d.   15 %
Answer: a, Reference: Chapter 3, P. 114, Difficulty: M

127. At birth, the average baby born in the United States weighs
    a.   5 Ω-6 pounds
    b.   8-9 pounds
    c.   7-7 Ω pounds
    d.   9 Ω- 1 0 pounds
Answer: c, Reference: Chapter 3, P. 115, Difficulty: M

128. A newborn's vital signs are evaluated at one and at five minutes after birth using the
    a.   Apgar scale
    b.   Gesell scale
    c.   Lamaze method
    d.   Brazelton Neonatal Assessment Scale
Answer: a, Reference: Chapter 3, P. 115, Difficulty: E

129.   Using the APGAR scale, at one and five minutes after birth, which of the following
        is evaluated?
        a.   temperament
        b.   learning ability
        c.   reflex responsivity
        d.   psychological condition
Answer: c, Reference: Chapter 3, P. 115, Difficulty: E

130.   On the APGAR scale a baby with a score of less than _____ is considered to be in
        poor condition.
        a.   4
        b.   8
        c.   10
        d.   100
Answer: a, Reference: Chapter 3, P. 116, Difficulty: M

131.   The Brazelton Neonatal Assessment Scale evaluates newborns'
        a.   vital signs
        b.   neurological condition
        c.   psychological condition
        d.   attachment to their mothers
Answer: b, Reference: Chapter 3, P. 116, Difficulty: E

132.   Which of the following newborn assessments includes a test of "cuddliness"?
        a.   the APGAR
        b.   the Loveness test
        c.   the Brazelton Neonatal Assessment Scale
        d.   The Personality Inventory for Children
Answer: c, Reference: Chapter 3, P. 116, Difficulty: D

133.   Scales for evaluating newborns' behavior are most useful for
        a.   predicting later development
        b.   predicting intelligence in school
        c.   screening for later behavior problems
        d.   predicting when medical intervention is needed
Answer: d, Reference: Chapter 3, P. 116, Difficulty: E

134.   Babies born between 37 and 43 weeks after conception are considered to be
        a.   preterm
        b.   posterm
        c.   of normal gestational age
        d.   at special risk for developmental problems
Answer: c, Reference: Chapter 3, P. 117, Difficulty: M

135.   Most deaths among preterm infants are caused by
        a.   their inability to digest food
        b.   the immaturity of their lungs
        c.   the weakness of their sucking reflex
        d.   their lack of an insulating layer of fat
Answer: b, Reference: Chapter 3, P. 117, Difficulty: M

136.   Premature birth is more likely to occur in women who
        a.   drink
        b.   are affluent
        c.   are carrying multiple fetuses
        d.   are pregnant for the first time
Answer: c, Reference: Chapter 3, P. 117, Difficulty: E

137.   "Fetal growth retardation" refers to
        a.   short length for birth weight
        b.   gestation of less than 37 weeks
        c.   very low birth weight for gestational age
        d.   birth weight of less than 2500 grams, regardless of gestational age
Answer: c, Reference: Chapter 3, P. 118, Difficulty: D

138.   Which of the following factors is most crucial in determining the effects of
        prematurity?
        a.   small head size
        b.   low birth weight
        c.   presence of medical difficulty
        d.   access to special education classes
Answer: c, Reference: Chapter 3, P. 119, Difficulty: E

139.   Premature babies are most likely to catch up developmentally with their full-term
        peers if
        a.   they are also small for their gestational age
        b.   their parents do not become overly attached to them
        c.   their families are well educated and well-off economically
        d.   they are left alone as much as possible, so that they do not become
                overstimulated
Answer: c, Reference: Chapter 3, P. 119, Difficulty: E

140.   The study by Greenberg and Crnic (1988) found that at one year of age premature
        infants
        a.   had mothers with especially positive attitudes to them
        b.   were either over or under stimulated by their mothers
        c.   cried more than a comparison group of full-term infants
        d.   had difficulty maintaining eye contact with their mothers
Answer: a, Reference: Chapter 3, P. 120, Difficulty: E

141.   Ethology is the study of
   a.   early infancy
   b.   human development
   c.   the influence of ethnicity on development
   d.   the evolutionary bases of animal behavior
Answer: d, Reference: Chapter 3, P. 120, Difficulty: E

142.   According to Konrad Lorenz, all of the following are signs of "babyness" except
   a.   round, protruding cheeks
   b.   large eyes relative to face
   c.   high, protruding forehead
   d.   small head relative to body
Answer: d, Reference: Chapter 3, P. 121, Difficulty: E

143.   According to Konrad Lorenz, features that signal "babyness" evoke caregiving
        behaviors from
   a.   adults
   b.   animals but not from humans
   c.   adults who already have children
   d.   females and indifference from males
Answer: a, Reference: Chapter 3, P. 121, Difficulty: M

144.   People switch from a preference for pictures of adults to a preference for pictures of
        infants at about what age?
   a.   5 years of age
   b.   the age of puberty
   c.   21 years of age
   d.   the time they are married
Answer: b, Reference: Chapter 3, P. 121, Difficulty: D

145.   Parents tend to interact more frequently and lovingly with babies who are
   a.   small
   b.   premature
   c.   physically attractive
   d.   physically handicapped
Answer: c, Reference: Chapter 3, P. 121, Difficulty: E

146.   Ideas about the importance of early contact for parent-infant. bonding came largely
        from
   a.   the ideas of Sigmund Freud
   b.   the writings of John Watson
   c.   studies of animal mothers and babies
   d.   well-controlled studies of human mothers and infants
Answer: c, Reference: Chapter 3, P. 121, Difficulty: D

147.   Klaus and Kennell speculated that close physical contact after birth helped mother and infant to "bond" because of
    a.   hormones formed by the mother's system during the birth process
    b.   the sharpness of the newborn's vision during the first hours of life
    c.   the sleepiness of both mother and infant immediately after the birth
    d.   the quiet of the delivery room compared to the noisiness of the womb
Answer: a, Reference: Chapter 3, P. 122, Difficulty: M

148.   Studies have shown that, in humans, extended parent-infant contact immediately after birth
    a.   is necessary for parent-infant attachment to occur
    b.   is not necessary for parent-infant attachment to occur
    c.   is all that is needed for parent-infant attachment to occur
    d.   may disrupt the normal formation of parent-infant attachment
Answer: b, Reference: Chapter 3, P. 122, Difficulty: D

149.   In a study by Sweeney and Bradbard (1988) parents describe their infants in sex-typed ways
    a.   while still in the womb
    b.   within one day of birth
    c.   once the babies are about 6 months of age
    d.   only when the babies display sex-typed characteristics
Answer: b, Reference: Chapter 3, P. 123, Difficulty: E

150.   A study by Rubin, Provenzano & Luria (1974) found than newborn infants are described in sex-typed ways by
    a.   both parents equally
    b.   doctors but not by parents
    c.   fathers more often than by mothers
    d.   mothers more often than by fathers
Answer: c, Reference: Chapter 3, P. 123, Difficulty: M

151.   Parental expectations based on the sex of their infants
    a.   occur only in primitive societies
    b.   occur only in industrialized societies
    c.   are usually harmful to the development of the infants
    d.   serve as a source of environmental continuity in development
Answer: d, Reference: Chapter 3, P. 125, Difficulty: M

Essay Questions

1. List the three periods of prenatal development and when they occur, describing the development which occurs in each.

2. Differentiate between the preformationist and epigenetic hypotheses of emergence of new forms during prenatal development. What is the current status of each hypothesis?

3. Name the three layers of the inner cell mass. Which structures develop from each layer?

4. Describe the changes that occur in a fertilized ovum during the germinal period.

5. How is the placenta formed, and what role does it play in prenatal development?

6. What have experiments with lower organisms indicated in regard to the function of fetal activity in development?

7. How much can fetuses hear while inside the uterus? What are the origins of the sound?

8. How has research indicated that fetuses are affected by sounds coming from outside their mothers' bodies?

9. What evidence from research indicates the capacity of the fetus for learning? Explain.

10. Discuss the ways in which maternal attitudes and psychological stress may influence pregnancy and birth.

11. How were pregnancies and births affected by conditions of maternal starvation in the Netherlands and in Leningrad during World War II? What role did the timing of starvation play in its effects?

12. List some of the factors which make it difficult to isolate and determine the extent to which prenatal and postnatal development are affected by malnutrition.

13. Describe ways in which food supplementation programs have influenced the development of children at risk for undernutrition. Explain.

14. Describe some ways in which the transition to fatherhood is marked by men in industrialized and preindustrial societies.

15.   What are teratogens? What are the most common teratogenic agents to which fetuses are exposed?

16.   What effect does the timing of exposure to teratogens have on developmental outcome?

17.   What is Rh incompatibility? Who does it affect? How can it be prevented?

18.   What general explanatory principles apply to our understanding of prenatal development?

19.   What are the amnion and the chorion? Describe their functions.

20.   List and describe the components of the bio-social-behavioral shift that occurs at birth.

21.   Name the three stages of labor. Describe the events during each.

22.   Compare the experience of childbirth in the United States to this experience in a less industrialized society.

23.   What types of medication are used to relieve discomfort during childbirth? Explain the advantages and disadvantages of their use, as well as any short or long-term side effects.

24.   What circumstances cause babies to be delivered by Caesarean section? Why do critics argue that such operations should be performed less often?

25.   What is "prepared childbirth"? Why is it difficult to assess the effectiveness of such techniques?

26.   Describe the physical characteristics of an average, full-term newborn.

27.   Describe what effect the physical process of birth has on the fetus. What physiological processes are stimulated by the birth process?

28.   What procedures are used to evaluate an infants physical condition shortly after birth?

29.   Describe the APGAR. Explain its use.

30.   What is the Brazelton Neonatal Assessment Scale? When is it used? Briefly describe the kinds of items it contains. To what extent do results predict future development?

31.   Describe some of the problems typically encountered by premature infants. What factors are associated with a greater risk of giving birth prematurely?

32.   Contrast prematurity and low birth weight. What factors are associated with low birth weight?

33.   Describe the possible long-term consequences of premature birth.

34.   What are endogenous activity, and exogenous activity? Explain.

35.   Describe Lee Salk's(1973) experiments studying fetal learning and resulting findings regarding the separation of hospitalized newborns and their mothers. Explain their implications.

36.   Do results of studies conducted by DeCasper and Spence support the claim that prenatal learning impacts later development? Explain and cite data.

37.   How have concepts derived from ethology helped psychologists understand early parent-infant interaction? Give an example and explain.

38.   It has been proposed that extended contact between parents and infants shortly after birth facilitates parent-infant attachment. Discuss evidence both for and against this view.

39.   In what ways might parents' expectations affect their reactions to their newborn infants? Provide an example.

Early Infancy: Initial Capacities and the Process of Change

Multiple-Choice Questions

1.   Compared to guinea pigs, human beings are born in a state of
   a.   wisdom
   b.   maturity
   c.   ignorance
   d.   immaturity
Answer: d, Reference: Chapter 4, P. 134, Difficulty: E

2.   In order for newborn babies to survive
   a.   they must be physically assisted
   b.   they only need to exercise inborn reflexes
   c.   they only need a minimal amount of support from the environment
   d.   their inborn behaviors must be coordinated exactly with the caretaking behavior of adults
Answer: a, Reference: Chapter 4, P. 134, Difficulty: E

3.   The statement made by William James in 1890 that the newborn child experiences
      the world as a "buzzing, blooming, confusion"
      a.   has been supported by empirical research
      b.   is consistent with viewing infants as "blank slates"
      c.   is a direct contradiction to Locke's concept of a tabula rasa
      d.   supports the idea that infants are primed by genetic endowment for their new
            environments
Answer: b, Reference: Chapter 4, P. 134, Difficulty: D

4.   Researchers assume that infants can tell the difference between two stimuli if they
      a.   only look at one stimulus
      b.   refuse to look at either stimulus
      c.   pay more attention to one stimulus than to the other
      d.   they spend equal amounts of time looking at both stimuli
Answer: c, Reference: Chapter 4, P. 135, Difficulty: M

5.   The habituation/dishabituation technique is used primarily to
      a.   measure infants' sensory capacities
      b.   teach infants early sensory-motor skills
      c.   measure infants' rate of physical growth
      d.   predict infants' later aptitude for learning
Answer: a, Reference: Chapter 4, P. 135, Difficulty: M

6.   Which of the following has occurred when a newborn stops attending to a
      repeatedly presented stimulus?
      a.   modeling
      b.   habituation
      c.   operant conditioning
      d.   classical conditioning
Answer: b, Reference: Chapter 4, P. 135, Difficulty: E

7.   Which is an example of habituation?
      a.   a newborn cries because she is hungry
      b.   an infant tires of looking at his mobile
      c.   a newborn is startled by a loud truck horn
      d.   an infant cannot differentiate between two round objects
Answer: b, Reference: Chapter 4, P. 135, Difficulty: D

8.   Habituation and dishabituation in an infant are important because they show that
      the infant
      a.   can perceive change
      b.   is too young to learn
      c.   is overwhelmed by his world
      d.   is able to think about what she is doing
Answer: a, Reference: Chapter 4, P. 135, Difficulty: M

9. Studies conducted by Weiss, Zelazo, and Swain (1988), indicate that infants only minutes old
   a. have color vision equal to that of adults
   b. are not startled by a loud noise close by
   c. turn their head toward the source of sound
   d. first scan the boundaries of an object or picture
Answer: c, Reference: Chapter 4, P. 135, Difficulty: M

10. According to Werner and Vanden Boss (1993)
    a. newborns are practically deaf for 3-4 weeks after birth
    b. newborn hearing is just about as good as older children's hearing
    c. newborn hearing is actually better than older children and adults for some parts of the sound spectrum
    d. newborn hearing is not as acute as hearing among older children and adults for some parts of the sound spectrum
Answer: d, Reference: Chapter 4, P. 135, Difficulty: M

11. How developed is a newborn's auditory system?
    a. he or she can hear many different sounds
    b. he or she can recognize melodies which are similar to one another
    c. he or she can often differentiate the human voice from other sounds
    d. he or she can understand the meaning of a story if it is short and simple
Answer: c, Reference: Chapter 4, P. 135, Difficulty: M

12. Newborns have been found to show a preference for the sound of
    a. human voices
    b. low-pitched tones
    c. instrumental music
    d. very loud noises to very soft noises
Answer: a, Reference: Chapter 4, P. 135, Difficulty: E

13. Cooper and Aslin found that infants are especially interested in listening to
    a. rock and roll music
    b. recorded speech of all kinds
    c. other babies cooing and babbling
    d. high-pitched and slow exaggerated speech
Answer: d, Reference: Chapter 4, P. 135, Difficulty: E

14. One of the most striking discoveries (Eimas, 1985) about the hearing of very young infants is that they are particularly sensitive to the sound category known as
    a. phonemes
    b. the purr of a cat
    c. baby talk register
    d. their mother's voice
Answer: a, Reference: Chapter 4, P. 135, Difficulty: M

15.   Which of the following is an example of a phoneme?
       a.   the word "sap"
       b.   the sound of /t/
       c.   the sound of the syllable /so/
       d.   the sound of middle C on the piano
Answer: b, Reference: Chapter 4, P. 135, Difficulty: D

16.   Studies conducted by Peter Eimas and others indicate that
       a.   newborns do not have the ability to make phonemic distinctions
       b.   the ability to perceive basic language sounds is present very early
       c.   the ability to make phonemic distinctions is only slight at birth and grows to
             its greatest capacity by the age of 6 to 8 months
       d.   a newborn's sense of hearing is poor until absorption of amniotic fluid, which
             is present in ears at birth, is complete
Answer: b, Reference: Chapter 4, P. 135, Difficulty: D

17.   The ability to make phonemic distinctions begins to narrow to just those distinctions
       that are present in one's native language at about what age?
       a.   birth
       b.   3 - 4 months
       c.   6 - 8 months
       d.   12 months
Answer: c, Reference: Chapter 4, P. 136, Difficulty: M

18.   An infant's color vision appears to be roughly that of adults by what age?
       a.   two hours
       b.   two days
       c.   two weeks
       d.   two months
Answer: d, Reference: Chapter 4, P. 137, Difficulty: M

19.   The visual system of newborns
       a.   is very near-sighted
       b.   tends to be far-sighted
       c.   is comparable to that of adults
       d.   shows excellent acuity but no color vision capability
Answer: a, Reference: Chapter 4, P. 137, Difficulty: D

20.   Which would a newborn see most clearly?
       a.   the face of a person standing beside her crib
       b.   a person standing outside, seen through a window
       c.   her mother's face while held in position for nursing
       d.   a person standing in the doorway of her room - about 10 feet away
Answer: c, Reference: Chapter 4, P. 137, Difficulty: E

21. Visual acuity in children is close to adult levels
    a. at birth
    b. sometime after they learn to walk
    c. around the time they are able to crawl
    d. around the same time they can talk in complete sentences
Answer: c, Reference: Chapter 4, P. 138, Difficulty: M

22. According to studies by Haith and his colleagues, which of the following is thought to be the primitive basis for looking behavior?
    a. long scanning movements
    b. exogenous eye movements
    c. endogenous eye movements
    d. sensitivity to changes in illumination
Answer: c, Reference: Chapter 4, P. 138, Difficulty: D

23. In the early 1960's Robert Franz demonstrated that babies can distinguish visual forms at what age?
    a. less than two hours old
    b. less than two days old
    c. less than two weeks old
    d. less than two months old
Answer: b, Reference: Chapter 4, P. 138, Difficulty: M

24. When infants around the age of two weeks are shown drawings of simple figures, they tend to
    a. scan the entire outside boundaries of the figures
    b. focus on lines, angles and other areas of high contrast
    c. scan the interior of the figures and ignore the boundaries
    d. give no indication that they perceive the figures in any way
Answer: b, Reference: Chapter 4, P. 139, Difficulty: D

25. Bronson argues that the increase in scanning competence seen in 3-month-old infants is due to
    a. global growth
    b. brain maturation
    c. experience seeing objects
    d. seeing their mother's face during nursing
Answer: b, Reference: Chapter 4, P. 139, Difficulty: M

26. Franz's early studies on face perception found that newborns
    a. preferred to look at a jumbled face
    b. had a learned preference for human faces
    c. preferred to look at a schematic human face
    d. could not distinguish between jumbles and schematic faces
Answer: c, Reference: Chapter 4, P. 139, Difficulty: M

27. Research by Sherrod (1979) and others suggest that newborns prefer looking at pictures of faces to other forms because
    a. they are attracted to round and oval figures
    b. they are biologically primed to be attracted to the human face
    c. faces contain many complex elements of areas of high contrast
    d. they cannot tell the difference between real faces and pictures of faces
Answer: c, Reference: Chapter 4, P. 140, Difficulty: M

28. Newborns are especially attracted to pictures of faces that are
    a. moving
    b. scrambled
    c. featureless
    d. upside down
Answer: a, Reference: Chapter 4, P. 140, Difficulty: M

29. Which statement about infant perception is true?
    a. Infants prefer stationary objects to moving objects.
    b. Infants prefer visual stimuli characterized by low contrast.
    c. Infants are biologically predisposed to recognize simple figures.
    d. Infants only a few days old can recognize their own mother's face.
Answer: d, Reference: Chapter 4, P. 140, Difficulty: E

30. A stabilometer is used in infant research
    a. to measure dishabituation
    b. to measure physical activity
    c. to provide an indication of habituation
    d. in studies of neonate's visual perceptual abilities
Answer: b, Reference: Chapter 4, P. 140, Difficulty: M

31. Researchers measure newborns' responses to odors by
    a. observing their vocalizations in response to each odor
    b. measuring changes in activity in response to each odor
    c. teaching them to perform behaviors that are rewarded by presentation of an odor
    d. pairing each odor with a visual stimulus, then measuring responses to the visual stimuli
Answer: b, Reference: Chapter 4, P. 140, Difficulty: D

32. Newborn infants demonstrate a preference for the odor of their own mother's milk at
    a. birth
    b. 5 days old
    c. 10 days old
    d. 3 weeks old
Answer: c, Reference: Chapter 4, P. 141, Difficulty: D

33.   When tested, which of the following tastes do neonates show a preference for?
    a.   sour
    b.   sweet
    c.   slightly salty
    d.   they cannot differentiate different tastes
Answer: b, Reference: Chapter 4, P. 141, Difficulty: E

34.   When there is a sudden drop in the temperature of their surroundings, newborns
    a.   become less active
    b.   become more active
    c.   give no indication that they are uncomfortable
    d.   reflexively draw up their legs and cross their arms across their chest
Answer: b, Reference: Chapter 4, P. 141, Difficulty: D

35.   In which of the following ways do newborns react to sudden changes in their position?
    a.   they prefer it
    b.   they ignore it
    c.   they are soothed
    d.   they respond reflexively
Answer: d, Reference: Chapter 4, P. 141, Difficulty: E

36.   A reflex is
    a.   one of the newborn's first voluntary behaviors
    b.   an automatic response to specific kinds of stimuli
    c.   the tendency for newborns to ignore a repeated stimulus
    d.   a response made by newborns to a wide variety of stimuli
Answer: b, Reference: Chapter 4, P. 142, Difficulty: E

37.   In newborn infants, rooting
    a.   refers to the same behavior as nursing
    b.   must be learned over the first few weeks of life
    c.   is a reflex that causes the head to turn in the direction of a touch on the cheek
    d.   is a voluntary behavior which the infant uses in order to locate the nipple while feeding
Answer: c, Reference: Chapter 4, P. 142, Difficulty: M

38.   Which of the following reflexes has disappeared by the time an infant is three to six months of age?
    a.   rooting
    b.   sucking
    c.   eyeblink
    d.   breathing
Answer: a, Reference: Chapter 4, P. 142, Table 4.1, Difficulty: E

39.   Which reflexes are important components of nursing?
       a.   sucking and Moro
       b.   Moro and grasping
       c.   rooting and sucking
       d.   rooting and grasping
Answer: c, Reference: Chapter 4, P. 142, Table 4.1, Difficulty: E

40.   Which of the following reflexes do some psychologists think is a holdover from early
       evolutionary stages, but with no current purpose?
       a.   Moro
       b.   rooting
       c.   sucking
       d.   eyeblink
Answer: a, Reference: Chapter 4, P. 143, Difficulty: M

41.   When Carroll Izard and his colleagues videotaped infant responses to a number of
       situations designed to elicit different emotions, they found
       a.   infants were incapable of displaying surprise
       b.   emotional expression varies from culture to culture
       c.   adults were consistent about identifying some facial expressions
       d.   adults varied widely on which facial expressions showed which emotions
Answer: c, Reference: Chapter 4, P. 143, Difficulty: M

42.   Newborns' facial expressions are
       a.   similar to those of adults
       b.   extremely culture-specific
       c.   very difficult to differentiate
       d.   controlled by higher brain centers
Answer: a, Reference: Chapter 4, P. 143, Difficulty: D

43.   Research by Ekman on facial expressions has found that
       a.   emotional expression varied from culture to culture
       b.   the ways in which emotions are expressed facially are universal
       c.   infants demonstrated the same facial expression of emotion as adults
       d.   infants had a much more limited range of emotional expressions than adults
Answer: b, Reference: Chapter 4, P. 143, Difficulty: D

44.   Emotions in the infant are thought to develop through the process of
       a.   learning
       b.   maturation
       c.   differentiation
       d.   the application of labels to feelings
Answer: c, Reference: Chapter 4, P. 144, Difficulty: D

45. According to Fischer, Lewis, and others, newborn infants experience
    a. fear, anger, and joy
    b. contentment and distress
    c. love, anger, and surprise
    d. surprise, joy, and distress
Answer: b, Reference: Chapter 4, P. 144, Difficulty: M

46. Differences between people in their responses to the environment and in the quality of their dominant mood are referred to as
    a. culture
    b. emotion
    c. temperament
    d. inherited characteristics
Answer: c, Reference: Chapter 4, P. 145, Difficulty: E

47. Temperamental characteristics such as activity level or intensity of reaction to a situation are thought to be
    a. present at birth
    b. established during the first month of life
    c. established by one year of age
    d. established by two years of age
Answer: a, Reference: Chapter 4, P. 145, Difficulty: M

48. According to the Thomas and Chess ratings of temperament, babies who adapt quickly to circumstances, who are playful, and who are regular in their biological functions are labeled
    a. easy
    b. pleasant
    c. emotional
    d. unemotional
Answer: a, Reference: Chapter 4, P. 145, Difficulty: E

49. Babies labeled by Thomas and Chess as "difficult" tend to
    a. have low activity levels
    b. be more playful than other babies
    c. adapt easily to new circumstances
    d. be irritable and to react negatively to new situations
Answer: d, Reference: Chapter 4, P. 145, Difficulty: E

50. Thomas and Chess and their colleagues classified babies' temperaments as
    a. trusting, wary, and suspicious
    b. happy, irritable, and unresponsive
    c. easy, difficult, and slow to warm up
    d. responsive, unresponsive, and depressed
Answer: c, Reference: Chapter 4, P. 145, Difficulty: M

51.   Babies with low activity levels who tend to withdraw while getting used to new situations are labeled by Thomas and Chess ratings as
        a.   easy
        b.   difficult
        c.   unresponsive
        d.   slow to warm up
Answer: d, Reference: Chapter 4, P. 145, Difficulty: E

52.   Genetic contributions to temperament are best measured by
        a.   measuring different children's reactions to the same test situations
        b.   observing parents and their children for similarities in temperament
        c.   testing whether all children raised in a particular culture show similar temperament
        d.   comparing the relative degree of similarity in temperament between identical and fraternal twins
Answer: d, Reference: Chapter 4, P. 145, Difficulty: E

53.   Daniel Freedman's 1974 study of ethnic differences in excitability among newborns suggests
        a.   excitability has a significant genetic component
        b.   excitability is entirely dependent on environment
        c.   black American babies are more placid than Anglo-American and Chinese babies
        d.   there is no difference in excitability between Chinese-American and Anglo-American babies
Answer: a, Reference: Chapter 4, P. 145, Difficulty: M

54.   There is evidence that temperament is stable over time
        a.   for boys but not for girls
        b.   in some cultures but not others
        c.   only when the environment remains stable
        d.   even when a child's environment undergoes many changes
Answer: c, Reference: Chapter 4, P. 147, Difficulty: D

55.   To fit an infant into the pattern of their household and community, parents are most likely to try to modify their newborn's
        a.   cries
        b.   temperament
        c.   food preferences
        d.   patterns of eating and sleeping
Answer: d, Reference: Chapter 4, P. 148, Difficulty: E

56. Observations of the activity levels of newborns indicate that
    a. they are extremely active most of the time
    b. they are always in one of several sleep states
    c. their range from extreme activity to quiet sleep
    d. they are never very active nor very deeply asleep
Answer: c, Reference: Chapter 4, P. 148, Difficulty: M

57. Changes in a newborn's states of arousal during sleep are monitored by
    a. habituation
    b. a sonogram
    c. an electroencephalograph
    d. the galvanic skin response
Answer: c, Reference: Chapter 4, P. 148, Difficulty: M

58. REM sleep is characterized by
    a. almost no motor activity
    b. motor activity and rapid brain activity
    c. slow regular breathing and slower brain waves
    d. awareness of everything going on around the individual
Answer: b, Reference: Chapter 4, P. 148, Difficulty: M

59. The breathing of a newborn is regular and slow and the body rarely moves during
    a. drowsiness
    b. REM sleep
    c. NREM sleep
    d. active periodic
Answer: c, Reference: Chapter 4, P. 148, Difficulty: M

60. After 2 or 3 months, an infant's sleep patterns change so that
    a. REM sleep precedes NREM sleep
    b. NREM sleep precedes REM sleep
    c. the infant sleeps only about 8 hours per day
    d. the infant sleeps in larger numbers of shorter periods
Answer: a, Reference: Chapter 4, P. 148, Difficulty: D

61. During the first week of life infants sleep about how many hours per day?
    a. 12
    b. 16
    c. 20
    d. 22
Answer: b, Reference: Chapter 4, P. 148, Difficulty: E

62.   An infant's sleep/wake cycles
        a.   are not modified by social pressure
        b.   are easily modified by adult social pressure
        c.   do not change during the first 6 months of life
        d.   are modified both by increases in brain maturity and by social pressure
Answer: d, Reference: Chapter 4, P. 150, Difficulty: D

63.   Among American infants, the length of the longest sleep period can be viewed as a
        measure of
        a.   fatigue
        b.   maturation
        c.   intelligence
        d.   brain activity
Answer: b, Reference: Chapter 4, P. 150, Difficulty: M

64.   Research by John Whiting on co-sleeping found that it
        a.   was rarely observed
        b.   occurs in about half the societies
        c.   occurs in about two-thirds of societies
        d.   occurs in most societies
Answer: c, Reference: Chapter 4, P. 151, Box 4.1, Difficulty: M

65.   Burton and Whiting (1961) found that separate quarters for young babies are usual
        in
        a.   Italy
        b.   Japan
        c.   the United States
        d.   non-technological countries
Answer: c, Reference: Chapter 4, P. 151, Box 4.1, Difficulty: M

66.   American mothers argue that sleeping alone is important for an infant because
        a.   the infant gets more sleep
        b.   it promotes independence in the infant
        c.   it teaches sensitivity to the needs of others
        d.   the baby needs to learn to be interdependent
Answer: b, Reference: Chapter 4, P. 151, Box 4.1, Difficulty: M

67.   Newborn babies who are fed "on demand" prefer to eat about every
        a.   hour
        b.   2 hours
        c.   3 hours
        d.   4 hours
Answer: c, Reference: Chapter 4, P. 152, Difficulty: E

68. Average infants eat only four times per day by approximately age
    a. 1 month
    b. 3 months
    c. 5 months
    d. 8 months
Answer: d, Reference: Chapter 4, P. 152, Difficulty: M

69. Parents react with signs of anxiety when
    a. feeding their infants
    b. carrying their infants
    c. looking at their infants
    d. hearing their infants cry
Answer: d, Reference: Chapter 4, P. 152, Difficulty: E

70. Who responds to babies' cries most strongly with increases in heart rate and blood pressure?
    a. new parents
    b. childless adults
    c. siblings of infants
    d. experienced parents
Answer: a, Reference: Chapter 4, P. 152, Difficulty: M

71. Nursing mothers may feel their milk flow when they
    a. are fatigued
    b. hear their baby crying
    c. know babies are asleep
    d. are under any kind of stress
Answer: b, Reference: Chapter 4, P. 152, Difficulty: E

72. Which distinct type of cry has not been identified in newborns by adult listeners?
    a. a pain cry
    b. an anger cry
    c. a hunger cry
    d. a rhythmic cry
Answer: b, Reference: Chapter 4, P. 152, Difficulty: M

73. The crying of infants who are "at risk" for developmental disorders
    a. is acoustically different from that of "normal" infants
    b. enables parents to know exactly what is wrong with their infants
    c. does not differ in acoustic quality or frequency from that of "normal" infants
    d. is acoustically the same as that of "normal" infants but occurs more frequently
Answer: a, Reference: Chapter 4, P. 152, Difficulty: M

74.   A study by Wolff (1969) demonstrated that
        a.   hunger is the only cause of crying in newborns
        b.   newborn babies do not cry when their diapers are wet
        c.   once babies are crying, changing their diapers does not cause them to stop
        d.   when babies stop crying because their diapers are changed, it is the handling
                they receive during changing that is mainly responsible
Answer: d, Reference: Chapter 4, P. 155, Box 4.2 Difficulty: D

75.   Reducing the amount of stimulation babies receive from their own movements
        a.   causes them to cry frantically
        b.   is ineffective in soothing them
        c.   can be accomplished by swaddling them
        d.   has temporary positive effects, but long term negative effects
Answer: c, Reference: Chapter 4, P. 155, Box 4.2 Difficulty: E

76.   All of the following are effective means of soothing crying newborns except
        a.   giving them pacifiers to suck on
        b.   wrapping them up tightly in a blanket
        c.   holding them up to an adult's shoulder
        d.   allowing their arms and legs to move without restriction
Answer: d, Reference: Chapter 4, P. 155, Box 4.2 Difficulty: E

77.   Nursing involves coordination of
        a.   the rooting and sucking reflexes alone
        b.   sucking, breathing, and swallowing by the infant
        c.   infants' sucking behaviors with the behaviors of their caregivers
        d.   infants' mothers' behaviors, with little contribution from the infants
Answer: b, Reference: Chapter 4, P. 153, Difficulty: E

78.   The small space between interconnecting neurons across which nerve impulses must
        flow is the
        a.   myelin
        b.   synapse
        c.   parietal lobe
        d.   primary motor area
Answer: b, Reference: Chapter 4, P. 154, Difficulty: E

79.   A sensory receptor, a motor neuron, and a synapse in the spinal cord are involved in
        a.   any reflex
        b.   a simple reflex
        c.   the sucking reflex
        d.   the central nervous system
Answer: b, Reference: Chapter 4, P. 155, Difficulty: M

80. Such reflexes as rooting and sucking are controlled by one of the most highly developed areas of the brain at birth, the
    a. brain stem
    b. cerebellum
    c. spinal cord
    d. cerebral cortex
Answer: a, Reference: Chapter 4, P. 157, Difficulty: D

81. The network of neurons that integrates information from several sensory sources with memories of past experiences is called the
    a. brain stem
    b. cerebellum
    c. cerebral cortex
    d. sensory receptors
Answer: c, Reference: Chapter 4, P. 157, Difficulty: E

82. Which structure has "uncommitted" areas that can synthesize sensory information and give rise to higher psychological functions?
    a. brain stem
    b. spinal cord
    c. hypothalamus
    d. cerebral cortex
Answer: d, Reference: Chapter 4, P. 157, Difficulty: D

83. The hippocampus, which plays an important role in memory, is estimated to be about _____ % mature at birth.
    a. 20
    b. 40
    c. 60
    d. 80
Answer: b, Reference: Chapter 4, P. 157, Difficulty: M

84. Myelin is
    a. present early in the prenatal period
    b. a fatty substance that coats neurons
    c. a process by which neurons multiply
    d. a substance in nerve cells that aids conduction
Answer: b, Reference: Chapter 4, P. 157, Difficulty: M

85. Neurons are assisted in transmitting nerve impulses more quickly by
    a. motor reflexes
    b. the process of myelination
    c. voluntary control of movement
    d. the lengthening of nerve impulses
Answer: b, Reference: Chapter 4, P. 157, Difficulty: M

86.   The cerebral cortex continues to mature throughout
        a.   the first year
        b.   the first five years
        c.   childhood and adolescence
        d.   the life span
Answer: c, Reference: Chapter 4, P. 158, Difficulty: M

87.   The first brain area to undergo important developmental change after birth is the
        a.   brain stem
        b.   primary motor area
        c.   primary sensory area
        d.   speech center in the temporal lobe
Answer: b, Reference: Chapter 4, P. 158, Difficulty: D

88.   The motor neurons that are myelinated the earliest are those going to the
        a.   toes
        b.   hands
        c.   legs and feet
        d.   arms and trunk
Answer: d, Reference: Chapter 4, P. 158, Difficulty: M

89.   Postnatal changes in the motor cortex allow infants to
        a.   remember past events
        b.   develop new motor reflexes
        c.   hear and see more accurately
        d.   perform voluntary movements
Answer: d, Reference: Chapter 4, P. 158, Difficulty: M

90.   Which of the following do infants become able to control earliest?
        a.   legs
        b.   heads
        c.   trunks
        d.   shoulders
Answer: b, Reference: Chapter 4, P. 158, Difficulty: E

91.   The first sensory nerve fibers to become active during the postnatal period are those responsible for
        a.   touch
        b.   vision
        c.   hearing
        d.   balance
Answer: a, Reference: Chapter 4, P. 158, Difficulty: D

92. It is known from studying babies born without cerebral cortexes that the cortex
    a. controls simple reflexes
    b. plays a minor role in development
    c. governs newborns' abilities to suck, cry, and yawn
    d. is necessary for the development of coordinated actions

Answer: d, Reference: Chapter 4, P. 159, Difficulty: D

93. In the Moro reflex, infants
    a. close their fingers on objects which touch their palms
    b. turn their heads in the direction of a touch on the cheek
    c. fling out their arms, then "hug" them in again toward their bodies
    d. make rhythmic leg movements when held with their feet touching a flat surface

Answer: c, Reference: Chapter 4, P. 159, Difficulty: E

94. The stepping reflex is thought by some theorists to be related to
    a. voluntary walking
    b. the righting reflex
    c. later proficiency in sports
    d. the ability to walk down stairs

Answer: a, Reference: Chapter 4, P. 159, Difficulty: E

95. According to Thelen and colleagues, the stepping reflex disappears because of
    a. changes in the cortex
    b. changes in the infant's muscle mass and weight
    c. the appearance of alternative incompatible behaviors
    d. difficulty in the ability to balance upright on two legs

Answer: b, Reference: Chapter 4, P. 159, Difficulty: M

96. Prereaching, also called visually initiated reaching,
    a. develops out of visually guided reaching
    b. is a behavior in which reaching and grasping are smoothly coordinated
    c. eventually becomes transformed into coordinated reaching and grasping
    d. comes about as a direct result of maturational changes in the cerebral cortex

Answer: c, Reference: Chapter 4, P. 160, Difficulty: D

97. Animals deprived of normal visual experience during infancy
    a. develop less complex visual cortexes
    b. develop more acute hearing as a compensation
    c. are indistinguishable from animals reared normally
    d. have normal vision but are less adept at problem solving

Answer: a, Reference: Chapter 4, P. 160, Box 4.3, Difficulty: D

98. Kittens who were reared in environments containing only horizontal lines
    a.   were not different from kittens raised in normal visual environments
    b.   developed fewer than normal of the cortical cells that respond to vertical lines
    c.   developed fewer than normal of the cortical cells that respond to horizontal lines
    d.   were better than average at detecting vertical lines when they were placed in normal visual environments

Answer: b, Reference: Chapter 4, P. 160, Box 4.3, Difficulty: E

99. Rosenzweig and his colleagues found heavier cerebral cortexes, greater amounts of a brain enzyme, and increased rates of learning among rats that were
    a.   housed singly in cages within an enriched environment
    b.   allowed to actively interact with an enriched environment
    c.   housed singly in cages within a standard laboratory environment
    d.   allowed to interact with another rat within a standard laboratory environment

Answer: b, Reference: Chapter 4, P. 160, Box 4.3, Difficulty: D

100. Animal studies testing the relationship between brain development and behavior indicate that
    a.   brain and behavior develop independently
    b.   for the most part, brain development is the direct result of behavioral changes
    c.   for the most part, changes in behavior are direct results of changes in the brain
    d.   developmental changes in the brain are stimulated by behavioral changes and lead to further changes in behavior

Answer: d, Reference: Chapter 4, P. 160, Box 4.3, Difficulty: M

101. Imitation in newborns
    a.   is easily observed in nearly all infants
    b.   seems sometimes to occur for facial gestures
    c.   is among the important learning mechanisms present at birth
    d.   is impossible because newborns are not yet able to represent actions and events mentally

Answer: b, Reference: Chapter 4, P. 163, Box 4.4, Difficulty: M

102. Research by Tiffany Field and her colleagues has demonstrated that, when shown different adult facial expressions, newborn infants
    a.   paid little attention
    b.   only responded to "happy" faces
    c.   smiled, regardless of the expression they saw
    d.   distinguished among and appeared to imitate expressions

Answer: d, Reference: Chapter 4, P. 163, Box 4.4, Difficulty: M

103. Classical conditioning establishes an association between stimuli that are
    a. biologically related
    b. identical to one another
    c. repeatedly presented together
    d. not presented together in nature
Answer: c, Reference: Chapter 4, P. 164, Difficulty: E

104. In Pavlov's conditioning experiments with dogs, the bell rung before food presentation served as a(n)
    a. conditional response
    b. conditional stimulus
    c. unconditional stimulus
    d. unconditional response
Answer: b, Reference: Chapter 4, P. 164, Difficulty: M

105. In classical conditioning, a conditional response is
    a. elicited by a conditional stimulus
    b. followed by a conditional stimulus
    c. identical in form to an unconditional response
    d. performed after an unconditional stimulus has been presented
Answer: a, Reference: Chapter 4, P. 164, Difficulty: E

106. In classical conditioning
    a. infants match the behavior of a model
    b. infants learn which events in their environments "go together"
    c. infants learn to ignore repeated presentations of the same stimulus
    d. infants' responses to stimuli are strengthened through reinforcement
Answer: b, Reference: Chapter 4, P. 164, Difficulty: E

107. When Elliot Blass and his colleagues gave newborns sugar water after stroking their foreheads the infants
    a. learned to make sucking movements when their foreheads were stroked
    b. made sucking movements, but not necessarily when their foreheads were stroked
    c. became less likely to make sucking movements when their foreheads were stroked
    d. learned no differently from those in a control group, for whom the sugar water was not paired with stroking
Answer: a, Reference: Chapter 4, P. 165, Difficulty: E

108.   The study conducted by Lipsett and his colleagues (1990) which demonstrated that neonates can learn to shut their eyes in anticipation of an airpuff which follows a sound of a tone is evidence for which of the following in young infants?
   a.   sensory reflex
   b.   operant conditioning
   c.   classical conditioning
   d.   experimental learning
Answer: c, Reference: Chapter 4, P. 165, Difficulty: M

109.   Infants form expectancies about connections between events in their environments through
   a.   imitation
   b.   habituation
   c.   operant conditioning
   d.   classical conditioning
Answer: d, Reference: Chapter 4, P. 165, Difficulty: M

110.   Operant conditioning is a way that infants
   a.   anticipate aversive events
   b.   learn to ignore repeated events
   c.   form expectations about events
   d.   add new behaviors to their repertoires
Answer: d, Reference: Chapter 4, P. 165, Difficulty: M

111.   Through operant conditioning, infants learn to
   a.   anticipate aversive events
   b.   ignore repeatedly presented stimuli
   c.   match their actions to those of a model
   d.   repeat behaviors that have positive outcomes
Answer: d, Reference: Chapter 4, P. 165, Difficulty: E

112.   What will make an infant more likely to repeat a particular action?
   a.   habituation
   b.   punishment
   c.   reinforcement
   d.   classical conditioning
Answer: c, Reference: Chapter 4, P. 165, Difficulty: E

113.   Einar Siqueland demonstrated that newborns learned to turn their heads more often when
   a.   music followed the head-turning
   b.   a pacifier was withdrawn if they turned their heads
   c.   the head-turning was elicited by a stroke on the forehead
   d.   the head-turning was followed by the opportunity to suck on a pacifier
Answer: d, Reference: Chapter 4, P. 166, Difficulty: M

114.   A shortcoming of the environmental-learning approach to development is that
   a.   it overemphasizes individual differences in temperament
   b.   it does not distinguish between learning and development
   c.   its explanations depend too much on biological maturation
   d.   it attempts to explain how existing behaviors are combined in new ways to produce new behaviors
Answer: b, Reference: Chapter 4, P. 166, Difficulty: M

115.   The basic units of psychological functioning in Piaget's theory are
   a.   schemas
   b.   operants
   c.   adaptations
   d.   conditioned reflexes
Answer: a, Reference: Chapter 4, P. 167, Difficulty: E

116.   According to Piaget, infants' earliest schemas are
   a.   the reflexes they have at birth
   b.   learned through reinforcement or lack of reinforcement
   c.   sensory in nature, not yet including a motor component
   d.   conditioned responses learned during the first few months after birth
Answer: a, Reference: Chapter 4, P. 167, Difficulty: M

117.   The process by which children transform experiences to fit their existing schemas is called
   a.   imitation
   b.   maturation
   c.   assimilation
   d.   accommodation
Answer: c, Reference: Chapter 4, P. 167, Difficulty: M

118.   Through the process of assimilation, infants
   a.   match their actions to those of a model
   b.   modify existing schemas to fit new information
   c.   transform new experiences to fit existing schemas
   d.   change their behavior as their nervous systems change
Answer: c, Reference: Chapter 4, P. 167, Difficulty: M

119.   As an infant learns to suck on a pacifier, which of the following best describes the relationship of the pacifier to the sucking?
   a.   assimilating
   b.   conditioning
   c.   internalizing
   d.   accommodating
Answer: a, Reference: Chapter 4, P. 167, Difficulty: D

120. The process in which infants modify schemas so as to apply them to new situations is called
     a.   assimilation
     b.   internalization
     c.   accommodation
     d.   behavior modification
Answer: c, Reference: Chapter 4, P. 167, Difficulty: M

121. What has an infant who sucks his fist done to his sucking schema to fit fist sucking?
     a.   habituated
     b.   assimilated
     c.   conditioned
     d.   accommodated
Answer: d, Reference: Chapter 4, P. 167, Difficulty: D

122. According to Piaget's theory, a new level of development is achieved when
     a.   a behavior is strengthened through reinforcement
     b.   equilibrium between assimilation and accommodation occurs
     c.   an infant assimilates a new experience to an existing schema
     d.   an infant associates two events through classical conditioning
Answer: b, Reference: Chapter 4, P. 168, Difficulty: M

123. The balance between assimilation and accommodation that brings the child to a new level of development is called
     a.   a schema
     b.   maturation
     c.   equilibrium
     d.   transformation
Answer: c, Reference: Chapter 4, P. 168, Difficulty: E

124. According to Piaget's theory, which stage is the first of four major developmental periods between birth and adulthood?
     a.   oral
     b.   autistic
     c.   sensorimotor
     d.   preoperational
Answer: c, Reference: Chapter 4, P. 168, Difficulty: E

125. New forms of behavior other than reflexes make their appearance during Piaget's sensorimotor substage
     a.   1
     b.   2
     c.   3
     d.   4
Answer: b, Reference: Chapter 4, P. 170, Difficulty: M

126.   In Piaget's theory, sensorimotor substage 2 is characterized by the appearance of
   a.   habituation
   b.   operant conditioning
   c.   primary circular reactions
   d.   secondary circular reactions
Answer: c, Reference: Chapter 4, P. 170, Difficulty: M

127.   When they perform primary circular reactions, infants
   a.   repeat pleasurable actions for their own sake
   b.   perform reflexes elicited by environmental events
   c.   perform actions in order to receive reinforcement from adults
   d.   avoid performing actions that lead to unpleasant consequences
Answer: a, Reference: Chapter 4, P. 170, Difficulty: M

128.   Which is an example of a primary circular reaction?
   a.   a newborn sticks out her tongue when she sees an adult model do so
   b.   an infant repeatedly brings his hand to his mouth and sucks his fingers
   c.   an infant learns to open her mouth in anticipation of feeding when her
           mother picks her up
   d.   an infant turns his head to the side more frequently when head turning is
           followed by a sip of sugar solution
Answer: b, Reference: Chapter 4, P. 170, Difficulty: D

129.   An infant clasping and unclasping her hands is an example of
   a.   imitative behavior
   b.   tertiary circular reaction
   c.   primary circular reaction
   d.   secondary circular reaction
Answer: c, Reference: Chapter 4, P. 170, Difficulty: M

130.   According to Piaget, primary circular reactions
   a.   are later signs of cognitive development
   b.   are the basic action structures of the infant
   c.   undergo differentiation during the first few months of life
   d.   become integrated between four and six months after birth
Answer: c, Reference: Chapter 4, P. 170, Difficulty: E

131.   Kenneth Kaye's investigation of mutual facilitation found that during nursing,
        mothers are most likely to jiggle their babies
   a.   while the baby sucks
   b.   in order to elicit the rooting reflex
   c.   during pauses in the baby's sucking
   d.   while placing the nipple in their mouths
Answer: c, Reference: Chapter 4, P. 172, Difficulty: E

132. According to Kenneth Kaye, an infant's seemingly automatic response of sucking in response to being jiggled is
      a.   a reflex just like rooting or grasping
      b.   explicitly taught to babies by their mothers
      c.   "preadapted," the result of evolutionary change
      d.   not related to the increasing efficiency of their nursing behavior
Answer: c, Reference: Chapter 4, P. 172, Difficulty: D

133. Piaget's theory for explaining development is associated with the
      a.   interactional perspective
      b.   psychodynamic perspective
      c.   biological-maturation perspective
      d.   environmental-learning perspective
Answer: a, Reference: Chapter 4, P. 172, Difficulty: E

134. Research by Margaret Mead and Frances MacGregor has found
      a.   babies are not nursed in all cultures
      b.   in all cultures mothers are the ones who nurse the infant, either with the bottle or breast
      c.   all cultures make some arrangement for the infant sucking reflex to become part of nursing
      d.   there is little variety in the way babies' nursing behavior is organized to fit with parental activities
Answer: c, Reference: Chapter 4, P. 173, Difficulty: M

135. American mothers observed by Brazelton and his colleagues react to their unresponsive infants as if the infants are
      a.   not present
      b.   just like adults
      c.   helpless and "without understanding"
      d.   engaging in significant interaction with them
Answer: d, Reference: Chapter 4, P. 175, Difficulty: D

136. Cross-cultural research has shown that the Kaluli who live in the rain forests of New Guinea see their babies as
      a.   little adults
      b.   helpless creatures
      c.   competent individuals
      d.   creatures of great understanding
Answer: b, Reference: Chapter 4, P. 175, Difficulty: M

137.   In full-term babies, the first postnatal bio-social-behavioral shift occurs at
    a.   two weeks
    b.   2 months
    c.   six months
    d.   one year
Answer: b, Reference: Chapter 4, P. 175, Difficulty: D

138.   An infant's first smiles
    a.   are endogenous, or REM, smiles
    b.   are triggered by seeing their mothers' faces
    c.   usually occur only when they are wide awake
    d.   are exogenous, or in response to environmental stimuli
Answer: a, Reference: Chapter 4, P. 177, Difficulty: M

139.   REM smiles in infants
    a.   are the same as social smiles
    b.   occur in response to the smiles of other people
    c.   are triggered by nearly any kind of outside stimulation
    d.   occur in response to activity of the infants' own brain waves
Answer: d, Reference: Chapter 4, P. 177, Difficulty: D

140.   An infant's smiles are truly social when they
    a.   occur in response to changes in brain waves
    b.   are triggered by sights and sounds from outside
    c.   occur during sleep as well as during waking times
    d.   occur in response to and elicit the smiles of another person
Answer: d, Reference: Chapter 4, P. 177, Difficulty: E

141.   An important part of the first postnatal bio-social-behavioral shift is the emergence
    of
    a.   REM smiling
    b.   social smiling
    c.   reflexive smiling
    d.   endogenous smiling
Answer: b, Reference: Chapter 4, P. 177, Difficulty: M

142.   In sighted babies, the development of which of the following is, to some extent,
    dependent on maturation of the visual system?
    a.   nursing
    b.   social smiling
    c.   the Moro reflex
    d.   sucking in response to being jiggled
Answer: b, Reference: Chapter 4, P. 178, Difficulty: E

143.   Parents of blind babies often elicit social smiling from their infants by
        a.   using touch to interact with their infants
        b.   smiling in response to the infants' smiling
        c.   verbally conditioning their infants to smile
        d.   leaving the infants alone and letting maturation take its course
Answer: a, Reference: Chapter 4, P. 178, Difficulty: E

144.   The emergence of social smiling is an important sign of the
        a.   strengthening of early reflexes
        b.   first postnatal bio-social-behavioral shift
        c.   appearance of primary circular reactions
        d.   increasing efficiency of nursing
Answer: b, Reference: Chapter 4, P. 178, Difficulty: E

Essay Questions

1.   What is the condition of the newborn's auditory system? What kinds of sounds do newborns prefer to listen to?

2.   Describe the vision capabilities of newborns. What type of "looking pattern" is employed?

3.   Describe the characteristics of visual stimuli which evoke a response from newborns. What changes occur in this area during the first three months of life?

4.   To what extent is it true that newborn infants have a preference for looking at human faces?

5.   How do researchers study newborn infants' capabilities for perceiving smells and tastes? Do the infants have any preferences?

6.   Describe three reflexes present at birth. What stimuli elicit each? Are these reflexes permanent features of behavior?

7.   What evidence is there that newborn infants experience emotions? Do these emotions differ from those of adults?

8.   Discuss the advantages and disadvantages of using facial expressions as indicators of emotional state in newborns and adults.

9.   What do psychologists mean by temperament? What categories of infant temperament have been identified by Thomas and Chess and their colleagues, and what are their characteristics? Discuss the stability of temperamental traits.

10. Discuss evidence of heritability for some aspects of temperament.

11. Describe the temperament classifications identified by Thomas & Chess and their colleagues.

12. What has research by Daniel Freedman demonstrated about the excitability differences of infants from various ethnic groups?

13. How do sleep patterns of infants change over the first several months of life? Explain how sleep patterns may be affected by cultural expectations.

14. Describe patterns of sleep in infants. Differentiate between REM and NREM sleep.

15. What kinds of cries can be distinguished in newborn infants, and what methods are used to distinguish them? What is the significance of unusual crying patterns?

16. Why do infants cry? What are some effective ways to stop babies from crying? How do the techniques work?

17. Differentiate between simple and complex reflexes. How do complex reflexes differ from simple reflexes?

18. What is myelination? How does it contribute to behavioral change during infancy? Explain.

19. Cite evidence for the idea that brain development is influenced by experience.

20. Describe several reflexes present in newborn infants. What happens to these behaviors over time?

21. What is classical conditioning? Describe an example of this kind of conditioning in infants.

22. Describe a classical conditioning study conducted with infants. Identify the conditioned stimulus, unconditioned stimulus, and the conditioned and unconditioned responses. What does this research tell us about the learning capabilities of young infants?

23. What evidence is there that newborn infants imitate facial expressions? Explain why this type of imitation is or is not the same as that performed by older babies.

24. Describe the role of operant conditioning in adding new or more complex behaviors to infants' repertoires.

25. What main difficulties do the biological-maturation and environmental-learning explanations of infant development pose for theorists?

26. According to Piaget, how do infants develop new behaviors?

27. Define equilibration and discuss its role in Piaget's theory of cognitive development.

28. Define assimilation and accommodation. What roles do they play in the acquisition of new behaviors? Give an example of each.

29. What is a schema? Provide an example.

30. Describe substages 1 and 2 of the sensorimotor period as proposed by Piaget. When do they occur? How long does each last? What are the main characteristics of the infant's behavior at each stage?

31. How are mothers' contributions to nursing behavior an example of the importance of the social environment for development?

32. Give an example of how parents' culturally influenced expectations about infants' abilities affect how they behave toward their infants.

33. Describe the first postnatal bio-social-behavioral shift. (Be sure to address biological, behavioral, and social components.)

34. Trace the development of smiling during the first several months of an infant's life. Discuss the role of visual feedback in the development of smiling.

35. How does nursing differ from sucking?

36. Discuss the debate regarding the disappearance of the stepping reflex.

37. What are some methodological problems that researchers encounter when studying learning and perception in the newborn?

The Achievements of the First Year

Multiple-Choice Questions

1.   During the first year of life most infants
      a.   triple their birth weights
      b.   double their birth lengths
      c.   double their birth weights
      d.   quadruple their birth weights
   Answer: a, Reference: Chapter 5, Pp. 187, Difficulty: E

2.   During the first year of life most infants increase in length by
      a.   half
      b.   double
      c.   triple
      d.   quadruple
   Answer: a, Reference: Chapter 5, Pp. 187, Difficulty: M

3.   Which factor is not thought to contribute to variability in the height and weight of children?
      a.   genetics
      b.   nutrition
      c.   exposure to sunlight
      d.   educational achievement
   Answer: d, Reference: Chapter 5, Pp. 187, Difficulty: M

4.   During the first year, children's heads
      a.   change little in size
      b.   grow to their full adult size
      c.   grow to be a larger proportion of total body length
      d.   grow to be a smaller proportion of total body length
   Answer: d, Reference: Chapter 5, P. 188, Difficulty: M

5.   By 1 year of age, the proportion of a child's body that is the head is about
    a.   6%
    b.   12%
    c.   20%
    d.   25%
Answer: c, Reference: Chapter 5, P. 188, Difficulty: M

6.   By adulthood the proportion of a person's body that is the head is about
    a.   6%
    b.   12%
    c.   20%
    d.   25%
Answer: b, Reference: Chapter 5, P. 188, Difficulty: M

7.   According to Thelen (1995), changes in body proportions by about 12 months of age make it easier for a child to
    a.   play with his or her toes
    b.   balance on two legs and begin to walk
    c.   reach for objects while in a squatting posture
    d.   bend over and pick up objects and return to a standing position without losing balance.
Answer: b, Reference: Chapter 5, P. 188, Difficulty: M

8.   Newborn's bones are
    a.   completely ossified
    b.   in the process of ossification
    c.   completely hard, but are not yet completely ossified
    d.   soft and do not harden until they are about 12 months of age
Answer: b, Reference: Chapter 5, P. 188, Difficulty: D

9.   The bones in an infant's hands and wrists are
    a.   ossified at birth
    b.   ossified by the end of the first year
    c.   not ossified until the end of infancy
    d.   among the last to ossify at about 6 months of age
Answer: b, Reference: Chapter 5, P. 188, Difficulty: M

10.   During the first postnatal year, an infant's muscles
    a.   do not increase in size
    b.   are adding new fibers each day
    c.   increase in length, thickness, and mass
    d.   are slightly decreased in total mass and length
Answer: c, Reference: Chapter 5, P. 188, Difficulty: E

11.   At birth the bones of female infants are more advanced than the bones of male infants by about
       a.   3 weeks
       b.   4 to 6 weeks
       c.   8 to 10 weeks
       d.   4 or more months
Answer: b, Reference: Chapter 5, P. 188, Difficulty: E

12.   By puberty, the bones of girls are more advanced than the bones of boys by about
       a.   3 weeks
       b.   4 to 6 weeks
       c.   8 to 10 months
       d.   2 years
Answer: d, Reference: Chapter 5, P. 188, Difficulty: E

13.   During the first year of life, changes in the brain are most striking in the
       a.   brain stem
       b.   cerebellum
       c.   hippocampus
       d.   frontal cortex
Answer: d, Reference: Chapter 5, P. 189, Difficulty: M

14.   The frontal cortex is important in
       a.   memory
       b.   simple reflexes
       c.   integrating information
       d.   smoothing motor movements
Answer: c, Reference: Chapter 5, P. 189, Difficulty: M

15.   A spurt of frontal cortical development has been observed to occur
       a.   in the first weeks of life
       b.   between 3 and 5 months
       c.   between 7 and 9 months
       d.   at the end of the first year
Answer: c, Reference: Chapter 5, P. 189, Difficulty: M

16.   According to Fischer and Rose (1994), increases in electrical activity and density of cell connections in the frontal lobes are important in
       a.   memory
       b.   simple reflexes
       c.   smoothing motor movements
       d.   coordinating more complex interactions
Answer: d, Reference: Chapter 5, P. 189, Difficulty: M

17.   According to Diamond, changes in the prefrontal area of the frontal cortex is important for the emergence of
a.   complex reflexes
b.   impulse inhibition
c.   coordinated actions
d.   integration of information
Answer: b, Reference: Chapter 5, P. 189, Difficulty: M

18.   The area of the brain thought to be crucial for the appearance of the ability to inhibit impulses is
a.   brain stem
b.   hippocampus
c.   frontal cortex
d.   prefrontal cortex
Answer: d, Reference: Chapter 5, P. 189, Difficulty: M

19.   According to Yonas and Hartman (1993), infants no longer reach for an object beyond their reach at about
a.   3 months
b.   5 months
c.   7 months
d.   9 months
Answer: b, Reference: Chapter 5, P. 190, Difficulty: M

20.   According to Matthew and Cook (1990), most babies can guide their movements with a single glance, and the movements with which they reach for and grasp objects look as well integrated and automatic as a reflex by the age of
a.   6 months
b.   9 months
c.   12 months
d.   15 months
Answer: b, Reference: Chapter 5, P. 190, Difficulty: D

21.   At what age are infants able to pick up objects using their thumb and forefinger?
a.   3 months
b.   6 months
c.   9 months
d.   12 months
Answer: d, Reference: Chapter 5, P. 190, Difficulty: M

22. Rachel Karniol (1989) found that as an infant's fine motor skills increase during the first 9 months of life, there is an invariable sequence in
    a. locomotion
    b. learning speech
    c. how they manipulate objects
    d. discovering right or left-handedness
Answer: c, Reference: Chapter 5, P. 191, Difficulty: E

23. According to Eleanor Gibson, as infants gain more control over their hands,
    a. they use the same actions on almost objects
    b. different objects can be explored differently
    c. adults need to structure the environment more
    d. variability between infants makes general conclusions about action difficult
Answer: b, Reference: Chapter 5, P. 191, Difficulty: E

24. Karniol (1989) found that although infants can hold their heads up from about 2 months of age, young infants still have difficulty moving their arms in a coordinated way until about the age of
    a. 3 to 4 months
    b. 5 to 6 months
    c. 7 months
    d. 8 months
Answer: a, Reference: Chapter 5, P. 191, Difficulty: D

25. Most babies have integrated the movements involved in crawling into a well-coordinated pattern by approximately how many months of age?
    a. 2
    b. 6
    c. 8
    d. 12
Answer: c, Reference: Chapter 5, P. 191, Difficulty: M

26. Examination of the ages at which children achieve motor milestones shows that
    a. practice has little effect on the ages at which babies master universal skills
    b. 90 percent of infants have begun walking by the time they are 12 months of age
    c. there are wide variations in the ages at which infants begin to sit, walk, and crawl
    d. infants are remarkably uniform in the ages at which they become able to sit, crawl, and walk
Answer: c, Reference: Chapter 5, P. 194, Table 5.1, Difficulty: M

27.   About 90% of infants are able to pull themselves up to stand by the age of
        a.   7 months
        b.   8 months
        c.   9 months
        d.   10 months
Answer: d, Reference: Chapter 5, P.194, Table 5.1, Difficulty: M

28.   During the first year, infants develop greater control over movements of their bodies beginning with their
        a.   feet
        b.   heads
        c.   hands
        d.   trunks
Answer: b, Reference: Chapter 5, P. 194, Table 5.1, Difficulty: M

29.   Wayne and Margaret Dennis found that traditionally raised Hopi infants who had been strapped to cradle boards
        a.   were significantly delayed in all aspects of motor development
        b.   learned to walk independently later than infants for whom cradle boards were not used
        c.   learned to walk independently earlier than infants for whom cradle boards had not been used
        d.   did not differ in age of independent walking from infants for whom cradle boards were not used
Answer: d, Reference: Chapter 5, P. 193, Difficulty: E

30.   Motor development during infancy
        a.   cannot be rushed or speeded up
        b.   can be sped up by extensive practice
        c.   does not affect communicative activity
        d.   does not affect an infant's relationship to his or her environment
Answer: b, Reference: Chapter 5, P. 193, Difficulty: M

31.   Kipsigi babies in Kenya, who are given training by parents in sitting, standing, and walking
        a.   reach these milestones at later ages than American children do
        b.   are advanced in these skills, and also in other motor skills which have not been taught
        c.   reach these motor milestones at the same ages as American children who have not received training
        d.   develop these skills earlier than American children, but are not advanced in motor skills which have not been taught
Answer: d, Reference: Chapter 5, P. 193, Difficulty: E

32. The infants of the Ache, who are discouraged from early acquisition of motor abilities, acquire the ability to walk
     a. earlier than American infants
     b. slightly later than American infants
     c. one year later than American infants
     d. about the same time as American infants
Answer: c, Reference: Chapter 5, P. 194, Difficulty: E

33. The greatest effect of practice in the development of motor skills appears in activities such as
     a. running and jumping
     b. standing and walking
     c. typing and roller skating
     d. crawling and rolling over
Answer: c, Reference: Chapter 5, P. 194, Difficulty: M

34. Between the ages of three and twelve months, there is evidence that infants are acquiring a greater ability to think systematically about their surroundings and to do all but which of the following?
     a. act accordingly
     b. recognize caretakers
     c. remember prior experiences
     d. employ deliberate variation of problem-solving means
Answer: d, Reference: Chapter 5, P. 195, Difficulty: E

35. According to Piaget, infants between the ages of 4 and 8 months act on the world through
     a. their inborn reflexes
     b. primary circular reactions
     c. secondary circular reactions
     d. a well-developed understanding of object permanence
Answer: c, Reference: Chapter 5, P. 195, Difficulty: M

36. Infants begin to perform secondary circular reactions during which substage of Piaget's stage of sensorimotor development?
     a. substage 1
     b. substage 2
     c. substage 3
     d. substage 4
Answer: c, Reference: Chapter 5, P. 195, Difficulty: M

37.   According to Piaget, if an infant discovers that when she kicks the mobile above her crib the fairy-tale characters flutter, then repeats this action many times, this is an example of
      a.   habituation
      b.   classical conditioning
      c.   a primary circular reaction
      d.   a secondary circular reaction
Answer: d, Reference: Chapter 5, P. 195, Difficulty: M

38.   When performing secondary circular reactions, infants
      a.   systematically vary their behaviors to produce novel results
      b.   repeatedly perform activities, such as thumb sucking, that center on their own bodies
      c.   repeatedly perform behaviors that cause interesting results in the outside environment
      d.   avoid performing behaviors that produce already known results in the outside environment
Answer: c, Reference: Chapter 5, P. 195, Difficulty: M

39.   The hallmark of the fourth sensorimotor substage is
      a.   simple reflexive activity
      b.   focus on external objects
      c.   ability to prolong pleasurable activities
      d.   the ability to coordinate actions to achieve a goal
Answer: d, Reference: Chapter 5, P. 195, Difficulty: D

40.   According to Piaget, true problem solving first appears in sensorimotor stage
      a.   2
      b.   3
      c.   4
      d.   5
Answer: c, Reference: Chapter 5, P. 196, Difficulty: D

41.   In sensorimotor substage 4, infants coordinate secondary circular reactions mainly to
      a.   reach a goal
      b.   make interesting experiences last
      c.   to avoid unpleasant consequences
      d.   make interesting effects on the environment last
Answer: a, Reference: Chapter 5, P. 196, Difficulty: D

42.   In sensorimotor substage 4, infants
        a.   think, using mental symbols
        b.   practice and extend their inborn reflexes
        c.   perform only secondary circular reactions
        d.   coordinate secondary circular reactions to achieve goals
Answer: d, Reference: Chapter 5, P. 196, Difficulty: M

43.   Piaget's notion of object permanence refers to the idea that
        a.   particular objects will exist forever
        b.   an object's identification never changes even when its appearance changes
        c.   the existence of objects is dependent on a person's belief in their existence
        d.   objects exist apart from our actions on them, and still exist when out of sight
Answer: d, Reference: Chapter 5, P. 198, Difficulty: E

44.   In a study by Bower (1982) when infants who did not yet search for hidden objects
        were presented with images of "multiple mothers" (images that appear in more than
        one place at a time) these infants
        a.   become upset
        b.   lost interest and looked away
        c.   interacted happily with each mother in turn
        d.   did not seem to notice the unusual situation
Answer: d, Reference: Chapter 5, P. 198, Difficulty: M

45.   According to Piaget, we can infer that infants understand that objects' continue to
        exist when out of sight if they
        a.   are at least 6 months of age
        b.   actively search for the hidden objects
        c.   show no sign of worry when the objects disappear
        d.   can perform secondary circular reactions involving those objects
Answer: b, Reference: Chapter 5, P. 198, Difficulty: M

46.   Piaget observed that infants look toward the source of sound during the first ____
        months of life.
        a.   2
        b.   4
        c.   7
        d.   9
Answer: b, Reference: Chapter 5, P. 199, Difficulty: E

47.   During the first 4 months of life, infants confronted with a hidden object test usually
        a.   make the A-not-B error
        b.   conduct a manual search for a hidden object
        c.   search visually but not manually for hidden objects
        d.   stare at the spot where a hidden object was last visible
Answer: d, Reference: Chapter 5, P. 199, Difficulty: E

48.   In which stage of developing object permanence will an infant first reach for objects which are only partly hidden?
        a.   stage 1
        b.   stage 2
        c.   stage 3
        d.   stage 4
Answer: c, Reference: Chapter 5, P. 199, Difficulty: M

49.   Infants first show that they are able to search actively for hidden objects during which stage of developing object permanence?
        a.   stage 1
        b.   stage 2
        c.   stage 3
        d.   stage 4
Answer: d, Reference: Chapter 5, P. 199, Difficulty: M

50.   What is the A-not-B error?
        a.   the tendency of infants 8 to 12 months of age to grasp objects which their parents prefer them not to have
        b.   the tendency of infants less than 8 to 12 months of age to turn their heads in the opposite direction from a sound
        c.   the tendency of infants under 8 to 12 months of age to persist in searching for a hidden object rather than turning their attention to a distractor
        d.   the tendency for infants 8 to 12 months of age to search for an object in a place it has previously been found rather than in second place where they have seen it being hidden
Answer: d, Reference: Chapter 5, P. 200, Difficulty: E

51.   Infants in stage 4 of developing object permanence
        a.   make the A not B error
        b.   recover a partially hidden object for the first time
        c.   turn their attention quickly away from a hidden object
        d.   stare at the place where they have seen an object disappear
Answer: a, Reference: Chapter 5, P. 200, Difficulty: E

52.   Studies by Baillargeon and colleagues indicate that infants typically realize that objects do not cease to exist simply because they are out of sight, by the age of
        a.   2 months
        b.   4 months
        c.   5 months
        d.   6 months
Answer: b, Reference: Chapter 5, P. 200, Difficulty: D

53. Baillargeon and her colleagues found that when 3-1/2 month-old infants were shown a rotating screen that appeared to pass through the place where a hidden box was located
   a. they were not surprised, even though this was a novel event
   b. they were more attentive than when the screen appeared to bump the hidden box, showing that they believed the box was still there
   c. they were less attentive than when the screen appeared to bump the box, showing that they no longer believed in the existence of the box once it was hidden
   d. they were equally as attentive as they were when the screen appeared to bump the box, so no conclusions about their understanding could be drawn

Answer: b, Reference: Chapter 5, P. 201, Difficulty: M

54. An important reason for infants' failure to pass hidden object tasks seems to be
   a. memory limitations
   b. lack of motor skills
   c. lack of linguistic skills
   d. inability to coordinate two actions

Answer: a, Reference: Chapter 5, P. 201, Difficulty: M

55. Adele Diamond (1991) has championed the view that young infants behave as they do on object permanence tests because they
   a. are confused
   b. quickly forget
   c. do not have the motor ability to remove a cloth cover
   d. cannot keep in mind the continued existence of something they can't see

Answer: d, Reference: Chapter 5, P. 201, Difficulty: D

56. Infants who have not yet learned to search for hidden objects
   a. do not yet have the motor skills to do so
   b. have trouble inhibiting a previously successful action
   c. are not capable of removing see-through covers from the same objects
   d. give no other indication that they understand that objects still exist when hidden

Answer: b, Reference: Chapter 5, P. 201, Difficulty: D

57. When Elizabeth Spelke tested 4-month-olds to see if they knew what sorts of sounds should accompany different pictures, she found that they
   a. consistently picked women's voices
   b. looked more often at films for which the correct soundtrack was being played
   c. did not yet understand the connections between the visual and auditory properties of objects
   d. could not connect people's voices and actions, but could make connections between mechanical sounds and pictures

Answer: b, Reference: Chapter 5, P. 204, Difficulty: E

58.   A study by Strei and Spelke (1988) found that 4-month-old infants were able to make
       a.   tactile discriminations based on visual habituation
       b.   visual discriminations based on tactile habituation
       c.   auditory discriminations based on visual habituation
       d.   tactile discriminations based on auditory habituation
Answer: b, Reference: Chapter 5, P. 204, Difficulty: M

59.   At what age has the habituation paradigm has shown infants to be sensitive to set size?
       a.   less than 6 months
       b.   7-9 months
       c.   10 months
       d.   12 months
Answer: a, Reference: Chapter 5, P. 205, Difficulty: M

60.   Research by Karen Wynn (1992) found that 4-month old infants
       a.   expected 1 + 1 to equal 2
       b.   could not differentiate sets of different sizes
       c.   looked more at a film with an appropriate sound track
       d.   could differentiate sets of various sizes as long as there were fewer than 5 elements
Answer: a, Reference: Chapter 5, P. 205, Difficulty: M

61.   When infants can tell that two somewhat different-looking objects are both balls, they are
       a.   categorizing
       b.   demonstrating habituation
       c.   demonstrating object permanence
       d.   coordinating secondary circular reactions
Answer: a, Reference: Chapter 5, P. 206, Difficulty: E

62.   In the study by Hayne, Rovee-Collier, and Perris (1987), 3-month-old infants were found to
       a.   look longer at a novel mobile than at a mobile they had seen
       b.   kick for a mobile with a different shape and different color as a trained mobile, but not for one with the same shape
       c.   kick for a mobile with the same shape but different color as a trained mobile, but not for one with a different shape
       d.   kick for a mobile the same amount as a trained mobile, but only if it had the same color, regardless of the shape
Answer: c, Reference: Chapter 5, P. 206, Difficulty: M

63.   A study by Eimas and Quinn (1994) found that 3-month-old infants were able to habituate for categories of
    a.   tools
    b.   birds
    c.   animals
    d.   clothing
Answer: c, Reference: Chapter 5, P. 207, Difficulty: E

64.   Mandler and McDonough (1993) present evidence that suggests the categorization of 7 month old infants is based on
    a.   shared behaviors
    b.   perceptual features
    c.   conceptual properties
    d.   actions that can be performed on objects
Answer: b, Reference: Chapter 5, P. 208, Difficulty: E

65.   Mandler and McDonough (1993) report evidence for conceptual categorization in infants of about
    a.   3-4 months
    b.   5-7 months
    c.   9-11 months
    d.   12 months
Answer: c, Reference: Chapter 5, P. 208, Difficulty: E

66.   Memory research with 3-month olds suggests that they remember how to move a mobile
    a.   for only one or two days
    b.   for only 3 or 4 days
    c.   for periods up to 2 weeks
    d.   up to a month if provided with a reminder
Answer: d, Reference: Chapter 5, P. 208, Difficulty: D

67.   Based upon studies of memory improvement, Rovee-Collier (1990) has concluded that improvement in memory over the course of the first year is
    a.   erratic and follows no set pattern
    b.   sporadic and involves no new principles
    c.   a continuous process involving new principles of learning or remembering
    d.   a continuous process and does not involve any new principles of learning or remembering
Answer: d, Reference: Chapter 5, P. 209, Difficulty: M

68.   Between 7 and 9 months of age, children become capable of which type of memory?
        a.   recall
        b.   rehearsal
        c.   mnemonic
        d.   recognition
Answer: a, Reference: Chapter 5, P. 209, Difficulty: D

69.   Which of the following is an example of recall memory?
        a.   a 3-month-old sees a rattle, picks it up, and puts it in her mouth
        b.   an infant becomes excited when his grandmother's face appears at the window
        c.   when a 1-month-old is picked up by his mother, he opens his mouth and
               turns toward the breast
        d.   a 9-month old sees his mother place an attractive pot in the kitchen
               cupboard, and after several minutes, he crawls over to the cupboard and
               removes the pot
Answer: d, Reference: Chapter 5, P. 209, Difficulty: D

70.   Meltzoff (1988) has observed that 9-month old infants
        a.   kick their legs to a familiar mobile two weeks later
        b.   spontaneously interact with toys in appropriate ways
        c.   imitate the facial gestures of an adult 24 hours later
        d.   imitate the behaviors of an adult with a toy 24 hours later
Answer: d, Reference: Chapter 5, P. 209, Difficulty: M

71.   About the same time that infants are able to remember well enough to compare the
        present situation with past situations
        a.   they become wary of familiar people
        b.   their enthusiasm for novel events increases
        c.   they become less interested in familiar events
        d.   they become wary of unfamiliar events and people
Answer: d, Reference: Chapter 5, P. 210, Difficulty: M

72.   Compared to younger infants, 9-month-olds' reactions to unfamiliar objects and
        people are characterized by
        a.   anger
        b.   wariness
        c.   frustration
        d.   enthusiasm
Answer: b, Reference: Chapter 5, P. 210, Difficulty: E

73.   Meltzoff and Moore (1994) have observed that 6-week old infants
    a.   kick their legs to a familiar mobile two weeks later
    b.   spontaneously interact with toys in appropriate ways
    c.   imitate the facial gestures of an adult 24 hours later
    d.   imitate the behaviors of an adult with a toy 24 hours later
Answer: c, Reference: Chapter 5, P. 210, Difficulty: M

74.   Meltzoff and Moore (1994) argue that the ability of 6-week old infants to imitate the facial gestures of an adult 24 hours later is evidence for
    a.   dishabituation
    b.   recall memory
    c.   recognition memory
    d.   operant conditioning
Answer: b, Reference: Chapter 5, P. 210, Difficulty: D

75.   Keiko Mizukami and her colleagues (1990) have observed that when an infant's mother disappears and a stranger appears over the crib
    a.   12 month old infants may become inconsolable
    b.   the skin temperature of 2 to 4 month old infants drops
    c.   the skin temperature of 2 to 4 month old infants increases
    d.   the skin temperature of the 6 to 8 month old infants drops
Answer: b, Reference: Chapter 5, P. 210, Difficulty: D

76.   When adult support allows children to accomplish with help what they are not yet able to do alone, the result is
    a.   the creation of a zone of proximal development
    b.   interference with the natural course of development
    c.   movement from one stage of development to the next
    d.   a lack of independence of the children from their parents
Answer: a, Reference: Chapter 5, P. 210, Difficulty: M

77.   Which illustrates a zone of proximal development?
    a.   a mother changes her infant son's diapers
    b.   a father vocalizes back at his infant when the child vocalizes
    c.   a mother guides her daughter's hand to her mouth as the infant holds a spoonful of cereal
    d.   an infant pushes away his father's hand when he sees a spoonful of medicine coming toward his mouth
Answer: c, Reference: Chapter 5, P. 211, Difficulty: D

78. What percent of the time did Mosler and Rogoff (1994) find that 6-month-old infants signaled their mothers to help them get a toy?
    a.   10%
    b.   40%
    c.   50%
    d.   75%
Answer: b, Reference: Chapter 5, P. 212, Difficulty: M

79. According to Joseph Campos and his colleagues, the critical factor in organizing a qualitative change in developmental processes late in the first year of life is
    a.   locomotion
    b.   increased communication abilities
    c.   the development of object permanence
    d.   being able to make categorical distinctions
Answer: a, Reference: Chapter 5, P. 212, Difficulty: D

80. Campos and his colleagues (1992) interview parents of 8-month-old infants who had begun to crawl about their feelings toward their infants and reported that
    a.   positive feelings were more intense in parents whose infants had begun to crawl
    b.   negative feelings were more intense in parents whose infants had begun to crawl
    c.   parents whose infants had begun to crawl reported fewer feelings of anger toward their infants
    d.   both positive and negative feelings were more intense in parents whose infants had begun to crawl
Answer: d, Reference: Chapter 5, P. 212, Difficulty: M

81. Which of the following does Eleanor Maccoby list as a sign that infants have become attached to their caretakers?
    a.   distress on separation
    b.   decreasing fear of strangers
    c.   crying when reunited after an absence
    d.   the ability to tolerate lengthy separations
Answer: a, Reference: Chapter 5, P. 213, Difficulty: M

82. When infants orient their actions to their caretaker even when he or she is absent, this is one of Maccoby's signs of
    a.   insecurity
    b.   attachment
    c.   independence
    d.   a difficult temperament
Answer: b, Reference: Chapter 5, P. 213, Difficulty: M

83.   Secondary intersubjectivity is a more complex way in which infants begin to react to others by
        a.   concentrating on the primary caretaker
        b.   ignoring the caretaker in favor of what interests them
        c.   interacting with the caretaker only when he or she is present
        d.   simultaneously paying attention to the caretaker and another object
Answer: d, Reference: Chapter 5, P. 213, Difficulty: M

84.   A study by Butterworth and Jarrett (1991) indicate that babies follow the line of their mothers' gaze and engage in joint visual attention with others by the age of
        a.   3 or 4 months
        b.   5 or 6 months
        c.   7 or 8 months
        d.   9 or 10 months
Answer: c, Reference: Chapter 5, P. 213, Difficulty: D

85.   Infants check the reactions of their caretakers to help them interpret unusual events when they engage in
        a.   imitation
        b.   attachment
        c.   self-recognition
        d.   social referencing
Answer: d, Reference: Chapter 5, P. 213, Difficulty: E

86.   Which of the following is an example of social referencing?
        a.   a child "shaves" alongside his father
        b.   a newborn cries when she hears another newborn in the nursery crying
        c.   a 1-year-old, approached by a strange cat, looks over to see her mother's reaction
        d.   a newborn sticks out his tongue immediately after seeing an adult perform the action
Answer: c, Reference: Chapter 5, P. 213, Difficulty: M

87.   Which develops first?
        a.   cooing
        b.   babbling
        c.   jargoning
        d.   first words
Answer: a, Reference: Chapter 5, P. 214, Difficulty: E

88.   An infant's first conversations
      a.   are examples of "jargoning"
      b.   are exchanges of vocalizations with other infants
      c.   take place during the second year of life, after they have learned a few words
      d.   take place at several months of age, as vocalizations are exchanged with familiar adults
Answer: d, Reference: Chapter 5, P. 214, Difficulty: E

89.   At about 4 months of age, an infant's vocalizations begin to include the consonant vowel combinations called
      a.   words
      b.   cooing
      c.   babbling
      d.   jargoning
Answer: c, Reference: Chapter 5, P. 214, Difficulty: E

90.   An infant's early babbling
      a.   consists of elongated vowel sounds
      b.   consists of meaningful word-like sounds
      c.   is completely dependent on auditory feedback
      d.   consists of consonant-vowel combinations repeated as a form of vocal play
Answer: d, Reference: Chapter 5, P. 214, Difficulty: E

91.   Until about 9 months of age, infants' babbling
      a.   consists only of vowel sounds
      b.   serves only as an attempt to communicate
      c.   is the same regardless of the language infants hear around them
      d.   contains only the sounds of the language infants hear around them
Answer: c, Reference; Chapter 5, P. 214, Difficulty: M

92.   Vocalizations that appear at the end of the first year of life that capture the intonation and stress of adult utterances are called
      a.   cooing
      b.   babbling
      c.   jargoning
      d.   first words
Answer: c, Reference: Chapter 5, P. 214, Difficulty: E

93.   At about the time infants begin to move around on their own, which of the following begins to play a greater role in their language development?
      a.   imitation
      b.   reinforcement
      c.   the environment
      d.   biological maturation
Answer: c, Reference: Chapter 5, P. 215, Difficulty: D

94.   Oller and Eiler's (1988) research has shown that
       a.   no deaf children babble
       b.   not all hearing children babble
       c.   only deaf children with residual hearing babble
       d.   all deaf and all hearing children babble similarly

Answer: c, Reference: Chapter 5, P. 215, Difficulty: M

95.   Among deaf infants, cooing and babbling
       a.   do not occur
       b.   follow the same course as they do in hearing infants
       c.   occur only if hearing aids provide infants with auditory feedback
       d.   occur at the same time as they do in hearing infants, but eventually die out

Answer: d, Reference: Chapter 5, P. 215, Difficulty: M

96.   At about the same time that the babbling of hearing children acquires intonation and
       expressiveness, deaf children
       a.   begin to "babble" with their hands
       b.   give up any attempts to communicate linguistically
       c.   continue to babble without expression or intonation
       d.   also develop expression and intonation in their babbling

Answer: a, Reference: Chapter 5, P. 215, Difficulty: E

97.   The bio-social-behavioral shift which takes place between the ages of 7 and 9
       months involves changes in which of the following parts of the brain?
       a.   the visual pathways
       b.   the areas important for planning and executing action
       c.   the areas important for the formation of higher reflexes
       d.   the areas involved in respiration and other vital functions

Answer: b, Reference: Chapter 5, P. 215, Difficulty: M

98.   At about 7 to 9 months of age, which of the following behavioral characteristics is
       thought to organize the bio-social-behavior shift?
       a.   attachment
       b.   locomotion
       c.   searching for hidden objects
       d.   memory based on categories

Answer: b, Reference: Chapter 5, P. 215, Difficulty: M

99.   Changes in the central nervous system, increases in size and strength, and new emotional responses to caretakers are involved in a bio-social-behavioral shift which occurs at approximately how many months of age?

a.   2-1/2
b.   5
c.   7 to 9
d.   12 to 14

Answer: c, Reference: Chapter 5, P. 215, Difficulty: E

100.   In Held and Hein's research, kittens who were reared in the dark were given visual experience in a "kitten carousel." Their study showed

a.   visual experience alone allows visual-motor coordination to develop
b.   active movement is necessary for developing visual-motor coordination
c.   neither visual nor motor experience is necessary for the development of visual-motor coordination
d.   in the absence of normal visual stimulation, the kittens' visual cortexes failed to develop and they became blind

Answer: b, Reference: Chapter 5, Box 5.1, Difficulty: M

101.   Campos and his colleagues have demonstrated that infants are more skilled at locating hidden objects when given extra experience with

a.   locomotion
b.   using external direction cues
c.   removing covers from objects
d.   none of the above, the skill seems to depend solely on simple maturation

Answer: a, Reference: Chapter 5, Box 5.1, Difficulty: M

102.   Campos and his colleagues have shown that experience in moving around in baby walkers prior to the onset of crawling were more advanced in

a.   locomotion
b.   babbling behavior
c.   attachment behavior
d.   object permanence tests

Answer: d, Reference: Chapter 5, Box 5.1, Difficulty: M

Essay Questions

1.   Describe the major changes that occur in infants' motor development during the first year of life.

2.   Discuss the role of practice in the development of early motor skills.

3.   What is the primary difference between substages 3 and 4 of Piaget's sensorimotor period?

4.   In what ways are primary circular reactions and secondary circular reactions alike? Give and describe an example of each. What substage is characterized by each?

5.   How do researchers test for object permanence?

6.   Explain why some psychologists think that infants 4 to 8 months old believe that objects continue to exist when they are hidden. Cite examples.

7.   Describe the A-not-B error. What factors may contribute to infants making this error on object permanence tests?

8.   Explain the relationship between experience with locomotion and the ability to search for hidden objects. What evidence is there that understanding spatial relations, including the ability to search for hidden objects, is affected by experience with locomotion?

9.   What is known about how infants put together different properties of objects, for example, sound and sight, to develop overall impressions of them?

10. How have changes in research paradigms given new insight into what children do and do not know about hidden objects?

11. Have later investigations of object permanence confirmed Piaget's beliefs about when it occurs? Explain.

12. How does an infant's ability to make categorical distinctions change over the first year of life? How do psychologists study these changes?

13. Discuss the memory development that occurs during the period between 2-1/2 and 12 months of age.

14. During the last part of the first year of life, what cognitive changes contribute to infants' increasing wariness?

15. Explain what is meant by a zone of proximal development. Describe an example. How can infants' wariness of unfamiliar people and objects be explained?

16. How have psychologists defined attachment of infants to their caretakers? When is it thought to develop?

17. What is primary intersubjectivity? How does it differ from secondary intersubjectivity?

18. What is social referencing? Describe the circumstances under which it is likely to occur.

19. What is babbling? When does it occur? Explain its development in both deaf and hearing infants.

20. Briefly describe infants' developing linguistic abilities during the first year of life.

21. Contrast infant babbling with jargoning.

22. Infants acquire new skills and abilities between 7 and 9 months of age, and achieve a new level of development. Describe the changes in the biological, behavioral, and social domains that converge to create this reorganization of behavior.

23. Certain psychologists believe changes in brain structure provide the physical basis for more complex motor behavior, and for increases in the ability to learn and solve problems. Explain these views and give examples.

24. Perceptual motor exploration is essential for increasing knowledge about and control over the environment. Discuss studies of the development of reaching and grasping skills as they relate to an increased knowledge of and greater control over an infant's environment.

25. Development emerges from interplay between assimilation and accommodation. Discuss each of these and what role the term "stages" plays in the structure of the cognitive process.

26. Explain the developmental progression of crawling. Be sure to include the integration of movements of many parts of the body which infants must master in order to locomote any distance.

27. Give convincing evidence that the data on object permanence, categorization, and the changing bases of remembering are not separate from each other.

28. You are going out for the evening with your friends, who are parents of a 10-month-old girl. The babysitter is new, and the baby is asleep when she arrives, so the parents decide not to wake the baby to say goodbye. Lately the baby has been increasingly grumpy about being left at home and, they reason, there's no point in causing a scene unnecessarily. The movie is great, but when you return at 11:00, the sitter tells your friends the baby awoke two hours earlier, screamed hysterically for 45 minutes without letting herself be comforted, and finally fell asleep. The sitter is exhausted too. From what you have learned about infants, why do you think the baby was crying, and what could her parents do to prevent such a situation from occurring again?

The End of Infancy

Multiple-Choice Questions

1. Compared to the first year of life, children's physical growth rate during the second year is
    a. slower
    b. a little faster
    c. about the same
    d. about twice as fast
    Answer: a, Reference: Chapter 6, P. 223, Difficulty: E

2. By the end of the third year, the average height of children raised in the U.S. is about
    a. 29 inches
    b. 33 inches
    c. 38 inches
    d. 43 inches
    Answer: c, Reference: Chapter 6, P. 223, Difficulty: M

3. By the end of the third year, children raised in the U.S. have increased their birth length by almost
    a. double
    b. two and 1/2 times
    c. triple
    d. quadruple
    Answer: a, Reference: Chapter 6, P. 223, Difficulty: D

4.   By the end of the third year, the average weight of children raised in the U.S. is
     about
     a.   29 pounds
     b.   33 pounds
     c.   38 pounds
     d.   43 pounds
Answer: b, Reference: Chapter 6, P. 223, Difficulty: M

5.   Brain development during the second year of life
     a.   does not appreciably affect cortical development
     b.   results in myelination of connections between different areas of the brain
     c.   does not include increases in brain weight, which has already reached adult
          levels
     d.   results, for the first time, in an imbalance between systems with respect to
          level of development
Answer: b, Reference: Chapter 6, P. 223, Difficulty: M

6.   In a study by Adolph and colleagues (1993), when 14-month-old infants were
     presented with ramps of various steepness, they
     a.   refused to try to maneuver down them
     b.   tumbled down the ramps into their mother's arms
     c.   tried alternative methods of maneuvering on them
     d.   spent more time feeling the surface of steeper ramps
Answer: c, Reference: Chapter 6, P. 225, Difficulty: M

7.   In a study by Adolph and colleagues (1993), when 8 1/2-month-old infants were
     presented with ramps of various steepness, they
     a.   climbed them without difficulty
     b.   tumbled down the ramps into their mother's arms
     c.   tried alternative methods of maneuvering on them
     d.   adjusted their movements after falling several times
Answer: b, Reference: Chapter 6, P. 225, Difficulty: M

8.   In a series of studies tracing the convergence of separately developing actions that
     results in the ability to walk, Esther Thelen and her colleagues found infants can
     execute the pattern of coordinated leg movements if placed on a treadmill and
     supported to stand by as early as
     a.   2 months of age
     b.   4 months of age
     c.   7 months of age
     d.   9 months of age
Answer: c, Reference: Chapter 6, P. 225, Difficulty: M

9.   At what age are most American children able to kick a ball forward?
       a.   15 months
       b.   17 months
       c.   20 months
       d.   24 months
Answer: c, Reference: Chapter 6, P. 226, Difficulty: M

10.   Which of the following motor abilities appears latest in development?
       a.   walking
       b.   jumping
       c.   kicking a ball
       d.   climbing stairs
Answer: b, Reference: Chapter 6, P. 226, Difficulty: M

11.   Manual dexterity increases significantly
       a.   around 6-months of age
       b.   after 12 months of age
       c.   not until 2 years of age
       d.   not until 3 years of age
Answer: b, Reference: Chapter 6, P. 226, Difficulty: M

12.   According to studies by Kevin Connolly and Mary Dalgleish that examined the
       development of the ability to use a spoon children cannot feed themselves with a
       spoon until approximately
       a.   9 months of age
       b.   1 year of age
       c.   2 years of age
       d.   4 years of age
Answer: c, Reference: Chapter 6, P. 226, Difficulty: E

13.   During the second year of life
       a.   visually guided reaching develops
       b.   voluntary control of elimination is mastered by most children
       c.   motor movements of the hands become more finely coordinated
       d.   children's rate of growth increases compared to its rate during the first year
Answer: c, Reference: Chapter 6, P. 226, Difficulty: D

14.   According to deVries & deVries (1977) children are not usually capable of voluntary
       postponement of elimination until at least age _____, but can be taught to eliminate
       when placed on a potty at age _____.
       a.   8 months; 4 months
       b.   12 months; 8 months
       c.   15 months; 6 months
       d.   24 months; 15 months
Answer: c, Reference: Chapter 6, P. 227, Difficulty: D

15.   In toilet training
       a.   it is best to start at 6 months of age or earlier
       b.   beginning at 12 months of age results in the quickest training.
       c.   delaying training until 2 years of age causes it to go more quickly
       d.   children can be taught to remain dry during the day only after they
             consistently remain dry at night
Answer: c, Reference: Chapter 6, P. 227, Difficulty: E

16.   With regard to toilet training, most children are able to
       a.   remain dry during the day by 2-3 years of age
       b.   learn more quickly the earlier training is begun
       c.   remain dry at night before they can remain dry during the day
       d.   remain dry at night at about the same time they can remain dry during the
             day
Answer: a, Reference: Chapter 6, P. 228, Difficulty: E

17.   Which circular reactions are characterized by the use of systematically varied action
       sequences?
       a.   tertiary
       b.   primary
       c.   secondary
       d.   coordinated
Answer: a, Reference: Chapter 6, P. 228, Difficulty: M

18.   Sensorimotor substage 5 in Piaget's theory is characterized by
       a.   representational thought
       b.   tertiary circular reactions
       c.   secondary circular reactions
       d.   coordination of secondary circular reactions
Answer: b, Reference: Chapter 6, P. 228, Difficulty: E

19.   Tertiary circular reactions differ from earlier forms of circular reactions because they
       a.   make interesting sights last
       b.   are examples of representational thought
       c.   involve deliberate varying of action sequences
       d.   involve actions on the infant's own body (thumb-sucking, for example)
Answer: c, Reference: Chapter 6, P. 228, Difficulty: M

20.   Tertiary circular reactions are novel for the infant because they
       a.   make interesting sights last
       b.   are carried out on the infant's body
       c.   make use of varied action sequences
       d.   have their effect on the mental world of the infant rather than the physical
             world
Answer: c, Reference: Chapter 6, P. 228, Difficulty: M

21.   In problem solving, substage 6 children seem to rely more upon
    a.   trial and error
    b.   symbolic combinations
    c.   coordination of circular reactions
    d.   overt, physical attempts to solve the problem
Answer: b, Reference: Chapter 6, P. 228, Difficulty: D

22.   In Piaget's theory, the appearance of representational thought is characteristic of
    a.   the preoperational period
    b.   the stage of concrete operations
    c.   substage 5 of the sensorimotor period
    d.   substage 6 of the sensorimotor period
Answer: d, Reference: Chapter 6, P. 229, Difficulty: E

23.   Being able to think about the relations between objects without actually acting on
        them physically is, according to Piaget, evidence that children are
    a.   making interesting sights last
    b.   engaging in representational thought
    c.   performing tertiary circular reactions
    d.   coordinating secondary circular reactions
Answer: b, Reference: Chapter 6, P. 230, Difficulty: D

24.   In Stage 5 of the object concept, children
    a.   are first able to search for an object that has just been covered by a cloth
    b.   tend to search for an object where they have previously found it, even though
            they see it moved to a new place
    c.   are able to search for an object in a new place, so long as they see it being
            moved from the place where they have previously found it
    d.   can search for an object in a new place even if they have not seen it moved
            from the place where they have previously found it
Answer: c, Reference: Chapter 6, P. 231, Difficulty: D

25.   A child who sees a wind-up toy move under the bed runs around to meet it on the
        other side. This is behavior we might see in a child whose understanding of the
        object concept is at a level of
    a.   substage 3
    b.   substage 4
    c.   substage 5
    d.   substage 6
Answer: d, Reference: Chapter 6, P. 231, Difficulty: D

26.   The problem-solving behavior of children in which of Piaget's sensorimotor substages show noticeable increase in planning?
    a.   3
    b.   4
    c.   5
    d.   6
Answer: d, Reference: Chapter 6, P. 232, Difficulty: D

27.   In substage 6 of the sensorimotor period, children's play becomes more
    a.   rigid
    b.   concrete
    c.   impulsive
    d.   imaginative
Answer: d, Reference: Chapter 6, P. 232, Difficulty: M

28.   We can tell that children are using representational thought when they
    a.   engage in pretend play
    b.   can perform circular reactions
    c.   are able to make interesting sights last
    d.   can recognize an object from one part which is sticking out
Answer: a, Reference: Chapter 6, P. 232, Difficulty: M

29.   Which is an example of locomotor play?
    a.   building a tall tower with blocks
    b.   climbing to the top of the jungle gym
    c.   pretending to be the engineer of a train
    d.   sniffing a paper flower as though it were real
Answer: b, Reference: Chapter 6, P. 232, Difficulty: M

30.   According to Peter Smith (1990) which of the following play types occurs both among humans and among the young of other species?
    a.   social
    b.   fantasy
    c.   pretend
    d.   symbolic
Answer: a, Reference: Chapter 6, P. 232, Difficulty: E

31.   According to Peter Smith, which form of play is uniquely human?
    a.   social play
    b.   object play
    c.   fantasy play
    d.   locomotor play
Answer: c, Reference: Chapter 6, P. 232, Difficulty: E

32. In play, babies use objects in the ways adults use them beginning at about how many months of age?
     a.   8
     b.   12
     c.   18
     d.   24

Answer: b, Reference: Chapter 6, P. 232, Difficulty: D

33. In symbolic play, children
     a.   shake, push, and pull objects
     b.   chase, tease, and imitate one another
     c.   practice running, jumping, and climbing
     d.   use an object to "stand for" something else

Answer: d, Reference: Chapter 6, P. 232, Difficulty: E

34. Which of the following is an example of symbolic play?
     a.   shaking a rattle
     b.   dropping peas on the floor
     c.   banging a peg with a hammer
     d.   making truck noises while moving a pine cone

Answer: d, Reference: Chapter 6, P. 232, Difficulty: E

35. A 2-year-old boy gallops his toy horse across the room and jumps it over a block "fence." He is
     a.   engaging in symbolic play
     b.   engaged in deferred imitation
     c.   performing a tertiary circular reaction
     d.   showing his mastery of the object concept

Answer: a, Reference: Chapter 6, P. 233, Difficulty: D

36. In play, children practice such activities as "cooking" or "taking care of the baby"
     a.   under adult supervision
     b.   by really carrying them out
     c.   because adults tell them to practice these things
     d.   without dangerous consequences of real-world practice

Answer: d, Reference: Chapter 6, P. 233, Difficulty: E

37. Symbolic play serves as a "zone of proximal development," according to
     a.   Jean Piaget
     b.   Peter Smith
     c.   John Bowlby
     d.   Lev Vygotsky

Answer: d, Reference: Chapter 6, P. 233, Difficulty: M

38. Vygotsky, observing the actions performed by children in play, found these actions to be _____ than those performed by children ordinarily.
     a. educationally less useful
     b. potentially more dangerous
     c. developmentally less advanced
     d. developmentally more advanced
Answer: d, Reference: Chapter 6, P. 233, Difficulty: M

39. Findings of Gaskin's (1990) cross-cultural studies exploring the beneficial effects of play indicated that while Central American Mayan infants engage in play in the first 2 years of life ___ than North American infants they are ___ in their performance on standardized tests of development.
     a. less; equal
     b. more; equal
     c. less; superior
     d. more; superior
Answer: a, Reference: Chapter 6, P. 234, Difficulty: M

40. Deferred imitation is considered to be a sign of
     a. assimilation
     b. reflexive behavior
     c. object permanence
     d. representational thought
Answer: d, Reference: Chapter 6, P. 234, Difficulty: M

41. Pretend play and deferred imitation are indicators of
     a. logical reasoning
     b. object permanence
     c. mental representation
     d. tertiary circular reactions
Answer: c, Reference: Chapter 6, P. 234, Difficulty: E

42. Eighteen-month-old children
     a. are just beginning to be afraid of strangers
     b. can imitate actions they have observed at earlier times
     c. have enough control over elimination to remain dry during the day and at night
     d. seem to recognize categories in an array of objects, but do not yet put like objects together
Answer: b, Reference: Chapter 6, P. 234, Difficulty: D

43.   A girl twirls and hits a tambourine after having seen a Spanish dancer on TV the
        night before. She is engaging in
        a.   assimilation
        b.   symbolic play
        c.   categorization
        d.   deferred imitation
Answer: d, Reference: Chapter 6, P. 234, Difficulty: D

44.   According to Piaget, deferred imitation appears in children's behavior at about the
        same time as
        a.   symbolic play
        b.   object permanence
        c.   tertiary circular reactions
        d.   the first imitations of adult speech sounds
Answer: a, Reference: Chapter 6, P. 234, Difficulty: M

45.   Piaget believed that imitation is closely linked to
        a.   adaptation
        b.   assimilation
        c.   accommodation
        d.   molding the world to internal schemas
Answer: c, Reference: Chapter 6, P. 234, Difficulty: D

46.   Piaget emphasized that imitation allowed children to
        a.   practice "real-life" activities in a comparatively safe setting
        b.   assimilate the world to their goals without needing to accommodate to reality
        c.   perform actions, with the help of other children, that they cannot yet
                perform alone
        d.   accommodate to reality without the need to assimilate information to
                previous ideas
Answer: d, Reference: Chapter 6, P. 234, Difficulty: D

47.   Research by Mandler (1990) and Meltzoff (1990) indicates that deferred imitation
        a.   appears late in the first year of life
        b.   occurs later than Piaget has suggested
        c.   develops much as described by Piaget
        d.   appears in conjunction with the ability to recognize objects
Answer: a, Reference: Chapter 6, P. 234, Difficulty: E

48.   Researchers who study mental representations in young children
        a.   use EEG's
        b.   use habituation techniques
        c.   use clues provided by children's behaviors
        d.   interview children about their thoughts and experiences
Answer: c, Reference: Chapter 6, P. 235, Difficulty: E

49.   An important difference between the behavior of child 18 months of age and that of
      a younger child is the creation of _____, when confronted with a collection of
      objects to be categorized.
      a.   subcategories
      b.   a work space
      c.   adult-like categories
      d.   exhaustive categories
Answer: b, Reference: Chapter 6, P. 235, Difficulty: D

50.   At what age did Sugarman find that children were able to divide the objects into
      more than one distinct group when presented with an array of different objects to
      categorize?
      a.   12 months
      b.   18 months
      c.   24 months
      d.   30 months
Answer: c, Reference: Chapter 6, P. 235, Difficulty: M

51.   In the second year of life, children become able to_____ categories in an
      array of objects.
      a.   recognize
      b.   create multiple
      c.   flexibly create and change
      d.   specify the critical features of
Answer: b, Reference: Chapter 6, P. 235, Difficulty: M

52.   Studies by DeLoache (1987, 1995) have reported that children can use a model of
      objects in a space to find an object hidden in the real space by about
      a.   24 months
      b.   30 months
      c.   36 months
      d.   42 months
Answer: c, Reference: Chapter 6, P. 237, Difficulty: M

53.   According to a longitudinal study by McCall, Eichorn, and Hogarty (1977) children
      are able to follow relatively complex verbal instructions by age
      a.   12 months
      b.   15 months
      c.   21 months
      d.   30 months
Answer: c, Reference: Chapter 6, P. 237, Difficulty: D

54.   Which of the following indicates the presence of representational thought?
   a.   pretend play
   b.   using words to stand for objects
   c.   imitating events that are not present
   d.   all of these
Answer: d, Reference: Chapter 6, P. 237, Difficulty: E

55.   By about 18 months of age toddlers begin to
   a.   use complete sentences
   b.   combine two actions in play
   c.   restrict fantasy play to single action
   d.   imitate single words they heard their parents use
Answer: b, Reference: Chapter 6, P. 237, Difficulty: M

56.   Children who can put two words together to form short sentences can usually also
   a.   combine symbolic actions in their play
   b.   categorize objects along two dimensions
   c.   represent the world to themselves mentally
   d.   all of these
Answer: d, Reference: Chapter 6, P. 237, Difficulty: M

57.   Children begin to demonstrate wariness of strangers
   a.   at birth
   b.   during the second year of life
   c.   between about 7 to 9 months of age
   d.   only if they are insecurely attached to their caretakers
Answer: c, Reference: Chapter 6, P. 238, Difficulty: M

58.   An example of a biological drive is
   a.   hunger
   b.   attachment
   c.   myelination
   d.   physical growth
Answer: a, Reference: Chapter 6, P. 238, Difficulty: M

59.   Freud suggested that babies become attached to those who satisfy their need for
   a.   food
   b.   sleep
   c.   exploration
   d.   contact comfort
Answer: a, Reference: Chapter 6, P. 239, Difficulty: E

60. According to Freud, during the oral stage infants usually become attached to
    a. their fathers
    b. their siblings
    c. their mothers
    d. any caregiver
Answer: c, Reference: Chapter 6, P. 239, Difficulty: E

61. During the second year of life, children's pursuit of which of the following often centers on toilet training?
    a. conflict
    b. security
    c. self-control
    d. gratification
Answer: c, Reference: Chapter 6, P. 239, Difficulty: E

62. Freud's theory implies that once children enter the anal stage they would begin to act more
    a. contrary
    b. distressed
    c. dependent
    d. independent
Answer: d, Reference: Chapter 6, P. 239, Difficulty: M

63. Which theorist proposed that the resolution of conflicts at each stage of development throughout the lifetime allows people to acquire new skills?
    a. Freud
    b. Piaget
    c. Erikson
    d. Bowlby
Answer: c, Reference: Chapter 6, P. 239, Difficulty: M

64. According to Erikson, during the first year of life, children must resolve the conflict between
    a. trust and mistrust
    b. initiative and guilt
    c. exploration and security
    d. autonomy and shame and doubt
Answer: a, Reference: Chapter 6, P. 239, Difficulty: M

65.   According to Erikson's view of development, the question "Can I trust my mother to take care of me?" is faced by children
    a.   during the first year of life
    b.   during the second year of life
    c.   during the third year of life
    d.   throughout their lives
Answer: a, Reference: Chapter 6, P. 239, Difficulty: M

66.   Erikson suggested that infants become attached to those
    a.   they trust
    b.   who feed them
    c.   who talk to them
    d.   who give them opportunities to explore
Answer: a, Reference: Chapter 6, P. 239, Difficulty: E

67.   According to Bowlby's observations, children who were separated from their parents for long periods of time eventually
    a.   fell into a permanent state of despair
    b.   became indifferent to other people, unless new relationships were formed
    c.   became, and stayed, frantic with fear until the new caretakers were found
    d.   forgot about their parents and learned to interact happily with multiple caretakers
Answer: b, Reference: Chapter 6, P. 240, Difficulty: D

68.   Who has contributed an evolutionary perspective to the study of attachment?
    a.   Piaget
    b.   Fischer
    c.   Erikson
    d.   Bowlby
Answer: d, Reference: Chapter 6, P. 240, Difficulty: M

69.   In Bowlby's explanation of attachment, a balance is established between the infant's need for proximity to its mother and its need for
    a.   food
    b.   sleep
    c.   comfort
    d.   learning experiences
Answer: d, Reference: Chapter 6, P. 240, Difficulty: M

70. Bowlby's hypothesized mechanism that provides a balance between an infant's need for safety and desire for learning experiences is called
    a.   autonomy
    b.   attachment
    c.   secure base
    d.   disattachment
Answer: b, Reference: Chapter 6, P. 240, Difficulty: E

71. Bowlby believed that the process of mother-infant attachment works similarly to the operation of a
    a.   telephone
    b.   computer
    c.   generator
    d.   thermostat
Answer: d, Reference: Chapter 6, P. 240, Difficulty: D

72. According to Bowlby's attachment theory, the mother serves as a
    a.   model
    b.   secure base
    c.   source of conflict
    d.   vehicle for needs reduction
Answer: b, Reference: Chapter 6, P. 240, Difficulty: M

73. Harrow's initial monkey studies using wire and cloth "mothers," were carried out in order to test the role of which of the following in the formation of attachment?
    a.   trust
    b.   memory
    c.   autonomy
    d.   drive reduction
Answer: d, Reference: Chapter 6, P. 241, Difficulty: E

74. In their studies of infant monkeys, how could Harlow and his colleagues tell when monkeys were attached to their surrogate mothers?
    a.   they would prefer to look at the surrogate mother that had fed them
    b.   they would only take milk from the mother to which they were attached
    c.   they would run to the surrogate mother when frightened by a strange object, then use the mother as a base from which to explore
    d.   their later social interactions with other monkeys were normal if they had been raised by a surrogate to which they had become attached
Answer: c, Reference: Chapter 6, P. 242, Difficulty: D

75.   Which theory of attachment did Harlow's monkey studies helped to rule out?
       a.   the social theory
       b.   the evolutionary theory
       c.   the drive-reduction theory
       d.   the behavioral-learning theory
Answer: c, Reference: Chapter 6, P. 242, Difficulty: M

76.   From observations of the adult behavior of surrogate-raised monkeys, it has been concluded that
       a.   inanimate surrogates can make perfectly acceptable mother substitutes for infant monkeys
       b.   an adequate amount of milk is both necessary and sufficient for monkeys' normal development
       c.   social interaction with other monkeys is necessary for infant monkeys' healthy social development
       d.   an adequate amount of contact comfort is both necessary and sufficient for monkeys' normal development
Answer: c, Reference: Chapter 6, P. 242, Difficulty: D

77.   Mary Ainsworth and her colleagues have studied attachment in human infants using
       a.   strange objects
       b.   surrogate mothers
       c.   the "strange situation"
       d.   frame-by-frame film analysis
Answer: c, Reference: Chapter 6, P. 243, Difficulty: E

78.   In the absence of their mothers in the "strange situation," which children are as likely to be comforted by a stranger as they would be by their mothers?
       a.   anxious/resistant
       b.   anxious/avoidant
       c.   securely/attached
       d.   no children can be comforted as well by a stranger
Answer: b, Reference: Chapter 6, P. 245, Difficulty: D

79.   In anxious/avoidant attachment, as measured in the "strange situation,"
       a.   infants cry when their mothers leave the room, and seek them out for comfort when they return
       b.   infants appear anxious in their mothers' presence, and are more relaxed and playful when their mothers leave the room
       c.   infants may or may not cry when their mothers leave the room, and do not seek them out for comfort when they return
       d.   infants become upset when their mothers leave the room, but alternately seek and pull away from them when they return
Answer: c, Reference: Chapter 6, P. 245, Difficulty: D

80.   When reunited with their mothers in the "strange situation," which type children
       are fairly easily consoled and soon resume playing?
       a.   detached
       b.   anxious/resistant
       c.   anxious/avoidant
       d.   securely attached
Answer: d, Reference: Chapter 6, P. 245, Difficulty: E

81.   American middle-class children display behavior classified as "securely attached" in
       the "strange situation" about what percent of the time?
       a.   12
       b.   25
       c.   65
       d.   95
Answer: c, Reference: Chapter 6, P. 245, Difficulty: M

82.   In the "strange situation," these children tend to be upset, even in their mothers'
       presence.
       a.   detached
       b.   anxious/resistant
       c.   anxious/avoidant
       d.   securely/attached
Answer: b, Reference: Chapter 6, P. 245, Difficulty: M

83.   Mothers are more likely to _____ and fathers are more likely to _____
       in interactions with their infants.
       a.   protect; play
       b.   comfort; feed
       c.   perform caretaking activities; play
       d.   play; perform caretaking activities
Answer: c, Reference: Chapter 6, P. 246, Box 6.1, Difficulty: M

84.   Recent analysis of research comparing attachment to mothers and fathers in the
       "strange situation" found that infants who were attached to one parent
       a.   cried at the sight of the other parent
       b.   were also attached to the other parent
       c.   clung to that parent during the assessment
       d.   were less likely to be attached to the other parent
Answer: b, Reference: Chapter 6, P. 247, Box 6.1, Difficulty: M

85.   A recent study with a large group of 15 month old Dutch infants comparing the attachment behavior of infants toward mothers, fathers, and day care workers in the "strange situation" found
        a.   secure attachment only to mothers
        b.   similar attachment patterns toward mothers, fathers, and day care workers
        c.   similar attachment patterns to mother and fathers but not day care workers
        d.   similar attachment patterns to mothers and day care workers but not fathers
Answer: c, Reference: Chapter 6, P. 247, Box 6.1, Difficulty: M

86.   Ainsworth and Bell found that infants who later behaved as though they were securely attached had mothers who had been rated during early infancy as more
        a.   verbal
        b.   passive
        c.   controlling
        d.   responsive
Answer: d, Reference: Chapter 6, P. 248, Difficulty: E

87.   In order to develop a secure attachment, mothers and infants need to be
        a.   part of a cohesive family
        b.   together most of the time
        c.   responsive to one another
        d.   frequently left alone together
Answer: c, Reference: Chapter 6, P. 248, Difficulty: M

88.   What behavior at 3 months of age, according to a study by Candice Feiring, is related to insecure attachment at 9 months of age?
        a.   more time interacting with mothers than objects
        b.   quick responses by the mother to the infant's signals
        c.   more time playing with objects than interacting with mothers
        d.   more time spent looking at the mother's face and engaging in mutual imitation
Answer: c, Reference: Chapter 6, P. 248, Difficulty: M

89.   Infants from Israeli kibbutz who are raised communally from an early age when compared with U.S. infants
        a.   do not differ in their patterns of attachment
        b.   were more often judged to be anxious/resistant
        c.   were more often judged to be anxious/avoidant
        d.   were more often judged to be securely attached
Answer: b, Reference: Chapter 6, P. 248, Difficulty: M

90.   The reason researchers have suggested for a finding of a low percentage of securely attached German babies is
    a.   a large portion of German parents are insensitive or indifferent to their children
    b.   unclear, as German and American parents interact with their infants in similar ways
    c.   German mothers behave toward their infants in ways calculated to foster dependence
    d.   German parents adhere to a cultural value that babies should be weaned from bodily contact as soon as they become mobile
Answer: d, Reference: Chapter 6, P. 248, Difficulty: M

91.   Compared to Japanese children of working mothers, traditionally-raised Japanese children whose mothers rarely leave them in the care of others are more often rated as which of following in the "strange situation"?
    a.   unattached
    b.   anxious/resistant
    c.   anxious/avoidant
    d.   securely attached
Answer: b, Reference: Chapter 6, P. 249, Difficulty: D

92.   In the "strange situation" Miyake and others identified no Japanese infants who were
    a.   dependent
    b.   anxious/resistant
    c.   anxious/avoidant
    d.   securely attached
Answer: c, Reference: Chapter 6, P. 249, Difficulty: M

93.   At about what age do the first overt signs of distress upon separation from their mothers appears in infants?
    a.   3 months
    b.   5 months
    c.   7 months
    d.   10 months
Answer: c, Reference: Chapter 6, P. 251, Difficulty: M

94.   Chimpanzees, when shown their images in a full-length mirror,
    a.   passively observed their mirror images
    b.   completely ignored their mirror images
    c.   always reacted as though the images were other chimps
    d.   at first acted as though the images were other chimps, but later recognized themselves in the mirror
Answer: d, Reference: Chapter 6, P. 251, Difficulty: M

95.   Children demonstrate that they can recognize themselves in the mirror when they
       a.   try to touch their mirror images
       b.   vocalize and point at their mirror images
       c.   use mirror images to detect toys placed behind them
       d.   use mirror images to find spots of color placed on their faces
Answer: d, Reference: Chapter 6, P. 252, Difficulty: E

96.   The ability to recognize themselves in the mirror
       a.   has been observed in all species of primates
       b.   is demonstrated by human infants from the first weeks of life
       c.   is demonstrated by human infants beginning at about 18 months of age
       d.   is demonstrated by human children beginning at about 36 months of age
Answer: c, Reference: Chapter 6, P. 252, Difficulty: M

97.   Children will use the information from their mirror images to rub spots of rouge off
       their noses, but not until about the age of
       a.   3 months
       b.   9 months
       c.   18 months
       d.   36 months
Answer: c, Reference: Chapter 6, P. 252, Difficulty: E

98.   At what age does a child become able to refer to her self in speech?
       a.   9 months
       b.   12 months
       c.   18 months
       d.   30 months
Answer: c, Reference: Chapter 6, P. 252, Difficulty: E

99.   A child who says "I make house" while building with blocks is demonstrating
       a.   imitation
       b.   self-description
       c.   self-recognition
       d.   more accommodation than assimilation
Answer: b, Reference: Chapter 6, P. 252, Difficulty: D

100.   At what age is a child first likely to be disturbed if given a horse missing its tail to
       play with?
       a.   6 months old
       b.   1 year old
       c.   2 years old
       d.   3 years old
Answer: c, Reference: Chapter 6, P. 253, Difficulty: M

101. Jerome Kagan performed a study in which an adult modeled pretend activities and 18-month-olds' responses were studied. The children
    a. ignored all of the adult model's actions
    b. were able to imitate even the most difficult actions
    c. simply ignored those activities that were too complex for them to imitate
    d. became disturbed, possibly because they felt they were expected to imitate the actions
Answer: d, Reference: Chapter 6, P. 253, Difficulty: D

102. A study by Bullock and Lutkenhaus (1989) traced the ability of infants to adhere to task standards set by adults. They found that infants were *not* regularly capable of sticking to the task until adult standards were met until approximately
    a. 18 months
    b. 24 months
    c. 30 months
    d. 36 months
Answer: d, Reference: Chapter 6, P. 253, Difficulty: M

103. Secondary emotions are thought to be
    a. direct responses to events
    b. caused by social interactions
    c. differentiated out of simple emotions
    d. reflective and not just direct responses to events
Answer: d, Reference: Chapter 6, P. 253, Difficulty: M

104. Which of the following is an example of a secondary emotion?
    a. love
    b. fear
    c. pride
    d. surprise
Answer: c, Reference: Chapter 6, P. 253, Difficulty: M

Essay Questions

1. Describe the changes that take place in an infant's nervous system during the second year of life.

2. Describe several physical behaviors that become possible during the period from 12 to 30 months of age.

3. Describe the development of problem-solving behavior that accompanies sensorimotor substages 5 and 6.

4.   How does a child's understanding of object permanence change during stages 5 and 6?

5.   What is meant by the statement that, "in late infancy, children begin to think representationally?"

6.   Discuss several developments that occur in late infancy that allow infants greater autonomy.

7.   Describe the relationship between symbolic play and deferred imitation. Give an example of each.

8.   What developments in classification and in symbolic play accompany children's ability to speak in two-word phrases?

9.   Give several examples of how a child's play might facilitate the child's development.

10. How does the play of children change as the child approaches late infancy?

11. Provide a brief overview of areas of cognitive change between 12 and 30 months of age.

12. Trace the development of infants' ability to categorize objects between 20 and 30 months of age.

13. What is "attachment"? What are signs of attachment between a child and the child's caretaker?

14. Discuss the predictors and antecedents of secure and insecure attachment.

15. How do Freud, Erikson, and Bowlby explain attachment?

16. According to evidence provided by Harlow's studies of monkeys, what is necessary for attachment to occur? What is necessary for normal social development to occur?

17. What is the drive-reduction theory of attachment? Describe the research paradigm used to investigate its premise. What were the findings?

18. What kinds of behaviors characterize the "securely attached," the "anxious/avoidant," and the "anxious/resistant" patterns of attachment?

19. What factors affect whether an infant remains in the same attachment classification when retested after several months?

20. Explain how temperamental and behavioral characteristics of infants and their parents can affect the quality of attachment.

21. Describe the "strange situation" used to assess patterns of attachment. Be sure to identify the three major attachment patterns.

22. What is the influence of culture associated with differences in infants' behavior in the "strange situation?"

23. What are some indications of the new sense of self that develops at the end of infancy?

24. What evidence would indicate that a 2-year-old has developed a "sense of self?"

25. Through what steps do infants pass in learning to recognize themselves in a mirror?

26. How do we know that, in late infancy, children are more sensitive to adult standards of what is proper and improper?

27. What are secondary emotions? How do they differ from primary emotions? What do they tell us about developmental changes in the child?

28. Describe changes occurring during the end of the second year and beginning of the third year of life that signal the end of infancy.

Early Experience and Later Life

Multiple-Choice Questions

1. The saying "As the twig is bent, so grows the tree" expresses the idea of the
   a. recency of infant experience
   b. importance of adult experience
   c. primacy of experience during infancy
   d. equal importance of all periods of development

   Answer: c, Reference: Chapter 7, P. 260, Difficulty: M

2. During the twentieth century, primacy has become associated with the idea that
   a. infancy occurs earlier than other stages of development
   b. the problems of infancy are not as important as those of later life
   c. the nature of children's first attachments influences their later relationships
   d. later experiences are progressively more important in influencing development

   Answer: c, Reference: Chapter 7, P. 260, Difficulty: E

3. Soren Kierkegaard says a sensitive mother
   a. helps her child every step of the way
   b. does not allow her child to take risks often
   c. tantalizes her child with promises of support
   d. encourages and supports her child with actions that lead to an independent child

   Answer: d, Reference: Chapter 7, P. 261, Difficulty: M

4.   What do White and Watts call mothers whose children become more competent than peers?
     a.   A mothers
     b.   sensitive mothers
     c.   competent mothers
     d.   just adequate mothers
Answer: a, Reference: Chapter 7, P. 261, Difficulty: E

5.   According to Burton White and Jean Watts, an important characteristic of A mothers is that they
     a.   are college educated
     b.   keep neat and attractive homes
     c.   talk to their children in ways they can understand
     d.   devote most of their time to attending to their children
Answer: c, Reference: Chapter 7, P. 261, Difficulty: D

6.   Burton White and Jean Watts found that children who were more competent than their peers in kindergarten tended to have mothers who
     a.   encouraged emotional dependence
     b.   respond excessively to their children
     c.   set reasonable limits on their behavior
     d.   favor children who are precocious, active, and demanding
Answer: c, Reference: Chapter 7, P. 261, Difficulty: E

7.   Effective parenting behaviors
     a.   aim, in any society, at promoting academic achievement
     b.   aim, in any society, at promoting cooperation with others
     c.   differ within societies but not between one society and another
     d.   differ, in different societies, according to the environment in which children will grow up
Answer: c, Reference: Chapter 7, P. 262, Difficulty: D

8.   In contrast to American mothers, Japanese mothers have been found to
     a.   encouraged emotional independence
     b.   respond excessively to their children
     c.   set reasonable limits on their behavior
     d.   favor children who are precocious, active, and demanding
Answer: b, Reference: Chapter 7, P. 262, Difficulty: E

9. In contrast to American and Japanese mothers, Scheper-Hughes (1992) has observed mothers in a poor area of Brazil to
   a. neglect a sick child and let it die
   b. encouraged emotional dependence
   c. respond excessively to their children
   d. set reasonable limits on their behavior

Answer: a, Reference: Chapter 7, P. 263, Difficulty: E

10. Parents sometimes worry that they will spoil their children if they
    a. are too responsive to the children
    b. allow the children to cry too often
    c. do not give the children enough material goods
    d. fail to protect the children from the harsh realities of life

Answer: a, Reference: Chapter 7, P. 263, Difficulty: E

11. Bell and Ainsworth's study of infants in their homes revealed that infants whose mothers responded quickly to their crying
    a. cried just as often as those whose mothers responded more slowly
    b. cried less often than infants whose mothers responded more slowly
    c. began to perform other behaviors to attract their mothers' attention
    d. cried more often than infants whose mothers responded more slowly

Answer: b, Reference: Chapter 7, P. 264, Difficulty: D

12. According to Ainsworth and Bell, infants whose mothers let them cry for long periods of time
    a. eventually stop crying
    b. cry less often than infants whose mothers respond quickly
    c. cry more often than infants whose mothers respond quickly
    d. spend about the same total amount of time crying as children whose mothers respond quickly to their cries

Answer: c, Reference: Chapter 7, P. 264, Difficulty: D

13. Ms. Smith does not want her baby to cry very much. What would you advise her to do, according to research data?
    a. avoid stranger anxiety
    b. always keep the baby near her
    c. be responsive to the baby's cries
    d. ignore the babies cries, to avoid reinforcement

Answer: c, Reference: Chapter 7, P. 264, Difficulty: M

14. Seligman first demonstrated learned helplessness when he demonstrated that
    a. dogs exposed to inescapable shock would not learn to escape shock later
    b. infants who learned to control a mobile quickly learned to control a similar one
    c. dogs not exposed to inescapable shock would not learn to escape shock when they could
    d. infants whose movements did not control a mobile quickly learned to control a similar one

Answer: a, Reference: Chapter 7, P. 264, Difficulty: E

15. Learned helplessness results when children
    a. come to enjoy pretending to be helpless infants
    b. whose parents are responsive to crying learn to cry more often
    c. learn that by acting helpless, they can get their parents to do things for them
    d. learn that their actions do not influence events and become passive in those situations

Answer: d, Reference: Chapter 7, P. 264, Difficulty: E

16. Infants who find that, in a particular situation, their actions have little effect may
    a. become frustrated and angry
    b. become passive in those situations in the future
    c. try harder to influence their environments in some other situation
    d. respond more quickly when circumstances change so that their actions do have an effect

Answer: b, Reference: Chapter 7, P. 264, Difficulty: M

17. When John S. Watson exposed infants to a mobile that they could control with their head movements, he found that infants who had
    a. learned to control a similar mobile quickly learned how to control the new one
    b. learned to control a similar mobile became confused and were unable to control this one
    c. been unable to control a similar mobile tried harder and quickly learned to control this one
    d. been unable to control a similar mobile learned to control this one just as quickly as infants who had been able to control a similar mobile

Answer: a, Reference: Chapter 7, P. 265, Difficulty: M

18.   According to John S. Watson, infants who were exposed to a mobile whose movements they could not control
        a.   later failed to learn to control a similar mobile which was controllable
        b.   continued to attempt to control the mobile in various ways, even though it was not physically possible
        c.   learned to control a similar but controllable mobile more quickly than infants who had been able to control the first mobile
        d.   learned to control a similar but controllable mobile just as quickly as infants who had already been exposed to controllable mobiles
Answer: a, Reference: Chapter 7, P. 265, Difficulty: M

19.   Finkelstein and Ramey (1977) demonstrated that 8-month-olds who had learned to activate a stimulus by pushing a panel
        a.   became disturbed when the experiment was altered so that vocalizing activated the stimulus
        b.   were equally fast at learning to activate the stimulus by vocalizing as were infants who had not learned to push the panel
        c.   were quicker to learn to activate the same stimulus by vocalizing than were infants who had not learned to push the panel
        d.   were slower to learn to activate the stimulus by vocalizing than infants who had not learned another method of activating the same stimulus
Answer: c, Reference: Chapter 7, P. 265, Difficulty: M

20.   There is lack of agreement across studies about whether daycare during the first year of infancy
        a.   causes learned helplessness
        b.   contributes to learning disabilities
        c.   leads to severe behavior problems
        d.   negatively affects infants' later development
Answer: d, Reference: Chapter 7, P. 266, Difficulty: M

21.   With regard to infant daycare during the first year of life, experts
        a.   disagree on the effects of early care experience
        b.   agree there is little or no risk associated with high quality care
        c.   are unwilling to make claims about the effects of daycare without further study
        d.   agree that early infant daycare puts children at considerable risk for long-term socioemotional difficulties
Answer: a, Reference: Chapter 7, P. 266, Box 7.1, Difficulty: M

22.   According to some investigators, a hazard of out-of-home care for infants during the first year of life is
      a.   insecure attachment to parents
      b.   lowered intelligence at school age
      c.   failure to become attached to parents
      d.   the development of severe emotional disorders
Answer: a, Reference: Chapter 7, P. 268, Box 7.1, Difficulty: E

23.   Jay Belsky is prominent among those who believe infant daycare during the first year of life
      a.   has no significant effect
      b.   is more likely to lead to insecure patterns of attachment
      c.   can be beneficial in developing the social skills of the infant
      d.   can not be investigated due to too many other intervening variables
Answer: b, Reference: Chapter 7, P. 268, Box 7.1, Difficulty: M

24.   Allison Clarke-Stewart has suggested all of the following regarding infant daycare except
      a.   negative effects are very small in terms of real life
      b.   children enrolled in daycare during the first year of life have higher scores on tests of intellectual development
      c.   behaviors of daycare children labeled "noncompliant" might really reflect increased independence and self-confidence
      d.   children enrolled in daycare during the first year of life are more securely attached to their mothers than children not in day care
Answer: d, Reference: Chapter 7, P. 268, Box 7.1, Difficulty: D

25.   The 1990 study by Carollee Howes that examined the age of children and quality of daycare they received found
      a.   neither low quality nor high quality daycare programs posed a risk for children in daycare under age one year
      b.   both low quality and high quality daycare posed a risk for children under one year of age for later behavior problems
      c.   age at entry into daycare made no difference, and the daycare experience in general posed risks for later behavior problems
      d.   low quality daycare posed a risk for children under 1 year of age for later behavior problems, but high quality daycare did not
Answer: d, Reference: Chapter 7, P. 268, Box 7.1, Difficulty: D

26. The 1990 study by Carollee Howes found that children who were in low quality daycare were more likely to also experience
    a. higher socioeconomic levels
    b. poor nutrition and health care
    c. families with more problems and few social networks
    d. extended families with strong support networks in the community

Answer: c, Reference: Chapter 7, P. 269, Box 7.1, Difficulty: D

27. While studying the later emotional development of children hospitalized before 5 years of age, Michael Rutter found that
    a. hospitalization was associated with no emotional ill effects
    b. children suffered emotional ill effects only if hospitalized a dozen times or more
    c. hospitalization produced later emotional disturbance because of children's separation from their parents
    d. one hospitalization produced no ill effects, but a history of several hospitalizations was associated with later behavior problems

Answer: d, Reference: Chapter 7, P. 266, Difficulty: M

28. A confounding factor in studies of the effects of hospitalization upon children is that
    a. hospitalized children usually come from wealthier families than those who are not hospitalized
    b. hospitalized children are somewhat more likely to come from economically disadvantaged families
    c. hospitalized children usually have nervous system damage which accounts for any behavioral differences discovered
    d. children who have been hospitalized are usually more cooperative than others and so are less likely to have behavioral problems

Answer: b, Reference: Chapter 7, P. 266, Difficulty: D

29. British children who had been separated from their families while quite young in order to avoid World War II bombing were later found to
    a. have no markedly abnormal characteristics
    b. be impaired in their later social relationships
    c. be more likely than the general population to suffer mental illness
    d. be emotionally better adjusted than those who had not been separated from their families

Answer: a, Reference: Chapter 7, P. 266, Difficulty: M

30.   British children 4 years of age and under who were separated from their parents to escape World War II bombing
       a.   were not distressed by the separation
       b.   were distressed by the separation and suffered disturbances of their later social relationships as a result
       c.   were distressed by the separation and as young adults were found to have, a high incidence of mental illness
       d.   were distressed by the separation, but as young adults had not developed psychological problems as a result
Answer: d, Reference: Chapter 7, P. 266, Difficulty: M

31.   A study by Wayne Dennis found that harmful effects of a low level of both stimulation and human contact were
       a.   not evident until age 5
       b.   evident within one year
       c.   noticed at 2 months of age
       d.   not noticed until the child left the orphanage
Answer: b, Reference: Chapter 7, P. 267, Difficulty: M

32.   Wayne Dennis found that children raised in an unstimulating Lebanese orphanage
       a.   developed better the longer they remained in the orphanage
       b.   developed at the same rate as home-reared Lebanese children
       c.   developed well until they were about 4 years old, then began to fall behind the developmental norms
       d.   quickly fell behind developmental norms but recovered if they were adopted by the time they were two years of age
Answer: d, Reference: Chapter 7, P. 267, Difficulty: D

33.   What has the study of Lebanese orphans by Wayne Dennis told us about the importance of early experience for later intellectual functioning?
       a.   the earlier an experience occurs, the more influential it is for later development
       b.   the later in development an experience occurs, the more important are its effects
       c.   the experiences of all periods of development contribute equally to developmental outcome
       d.   early experiences are important, but their effects can be modified by experiences that occur later
Answer: d, Reference: Chapter 7, P. 269, Difficulty: D

34. Tizard and Hodges estimated that English children raised in residential nurseries from just after birth had
    a. consistent caregivers the first two years
    b. an ability to form many multiple attachments
    c. as many as 50 different care-takers by 4 1/2 years of age
    d. formed attachments to peers in the absence of appropriate adult figures

Answer: c, Reference: Chapter 7, P. 270, Difficulty: E

35. According to Tizard, leaving institutional care
    a. had a positive effect on the child
    b. produced emotional or behavioral disturbances if done before ten years of age
    c. had a varying degree of effect, depending on whether the child was a boy or a girl
    d. was detrimental to psychological and emotional ties formed by the child before two years of age

Answer: a, Reference: Chapter 7, P. 270, Difficulty: E

36. Psychologists found that English children raised in residential nurseries from birth until at least 2 years of age
    a. had formed attachments to most of the 24 nurses who had cared for them during their first two years
    b. did not form attachments to their caretakers, and did not form attachments to their adoptive parents
    c. were better adjusted than those who went to live with their biological parents, if they were adopted between the ages of 2 and 8
    d. were better adjusted than those who were adopted, if they went to live with their biological parents between the ages of 2 and 8

Answer: c, Reference: Chapter 7, P. 270, Difficulty: D

37. Tizard found that children leaving institutional care who were adopted between 2 and 8 years of age
    a. did not fare as well as children returned to their original families
    b. scored higher on achievement tests than children returned to their original families
    c. related as well to their adoptive parents as did those who returned to their biological parents
    d. did not relate as well to their adoptive parents as did those returned to their biological parents

Answer: b, Reference: Chapter 7, P. 270, Difficulty: M

38.   When Howard and Tizard contacted previously institutionalized children at age 16 they found
       a.   both adopted and biologically restored children formed mutual attachments with their parents
       b.   neither adopted nor biologically restored children form mutual attachment with their parents
       c.   most of the adopted children formed mutual attachments with their adoptive parents regardless of age
       d.   most of the children returned to their biological parents formed mutual attachments with their parents regardless of age
Answer: c, Reference: Chapter 7, P. 271, Difficulty: M

39.   Tizard and Howard's research on the later effects of children previously institutionalized found
       a.   children who went to adoptive homes were better socially adjusted at school
       b.   children who went to their original families were better socially adjusted at school
       c.   both adopted children and children returned to their biological parents had trouble with social relations at school
       d.   both adopted children and children returned to their biological parents formed good relationships with their peer groups
Answer: c, Reference: Chapter 7, P. 271, Difficulty: M

40.   Tizard's research on children raised in residential nurseries showed that
       a.   if children do not form attachments before 2 years of age, they will never form attachments to anyone
       b.   given a supportive environment, children can form attachments to parents even if the children are beyond infancy
       c.   children are more likely to become attached to their biological parents than to adoptive parents, regardless of the children's ages
       d.   institutional care results in children who are just as well adjusted as children who are adopted or who are raised by their biological parents
Answer: b, Reference: Chapter 7, P. 271, Difficulty: M

41.   How were twin boys in Czechoslovakia who were isolated at a young age treated after they were found?
       a.   they were adopted by a caring family
       b.   they were sent to live among a group of younger children
       c.   they were institutionalized with other children of their age
       d.   they were left with their biological father and the family was given intensive counseling
Answer: b, Reference: Chapter 7, P. 271, Difficulty: M

42.   Twin boys in Czechoslovakia who were raised in isolation until age 6, were found at age 14 to
        a.   have normal intelligence
        b.   be severely mentally retarded
        c.   to have significantly impaired language skills
        d.   to have strong spatial skills relative to other skills
Answer: a, Reference: Chapter 7, P. 272, Difficulty: M

43.   Genie, a child who lived in nearly total isolation for more than 11 years, when given rehabilitation
        a.   recovered to the point of nearly normal behavior
        b.   recovered somewhat, but never developed normal language skills
        c.   developed normal language skills but never showed affection to other people
        d.   made little progress in any area of development despite years of rehabilitation
Answer: b, Reference: Chapter 7, P. 272, Difficulty: D

44.   According to Curtiss, 13 year old Genie, who had been severely neglected, once liberated, developed ways to
        a.   communicate well
        b.   rehabilitate herself
        c.   manipulate visitors
        d.   substantiate her existence
Answer: c, Reference: Chapter 7, P. 272, Difficulty: D

45.   Twin boys in Czechoslovakia may have made a good recovery from severe isolation because they
        a.   were in puberty when they were rescued
        b.   had one another for company when they were in isolation
        c.   were sent to live among a group of children their own age
        d.   had developed good language skills in interaction with each other when isolated from others
Answer: b, Reference: Chapter 7, P. 272, Difficulty: D

46.   Studies of isolated children leave little doubt that early deprivation of caretaking
        a.   produces negligible effects
        b.   produces severe psychopathology
        c.   always disrupts normal development
        d.   is not necessarily devastating to later development
Answer: d, Reference: Chapter 7, P. 272, Difficulty: D

47.   Which of the following is associated with childhood behavior problems and psychiatric disorders, according to Michael Rutter and his colleagues?
   a.   family harmony
   b.   small family size
   c.   social disadvantage
   d.   attendance at a large school
Answer: c, Reference: Chapter 7, P. 273, Difficulty: E

48.   Research on risk factors for childhood psychiatric disorders such as family discord and social deviance shows that
   a.   the combination of two or more risk factors makes psychiatric problems more likely
   b.   the presence of even one risk factor is associate with a vastly increased incidence of psychiatric illness
   c.   children exposed to two or more risk factors are in general better adjusted than those exposed to only one
   d.   risk factors-alone or in combination-have been shown to be unrelated to the development of psychiatric disorders
Answer: a, Reference: Chapter 7, P. 273, Difficulty: M

49.   Children who live in stressful environments but do not develop problems are considered to be
   a.   resilient
   b.   canalized
   c.   vulnerable
   d.   immunized
Answer: a, Reference: Chapter 7, P. 273, Difficulty: E

50.   Children who are labeled resilient are likely to
   a.   be temperamentally "slow to warm up"
   b.   not respond to environmental simulation
   c.   live in relatively stress-free environments
   d.   develop in healthy ways despite living in stressful environments
Answer: d, Reference: Chapter 7, P. 273, Difficulty: E

51.   Which of the following has not been found to be true in studies of children with behavior problems and psychiatric disorders?
   a.   time plays a significant role in the causes of disorders
   b.   family discord is among the leading risk factors behind disorders
   c.   individual children living in highly stressful circumstances have reasonably similar reactions
   d.   there is an increase in the likelihood of children suffering if they face more than one risk factor
Answer: c, Reference: Chapter 7, P. 273, Difficulty: E

52. An important longitudinal study of multiracial children born on Kauai likely to suffer developmental problems found all of the following reduced the risk of developmental difficulties except
   a. a sibling was available as a caretaker or confidant
   b. the child had substantial caretaker attention during infancy
   c. alternate caretakers were available to the mother within the household
   d. the spacing between the child studied and the closest sibling was less than two years

Answer: d, Reference: Chapter 7, P. 273, Difficulty: D

53. Children from families in which there are four or fewer children and a supportive network of family and friends are more likely to exhibit
   a. less adaptability than children without these advantages
   b. resilience when faced with stressful events in childhood
   c. vulnerability to difficulties caused by stressful events in childhood
   d. no advantages or disadvantages relative to children without these family characteristics

Answer: b, Reference: Chapter 7, P. 274, Difficulty: M

54. Research in Kauai showed that children from cohesive families that provided them with structure and alternate caretakers were
   a. more resilient than other children in the face of stressful life circumstances
   b. equally likely compared to other children to have developmental difficulties
   c. more vulnerable than other children to stressful environmental circumstances
   d. more likely than other children to undergo a large amount of stress during childhood

Answer: a, Reference: Chapter 7, P. 274, Difficulty: E

55. In the face of risk factors for developmental problems, children who come from supportive, cohesive families are more likely to be
   a. logical
   b. resilient
   c. vulnerable
   d. hospitalized

Answer: b, Reference: Chapter 7, P. 274, Difficulty: E

56. The longitudinal study by Werner and Smith of the children of Kauai found the risk of developmental difficulties was reduced under what circumstances when
   a. there were four or more children
   b. siblings interacted little with one another
   c. the family was cohesive and provided structure and rules
   d. the mother worked outside the home and work demands were large

Answer: c, Reference: Chapter 7, P. 274, Difficulty: M

57.   Children from what environment are more likely to develop psychological disorders
       than those from other places?
       a.   poor rural areas
       b.   poor, inner-city neighborhoods
       c.   suburban areas outside large cities
       d.   middle-class neighborhoods of small towns
Answer: b, Reference: Chapter 7, P. 274, Difficulty: E

58.   Attending a school with a good academic record and attentive teachers
       a.   does not help or hurt children from disadvantaged or discordant homes
       b.   can help buffer children from deprived backgrounds from some the stresses
             of their environment
       c.   can be more stressful for deprived children than attending a school that is less
             demanding academically
       d.   improves the academic performance of children from disadvantaged homes,
             but does not lessen their risk of developing psychological disorders
Answer: b, Reference: Chapter 7, P. 275, Difficulty: M

59.   Children with which of the following types of temperament are more likely to
       experience psychological problems as adults, than are children with other types of
       temperament?
       a.   easy
       b.   difficult
       c.   vulnerable
       d.   slow to warm up
Answer: b, Reference: Chapter 7, P. 275, Difficulty: E

60.   Depressed mothers differ from non-depressed mothers in that the depressed
       mothers
       a.   talk to their infants less
       b.   look at their infants more
       c.   are more intrusive with their infants
       d.   provide more physical stimulation to their infants
Answer: a, Reference: Chapter 7, P. 276, Box 7.2, Difficulty: M

61.   Infants of depressed mothers are more likely than infants of non-depressed mothers
       to
       a.   sleep more
       b.   be insecurely attached
       c.   play more with objects
       d.   interact more readily with strange adults
Answer: b, Reference: Chapter 7, P. 276, Box 7.2, Difficulty: M

62.   What behavior did Field and her colleagues observe in newborn infants of mothers who were depressed during pregnancy on the Brazelton Neonatal Assessment Scale?
    a.   absence of crying
    b.   elevated activity levels
    c.   increased ratings of cuddliness
    d.   limited responses to social stimulation
Answer: d, Reference: Chapter 7, P. 276, Box 7.2, Difficulty: M

63.   What factor has been found to protect a child from the negative effects of being raised by a depressed mother?
    a.   high intelligence
    b.   high family income
    c.   socially engaging personality
    d.   the presence of siblings in the household
Answer: c, Reference: Chapter 7, P. 276, Box 7.2, Difficulty: M

64.   A supportive adult other than the mother is most important for infants whose depressed mother
    a.   shows persistent
    b.   has cycles of depression
    c.   recovers from her depression
    d.   has either cyclic or persistent depression
Answer: d, Reference: Chapter 7, P. 276, Box 7.2, Difficulty: M

65.   What technique has Field described as a useful intervention to teach a depressed mother to improve her interactions with her infant?
    a.   imitate her infant
    b.   provide facial expressions for her infant to imitate
    c.   speak somewhat more quickly when speaking to her infant
    d.   teach the mother to administer the Brazelton Neonatal Assessment Scale to her infant
Answer: a, Reference: Chapter 7, P. 276, Box 7.2, Difficulty: M

66.   A study by De Vries (1987) on infants in Masai found that
    a.   infants with an easy temperament showed the best survival rate
    b.   infants with a difficult temperament showed the best survival rate
    c.   there was no difference in survival rate as a function of temperament
    d.   infants who were rated as slow to warm up showed the best survival rate
Answer: b, Reference: Chapter 7, P. 275, Difficulty: M

67.   According to Werner and Smith's study of disadvantaged Hawaiian children, which characteristics of infants were associated with a good developmental outlook?
       a.   frequently fussy
       b.   low activity level
       c.   social responsiveness
       d.   irregular eating and sleeping
Answer: c, Reference: Chapter 7, P. 275, Difficulty: M

68.   Models of development used to trace the interaction of children's characteristics and various influences on their development over time are called
       a.   biological
       b.   ethological
       c.   transactional
       d.   environmental
Answer: c, Reference: Chapter 7, P. 277, Difficulty: E

69.   Transactional models of development help to account for the
       a.   influence of generic factors on developmental outcome
       b.   ways in which development is shaped by reinforcement
       c.   ways children's characteristics interact with changing characteristics of their environments
       d.   way improvements in some areas of psychological functioning are accompanied by regressions in others
Answer: c, Reference: Chapter 7, P. 278, Difficulty: D

70.   Which type of model best accounts for the fact that temperamentally "difficult" children are more likely than others to suffer developmental problems when their families are under stress?
       a.   ethological
       b.   transactional
       c.   biological-maturation
       d.   environmental-learning
Answer: b, Reference: Chapter 7, P. 278, Difficulty: M

71.   Rutter and his colleagues explained poor later life adjustments of young adults who spent significant parts of their infancy and early childhoods in institutions using a
       a.   learning model
       b.   risk factor ratio
       c.   transactional model
       d.   deprivation classification model
Answer: c, Reference: Chapter 7, P. 279, Difficulty: M

72. In terms of the transactional model, early misfortune
    a. led to a resilient adulthood
    b. did not constitute a life-long path of continual misfortune
    c. led only to immediate misfortune that was not perpetuated in adult life
    d. set in motion a series of events that tended to perpetuate the early difficulty

Answer: d, Reference: Chapter 7, P. 279, Difficulty: D

73. Rutter and his colleagues found that young men who spent time in child care institutions were
    a. more likely than women to find a supportive spouse
    b. similar to woman in showing few positive later live experiences
    c. unable to successfully block transmission of early negative experiences to the next generation
    d. similar to the women in showing high risk of long term difficulties even after positive later life experiences

Answer: a, Reference: Chapter 7, P. 279, Difficulty: D

74. A key element in any effort to repair developmental damage caused by early social or intellectual deprivations is
    a. monitoring by parents
    b. increased sibling interaction
    c. instruction in basic needs and self-care
    d. removal from the damaging environment

Answer: d, Reference: Chapter 7, P. 279, Difficulty: D

75. According to research by Harlow and others, what might have been an intervention that would have been effective with Genie?
    a. letting her play with younger children
    b. providing her with intense language therapy
    c. giving her intense interaction playing with objects
    d. providing her with opportunities to interact with peers

Answer: a, Reference: Chapter 7, P. 281, Difficulty: D

76. Rigler and his colleagues have been criticized in their treatment of Genie because they focus primarily on
    a. attachment
    b. language development
    c. cognitive development
    d. social and emotional development

Answer: b, Reference: Chapter 7, P. 281, Box 7.3, Difficulty: D

77.   Harry Harlow's study of monkeys raised in isolation with inanimate surrogate
        mothers, found that when monkeys were moved to a group cage after being isolated
        for the first three months of life they
        a.   immediately adapted
        b.   were permanently affected by the experience
        c.   showed no effects whatsoever of the isolation
        d.   were initially overwhelmed but adapted within a month
Answer: d, Reference: Chapter 7, P. 279, Difficulty: E

78.   Monkeys kept in total isolation for the first six months of life, who were then placed
        in group cages
        a.   rocked, bit, or scratched themselves compulsively
        b.   were not significantly different from normal monkeys
        c.   were affected the same as monkeys isolated for three months
        d.   had developed better adaptive skills than monkeys isolated for three months
Answer: a, Reference: Chapter 7, P. 280, Difficulty: M

79.   Monkeys who were isolated for the second 6-months of life
        a.   showed increased adaptive skills
        b.   were not significantly affected by their isolation
        c.   became fearful and aggressive when placed in group cages
        d.   reacted in the same way as those isolated for the first 3-months of life
Answer: c, Reference: Chapter 7, P. 280, Difficulty: M

80.   Harlow and his colleagues discovered that monkeys isolated for their first 6 months
        of life
        a.   were not significantly affected by their isolation
        b.   reacted to infant monkeys, but not adults, in completely normal ways
        c.   had severe and long-lasting difficulty in interacting with other monkeys
        d.   reacted normally to adult monkeys but did not know how to react to infants
Answer: c, Reference: Chapter 7, P. 280, Difficulty: D

81.   Initially, research by Harlow and his colleagues on the effect of early isolation in
        monkeys suggested the first _____ was/were critical for social development
        a.   3 months
        b.   6 months
        c.   1 year
        d.   2 years
Answer: b, Reference: Chapter 7, P. 280, Difficulty: M

82.   When Harlow's formerly isolated monkeys first gave birth to infants, they
       a.   behaved normally toward them
       b.   behaved abusively toward their infants
       c.   tolerated the infants but did not initiate interactions
       d.   were initially abusive but shortly came to interact with them in normal ways
Answer: b, Reference: Chapter 7, P. 282, Difficulty: E

83.   Harlow found it was possible to reverse the social pathologies of previously isolated
       monkeys by
       a.   punishing inappropriate behaviors
       b.   providing nurturing human contact
       c.   introducing them to new environments slowly
       d.   introducing them into a mother-infant type of relationship with a younger
             monkey
Answer: d, Reference: Chapter 7, P. 282, Difficulty: D

84.   Harlow and his colleagues found that formerly isolated monkeys were helped to
       regain normal social functioning by
       a.   finding mates
       b.   interacting with much younger monkeys
       c.   interacting with a large group of monkeys
       d.   giving birth to an offspring that was removed at birth
Answer: b, Reference: Chapter 7, P. 282, Difficulty: M

85.   Studies have shown that both formerly isolated monkeys and socially isolated
       children become better socially adjusted if they
       a.   spend more time with sympathetic adults
       b.   are allowed to play regularly with same-age peers
       c.   are allowed to play regularly with younger monkeys or children
       d.   are left alone until they feel comfortable joining their peer groups for play
Answer: c, Reference: Chapter 7, P. 282, Difficulty: M

86.   In a study by Furman, Rahe, and Hartup, socially isolated children who participated
       in a series of play sessions with younger children
       a.   behaved abusively toward the younger children
       b.   began to interact much more with their peers in day care
       c.   began to interact more with younger children and less with their peers in day
             care
       d.   did not increase in their interaction with peers as much as a group of children
             whose play sessions were with age- mates
Answer: b, Reference: Chapter 7, P. 283, Difficulty: M

87.   Evidence suggests the effects of severe, extended protein malnutrition remain with the child
       a.   well into adulthood
       b.   a relatively short time
       c.   at least into adolescence
       d.   until the child starts school
Answer: c, Reference: Chapter 7, P. 283, Difficulty: M

88.   When Matas, Arend, and Sroufe presented mother-child pairs with a difficult problem-solving task, they found that children who cooperated best with their mothers were those rated as having a(n)
       a.   secure attachment
       b.   anxious/resistant attachment
       c.   anxious/avoidant attachment
       d.   slow to warm up temperament
Answer: a, Reference: Chapter 7, P. 284, Difficulty: E

89.   In an extensive research project Alan Sroufe and his colleagues found that attachment classification during infancy predicted all of the following, except
       a.   performance of cognitive tests at age 10
       b.   quality of interactions between 10 year old children and their peers
       c.   quality of interactions between 10 year old children and their camp counselors
       d.   social skills at age 10
Answer: a, Reference: Chapter 7, P. 285, Difficulty: E

90.   A research project by Sroufe and his colleagues found that when children who had been classified as securely attached as infants attended a summer camp at age 10, they were
       a.   less able to express their feelings than other children
       b.   more skilled in social interactions than other children
       c.   more likely to experience homesickness than other children
       d.   more dependent on the adults for attention than other children
Answer: b, Reference: Chapter 7, P. 285, Difficulty: E

91.   A study by John Bates and his colleagues found
       a.   no relationship between infant attachment classification and behavior problems at 3 years
       b.   difficult peer relations at age three years for infants who were classified as insecure/resistant
       c.   higher levels of independent behavior at age three years for infants who were classified as insecure/resistant
       d.   higher levels of dependent behavior on a teacher at age three years for infants who were classified as insecure/avoidant
Answer: a, Reference: Chapter 7, P. 285, Difficulty: D

92.   According to Inge Bretherton, as long as the environment supports the use of their internal working models of how to behave toward others
       a.   children will be psychologically well adjusted
       b.   any changes in children's behavior should be due to heredity factors
       c.   there should be continuity over time in the way children relate to others
       d.   the ways in which children relate to others will undergo no changes at all
Answer: c, Reference: Chapter 7, P. 285, Difficulty: D

93.   Infant developmental scales
       a.   are not useful in predicting later IQ
       b.   measure infants' genetically programmed potential
       c.   can predict IQ in adulthood, though not necessarily in later childhood
       d.   are good predictors of IQ in later childhood but not necessarily in adulthood
Answer: a, Reference: Chapter 7, P. 286, Difficulty: D

94.   According to McCall and to Sameroff, intelligence tests given to young children are most useful in predicting later behavior if
       a.   they are related to rates of habituation
       b.   the scores are at the extremes of the continuum
       c.   the abilities measured at both ages are the same
       d.   the environment of the children undergoes no drastic change
Answer: b, Reference: Chapter 7, P. 286, Difficulty: D

95.   A problem with drawing conclusions about continuities and discontinuities in development on the basis of tests given in infancy is that
       a.   there are no real continuities in development between infancy and later childhood
       b.   a large amount of physical growth takes place between infancy and later childhood
       c.   the tests used at different ages often do not really measure the same psychological functions
       d.   the environments of most children undergo drastic changes between infancy and later childhood
Answer: c, Reference: Chapter 7, P. 286, Difficulty: D

96.   Support for claims of cognitive continuity between infancy and childhood comes from studies that examine
       a.   the age of onset of first words
       b.   an infant's success at finding a hidden object
       c.   an infant's preference for looking at novel pictures
       d.   the rate at which infants process visual information
Answer: d, Reference: Chapter 7, P. 286, Difficulty: M

97.   Children who tend to be proficient at problem-solving and concept-formation tasks during early childhood, as infants
      a.   are quick to habituate to repeated events
      b.   score well on infant developmental scales
      c.   experience many environmental discontinuities
      d.   respond in an angry way when their sucking is interrupted
Answer: a, Reference: Chapter 7, P. 286, Difficulty: D

98.   According to Bornstein and Sigman (1986), children how play in relatively sophisticated ways are more likely as infants to have
      a.   habituated rapidly
      b.   been easily consoled when upset
      c.   demonstrated intermodal coordination
      d.   demonstrated strong preferences for novelty
Answer: a, Reference: Chapter 7, P. 286, Difficulty: D

99.   Correlations between cognition in infancy and later behavior are generally
      a.   strong
      b.   very modest
      c.   beyond any reasonable doubts
      d.   so slight as to indicate no significant continuities
Answer: b, Reference: Chapter 7, P. 286, Difficulty: D

100. Freud pointed out that, when development is viewed backwards, from outcome to beginning
      a.   all of behavior appears to be motivated by sexual desire
      b.   it is more difficult to discern what events led to particular outcomes
      c.   it becomes easier to spot developmental discontinuities than continuities
      d.   sequences of events and outcomes appear more inevitable than they otherwise would
Answer: d, Reference: Chapter 7, P. 287, Difficulty: M

Essay Questions

1.   What is meant by "optimal conditions" for infant development? Include how the cultural and historical settings into which a child is born affect these "conditions."

2.   Discuss the implications of extreme maternal responsiveness to infants' cries.

3.   What is learned helplessness? Include the evidence that it does or does not occur among infants.

4.   What are the effects on infants of temporary separations from their parents, i.e., vacation, a night out, or hospitalization.

5.   What research supports the effects, if any, of the extensive daycare experience on infants less than 1 year of age?

6.   Discuss the prevailing views about the effects of infant daycare for infants under one year of age.

7.   Name two major researchers in the area of infant daycare. Compare and contrast their views. Do they agree or disagree on its effects? Explain.

8.   Wayne Dennis studied orphanage-raised children in Lebanon. How did the institutional care they received affect these children's development? How did this experience affect later development?

9.   Barbara Tizard conducted a study of children in English residential nurseries. How did her conclusions support the hypothesis, "no single temperamental trait in infancy positively predicts adult psychological adjustment?"

10.   Compare the results of Wayne Dennis's study of Lebanese orphanage children and the Barbara Tizard study of children in English residential nurseries. What were the outcomes that support or disprove acquired developmental difficulties?

11.   Once in a while a child is discovered who has been socially isolated for several years. What do the successes and/or failures of rehabilitation efforts tell us about the role of early experiences in later development?

12.   What are transactional models of development. How are they helpful in studying the effects of early childhood experiences?

13.   Using one of the examples of "transactional" models, trace the evolution of a "difficult" child to a positively functioning "easy" adult.

14.   Why might difficult children fare better in development? Explain and cite examples.

15.   Explain how the rehabilitation methods applied to Harlow's monkeys influenced effective rehabilitation of socially isolated children.

16.   In what ways did isolation effect the social behavior of Harlow's monkeys? What was the most effective method of rehabilitating these monkeys? Why?

17.   Cite evidence that Harlow's "therapy" with isolated reared monkeys might work with children. Explain.

18.   What kinds of social interactions have been shown to be therapeutic for socially isolated monkeys, as well as socially isolated children? Describe the effects.

19.   Why are we limited in the prediction of later psychological functioning by examining behavior in infancy? Explain.

20.   To what extent does the proverb "As the twig is bent, so grows the tree," apply to human development?

21.   Three factors evolved from the "Bent Twig" theory. Based upon these factors, what conclusion did psychologists draw about a child's developing capacities?

22.   Glenn and Mary Jones adopt a one-year-old baby who was born overseas and cared for in an orphanage of unknown quality for the first 4 months of life. Glenn and Mary are concerned about what the long-term effects this orphanage experience may have on the baby's development. What can you tell them to reassure them?

23.   What do think is the meaning of Alan Sroufe's statement that "continuity of development takes the form of coherence across transformations"? What are some of the implications of this concept?

24.   Discuss the concepts of vulnerability and resilience. How do these concepts relate to critical periods (the timing of experiences)?

25.   Evaluate the following statement: "Infancy is the most formative time in a person's life. In particular, the child's relationship with his mother during his first year is the foundation of his personality and will affect every later relationship." What evidence supports and refutes this statement?

26.   Discuss the role of stress and children's vulnerability. How do they interact?

27.   What family characteristics predispose children to developmental difficulties?

28.   Discuss the circumstances that have been found to reduce the risk of developmental difficulties and promote resilience.

29.   Considering the inconsistencies in predicting child development, how does the concept of an "internal working model" make sense?

30.   What is the relationship between measures of intelligence in infancy and childhood to intelligence measured later in life? What factors contribute to stability? What factors contribute to change?

Language Acquisition

CHAPTER **8**

Multiple-Choice Questions

1. Between the ages of 2 and 6, language growth plays a significant part in which area of children's development?
   a. mental and social
   b. physical and emotional
   c. sensorimotor and social
   d. mental and sensorimotor
   Answer: a, Reference: Chapter 8, P. 296, Difficulty: E

2. By age 6 years, a child will usually have a vocabulary of
   a. 5 to 10 thousand words
   b. 8 to 14 thousand words
   c. 15 to 20 thousand words
   d. more than 20 thousand words
   Answer: b, Reference: Chapter 8, P. 296, Difficulty: E

3. At birth children
   a. must be taught to attend to language
   b. show a preference for language over other sounds
   c. produce basic sounds in all languages through babbling
   d. can differentiate the basic sound categories of only their language
   Answer: b, Reference: Chapter 8, P. 296, Difficulty: E

4. Which of the following is clearly linked to social referencing
   a. babbling
   b. social smiling
   c. primary intersubjectivity
   d. secondary intersubjectivity
   Answer: d, Reference: Chapter 8, P. 297, Difficulty: M

5.   When babies and mothers talk, they share knowledge about objects to which they
      jointly attend. This is an example of _____ as a precursor to language
      a.   social referencing
      b.   primary intersubjectivity
      c.   pragmatic communication
      d.   secondary intersubjectivity
Answer: d, Reference: Chapter 8, P. 297, Difficulty: D

6.   Babies begin pointing at objects at age
      a.   3 to 5 months old
      b.   6 to 8 months old
      c.   9 to 12 months old
      d.   15 to 18 months old
Answer: c, Reference: Chapter 8, P. 297, Difficulty: M

7.   Which of the following would be considered a form of prelinguistic communication
      a.   pointing
      b.   babbling
      c.   first words
      d.   banging with a spoon
Answer: a, Reference: Chapter 8, P. 297, Difficulty: E

8.   Which statement is most true of the current study of language development?
      a.   both the development of grammar and reference are well understood
      b.   both the development of reference and grammar have proven difficult to
            understand
      c.   the development of reference is well understood but the development of
            grammar is not
      d.   the development of grammar is well understood but the development of
            reference is not
Answer: b, Reference: Chapter 8, P. 297, Difficulty: E

9.   The rules that govern both the sequence of words in a sentence and the ordering of
      parts of words are called
      a.   referents
      b.   grammar
      c.   semantics
      d.   deep structure
Answer: b, Reference: Chapter 8, P. 297, Difficulty: E

10.   Utterances such as: "Sarah eated fast"
       a.   are usually learned by imitation
       b.   are rarely if ever made by children
       c.   show that children have some grasp of grammatical rules
       d.   provide evidence that children rarely confuse grammatical forms
Answer: c, Reference: Chapter 8, P. 299, Difficulty: D

11.   The ability to embed sentences within each other, as when "I went to the park." "I played on the swings." "I played in the sandbox" becomes, "I went to the park and played on the swings and in the sandbox." is referred to as
       a.   recursion
       b.   fast mapping
       c.   overextension
       d.   abstract modeling
Answer: a, Reference: Chapter 8, P. 299, Difficulty: M

12.   Which of the following illustrates the property of recursion?
       a.   lion eats giraffe
       b.   what's your name?
       c.   the fish swam in the stream
       d.   the bird who sang the song built the nest
Answer: d, Reference: Chapter 8, P. 300, Difficulty: D

13.   Webster's definition of language identifies four central aspects of language including all of the following except
       a.   words
       b.   sounds
       c.   utterances
       d.   methods of combining words
Answer: c, Reference: Chapter 8, P. 300, Difficulty: E

14.   Children change from babbling to pronouncing words at about what age?
       a.   late in the first year
       b.   around 18 months
       c.   at the end of the second year
       d.   around 36 months
Answer: a, Reference: Chapter 8, P. 300, Difficulty: E

15.   Lieberman's study involving the organization of set of sounds and sound
       combinations found that adults can easily produce about how many sounds per
       second
       a.   12
       b.   36
       c.   50
       d.   100
Answer: a, Reference: Chapter 8, P. 300, Difficulty: D

16.   Humans have the ability to produce high rates of speech because
       a.   language learning is innate
       b.   sound combinations are not organized
       c.   the number of permissible combinations of sounds approaches infinity
       d.   sound combinations are organized and permissible combinations are reduced
Answer: d, Reference: Chapter 8, P. 300, Difficulty: D

17.   The length of time it takes children to master the pronunciation of separate sounds
       of their native language is
       a.   3 months
       b.   6 months
       c.   one year
       d.   several years
Answer: d, Reference: Chapter 8, P. 300, Difficulty: E

18.   When a child between the ages of two and three years old cannot produce a
       particular sound she will typically
       a.   substitute another sound
       b.   become frustrated and angry
       c.   refuse to use words that include the sound
       d.   misunderstand words that include the sound when she hears them
Answer: a, Reference: Chapter 8, P .300, Difficulty: D

19.   A child says "puzzle" instead of "puddle." Later the same child says "puggle" instead
       of "puzzle." Examples of this type provide evidence that
       a.   children cannot understand a word they cannot pronounce
       b.   the basic sounds of a language are learned as particular instances
       c.   the basic sounds of a language are not isolated instances of pronunciation
       d.   children are not capable of producing sounds for which they sometimes make
             substitutions
Answer: c, Reference: Chapter 8, P. 300, Difficulty: E

20.   The basic sounds of a language are known as
       a.   letters
       b.   syllables
       c.   phonemes
       d.   morphemes
Answer: c, Reference: Chapter 8, P. 301, Difficulty: M

21.   A child's attention to the sound differences of a language
       a.   is independent of the acquisition of phonemes
       b.   is independent of the acquisition of word meaning
       c.   uses a basic mechanical skill involving mouth shape
       d.   develops along with the acquisition of word meaning
Answer: d, Reference: Chapter 8, P. 301, Difficulty: M

22.   The term morpheme
       a.   is synonymous with phoneme
       b.   refers to children's first words
       c.   refers to a basic unit of meaning in a language
       d.   refers to units of sound which are the same for all languages
Answer: c, Reference: Chapter 8, P. 301, Difficulty: M

23.   The basic unit of meaning in language is called a
       a.   noun
       b.   word
       c.   phoneme
       d.   morpheme
Answer: d, Reference: Chapter 8, P. 301, Difficulty: E

24.   How many morphemes are contained in the sentence, "The boy danced all night long."
       a.   5
       b.   6
       c.   7
       d.   8
Answer: c, Reference: Chapter 8, P. 301, Difficulty: D

25.   Children begin to use their first real words
       a.   at birth
       b.   when they begin to babble
       c.   just before their first birthday
       d.   just after their second birthday
Answer: c, Reference: Chapter 8, P. 301, Difficulty: E

26. Which of the following is the most accurate description of development in relation to the acquisition of language?
    a.   words enable children to organize their activity in a new way
    b.   children learn to mediate with words after they acquire language
    c.   a child's activity and the organization of words are in no way related
    d.   general nominals are learned after the child has acquired many words as mediators

Answer: a, Reference: Chapter 8, P. 302, Difficulty: D

27. Research by Katherine Nelson on children's early vocabularies found most of children's early words were
    a.   verbs
    b.   nouns
    c.   adverbs
    d.   adjectives

Answer: b, Reference: Chapter 8, P. 303, Difficulty: M

28. Which of the following is a relational word that appears early in children's vocabularies?
    a.   "no"
    b.   "juice"
    c.   "doggie"
    d.   "mommy"

Answer: a, Reference: Chapter 8, P. 303, Difficulty: D

29. The form of mislabeling in which many examples in a category are referred to be a single term that adults use to label only one of the examples is called
    a.   expanding
    b.   overextension
    c.   underextension
    d.   protosentencing

Answer: b, Reference: Chapter 8, P. 304, Difficulty: M

30. Which of the following is an example of an overextension?
    a.   calling a rose "flower"
    b.   calling a bird "animal"
    c.   calling a horse "doggie"
    d.   using the word "doggie" only for the family pet

Answer: c, Reference: Chapter 8, P. 304, Difficulty: D

31. A child calls all farm animals "horsey." This is an example of
     a.   overextension
     b.   underextension
     c.   intermediate abstraction
     d.   the mediated character of language

Answer: a, Reference: Chapter 8, P. 304, Difficulty: M

32. When children use words in a narrower way than adults do, it is referred to as
     a.   jargoning
     b.   telegraphic
     c.   overextension
     d.   underextension

Answer: d, Reference: Chapter 8, P. 304, Difficulty: E

33. A child uses the word "doggy" only for his own family's dog, not for other dogs.
     This is an example of
     a.   imitation
     b.   mediating
     c.   overextension
     d.   underextension

Answer: d, Reference: Chapter 8, P. 304, Difficulty: M

34. The words children acquire first can be best described as what level of generality?
     a.   low
     b.   high
     c.   intermediate
     d.   nonconceptual

Answer: c, Reference: Chapter 8, P. 305, Difficulty: D

35. Two-year-old Amanda uses the word "flower" to refer to lilies, carnations, pansies,
     and dandelions. She probably does this because
     a.   she is overextending the word "flower"
     b.   her visual system cannot differentiate among the flowers
     c.   her first words are at an intermediate level of abstraction
     d.   she has only learned very specific levels and no abstract terms as yet

Answer: c, Reference: Chapter 8, P. 306, Difficulty: D

36. A child says "cookie," meaning "I want a cookie." The word "cookie" is an example
     of a(n)
     a.   holophrase
     b.   overextension
     c.   underextension
     d.   explicit ordering

Answer: a, Reference: Chapter 8, P. 308, Difficulty: E

37.   The early one word utterance that may stand for a whole sentence is referred to as
        a.   phoneme
        b.   holophone
        c.   morpheme
        d.   holophrase
Answer: d, Reference: Chapter 8, P. 308, Difficulty: E

38.   Greenfield and Smith's interpretation of single word utterances is that they stand for
        a.   a whole idea
        b.   a whole sentence
        c.   differentiated language capacities
        d.   a particular element of what the child wants to discuss
Answer: d, Reference: Chapter 8, P. 308, Difficulty: D

39.   A child's new potential for creating meaning by varying the arrangement of linguistic
        elements marks the birth of
        a.   language
        b.   grammar
        c.   social words
        d.   interpretations
Answer: b, Reference: Chapter 8, P. 308, Difficulty: M

40.   Several features of the English language stand out in early "protosentences"
        including all of the following, *except*
        a.   ordering
        b.   explicitness
        c.   telegraphic quality
        d.   grammatical morphemes
Answer: d, Reference: Chapter 8, P. 309, Difficulty: E

41.   Which of the following is true of two-word speech?
        a.   it occurs before the use of syntax
        b.   interpretation is dependent on context
        c.   interpretation is independent of context
        d.   it does little to extend the child's ability to communicate
Answer: b, Reference: Chapter 8, P. 309, Difficulty: M

42.   A child's utterances are measured in terms of the average number of
        a.   words per sentence
        b.   concepts per sentence
        c.   phonemes per sentence
        d.   morphemes per sentence
Answer: d, Reference: Chapter 8, P. 310, Difficulty: D

43.   The little words and word parts that are systematically absent in two-word
        utterances are called
        a.   phonemes
        b.   surface structures
        c.   imitative complexities
        d.   grammatical morphemes
Answer: d, Reference: Chapter 8, P. 310, Difficulty: M

44.   Grammatical morphemes
        a.   are innate structures inherent in language
        b.   measure the complexity of children's utterances
        c.   create meaning by showing the relations between words
        d.   show that children do not understand the difference between verbs and nouns
Answer: c, Reference: Chapter 8, P. 310, Difficulty: M

45.   The elements that create meaning by showing the relations between other elements
        within the sentence are called
        a.   vowels
        b.   phonemes
        c.   extensions
        d.   grammatical morphemes
Answer: d, Reference: Chapter 8, P. 310, Difficulty: M

46.   An example of how young children use ordering rules to achieve language
        competence is evident in their use of
        a.   phonemes
        b.   holophrases
        c.   tag questions
        d.   two-word utterances
Answer: c, Reference: Chapter 8, P. 311, Difficulty: M

47.   "You brought the things, didn't you?" is an example of
        a.   a holophrase
        b.   a tag question
        c.   telegraphic speech
        d.   the use of grammatical phonemes
Answer: b, Reference: Chapter 8, P. 311, Difficulty: E

48.   Highly abstract rules of language are acquired by
        a.   linguists
        b.   all adults
        c.   all normal children
        d.   individuals in industrialized societies
Answer: c, Reference: Chapter 8, P. 311, Difficulty: E

49.   When learning to communicate effectively a child needs to learn
       a.   nothing more than the sounds of language
       b.   to rely solely on a language acquisition device
       c.   pragmatic as well as grammatical aspects of language
       d.   nothing more than grammatical rules and word meanings
Answer: c, Reference: Chapter 8, P. 312, Difficulty: E

50.   Pragmatics involves the ability to
       a.   imitate language
       b.   use grammatical morphemes
       c.   use speech forms to accomplish actions
       d.   understand the ordering of linguistic terms
Answer: c, Reference: Chapter 8, P. 312, Difficulty: D

51.   If an infant holds up her cup and says "more" in order to get more juice, she is using
       a.   recursion
       b.   a proto-imperative
       c.   a proto-declarative
       d.   the cooperative principle
Answer: b, Reference: Chapter 8, P. 312, Difficulty: M

52.   A proto-declarative is
       a.   always verbal
       b.   a way of referring
       c.   not considered conversational in nature
       d.   a way of engaging another person to achieve a desired object
Answer: b, Reference: Chapter 8, P. 312, Difficulty: M

53.   A baby points to a cat and says "kitty". This is an example of
       a.   overextension
       b.   underextension
       c.   proto-imperative
       d.   proto-declarative
Answer: d, Reference: Chapter 8, P. 312, Difficulty: E

54.   In her study of how children make use of language, Marilyn Shatz found that
       children as young as 2 were able to
       a.   imitate parental speech patterns
       b.   understand only direct commands
       c.   correct the grammatical errors of peers
       d.   respond correctly to indirect commands
Answer: d, Reference: Chapter 8, P. 313, Difficulty: D

55.   According to philosopher H. P. Grice, the master rule of ordinary conversation is
        a.   the cooperative principle
        b.   taking account of the listener
        c.   mastery of grammatical rules
        d.   the conversational act principle
Answer: a, Reference: Chapter 8, P. 313, Difficulty: E

56.   The maxims of quantity, quality, relevance, and clarity of speech are all aspects of
        a.   figurative language
        b.   complex constructions
        c.   the cooperative principle
        d.   taking account of the listener
Answer: c, Reference: Chapter 8, P. 313, Difficulty: M

57.   The onset of metaphorical language coincides with the onset of
        a.   syntax
        b.   holophrases
        c.   symbolic play
        d.   recursive utterances
Answer: c, Reference: Chapter 8, P. 314, Box 8.2, Difficulty: D

58.   The use of figurative language is rarely seen in children before the age of
        a.   2 years
        b.   4 years
        c.   5 years
        d.   7 years
Answer: a, Reference: Chapter 8, P. 314, Box 8.2, Difficulty: M

59.   The figurative use of words provides evidence that language is
        a.   innate
        b.   creative
        c.   imitative
        d.   independent of thought
Answer: c, Reference: Chapter 8, P. 314, Box 8.2, Difficulty: D

60.   Ellen Winner identified which of the following as the basis of children's metaphors?
        a.   similarities in action and syntax
        b.   perceptual similarities and similarities in action
        c.   similarities in syntax and perceptual similarities
        d.   perceptual similarities and imitative holophrases
Answer: b, Reference: Chapter 8, P. 314, Box 8.2, Difficulty: D

61.   Which of the following is true regarding metaphorical language?
       a.   it is thought to depend on the appearance of deferred imitation
       b.   it provides evidence that language production is a creative process
       c.   the appearance of metaphorical language is fairly late in childhood
       d.   when young children become able to use metaphorical language they also
             understand the figurative meaning of adult speech
Answer: b, Reference: Chapter 8, P. 314, Box 8.2, Difficulty: M

62.   The use of figurative speech
       a.   increases continuously until adulthood
       b.   is rarely based on perceptual attributes
       c.   decreases after children have mastered language
       d.   is easily understood by children after the age of 2
Answer: c, Reference: Chapter 8, P. 314, Box 8.2, Difficulty: M

63.   Shatz and Gelman found that children as young as 4 years of age were able to
       modify their speech
       a.   when talking to 2-year-olds
       b.   only if they had younger siblings
       c.   when talking to dolls but not to children
       d.   only when instructed to do so by their parents
Answer: a, Reference: Chapter 8, P. 315, Difficulty: M

64.   When 4-year-olds speak to 2-year-olds they
       a.   shorten their sentences
       b.   imitate the 2-year-olds' speech
       c.   pretend to be older than they are
       d.   increase the complexity of their speech
Answer: a, Reference: Chapter 8, P. 315, Difficulty: M

65.   The two divergent theories of language acquisition that dominated much of the
       twentieth century are
       a.   nativist and interactionist approaches
       b.   learning theory and nativist approaches
       c.   learning theory and interactionist approaches
       d.   nativist and biological-maturation approaches
Answer: b, Reference: Chapter 8, P. 315, Difficulty: M

66.   In recent decades which approach to language acquisition has gained prominence?
       a.   nativist
       b.   interactionist
       c.   learning-theory
       d.   environmentalist
Answer: b, Reference: Chapter 8, P. 316, Difficulty: E

67.   What is (are) the mechanism(s) proposed by the learning theory of language acquisition?
   a.   environment
   b.   script coordination
   c.   imitation, conditioning
   d.   assimilation, accommodation
Answer: c, Reference: Chapter 8, P. 316, Table 8.4, Difficulty: D

68.   Classical conditioning plays a major role in language acquisition, according to
   a.   nativist theory
   b.   learning theory
   c.   interactionist theory
   d.   cultural-context theory
Answer: b, Reference: Chapter 8, P. 316, Difficulty: M

69.   The meaning of a word is the sum of the associations it evokes after being paired with many different experiences, according to which explanation of language acquisition?
   a.   nativist
   b.   cognitive
   c.   interactionist
   d.   learning theory
Answer: d, Reference: Chapter 8, P. 317, Difficulty: D

70.   Classical conditioning can explain how children learn to
   a.   imitate language
   b.   produce language
   c.   comprehend language
   d.   understand "ordering"
Answer: c, Reference: Chapter 8, P. 317, Difficulty: M

71.   The operant conditioning explanation of language learning begins with the observation that children
   a.   emit a rich repertoire of sounds while babbling
   b.   do not emit sounds until they are ready to learn to talk
   c.   eventually pronounce only the phonemes of their own language
   d.   emit sounds while babbling which are unrelated to their later speech
Answer: a, Reference: Chapter 8, P. 317, Difficulty: D

72.   According to the operant conditioning explanation of language acquisition, sounds
      become words through
      a.   imitation
      b.   reinforcement
      c.   biological maturation
      d.   the process of association
Answer: b, Reference: Chapter 8, P. 317, Difficulty: M

73.   Which of the following is not learned by imitation according to learning theory
      views of language acquisition?
      a.   word referents
      b.   grammatical morphemes
      c.   complex grammatical patterns
      d.   phonemes particular to a language
Answer: c, Reference: Chapter 8, P. 317, Difficulty: E

74.   The term "abstract modeling" refers to children's ability to
      a.   verbally interpret their own scribbling
      b.   repeat the intonation contours of words
      c.   comprehend the meanings of novel utterances
      d.   imitate utterances while learning the linguistic principles underlying them
Answer: d, Reference: Chapter 8, P. 318, Difficulty: D

75.   Learning theorists propose that language is acquired through
      a.   overextensions
      b.   abstract modeling
      c.   cognitive achievements
      d.   a language acquisition device
Answer: b, Reference: Chapter 8, P. 318, Difficulty: M

76.   Noam Chomsky is associated with which view of language acquisition?
      a.   nativist
      b.   learning
      c.   cultural-context
      d.   cognitive-interactionist
Answer: a, Reference: Chapter 8, P. 318, Difficulty: E

77.   According to Noam Chomsky, all of the following are true of language development
      except
      a.   the capacity to comprehend and generate language is innate
      b.   the capacity to comprehend and generate language is learned
      c.   language develops by different principles than do other human behaviors
      d.   the capacity to comprehend and generate language is like a special human
             organ with its own structure and function
Answer: b, Reference: Chapter 8, P. 318, Difficulty: M

78. Chomsky refers to the actual sentences people produce as
    a. a form of imitation
    b. the deep structure of language
    c. the language acquisition device
    d. the surface structure of language
Answer: d, Reference: Chapter 8, P. 318, Difficulty: M

79. Chomsky refers to the restricted set of rules from which actual sentences can be derived as
    a. triggers
    b. deep structure
    c. surface structure
    d. linguistic devices
Answer: b, Reference: Chapter 8, P. 318, Difficulty: D

80. Brown and Hanlon's finding that parents fail to correct or even notice grammatical errors of their children's speech is evidence for which theory of language acquisition?
    a. nativist
    b. learning
    c. interactionist
    d. constructivist
Answer: a, Reference: Chapter 8, P. 318, Difficulty: M

81. In a study by Brown and Hanlon (1970) it was found that the typical parental reaction to their children's grammatical errors was that parents
    a. reacted with anger
    b. showed no reaction
    c. corrected their children's speech
    d. reacted calmly but showed disapproval
Answer: b, Reference: Chapter 8, P. 318, Difficulty: M

82. According to Chomsky, a language acquisition device
    a. is like a specialized organ for language learning
    b. develops out of the child's general cognitive structures
    c. is formed from a process of conditioning and imitation
    d. cannot account for how children living in different places learn different languages
Answer: a, Reference: Chapter 8, P. 319, Difficulty: E

83.   The nativist approach to language acquisition stresses
    a.   children's overall mental development
    b.   the need for specialized language training
    c.   parental roles in the acquisition of language
    d.   children's readiness to learn language from birth
Answer: d, Reference: Chapter 8, P. 319, Difficulty: M

84.   In language learning, according to Noam Chomsky, experience
    a.   determines the nature of language learning structures
    b.   plays a subordinate role to the evolutionary history of the species
    c.   modifies the general cognitive structures underlying language learning
    d.   modifies the way the language acquisition device works once it is activated
Answer: b, Reference: Chapter 8, P. 319, Difficulty: M

85.   Which view of language acquisition believes that children's language development is
      closely linked to their cognitive development?
    a.   nativist
    b.   interactionist
    c.   learning-theory
    d.   environmentalist
Answer: b, Reference: Chapter 8, P. 319, Difficulty: E

86.   Meltzoff and Gopnik suggest the way children use words changes in conjunction
      with a change in the nature of their deferred imitations around the age of
    a.   12 months
    b.   18 months
    c.   24 months
    d.   48 months
Answer: b, Reference: Chapter 8, P. 319, Difficulty: D

87.   Elizabeth Bates and her colleagues, believe that acquisition of grammar is primarily
    a.   the product of an innate rule system
    b.   a process of learning grammatical structures
    c.   a by-product of learning the rules of language
    d.   a by-product of learning how to do things with words
Answer: d, Reference: Chapter 8, P. 320, Difficulty: M

88.   Which approach to language acquisition stresses the importance of "formatted
      activities?"
    a.   nativist
    b.   interactionist
    c.   learning-theory
    d.   cultural-context
Answer: d, Reference: Chapter 8, P. 321, Difficulty: D

89. Bruner refers to socially pattered activities in which an adult and child do things to and with each other by the term
    a. format
    b. deep structure
    c. abstract modeling
    d. communicative interaction
Answer: a, Reference: Chapter 8, P. 321, Difficulty: M

90. According to Bruner, which of the following is a formatted activity?
    a. taking a nap
    b. eating a cookie
    c. playing pat-a-cake
    d. watching Sesame Street
Answer: c, Reference: Chapter 8, P. 321, Difficulty: D

91. The importance of a language acquisition support system is emphasized in which of the following views?
    a. nativist
    b. cognitive
    c. learning-theory
    d. cultural-context
Answer: d, Reference: Chapter 8, P. 321, Difficulty: M

92. Among nonhuman species, language is
    a. limited to noncommunicative grunts
    b. limited to noncommunicative gestures
    c. less powerful and flexible than human speech
    d. equally as powerful and flexible as human speech
Answer: c, Reference: Chapter 8, P. 321, Difficulty: M

93. When chimpanzees are reared with human children they
    a. make recursive utterances
    b. acquire oral language like that of their human counterparts
    c. acquire sign language like that of their human counterparts
    d. can acquire gestures that resemble some aspects of human language
Answer: d, Reference: Chapter 8, P. 322, Difficulty: M

94. After chimpanzees are included in every day human activities for an extended period of time they
    a. learn several thousand signs
    b. create word combinations similar to that of a 2-year-old
    c. produce speech comparable to the speech of 4-year-old children
    d. frequently use complex communicative language to coordinate actions
Answer: b, Reference: Chapter 8, P. 322, Difficulty: M

95. Research on children with William's syndrome who developed near normal speech patterns in spite of mental retardation suggests
    a. language functioning is entirely innate
    b. language functioning is the basis of normal cognitive functioning
    c. there is a close link between general cognitive ability and language functioning
    d. some aspects of language develop independently of general cognitive functioning

Answer: d, Reference: Chapter 8, P. 322, Difficulty: E

96. When children are deprived of human interaction they
    a. do not develop normal language
    b. invent a gestural system of communication
    c. can learn language from watching television
    d. can learn language if they watch TV programs portraying human interactions

Answer: a, Reference: Chapter 8, P. 323, Difficulty: M

97. Studies which examined cases where children were left alone for long periods of time with a television set broadcasting in a different language than that spoken in the home found
    a. children learned the language on television but not that spoken in the home
    b. language can be learned solely through imitation and the association of sound and action
    c. television exposure alone was adequate for normal linguistic ability in a second language to develop
    d. linguistic ability in the second language may be impaired when there is opportunity to interact with other speakers

Answer: d, Reference: Chapter 8, P. 323, Difficulty: M

98. Any delays in deaf children's language development can be explained by
    a. the absence of the ability to hear
    b. differences in their participation in language-mediated activities
    c. both the absence of hearing and different participation in language-mediated activities
    d. neither the absence of hearing nor different participation in language-mediated activities

Answer: b, Reference: Chapter 8, P. 324, Difficulty: M

99. Susan Goldin-Meadow and her colleagues found that "home sign"
    a. develops as far as pointing
    b. develops among hearing children of deaf parents
    c. develops among deaf children of hearing parents
    d. is idiosyncratic and does not resemble normal language in any way

Answer: c, Reference: Chapter 8, P. 324, Difficulty: M

100. Children who use "home sign"
   a. are unable to use recursion
   b. never make multi-word utterances
   c. make multi-word utterances around their fifth birthdays
   d. adhere to ordering principles similar to those used in normal language

Answer: d, Reference: Chapter 8, P. 324, Difficulty: M

101. Children who use "home sign" fail to
   a. communicate
   b. embed sentences
   c. make two and three word utterances
   d. master complex grammatical distinctions

Answer: d, Reference: Chapter 8, P. 324, Difficulty: D

102. Which of the following is both necessary and sufficient for children to develop normal language?
   a. pairing of sounds and actions
   b. hearing the sound of language
   c. hearing and seeing language interactions on television
   d. social interactions organized with the sights or sounds of language

Answer: d, Reference: Chapter 8, P. 325, Difficulty: M

103. Bartlett and Carey demonstrated children's developing vocabularies in the course of normal conversation by inventing the color "chromium." The findings of this study suggest
   a. children learn by imitation
   b. direct teaching of new vocabulary words is most effective
   c. children acquire language because adults explicitly reward their efforts
   d. children can learn new words when they occur in a close relationship with familiar action

Answer: d, Reference: Chapter 8, P. 325, Difficulty: M

104. When Bartlett and Carey arranged for preschool children to learn the word "chromium," the children
   a. learned it only after being tutored
   b. had difficulty learning the unfamiliar word
   c. learned to say the word but could not identify "chromium" objects
   d. learned the word after one experience with its use in a familiar situation

Answer: d, Reference: Chapter 8, P. 325, Difficulty: M

105.   When children hear an unfamiliar word in a familiar and highly structured situation
        they likely form an idea of the word's meaning and how that word might fit into
        their existing repertoire. This phenomenon has been termed
        a.   pragmatism
        b.   fast mapping
        c.   mental module
        d.   telegraphic ability
Answer: b, Reference: Chapter 8, P. 325, Difficulty: M

106.   According to the text there is wide agreement that all of the following are essential
        in language acquisition except
        a.   deliberate instruction in language
        b.   imitation of language behavior of others
        c.   a biologically programmed sensitivity to language present at birth
        d.   interaction with caretakers where language is used as a source of coordination
Answer: a, Reference: Chapter 8, P. 327, Difficulty: E

107.   The special high-pitched voice-varying intonation and simplified vocabulary adults
        use when they talk to small children is known as
        a.   recursion
        b.   motherese
        c.   holophrases
        d.   fast mapping
Answer: b, Reference: Chapter 8, P. 327, Difficulty: E

108.   High pitch, exaggerated intonation, slow speech, and distinct pauses between
        utterances are speech patterns of
        a.   children over the age of 3
        b.   adults speaking to children
        c.   children under the age of 3
        d.   hearing children of deaf parents
Answer: b, Reference: Chapter 8, P. 328, Table 8.6 Difficulty: M

109.   American adults are likely to modify their speech to children to
        a.   complicate their own utterances
        b.   increase the opportunity to use gestures
        c.   immediately correct children's grammatical errors
        d.   match the level of complexity in the children's own speech
Answer: d, Reference: Chapter 8, P. 328, Difficulty: M

110. When Courtney Cazden exposed children to numerous expansions of their speech, she found
    a. a positive effect on language development
    b. a negative effect on language development
    c. no special effects on language development
    d. a decrease in children's language errors that was inversely proportional to the number of expansions
Answer: c, Reference: Chapter 8, P. 328, Difficulty: M

111. Albert Bandura is a proponent of what view of language acquisition?
    a. nativist
    b. contextual
    c. cognitive-interactionist
    d. environmental-learning
Answer: d, Reference: Chapter 8, P. 329, Difficulty: E

112. Piaget's view of the relationship between language and thought is that
    a. language determines cognition
    b. cognition determines language
    c. language and cognition are independent
    d. cognition initially determines language but after language develops sufficiently language determines cognition
Answer: b, Reference: Chapter 8, P. 329, Difficulty: M

113. Which of the following, according to Piaget, is an example of egocentric speech?
    a. a 5-year-old explains to his mother what he did at school that day
    b. a 4-year-old simplifies her speech when talking to her 2- year-old brother
    c. two 3-year-olds have a "conversation" in which each is talking about a different topic
    d. two 4-year olds have a 'conversation' on a single topic, but keep interrupting each other
Answer: c, Reference: Chapter 8, P. 329, Difficulty: M

114. The failure of language training to influence problem-solving in the study of French speaking preschoolers by Sinclair de Zwart (1967) seems to confirm Piaget's theory that
    a. language does not affect thought
    b. preschool age children are not yet problem solvers
    c. language training during the preschool years is relatively ineffective
    d. children can not learn to solve problems until they move to a new level of cognitive development
Answer: a, Reference: Chapter 8, P. 330, Difficulty: M

115.   The concept of a "mental module" is associated with which theorist?
       a.   Piaget
       b.   Skinner
       c.   Chomsky
       d.   Vygotsky
Answer: c, Reference: Chapter 8, P. 330, Difficulty: E

116.   According to Chomsky the self-contained nature of the language-using capacity is
       called
       a.   a format
       b.   a schema
       c.   fast mapping
       d.   a mental module
Answer: d, Reference: Chapter 8, P. 330, Difficulty: M

117.   According to Noam Chomsky
       a.   there is no mental module for language
       b.   language is an outgrowth of sensorimotor abilities
       c.   there is no connection between language and thought
       d.   the linguistic ability of some severely retarded children provides support for
             his theory of language
Answer: d, Reference: Chapter 8, P. 330, Difficulty: D

118.   The most prominent cultural theory of language and thought was developed by
       a.   Piaget
       b.   Bandura
       c.   Chomsky
       d.   Vygotsky
Answer: d, Reference: Chapter 8, P. 331, Difficulty: D

119.   According to Lev Vygotsky,
       a.   children develop into social beings over time
       b.   psychological functions are first manifest in a social environment
       c.   children develop in contexts that are organized by adults and peers
       d.   changes in cognition are necessary precursors for changes in language
Answer: b, Reference: Chapter 8, P. 331, Difficulty: M

120.   Lev Vygotsky found that when preschoolers were surrounded by deaf-mute children
       their
       a.   language was unchanged
       b.   egocentric speech decreased
       c.   egocentric speech increased
       d.   non-egocentric speech increased
Answer: b, Reference: Chapter 8, P. 331, Difficulty: M

121.	Lev Vygotsky believed that before the age of 2,
	a.	language is asocial
	b.	language and thought are indistinguishable
	c.	language and thought develop independently
	d.	the transition from social to individual thought is completed

Answer: c, Reference: Chapter 8, P. 331, Difficulty: M

122.	According to Vygotsky, language and thought develop
	a.	along parallel, relatively unrelated lines throughout childhood
	b.	along parallel, relatively unrelated lines for about the first two years of life
	c.	simultaneously, each depending on the other for development throughout childhood
	d.	simultaneously, each depending on the other for development for about the first two years of life

Answer: b, Reference: Chapter 8, P. 331, Difficulty: M

123.	Which of the following statements best summarizes current scientific and theoretical knowledge about the language acquisition process?
	a.	learning theorists have put together the best normal description of how syntax works
	b.	linguists and psychologists have been able to agree and put together a complete theory of language acquisition
	c.	Noam Chomsky's approach provides a complete description of the experiences necessary to trigger language acquisition
	d.	though there is no single theory which explains all aspects of language acquisition, much is known about the overall process

Answer: d, Reference: Chapter 8, P. 332, Difficulty: M

Essay Questions

1.	List major characteristics of the learning-theory, nativist, and interactionist approaches to children's language acquisition.

2.	What is a phoneme? Give examples. Do all languages use the same set of phonemes? Discuss.

3.	Why might children's first words and word meanings best be described as collaborations between adults and children? Give examples.

4.	Describe common characteristics of a child's earliest words. What role do overextensions and underextensions play in language acquisition?

5. Do early words stand for sentences? Explain.

6. What is fast mapping? Give an example.

7. What are grammatical morphemes? Give examples. Which morphemes are most likely to be acquired first by English-speaking children?

8. How is children's early language not fully communicative? In what way do preschoolers speak to different aged listeners?

9. Compare Piaget's views of the relationship between language and thought during early childhood with those of Vygotsky.

10. Describe the development of figurative speech as part of children's language repertoire.

11. How is language a distinctively human accomplishment? In what ways is it an ability we share with animals of other species?

12. What is a holophrase? Why do psychologists disagree about the meanings of these utterances?

13. How do children raised in language-deprived environments learn to communicate? What do these situations demonstrate about necessary and sufficient conditions for language acquisition?

14. Describe how young children differ from adults in the level of abstraction of words they typically use.

15. How might the surface structures of a sentence differ from its deep structure? Explain.

16. What is overextension and underextension in young children's speech? Provide an example of each.

17. In what ways do adults modify children's language environments to help them acquire language? Is such modification necessary for children to learn language? If so, to what extent?

18. A toddler touches the cactus and says "hot." Which word category does the word "hot" fit into? How could this be an example of a holophrase?

19. What are proto-imperatives? Give an example.

20. Differentiate between a proto-imperative and a proto-declarative. Give examples of each.

21. Describe a language-rich environment for an infant or toddler, and discuss whether this type of environment aids in language growth.

22. What does "expansion" refer to with regard to children's speech? How does it impact language development?

23. What is a "collective monologue"? What Piagetian characteristic from the preoperational period is thought to influence it?

24. Describe Chomsky's concept of a mental module. What role does it play in language acquisition?

25. Describe the relationship between thought and language proposed by Vygotsky.

26. What is a "LASS"? With what theory of language development is it associated?

27. Do theorists use the classical conditioning model to account for how children learn to understand or produce language? Explain.

28. Summarize the results of research investigating the relationship between special adult behaviors to teach language and the rate of language acquisition. What role does culture play in this behavior?

29. How is animal language different from human language? Explain.

30. Compare and contrast early language development in deaf and hearing children. Explain.

31. What is the relationship of MLU to the level of language development? Explain.

Early Childhood Thought: Islands of Competence

Multiple-Choice Questions

1.   "Magical thinking" allows preschool aged children to do all of the following except
    a.   vacillate between insight and ignorance
    b.   say and believe things that violate logic and physics
    c.   answer scientific questions correctly without the use of logic
    d.   allow their thinking to "wobble" back and forth between the reasonable and the unreasonable
Answer: c, Reference: Chapter 9, P. 338, Difficulty: M

2.   Of the following, a preschooler would be most likely to remember
    a.   the details of a trip to the zoo
    b.   a list of unrelated but familiar words
    c.   a set of cars immediately after seeing them
    d.   a set of doll house toys immediately after seeing them
Answer: a, Reference: Chapter 9, P. 338, Difficulty: D

3.   Which of Piaget's developmental stages is characterized by the ability to reason through overt action?
    a.   sensorimotor
    b.   preoperational
    c.   formal operational
    d.   concrete operational
Answer: a, Reference: Chapter 9, P. 340, Difficulty: M

4.   According to Piaget, a preschooler's thought
      a.   can no longer be described as "primitive"
      b.   is fundamentally the same as an older infant's
      c.   is capable of allowing one thing to stand for another
      d.   relies exclusively on trial and error to solve problems
Answer: c, Reference: Chapter 9, P. 340, Difficulty: D

5.   Piaget used the term "preoperational" to describe children between the ages of 3 and
      5, because they do not yet have the ability to
      a.   learn language
      b.   understand simple commands
      c.   operate simple machines, such as staplers
      d.   combine, separate, and transform information mentally
Answer: d, Reference: Chapter 9, P. 340, Difficulty: M

6.   Piaget used the term "center" to refer to
      a.   a form of egocentrism
      b.   a form of operational thinking
      c.   the ability to overcome magical thinking
      d.   the ability to focus attention on a single feature
Answer: d, Reference: Chapter 9, P. 340, Difficulty: E

7.   Which of the following is a characteristic of preoperational thought?
      a.   perspective taking
      b.   the ability to think logically
      c.   the ability to distinguish appearance from reality
      d.   the ability to understand and follow simple commands
Answer: d, Reference: Chapter 9, P. 340, Difficulty: M

8.   As used by Piaget, the term egocentrism refers to
      a.   a form of confusion
      b.   a form of selfishness
      c.   the ability to use decentered thought
      d.   the inability to take another's point of view
Answer: d, Reference: Chapter 9, P. 341, Difficulty: M

9.   In Piaget and Inhelder's classic "three mountain problems" where preoperational
      children are asked to identify the doll's perspective, they almost always choose the
      picture that corresponds to
      a.   the doll's point of view
      b.   their own point of view
      c.   the first view that they saw
      d.   the experimenter's point of view
Answer: b, Reference: Chapter 9, P. 341, Difficulty: E

10.   All of the following are settings used to demonstrate egocentric thought except
    a.   collective monologues
    b.   the three mountain problem
    c.   comparison of two subsets with a superordinate set
    d.   cooperative problem solving with a screen between the two partners
Answer: c, Reference: Chapter 9, P. 341, Difficulty: D

11.   The ability to think about other people's mental states that develops in a child's 4th year of life, is referred to as
    a.   centering
    b.   theory of mind
    c.   egocentric reasoning
    d.   transductive reasoning
Answer: b, Reference: Chapter 9, P. 343, Difficulty: D

12.   The ability to think about the mental states of other people first appears during the _____ year of life.
    a.   second
    b.   third
    c.   fourth
    d.   fifth
Answer: c, Reference: Chapter 9, P. 343, Difficulty: E

13.   A study by Avis and Harris (1991) with Baka children in West Africa found that the Baka children
    a.   failed entirely to develop a theory of mind
    b.   developed a theory of mind later than English and American children
    c.   developed a theory of mind earlier than English and American children
    d.   developed a theory of mind at the same age as English and American children
Answer: d, Reference: Chapter 9, P. 343, Difficulty: M

14.   Halloween is likely to be frightening to 3-year-olds because
    a.   most three-year-olds are afraid of the dark
    b.   at that age many children are afraid of strangers
    c.   a child that age has difficulty distinguishing appearance from reality
    d.   a three-year-old is likely to believe that a mask can transform whatever it is covering
Answer: c, Reference: Chapter 9, P. 344, Difficulty: E

15.   When Rheta De Vries put a dog mask on a cat,
       a.   3-year-olds believed the cat was still a cat
       b.   all of the children believed that the cat remained a cat
       c.   4-and 5-year-olds showed significant signs of confusion
       d.   all children under the age of 7 believed the cat became a dog
Answer: c, Reference: Chapter 9, P. 344, Difficulty: M

16.   When John Flavell and his colleagues showed children objects that appeared to be
       one thing but were really another, they found that
       a.   5-year-olds were never fooled by the appearance of the objects
       b.   Chinese 3-year-olds were better able to distinguish appearance from reality
       c.   both American and Chinese 3-year-olds were able to solve the problem if
             given enough time
       d.   both American and Chinese 3-year-olds experienced similar difficulties
             distinguishing appearance from reality
Answer: d, Reference: Chapter 9, P. 344, Difficulty: E

17.   Which of the following is not true regarding young children's difficulties with the
       appearance/reality distinction?
       a.   training young children to recognize the distinctions have failed
       b.   simplifying the task does not help young children make the distinction
       c.   3-year-old children from many different cultures experience similar
             difficulties
       d.   young children's difficulties with the appearance/reality distinction are trivial
             and easily overcome
Answer: d, Reference: Chapter 9, P. 345, Difficulty: M

18.   As evidence that the difficulties which young children have with the
       appearance/reality distinction are "nontrivial, deep-seated, [and] genuinely
       intellectual ones", Flavell points out that
       a.   various attempts to simplify the task do not help a young child over their
             difficulties
       b.   attempts to train young children to make appropriate distinctions have been
             successful
       c.   Chinese, Japanese, and British three year olds differ in the degree to which
             they have difficulty with the task
       d.   various attempts to simplify the task contribute significantly to a young child's
             resolution of their difficulties
Answer: a, Reference: Chapter 9, P. 345, Difficulty: D

19. When young children think transductively they
    a. are at least six years of age
    b. are in the concrete operations stage
    c. are likely to confuse cause and effect
    d. have mastered the appearance-reality distinction
Answer: c, Reference: Chapter 9, P. 345, Difficulty: M

20. The text discusses a young child who thought that because there are no graveyards in New York City, people do not die there, as an example of
    a. centering
    b. egocentrism
    c. horizontal decalage
    d. transductive reasoning
Answer: d, Reference: Chapter 9, P. 346, Difficulty: M

21. One problem for Piaget's theory is
    a. magical thinking
    b. egocentric thought
    c. lack of total consistency in preschoolers problem solving
    d. large variations in the way preschoolers solve the same problems
Answer: d, Reference: Chapter 9, P. 346, Difficulty: D

22. The term horizontal dÈcalage refers to
    a. a common set of operations used to solve all problems
    b. variation in the abilities of several people to solve the same problem
    c. a transition state between the sensorimotor and preoperational stages
    d. variation in an individual's ability to solve different versions of the same problem
Answer: d, Reference: Chapter 9, P. 346, Difficulty: M

23. Uneven levels of performance on tasks examining cognitive abilities in preschool children has been referred to as
    a. theory of mind
    b. horizontal dÈcalage
    c. precausal reasoning
    d. transductive reasoning
Answer: b, Reference: Chapter 9, P. 346, Difficulty: E

24.   Having been shown a farm diorama, an egocentric child would
       a.   selfishly demand to play with it
       b.   be able to draw the diorama in perspective
       c.   correctly identify pictures of the diorama as seen from a viewpoint other than
             her own
       d.   indicate that from any angle the diorama looks the same as it appears from
             her own perspective
Answer: d, Reference: Chapter 9, P. 348, Difficulty: D

25.   Children aged 3 to 5 can solve the three mountain problem if
       a.   they receive extensive practice and coaching
       b.   they are permitted to walk around the diorama
       c.   the problem is presented in such a way that it makes "human sense"
       d.   the mountains each have a distinctive feature, such as a church, or a house or
             snow
Answer: c, Reference: Chapter 9, P. 348, Difficulty: E

26.   Meltzoff (1995) observed that 18-month-old infants would imitate
       a.   the intention of the actions of a machine but not a person
       b.   the intention of the actions of a person but not a machine
       c.   the intention of the actions of both a person and a machine
       d.   only completed actions, not uncompleted actions, of a person
Answer: b, Reference: Chapter 9, P. 348, Difficulty: E

27.   An experiment by Chandler and his colleagues used a puppet's footprints in a game
       of hiding treasure and asked 2- and 3-year-old children to help deceive a third party
       about the location of the treasure. They found
       a.   more than half of the 2- and 3-year-old children wiped away the footprints
       b.   3-year-old children, but not 2-year-old children, wiped away the footprints
       c.   all 2- and 3-years-old children were capable of deceiving a third party by
             wiping away footprints
       d.   both 2- and 3-year-old children were so distracted by the puppet that
             experimenters were unable to determine if the children understood the task
Answer: a, Reference: Chapter 9, P. 349, Difficulty: D

28.   Experiments that found 2- and 3-year-old children would wipe away a puppet's
       footprints to deceive an experimenter about the location of hidden treasure are
       evidence of
       a.   theory of mind
       b.   egocentric thought
       c.   horizontal decalage
       d.   transductive reasoning
Answer: a, Reference: Chapter 9, P. 349, Difficulty: M

29.   When Harris and his colleagues asked 4-year-olds to distinguish between the behavior and feelings of a character in a story they were able to make
    a.   the distinction but could not justify it
    b.   and justify the distinction most of the time
    c.   the distinction if given dolls to act out the scene
    d.   and justify the distinction approximately 50 percent of the time
Answer: a, Reference: Chapter 9, P. 349, Difficulty: M

30.   Michael Siegal's (1991) investigation into young children's understanding of appearance-reality problems suggests
    a.   3-year-old children are not easily confused with standard appearance-reality questions
    b.   young children are not capable of making appearance-reality distinctions much before six years of age
    c.   presenting a series of questions repeatedly to 3-year-old children demonstrated their ability to distinguish reality from appearance
    d.   3-year-old children are capable of making appearance-reality distinctions when presented with a single problem and not repeatedly questioned about their responses
Answer: d, Reference: Chapter 9, P. 350, Difficulty: M

31.   Recent studies by Michael Siegal and his colleagues support all of the following conclusions regarding appearance-reality distinctions in children, except
    a.   their ability to make such a distinction is fragile
    b.   many are able to make the distinction well before middle childhood
    c.   most are unable to make the distinction until well into middle childhood
    d.   their ability to make such a distinction may not appear unless special care is taken to avoid confusing them
Answer: d, Reference: Chapter 9, P. 350, Difficulty: E

32.   One of the better-known problems Piaget used to determine causal reasoning was the
    a.   three mountain problem
    b.   Snoopy and the marble box
    c.   stone that appeared to be an egg
    d.   description of how a bicycle works
Answer: d, Reference: Chapter 9, P. 350, Difficulty: E

33.   When Susan Isaacs tested Piaget's notion of precausal reasoning by asking a 5-year-old to describe how his tricycle worked, she found that he
    a.   was unable to explain
    b.   was able to explain how the tricycle worked
    c.   recognized that a demonstration would be an adequate explanation
    d.   was no better able than Piaget's subjects to give a causal explanation
Answer: b, Reference: Chapter 9, P. 351, Difficulty: M

34.   Bullock and Gelman demonstrated that when causation problems are simplified, preschoolers can
        a.   understand causation
        b.   correctly answer verbal problems
        c.   not give any causal explanation at age 5
        d.   understand causation and give explanations by age 3
Answer: a, Reference: Chapter 9, P. 351, Difficulty: D

35.   Piaget may have underestimated young children's cognitive competence in causal reasoning because
        a.   his problems deliberately tried to confuse young children
        b.   he relied on verbally presented problems and verbal justifications of reasoning
        c.   he used only interviews with his own children on which to base his conclusions
        d.   he required children to manipulate objects they were not yet capable of manipulating
Answer: b, Reference: Chapter 9, P. 351, Difficulty: M

36.   A problem when using young children as witnesses is that they
        a.   are incapable of remembering events
        b.   tend to persist adamantly with the first answer that pops into mind
        c.   may alter their testimony as a result of the questions they are asked
        d.   are unable to use dioramas or other diagrams as part of their testimony
Answer: c, Reference: Chapter 9, P. 352, Box 9.1, Difficulty: D

37.   Which of the following has been suggested as a reason children give inaccurate testimony in long criminal proceedings with many repeated questions?
        a.   they want to escape from an unpleasant situation
        b.   children have trouble remembering stressful events
        c.   children believe they have trouble remembering well
        d.   they assume there is something wrong with their first answer
Answer: d, Reference: Chapter 9, P. 352, Box 9.1, Difficulty: M

38.   According to Elizabeth Loftus adult witnesses
        a.   and preschoolers are equally good witnesses
        b.   are not susceptible to alteration by suggestion
        c.   are not susceptible to misinformation introduced by questioning
        d.   may alter their testimony as a result of the questions being asked
Answer: d, Reference: Chapter 9, P. 352, Box 9.1, Difficulty: E

39.   Neo-Piagetians believe that
      a.   development is a function of biological maturation
      b.   adults structure environments that foster development
      c.   children can best be viewed as limited-capacity systems
      d.   Piaget's theory can be modified to account for new data
Answer: d, Reference: Chapter 9, P. 354, Difficulty: M

40.   In recent studies, Flavell and his colleagues suggested that, in the process of
      adopting another's point of view, it is important to distinguish which levels of
      difficulty?
      a.   perceptual perspective taking and cognitive perspective taking
      b.   another cannot see what they see and when two people view an object at they
            same time they see it differently
      c.   another cannot see what they see and individual preferences will effect what
            two people see in the same situation
      d.   when two people view an object at the same time they see it differently and
            when two people are in different places they see objects from different angles
Answer: b, Reference: Chapter 9, P. 354, Difficulty: D

41.   The belief that development results from children's cognitive inventions is held by
      psychologists who take
      a.   a cultural-contextual view
      b.   a neo-Piagetian approach
      c.   a biological maturation view
      d.   an information-processing approach
Answer: b, Reference: Chapter 9, P. 355, Difficulty: E

42.   Jean Mandler said, "It may well be that in many areas of thinking there is no
      generalized competence, only hard-won principles wrested anew from each domain
      as it is explored." Which approach to cognitive development does this statement
      reflect?
      a.   modularity
      b.   neo-Piagetian
      c.   cultural-context
      d.   information-processing
Answer: b, Reference: Chapter 9, P. 355, Difficulty: D

43. According to neo-Piagetian theories of development
     a. assimilation and accommodation are no longer viable aspects of the theory
     b. knowledge gathered in one domain is not automatically used in a second domain
     c. there remains a single unitary competence that underlies children's problem solving ability
     d. horizontal decalage accounts for much of the new data that has been gathered in the past twenty years
Answer: b, Reference: Chapter 9, P. 355, Difficulty: D

44. According to Robbie Case, a problem for the task of defining global stages that are applicable in all domains is that
     a. biological maturation is not well enough understood
     b. synchronous change violates the principles of problem solving
     c. information-processing capacity is different for each cognitive domain
     d. precise understanding of the knowledge required by tasks in different cognitive domains must be achieved
Answer: d, Reference: Chapter 9, P. 355, Difficulty: D

45. Studies by Case have shown that when care is taken to equate the logical structure of two problems with content from different domains
     a. horizontal decalage is observed
     b. different levels of cognitive development are seen for different domains
     c. discontinuity in cognitive development is observed for the two kinds of problems
     d. same or similar levels of cognitive development are present for the two kinds of problems
Answer: d, Reference: Chapter 9, P. 355, Difficulty: M

46. The recent line of neo-Piagetian work maintaining that if researchers can gain a sufficient precise understanding of the knowledge required by each cognitive domain, they may eventually achieve Piaget's goal of defining global stages that apply to all domains is represented in the work of
     a. Case
     b. Klahr
     c. Siegler
     d. Flavell
Answer: a, Reference: Chapter 9, P. 355, Difficulty: D

47. Which framework for understanding cognitive development likens the child's thinking to that of a computer?
    a. neo-Piagetians
    b. modularity theorists
    c. cultural-context theorists
    d. information-processing theorists
Answer: d, Reference: Chapter 9, P. 356, Difficulty: E

48. David Klahr is a leading proponent of which approach?
    a. modularity
    b. neo-Piagetian
    c. cultural-context
    d. information-processing
Answer: d, Reference: Chapter 9, P. 356, Difficulty: M

49. David Klahr's objection to the concepts of assimilation and accommodation is that they are
    a. too vague
    b. too domain specific
    c. too narrowly defined to be useful
    d. appropriate for the sensorimotor stage, but not for other stages
Answer: a, Reference: Chapter 9, P. 356, Difficulty: E

50. Which of the following statements is most accurate regarding information processing psychologists?
    a. they all stand in opposition to neo-Piagetian views
    b. some believe in discontinuous stage-like changes in a child's overall functioning
    c. they represent a united approach to the continuity/discontinuity perspective of development
    d. they uniformly believe that development is a continuous process in which limitations on memory capacity are overcome
Answer: b, Reference: Chapter 9, P. 356, Difficulty: M

51. Which of the following is not a characteristic of short-term memory?
    a. information is stored for several days
    b. information is stored for several seconds
    c. it is continually monitored by control processes
    d. new information is combined with knowledge from long term memory
Answer: a, Reference: Chapter 9, P. 357, Difficulty: E

52. According to the information-processing view of development, preschool children have
     a.   limited information processing capacity
     b.   the ability to direct their attention at will
     c.   more than enough memory to solve problems
     d.   more than enough attention to solve problems
Answer: a, Reference: Chapter 9, P. 357, Difficulty: E

53. Information processing psychologists are united by a common view of capacity limitations, citing the causes of young children's difficulties to include all of the following except
     a.   limited memory
     b.   insufficient or uneven attention
     c.   no capacity for precausal reasoning
     d.   limited strategies for acquiring and using information
Answer: c, Reference: Chapter 9, P. 357, Difficulty: D

54. Which group of theorists proposes that young children's limitations in attention, memory and use of strategies are the reason for their cognitive
     a.   modularity
     b.   neo-Piagetian
     c.   cultural-context
     d.   information-processing
Answer: d, Reference: Chapter 9, P. 357, Difficulty: E

55. When not distracted, preschoolers are likely to explore a problem
     a.   systematically
     b.   unsystematically
     c.   with unlimited attention
     d.   in the same way as older infants
Answer: b, Reference: Chapter 9, P. 357, Difficulty: M

56. Vurpillot found that when they scanned pictures of houses preschoolers
     a.   were able to attend to relevant details
     b.   and 10-year-olds scanned differently
     c.   and 10-year-olds scanned in similar ways on all trials
     d.   and 10-year-olds scanned in similar ways only when the houses were alike
Answer: b, Reference: Chapter 9, P. 358, Difficulty: D

57. Vurpillot's study of 3 - to 10-year-old children's scanning patterns shows that
     a.   older children scan in a haphazard way
     b.   preschoolers have limited ability to select relevant details
     c.   preschoolers scan haphazardly only 50 percent of the time
     d.   information about processing capacity cannot be obtained from scan patterns
Answer: b, Reference: Chapter 9, P. 358, Difficulty: M

58.   Work by Chi and Klahr (1975) found the number of objects flashed simultaneously on a screen that 5-year-old children could perceive was
    a.   three
    b.   five
    c.   seven
    d.   the same as adults
Answer: a, Reference: Chapter 9, P. 358, Difficulty: M

59.   When Chi and Klahr showed 5-year-olds and adults objects flashed on a screen, they found that
    a.   both 5-year-olds and adults could detect 6
    b.   adults were only slightly better than 5-year-olds
    c.   5-year-olds could detect only 3 but adults could detect 6
    d.   neither adults nor preschoolers could detect more than 3
Answer: c, Reference: Chapter 9, P. 358, Difficulty: E

60.   Age-related increases in the ability to hold information in mind
    a.   do not seem to boost adult problem-solving skills
    b.   cease after the transition from infancy to early childhood
    c.   cannot account for increases in problem solving skill after the age of 5
    d.   enable adults to solve problems without losing track of what they are doing
Answer: d, Reference: Chapter 9, P. 358, Difficulty: M

61.   Information processing theorists have demonstrated
    a.   qualitatively different ways of thinking at different ages
    b.   changes in brain maturation related to different kinds of thought
    c.   age related changes from a reliance on short term memory to a reliance on long term memory
    d.   age-related increases in the ability to hold several items of information in the mind at one time
Answer: d, Reference: Chapter 9, P. 358, Difficulty: E

62.   Preschoolers do well on Piagetian tasks when
    a.   they are interested in the task
    b.   they are allowed to choose the domain of the task
    c.   the task is relatively novel and unconnected to prior events
    d.   information is presented quickly so they don't become bored
Answer: a, Reference: Chapter 9, P. 358, Difficulty: M

63.   By the beginning of the preschool period the brain will have attained what percentage of its adult weight?
        a.   25
        b.   50
        c.   75
        d.   90
Answer: b, Reference: Chapter 9, P. 359, Difficulty: M

64.   By the age of 6 years the brain will have attained what percentage of its adult weight?
        a.   50
        b.   75
        c.   90
        d.   100
Answer: c, Reference: Chapter 9, P. 359, Difficulty: M

65.   During the preschool period, more effective connections made between the temporal, occipital, and parietal areas of the brain allow for
        a.   fine motor control
        b.   short-term memory
        c.   increased auditory ability
        d.   temporal, visual, and spatial information
Answer: d, Reference: Chapter 9, P. 359, Difficulty: E

66.   Increases in short term memory are related to changes in which brain area(s) in the preschool years?
        a.   cerebellum
        b.   hippocampus
        c.   connections of cerebellum to cortex
        d.   connections between temporal, parietal, and occipital lobes
Answer: b, Reference: Chapter 9, P. 359, Difficulty: M

67.   Modularity theorists focus on the role of which of the following in cognitive development?
        a.   context
        b.   social factors
        c.   cultural factors
        d.   biological factors
Answer: d, Reference: Chapter 9, P. 360, Difficulty: M

68.   Highly specific mental faculties associated with particular domains of environmental input are referred to as
    a.   scripts
    b.   operations
    c.   theory of mind
    d.   mental modules
Answer: d, Reference: Chapter 9, P. 360, Difficulty: M

69.   All of the following are true of mental modules except
    a.   operations are domain specific
    b.   separate modules are only loosely connected
    c.   principles of operation are innately specified
    d.   different domains have strong direct connections to one another
Answer: d, Reference: Chapter 9, P. 360, Difficulty: D

70.   Research by modularity theorists on 6-month-olds sensitivity to causality sought to establish perception of causality as
    a.   a learned event
    b.   an innate primitive capacity
    c.   equivalent in infants and adults
    d.   too complex an event for infants
Answer: b, Reference: Chapter 9, P. 361, Difficulty: M

71.   When Alan Leslie showed 6-month-old infants an illusion in which one dot appeared to bump into another, he found that
    a.   the babies tracked only the first dot
    b.   the babies could not attend to both dots simultaneously
    c.   they looked longer at a non-causal event than a novel causal event after exposure to an initial causal event
    d.   there neither habituated to a repeatedly presented causal event nor dishabituated to a novel causal event or a non-causal event
Answer: c, Reference: Chapter 9, P. 361, Difficulty: M

72.   Which of the following is not a characteristic of autism?
    a.   inability to walk and run
    b.   inability to relate to others
    c.   lack of symbolic pretend play
    d.   rare use of language to communicate
Answer: a, Reference: Chapter 9, P. 361, Difficulty: M

73.   Baron-Cohon and his colleagues found that when children were asked to arrange
       pictures into a story, autistic children
       a.   could not sequences any of the pictures correctly
       b.   did not differ from normal or mentally retarded children
       c.   could sequence mechanical and behavioral stories, but not mentalistic ones
       d.   could sequence mechanical stories, but not behavioral or mentalistic stories
Answer: c, Reference: Chapter 9, P. 361, Difficulty: M

74.   Evidence that autistic children lack a theory of mind come from difficulties they
       experience
       a.   on the false belief task
       b.   sequencing pictures into stories demonstrating mechanical events
       c.   habituating to a causality problem and dishabituating to a non-causal
             problem
       d.   sequencing pictures into stories demonstrating behavioral events among
             people
Answer: a, Reference: Chapter 9, P. 362, Difficulty: M

75.   Samet has explained the behavior of autistic children as a failure to
       a.   develop a sense of self
       b.   develop normal language
       c.   develop a theory of mind
       d.   understand appropriate causal relations
Answer: a, Reference: Chapter 9, P. 363, Difficulty: D

76.   The theory of mental modules has
       a.   explained horizontal decalage
       b.   well delineated the boundaries between modules
       c.   difficulty identifying the full set of mental modules
       d.   provided an adequate account of unevenness in development
Answer: c, Reference: Chapter 9, P. 363, Difficulty: M

77.   Which of the following has not been used an example of a mental module?
       a.   face recognition
       b.   music perception
       c.   perception of causality
       d.   taking another's point of view
Answer: d, Reference: Chapter 9, P. 363, Difficulty: D

78. Cultural-context theories and Piaget's theory both
   a. emphasize the constructivist aspect of development
   b. deny any biological role in the development of mind
   c. emphasize the importance of the social environment on development
   d. reject information-processing approaches to obtaining information about children's modes of thinking

Answer: a, Reference: Chapter 9, P. 363, Difficulty: M

79. Which of the following is an example of "social co-construction"?
   a. a mother encouraging her toddler to walk
   b. a two year old playing with a four year old
   c. a three year old building houses out of blocks
   d. a toddler eating cereal his mother has poured for him

Answer: a, Reference: Chapter 9, P. 363, Difficulty: E

80. Context can be thought of as
   a. the opposite of a schema
   b. the support an adult can give to a child
   c. cultural meaning systems used to interpret experience
   d. the elements of a schema that form the child's own actions

Answer: c, Reference: Chapter 9, P. 363, Difficulty: M

81. According to context theory, organizing the relationships among different contexts is primarily a function of
   a. culture
   b. practice
   c. experience
   d. self-regulation

Answer: a, Reference: Chapter 9, P. 363, Difficulty: M

82. The term schema refers to
   a. an organized pattern of knowledge
   b. features of the environment that are universal
   c. a way of isolating behavior from environment
   d. the property of an environment that brings together disparate elements of behavior

Answer: a, Reference: Chapter 9, P. 364, Difficulty: M

83. According to Katherine Nelson, children construct scripts from
   a. their actions on objects
   b. participation in routine events
   c. participation in unorganized events
   d. their interactions with different people

Answer: b, Reference: Chapter 9, P. 364, Difficulty: E

84. Scripts are
    a. schemas for events
    b. the same as contexts
    c. the same as schemas
    d. never used to guide action
Answer: a, Reference: Chapter 9, P. 364, Difficulty: M

85. Script knowledge
    a. is not tied to particular events
    b. is organized into a general structure
    c. does not apparently emerge until about age 6
    d. provides the child with explicit prohibitions on behavior
Answer: b, Reference: Chapter 9, P. 365, Difficulty: E

86. All except which of the following are functions of scripts?
    a. a guide to action
    b. a guide to biological maturation
    c. allowing people to coordinate effectively
    d. provision for a framework within which abstract concepts can be acquired
Answer: b, Reference: Chapter 9, P. 365, Difficulty: M

87. Children's play between the ages of 1 and 2 years
    a. is primarily social
    b. is both solitary and imaginative
    c. can be described as socio-dramatic
    d. requires negotiation among the participants
Answer: b, Reference: Chapter 9, P. 368, Box 9.2, Difficulty: M

88. Socio-dramatic play
    a. involves little direct imitation
    b. depends strongly on direct imitation
    c. rarely uses material from familiar scenes
    d. is not considered especially important by Piaget
Answer: a, Reference: Chapter 9, P. 368, Box 9.2, Difficulty: M

89. For Piaget, egocentrism is to logical thought as
    a. egocentrism is to rule-bound play
    b. pretend play is to rule-bound play
    c. egocentrism is to concrete operations
    d. pretend play is to concrete operations
Answer: b, Reference: Chapter 9, P. 368, Box 9.2, Difficulty: M

90.   For Piaget, pretend play is an example of
        a.   imitation
        b.   adaptation
        c.   assimilation
        d.   accommodation
Answer: c, Reference: Chapter 9, P. 368, Box 9.2, Difficulty: M

91.   Jerome Singer and Dorothy Singer (1990) believe that once middle childhood is
        reached, pretend play
        a.   increases
        b.   disappears
        c.   goes underground
        d.   becomes more complex and detailed
Answer: c, Reference: Chapter 9, P. 368, Box 9.2, Difficulty: D

92.   According to Vygotsky, pretend play provides children with
        a.   a means of expressing egocentric behavior
        b.   a support system analogous to that provided by adults
        c.   an opportunity to act outside the zone of proximal development
        d.   an opportunity to exactly reproduce the behavior of an adult model
Answer: b, Reference: Chapter 9, P. 368, Box 9.2, Difficulty: D

93.   Studies by Dias and Harris found that pretending
        a.   increased young children's causal reasoning
        b.   increased young children's logical reasoning
        c.   decreased young children's logical reasoning
        d.   had no effect on young children's logical reasoning
Answer: b, Reference: Chapter 9, P. 368, Box 9.2, Difficulty: D

94.   Cross-cultural research on pretend play has found that in non industrialized cultures
        where schooling is absent, the socio-dramatic play of children
        a.   is absent
        b.   does not differ from industrialized cultures
        c.   involves more imaginative transformations
        d.   more closely resembles models provided by actual adult practices
Answer: d, Reference: Chapter 9, P. 368, Box 9.2, Difficulty: D

95.   Which approach suggests children must acquire a large repertoire of scripts and the
        knowledge needed to use them?
        a.   modularity
        b.   neo-Piagetian
        c.   cultural-context
        d.   information-processing
Answer: c, Reference: Chapter 9, P. 366, Difficulty: E

96.   The fact that children must acquire a large repertoire of scripts needed for appropriate contexts provides a natural explanation of
       a.   mental modules
       b.   growth of the brain
       c.   transductive reasoning
       d.   unevenness of development in early childhood
Answer: d, Reference: Chapter 9, P. 366, Difficulty: M

97.   Which approach attempts to partially explain unevenness in development by citing how adults regulate the difficulty of a child's role?
       a.   modularity
       b.   neo-Piagetian
       c.   cultural-context
       d.   information processing
Answer: c, Reference: Chapter 9, P. 366, Difficulty: D

98.   Barbara Rogoff, a prominent cultural context theorist calls the process by which adults shape children's development
       a.   context cooperation
       b.   guided participation
       c.   modular cooperation
       d.   scripted collaboration
Answer: b, Reference: Chapter 9, P. 367, Difficulty: M

99.   Modularity theorists see change as coming from
       a.   factors inside the child
       b.   factors outside the child
       c.   the interactions of culture and biology
       d.   the interactions of schemas and the environment
Answer: a, Reference: Chapter 9, P. 370, Difficulty: M

100.   Children's earliest scribbles often
       a.   represent their unformed thoughts
       b.   reflect a desire to produce a product
       c.   are made for the sake of the movements themselves
       d.   are carefully planned although somewhat uncontrolled
Answer: c, Reference: Chapter 9, P. 371, Difficulty: E

101.   Children seem to become aware that their drawings can represent things at about the age of
       a.   1 year
       b.   2 years
       c.   3 years
       d.   4 years
Answer: c, Reference: Chapter 9, P. 371, Difficulty: M

102.   Learning to draw in three dimensions
    a.   occurs spontaneously in all cultures
    b.   is a universal developmental phenomenon
    c.   involves the sequential addition of single dimensions
    d.   cannot be explained by information-processing theory
Answer: c, Reference: Chapter 9, P. 373, Difficulty: D

103.   Children who are deprived of the opportunity to draw
    a.   never recover from the deprivation
    b.   contradict the modularity view of drawing ability
    c.   provide evidence for the Piagetian view of drawing ability
    d.   may skip the initial stages of drawing if later given an opportunity to draw
Answer: d, Reference: Chapter 9, P. 374, Difficulty: E

104.   According to a cultural-context view, children learn to draw
    a.   primarily by watching others
    b.   according to a universal sequence of stages
    c.   by building up their skills one dimension at a time
    d.   in part by learning from scripted conversations with adults
Answer: d, Reference: Chapter 9, P. 374, Difficulty: D

105.   Which theoretical position would deny that constructive interactions play a prominent role in promoting cognitive development?
    a.   modularity
    b.   neo-Piagetian
    c.   cultural-context
    d.   information-processing
Answer: a, Reference: Chapter 9, P. 377, Difficulty: M

106.   According to the text, competing approaches to the development of cognitive processes are most usefully viewed as
    a.   complementary
    b.   mutually exclusive
    c.   a single comprehensive explanatory framework
    d.   major improvements over the inadequate research techniques of Piaget
Answer: a, Reference: Chapter 9, P. 377, Difficulty: M

Essay Questions

1.   What is Piaget's explanation of magical thinking?

2.   Describe Piaget's two classic experiments that he used to illustrate the differences between preoperational and concrete operational thought.

3. Describe the most salient characteristics of preschool thought processes.

4. What is transductive reasoning? Compare and contrast pre-causal and causal reasoning. Give an example of each.

5. Describe evidence of non-egocentric thought among 2- and 3-year-old children.

6. How does understanding the appearance/reality distinction help to explain cognitive development in the preschool period? Explain.

7. List and describe the three aspects of preschoolers' thought according to Piaget. Cite evidence from other psychologists' research supporting or modifying Piaget's views.

8. Explain the importance of limited capacity and short-term memory to information processing theories.

9. Cite evidence supporting an information-processing explanation of preschoolers' cognitive development.

10. Define mental modules, citing evidence supporting a modular view of development. What is the weakness of the modular view? What are the mechanisms of change in this view?

11. In one view, the event of taking a bath remains constant at all ages. In another view, the context in which this event occurs changes with development. Describe these two points of view and the implications of each developmental process.

12. Describe and discuss the functions of scripts in the thinking processes of preschool age children. Give two examples.

13. Describe several ways in which the unevenness of child development is influenced by culture. Explain.

14. Explain how Piaget's research techniques may have underestimated the cognitive competence of young children's causal reasoning.

15. Describe the roles of horizontal dÈcalage in Piagetian theory and in cultural-context theory. How are they similar? How do they differ?

16. Describe how contexts and schemas might work together to increase the complexity of the environment and the behavior of a child. Explain.

17. Compare and contrast Piaget's views of the importance of pretend play to that of Vygotsky.

18.   Discuss the role of biological maturation in the modularity theory, and cultural-context theory, in the cognitive development of a preschooler. How are they similar? How do they differ?

19.   Describe the stage-like sequence that occurs as children learn to draw.

20.   Briefly describe some of the ways neo-Piagetians differ from Piaget in their conceptualization of childhood cognitive development.

21.   How do cultural-context theorists differ from Piaget in their approach to cognitive development?

22.   How have cultural-context approaches included Piaget's concept of "schemas" in their explanation of development?

23.   What are scripts? Who uses them? Give examples.

24.   Describe the ways in which cultural-context influences the unevenness in children's development.

25.   What is "guided participation"? For which approach to development is it particularly important? Explain.

26.   What is socio-dramatic play? Discuss when it appears and how it differs from play in infancy.

Social Development in Early Childhood

Multiple-Choice Questions

1. According to Freud, individuals strive to achieve
   a. egoistic affiliation
   b. affiliation and cognitive integration
   c. both individualism and integration into the community
   d. either individualism or integration into the community

   Answer: c, Reference: Chapter 10, P. 382, Difficulty: M

2. Personality formation refers to
   a. a sense of self-awareness
   b. the process of becoming altruistic
   c. the process of acquiring social values and standards
   d. the development of an awareness of the thoughts and feelings of others

   Answer: a, Reference: Chapter 10, P. 382, Difficulty: D

3. Socialization begins at
   a. birth
   b. the end of infancy
   c. the beginning of childhood
   d. the beginning of adolescence

   Answer: a, Reference: Chapter 10, P. 382, Difficulty: E

4.   Peoples expectations about a child's rights, duties, obligations, and socially acceptable behaviors are embodied in the concept of
      a.   identity
      b.   social role
      c.   personality
      d.   temperamental traits
Answer: b, Reference: Chapter 10, P. 382, Difficulty: E

5.   Personality is
      a.   the same thing as a social role
      b.   a pattern of responsivity and associated emotional states
      c.   a unique pattern of temperament, emotions, and abilities
      d.   the sum total of the standards, values, and knowledge of the society
Answer: c, Reference: Chapter 10, P. 382, Difficulty: M

6.   A person's view of himself or herself is reflected in the concept of
      a.   social role
      b.   personality
      c.   self-concept
      d.   temperament
Answer: c, Reference: Chapter 10, P. 382, Difficulty: M

7.   The earliest visible manifestations of personality such as patterns of responsivity are referred to as
      a.   activity traits
      b.   concept traits
      c.   the self-concept
      d.   temperamental traits
Answer: d, Reference: Chapter 10, P. 383, Difficulty: M

8.   Personality and socialization are
      a.   opposites
      b.   synonymous
      c.   interdependent concepts
      d.   two separate stages of personality development
Answer: c, Reference: Chapter 10, P. 383, Difficulty: E

9.   Identification is a process that
      a.   is independent of sex roles
      b.   is independent of cognition
      c.   involves making the characteristics of another person one's one
      d.   involves consciously recognizing the personality characteristics of another person
Answer: c, Reference: Chapter 10, P. 383, Difficulty: M

10.   Identification is a process that
       a.   is uniquely family related
       b.   is uniquely gender related
       c.   involves the same sex parent only
       d.   can involve any significant social agent
Answer: d, Reference: Chapter 10, P. 383, Difficulty: M

11.   Which of the following mechanisms has not been proposed to explain the
       development of identification?
       a.   imitation
       b.   cognition
       c.   differentiation
       d.   inhibition of choice
Answer: d, Reference: Chapter 10, Pp. 383, Difficulty: D

12.   The overwhelming majority of research on identification in early childhood focuses
       on
       a.   religion
       b.   ethnicity
       c.   sex roles
       d.   family membership
Answer: c, Reference: Chapter 10, P. 384, Difficulty: D

13.   During the preschool years the dominant feelings about parents are
       a.   not liking a parent
       b.   hostility toward both parents
       c.   wanting to be like one's parents
       d.   wanting to be near one's parents
Answer: c, Reference: Chapter 10, P. 385, Difficulty: E

14.   According to Freud, "primary identification" refers to when infants
       a.   can identify themselves
       b.   recognize their mothers
       c.   can identify their primary love objects
       d.   recognize that someone else is like themselves
Answer: d, Reference: Chapter 10, P. 385, Difficulty: M

15.   The Meltzoff and Moore demonstration of neonatal imitation is an example of
       _____ according to Freudian theory.
       a.   primary identification
       b.   secondary identification
       c.   identification through affiliation
       d.   identification through differentiation
Answer: a, Reference: Chapter 10, P. 385, Difficulty: D

16.   According to Freud, secondary identification
       a.   occurs during latency
       b.   always involves a parent
       c.   begins during the first year of life
       d.   involves molding one's ego after a model
Answer: d, Reference: Chapter 10, P. 385, Difficulty: D

17.   Wanting to be a physician like dad would be an example of _____ according to
       Freudian theory.
       a.   primary identification
       b.   secondary identification
       c.   identification through affiliation
       d.   identification through differentiation
Answer: b, Reference: Chapter 10, P. 385, Difficulty: D

18.   Freud constructed a general theory of development based on
       a.   experiments
       b.   clinical data
       c.   longitudinal studies
       d.   interviews with children
Answer: b, Reference: Chapter 10, P. 386, Box 10.1, Difficulty: E

19.   According to Freud all biological drives
       a.   involve the ego
       b.   are ultimately unresolved
       c.   lead to resolution of the oedipal complex
       d.   aid in survival and propagation of the species
Answer: d, Reference: Chapter 10, P. 386, Box 10.1, Difficulty: E

20.   Freud believed that personality was a function of
       a.   instincts
       b.   imitation and identification
       c.   the situation in which the adult lived
       d.   conflict resolution in early stages of development
Answer: d, Reference: Chapter 10, P. 386, Box 10.1, Difficulty: M

21.   Which of the following represents the sequence of stages proposed by Freud?
       a.   oral, anal, latency, genital, phallic
       b.   anal, oral, phallic, genital, latency
       c.   oral, anal, phallic, latency, genital
       d.   oral, anal, phallic, genital, latency
Answer: c, Reference: Chapter 10, P. 387, Box 10.1, Difficulty: E

22. Freud believed that during the fourth year of life when children begin to focus their pleasure-seeking on the genital area, they are in the _____ stage.
    a. anal
    b. phallic
    c. genital
    d. latency
Answer: b, Reference: Chapter 10, P. 386, Box 10.1, Difficulty: M

23. According to Freud, conflict resolution in which stage of development produces the most basic form of sexual identification?
    a. anal
    b. phallic
    c. genital
    d. latency
Answer: b, Reference: Chapter 10, P. 387, Box 10.1, Difficulty: M

24. According to Freud, sexual desires are suppressed and sexual energy is channeled into the acquisition of technical skills during which stage?
    a. anal
    b. phallic
    c. genital
    d. latency
Answer: d, Reference: Chapter 10, P. 387, Box 10.1, Difficulty: M

25. According to the Freudian theory of development, the genital stage is marked by
    a. the repression of sexual urges
    b. control of the personality by the id
    c. sexual urges directed toward parents
    d. the physiological changes of puberty
Answer: d, Reference: Chapter 10, P. 387, Box 10.1, Difficulty: E

26. Sammy has just shot up 10 inches and become interested in girls. According to Freud, he is probably in the _____ stage.
    a. anal
    b. phallic
    c. genital
    d. latency
Answer: c, Reference: Chapter 10, P. 387, Box 10.1, Difficulty: D

27. According to Freud, which mental structure(s) strive(s) for self-preservation through adaptation, perception, and problem solving?
    a. id
    b. ego
    c. super-ego
    d. the id, ego, and the superego
Answer: b, Reference: Chapter 10, P. 387, Box 10.1, Difficulty: M

28. Which of the Freudian structures of personality battle for control of the person's mind and body?
    a. the id and the ego
    b. the id and the superego
    c. the id, ego and superego
    d. the ego and the superego
Answer: b, Reference: Chapter 10, P. 387, Box 10.1, Difficulty: M

29. According to Robert Emde, Freud contributed the following important emphasis to developmental psychology.
    a. the focus on conscious aspects of personality
    b. an insistence on the simplicity of individual behavior
    c. the importance of early experience in personality formation
    d. the need to study groups of various personality types before generalizations can be made
Answer: c, Reference: Chapter 10, P. 387, Box 10.1, Difficulty: M

30. The Oedipus complex occurs during the _____ stage.
    a. oral
    b. anal
    c. phallic
    d. genital
Answer: c, Reference: Chapter 10, P. 388, Difficulty: E

31. According to Freud, during the latency stage, a young boy
    a. suppresses his feelings toward his mother
    b. continues to experience a strong sense of guilt
    c. uses only the defense mechanism of repression
    d. rejects the defense mechanism of identification
Answer: a, Reference: Chapter 10, P. 388, Difficulty: M

32. According to Freud, when girls discover they do not have a penis, they
    a. blame their fathers
    b. blame their mothers
    c. withdraw their love from both parents
    d. refuse to compete with their mothers for their fathers' affection
Answer: b, Reference: Chapter 10, P. 388, Difficulty: E

33.   According to Freud, when compared with men, women
   a.   develop a weaker moral sense
   b.   possessed an equivalent sense of justice
   c.   were more willing to submit to the exigencies of life
   d.   were less often influenced in their judgments by feelings of hostility
Answer: a, Reference: Chapter 10, P. 388, Difficulty: M

34.   Nancy Chodorow's view of early social interaction between the two sexes differed
        from Freud in that
   a.   males achieve identity through intimacy
   b.   males achieve identity through attachment
   c.   females achieve identity through separation
   d.   females achieve identity through attachment
Answer: d, Reference: Chapter 10, P. 389, Difficulty: D

35.   Girls are to affiliation as boys are to
   a.   hostility
   b.   inhibition
   c.   socialization
   d.   differentiation
Answer: d, Reference: Chapter 10, P. 389, Difficulty: D

36.   According to Nancy Chodorow males achieve identity through _____ while
        female achieve it through _____.
   a.   intimacy; separation
   b.   separation; attachment
   c.   attachment; separation
   d.   differentiation; affiliation
Answer: b, Reference: Chapter 10, P. 389, Difficulty: D

37.   Current research on sex-role development suggests that
   a.   defense mechanisms do not really exist
   b.   all human embryos initially follow a male path of development
   c.   adults, not children, are the primary carriers of sexual fantasies
   d.   the aspects of identity formation that Freud said were a consequence of
          resolution of the Oedipus complex do not occur until middle childhood
Answer: c, Reference: Chapter 10, P. 389, Difficulty: M

38.   Chichette and Carlson's 1989 studies indicate that disturbances in identity formation
       result not from children's inability to resolve infantile sexual desires, but from
       a.   single parents assuming roles of both father and mother
       b.   mixed messages children are subject to while viewing television
       c.   sexually abusive or seductive parents causing psychological traumas
       d.   lack of parental guidance and attention, due to the necessity for both parents
             to work during the elementary school years
Answer: c, Reference: Chapter 10, P. 389, Difficulty: D

39.   According to social-learning theorists, sex-role identification is
       a.   an imitative process
       b.   driven by inner conflict
       c.   independent of attention
       d.   independent of the environment
Answer: a, Reference: Chapter 10, P. 389, Difficulty: E

40.   All of the following are factors in the ability to learn by imitation except
       a.   memory
       b.   affiliation
       c.   availability
       d.   motor reproduction
Answer: b, Reference: Chapter 10, P. 390, Difficulty: M

41.   Bandura believes that
       a.   behavior cannot be modeled from a book or television
       b.   during early childhood external payoff or motivation is unnecessary
       c.   children are automatically able to determine the salient features of a situation
       d.   children's observations are especially effective when they have a name for
             modeled events
Answer: d, Reference: Chapter 10, P. 390, Difficulty: D

42.   Which of the following did Beverly Fagot observed in the home of the children she
       observed?
       a.   imitation of sex-appropriate behavior
       b.   punishment of sex-appropriate behavior
       c.   reinforcement of sex-appropriate behavior
       d.   identification with the sex-appropriate behavior of the parents
Answer: c, Reference: Chapter 10, P. 390, Difficulty: M

43.   Which of the following is a problem for social-learning theory?
       a.   the concept of a reward is difficult to define
       b.   parents provide models for children to imitate
       c.   children often need to see a model more than once
       d.   behavior cannot be learned from a book or television
Answer: a, Reference: Chapter 10, P. 390, Difficulty: M

44. Kohlberg's theory of social development is best described as
    a. Freudian
    b. cognitive
    c. biological
    d. social learning
Answer: b, Reference: Chapter 10, P. 391, Difficulty: E

45. For which theorist is the crucial factor in sex-role identification the child's developing ability to categorize themselves as "boys" or "girls"
    a. Bem
    b. Piaget
    c. Bandura
    d. Kohlberg
Answer: d, Reference: Chapter 10, P. 391, Difficulty: D

46. Kohlberg believes that sex role concepts derive from
    a. a gender schema
    b. instinctual wishes
    c. passive social training
    d. children's active structuring of their experience
Answer: d, Reference: Chapter 10, P. 391, Difficulty: M

47. According to Kohlberg, the most important factor in children's sex-role identification is
    a. motivation
    b. the gender schema
    c. the ability to reproduce motor actions
    d. the ability to categorize themselves as boys and girls
Answer: d, Reference: Chapter 10, P. 391, Difficulty: M

48. The little boy that called Jeremy (the boy who wore a barrette) a girl, lacked _____ in Kohlberg's theory.
    a. sex-role stability
    b. a gender schema
    c. sex-role constancy
    d. basic sex-role identity
Answer: c, Reference: Chapter 10, P. 391, Difficulty: D

49. A piece of evidence that is troublesome for Kohlberg's theory is
    a. the existence of sex-role constancy
    b. the strength of sex-role stereotypes
    c. play with sex-appropriate toys at too young an age
    d. the tendency of boys to imitate sex-inappropriate behavior
Answer: c, Reference: Chapter 10, P. 391, Difficulty: D

50.   A mental model containing information about males and females is a
        a.   gender role
        b.   gender schema
        c.   gender identity
        d.   motor reproduction process
Answer: b, Reference: Chapter 10, P. 391, Difficulty: M

51.   Gender schema theory is an explanation of how children's sexual identity develops
        that includes elements of
        a.   psychoanalysis and social-learning theory
        b.   psychoanalysis and cognitive-developmental theory
        c.   classical and operant conditioning and humanistic theory
        d.   social-learning theory and cognitive-developmental theory
Answer: d, Reference: Chapter 10, P. 391, Difficulty: M

52.   According to Levy and Fivush, the development of gender schemas includes the
        formation of
        a.   scripts
        b.   conditioned responses
        c.   identity, stability, and constancy
        d.   a portion of the ego devoted to gender-related behaviors
Answer: a, Reference: Chapter 10, P. 392, Difficulty: M

53.   Gender schema theory deviates from Kohlberg's theory of gender development in
        the importance of
        a.   sex-role stability
        b.   sex-role constancy
        c.   gender differences
        d.   basic sex-role identity
Answer: b, Reference: Chapter 10, P. 392, Difficulty: M

54.   Children aged 2.5 years are more likely to be compatible with playmates who
        a.   are of the same sex
        b.   are of the opposite sex
        c.   are the same age independent of sex
        d.   have a well developed sense of identity
Answer: a, Reference: Chapter 10, P. 393, Difficulty: M

55.   According to Maccoby and Jacklin's work, boys and girls are developing distinct
        styles of play by the age of
        a.   2
        b.   3
        c.   4
        d.   5
Answer: a, Reference: Chapter 10, P. 393, Difficulty: E

56.   According to Maccoby and Jacklin's work, sex-typed toy preferences begin to emerge
       between the ages of
       a.   1 and 3
       b.   2 and 4
       c.   3 and 5
       d.   4 and 6
Answer: a, Reference: Chapter 10, P. 393, Difficulty: M

57.   Dunn has observed verbal expressions of gender awareness as early as the age of
       a.   3
       b.   4
       c.   5
       d.   6
Answer: a, Reference: Chapter 10, P. 394, Difficulty: E

58.   Fagot and her colleagues observed children correctly identifying the gender of
pictures of men and women as early as the age of
       a.   2
       b.   3
       c.   4
       d.   5
Answer: b, Reference: Chapter 10, P. 394, Difficulty: E

59.   By age 3 or 4 years of age children
       a.   are able to separate pictures of boys and girls
       b.   are still unable to say whether they are boys or girls
       c.   are always able to say whether they will be a mommy or daddy
       d.   have a stable conceptual understanding of male and female roles
Answer: a, Reference: Chapter 10, P. 394, Difficulty: M

60.   Mary Bradbard observed that labeling neutral toys as "things for boys" or "things for
       girls" affected childrens'
       a.   activity
       b.   play structure
       c.   play with each other
       d.   exploration of the toys
Answer: d, Reference: Chapter 10, P. 395, Difficulty: D

61.   According to Vivian Paley's observations in her preschool classroom, children seek to adhere to the cultural definition of what it means to be a boy or a girl by the age of
       a.   2
       b.   3
       c.   4
       d.   5
Answer: d, Reference: Chapter 10, P. 395, Difficulty: M

62.   Psychoanalytic theorists are likely to attribute preference for sex-typed toys to
       a.   sibling models
       b.   parental identification
       c.   biological predisposition
       d.   probabilities based on availability
Answer: c, Reference: Chapter 10, P. 396, Difficulty: D

63.   Social learning theorist are likely to attribute preference for sex-typed toys to
       a.   a gender schema
       b.   sex-role constancy
       c.   biological predisposition
       d.   imitation and reinforcement
Answer: d, Reference: Chapter 10, P. 397, Difficulty: M

64.   Recent studies compared families that sought to promote sex egalitarianism with families who adhered to existing cultural norms. What did they find with regard to sex-typed preferences for toys and friends among their children?
       a.   no differences
       b.   few differences
       c.   dramatic differences
       d.   differences only in the preference of females
Answer: b, Reference: Chapter 10, P. 397, Difficulty: M

65.   Sex-typed behavior attributes
       a.   vary across cultures
       b.   are all cross-cultural universals
       c.   do not include occupations and modes of attire
       d.   must be acquired before children can learn other roles
Answer: a, Reference: Chapter 10, P. 397, Difficulty: E

66. In a famous study of racial and ethnic identity which asked 3-year-old African-American children which of two dolls they would like to play with found these children seemed to prefer
     a.   the black doll
     b.   the white doll
     c.   any doll but the white doll
     d.   whichever doll was the same sex an the child
Answer: b, Reference: Chapter 10, P. 398, Difficulty: E

67. Later interpretation of early studies of the development of racial and ethnic identity casts doubt on which of the following?
     a.   minority group children acquire a generalized negative ethnic self-conception
     b.   African-American children define themselves in terms of their own racial group
     c.   minority children's choice of white dolls are an expression of their desire for the power and wealth of white people
     d.   children show a greater preference for dolls representing their own group when tested in their native language
Answer: a, Reference: Chapter 10, P. 398, Difficulty: D

68. Later studies which examined young children's preferences for dolls of various ethnic identities have found
     a.   minority children acquire a negative ethnic self-concept
     b.   African-American children define themselves in terms of the majority group
     c.   children show a greater preference for dolls representing their own group when tested in their native language
     d.   that despite their choice of dolls, children clearly identify with and value their own ethnic group and develop a strong sense of self-worth
Answer c, Reference: Chapter 10, P. 398, Difficulty: M

69. Which of the following has not been suggested as a reason that minority children choose white dolls in studies on ethnic identity?
     a.   minority children feel pressure from white interviewers
     b.   minority children desire the status and wealth of white people
     c.   minority children define themselves in terms of the majority group
     d.   minority children have acquired a generalized negative ethnic self-conception
Answer: a, Reference: Chapter 10, P. 398, Difficulty: M

70.   Experimental studies on shaping of children's ethnic preferences with rewards have
       found
       a.   black children can be trained to prefer white stimuli
       b.   it is not possible to shape children's ethnic preferences with rewards
       c.   ethnic preferences may be altered with rewards during training sessions but
             effects disappear in the absence of rewards
       d.   training can successfully change preferences from white to black stimuli with
             the effects lasting beyond the training session
Answer: d, Reference: Chapter 10, P. 399, Difficulty: E

71.   Studies of ethnic and racial identity indicate that children are aware of these
       differences by the time they are
       a.   2 years old
       b.   4 years old
       c.   6 years old
       d.   8 years old
Answer: b, Reference: Chapter 10, P. 399, Difficulty: M

72.   Adult evaluations of children's behavior
       a.   for the most part remain external to the child
       b.   become the basis for children's self-evaluations
       c.   become the basis for the latency stage, according to Freud
       d.   do not help children acquire the ability to regulate themselves
Answer: b, Reference: Chapter 10, P. 399, Difficulty: D

73.   Heteronomous morality refers to the belief of
       a.   Maccoby that children are inhibited
       b.   Freud that males and females adopt different moral values
       c.   Kohlberg that males and females adopt different moral values
       d.   Piaget that children internalize an externally imposed value system
Answer: d, Reference: Chapter 10, P. 400, Difficulty: D

74.   Moral decisions based on external considerations are referred to as
       a.   learned
       b.   internalized
       c.   autonomous
       d.   heteronomous
Answer: d, Reference: Chapter 10, P. 400, Difficulty: E

75. According to Piaget, the most important factor in preschool children's judgments about what makes one of two actions the "naughtiest" is the
    a. outcome of the action
    b. autonomous morality of peers
    c. intention of the person doing the action
    d. sex of the parent whose rule is being violate

Answer: a, Reference: Chapter 10, P. 401, Difficulty: M

76. According to Piaget, when children enter middle childhood their morality is described as
    a. independent
    b. autonomous
    c. heteronomous
    d. externally imposed

Answer: b, Reference: Chapter 10, P. 401, Difficulty: E

77. Morality which is based on an understanding that rules are arbitrary agreements that can be challenged is called
    a. cognitive morality
    b. Piagetian morality
    c. autonomous morality
    d. heteronomous morality

Answer: a, Reference: Chapter 10, P. 401, Difficulty: M

78. Children begin to feel guilt once they have
    a. acquired an ego
    b. experienced punishment
    c. passed their first birthdays
    d. internalized adult standards

Answer: d, Reference: Chapter 10, P. 401, Difficulty: M

79. The process by which external culturally organized experiences become transformed into inner psychological processes is called
    a. learning
    b. imitation
    c. internalization
    d. cognitive development

Answer: c, Reference: Chapter 10, P. 401, Difficulty: E

80. Culture is a part of which of the following aspects of conscience?
    a. content and suppression
    b. content and development
    c. suppression and aggression
    d. development and suppression

Answer: b, Reference: Chapter 10, P. 401, Difficulty: D

81.   Self-control arises out of a desire to balance
        a.   biological cravings
        b.   opposing cultural demands
        c.   desire and internalized social standards
        d.   inhibition of emotions and inhibition of movement
Answer: c, Reference: Chapter 10, P. 404, Difficulty: M

82.   Which of the following games would a preschooler find the most difficult?
        a.   pat-a-cake
        b.   Simon says
        c.   London bridge
        d.   ring-around-the-rosy
Answer: b, Reference: Chapter 10, P. 404, Difficulty: M

83.   Of the following, which do preschoolers find most difficult?
        a.   stopping an action
        b.   initiating an action
        c.   copying simple motor actions
        d.   accepting an immediate reward for an action
Answer: a, Reference: Chapter 10, P. 404, Difficulty: M

84.   Given a choice between eating the last small piece of pie immediately or getting a
        large piece of pie after shopping tomorrow, in general how old would you expect
        children to be before they choose to wait?
        a.   3 years
        b.   6 years
        c.   9 years
        d.   12 years
Answer: d, Reference: Chapter 10, P. 404, Difficulty: D

85.   Asking children to match a familiar figure with its mate in a set of confusing
        alternatives is a popular way to assess
        a.   inhibition of choice
        b.   inhibition of movement
        c.   inhibition of self-control
        d.   inhibition of conclusions
Answer: d, Reference: Chapter 10, P. 404, Difficulty: M

86.   William Gardner and Barbara Rogoff (1990) used mazes to study the link between
        self-control and
        a.   conscience
        b.   personality
        c.   symbolic thinking
        d.   the ability to plan ahead
Answer: d, Reference: Chapter 10, P. 404, Difficulty: M

87.	According to Kochanska and Aksan, between the ages of 1 and 2, children develop the ability to begin, maintain, modify, and inhibit actions in response to a direct command. This is called
	a.	situational compliance
	b.	committed compliance
	c.	internalized knowledge
	d.	the inhibition of compliance
Answer: a, Reference: Chapter 10, P. 405, Difficulty: M

88.	Most of the compliance demonstrated by the 26 to 41 month old children in the Kochanska and Aksan (1995) study was of the _____ kind.
	a.	defiant
	b.	situational compliance
	c.	committed compliance
	d.	internalized knowledge
Answer: b, Reference: Chapter 10, P. 405, Difficulty: M

89.	In the Kochanska and Aksan (1995) study, when children who were told not to touch attractive toys were left alone by their mother, they
	a.	played with the toys
	b.	did not touch the toys
	c.	examined the toys but did not play with them
	d.	looked at the toys but did not play with them
Answer: b, Reference: Chapter 10, P. 405, Difficulty: M

90.	According to work by, Kochanska and Aksan (1995), there appears to be a direct connection between
	a.	aggression and self-control
	b.	intelligence and self-control
	c.	parental power and self-control
	d.	cognitive development and self-control
Answer: d, Reference: Chapter 10, P. 405, Difficulty: M

91.	"Contagious crying" engaged in by newborn infants is widely believed to be related to newborn
	a.	anger
	b.	empathy
	c.	discomfort
	d.	self-awareness
Answer: b, Reference: Chapter 10, P. 406, Difficulty: M

92. Maccoby suggests that children cannot be aggressive until they are
    a. at least 6 months old
    b. capable of contagious crying
    c. able to show socially constructive behavior
    d. able to understand they can cause others to be distressed

Answer: d, Reference: Chapter 10, P. 406, Difficulty: E

93. Two kinds of aggression are
    a. social and prosocial
    b. generative and stagnant
    c. instrumental and hostile
    d. person-oriented and contagious

Answer: c, Reference: Chapter 10, P. 406, Difficulty: E

94. Which of the following types of aggression is sometimes called "person oriented" aggression
    a. social aggression
    b. hostile aggression
    c. contagious aggression
    d. instrumental aggression

Answer: b, Reference: Chapter 10, P. 406, Difficulty: E

95. All of the following are motives for hostile aggression except
    a. desire for revenge
    b. desire to obtain a toy
    c. desire to hurt another
    d. establishing dominance

Answer: b, Reference: Chapter 10, P. 406, Difficulty: M

96. Worrying about "ownership rights" has been proposed by Judy Dunn as a reason for young children's
    a. increasing self-control
    b. increases in aggression
    c. decreases in aggression
    d. increases in prosocial behavior

Answer: b, Reference: Chapter 10, P. 407, Difficulty: M

97. When watching for aggressive behavior in 2-year-olds, Bronson observed that
    a. physical altercations over possessions increase
    b. children were no longer interested in ownership rights, per se
    c. children sometimes struggled for a toy, then lost interest once the struggle was over
    d. a concern for possession emerged that is different from that observed in other societies

Answer: c, Reference: Chapter 10, P. 407, Difficulty: D

98. Between the ages of 3 and 6 years of age
   a. verbal aggression increases
   b. instrumental aggression appears
   c. physical altercations over possessions increase
   d. boys and girls display similar amounts of aggression

Answer: a, Reference: Chapter 10, P. 407, Difficulty: M

99. According to studies of Legault and Strayer (1990) the differences in levels of aggression between girls and boys seems to emerge when they are about
   a. 6 months old
   b. 1-2 years old
   c. 2-3 years old
   d. 4-5 years old

Answer: c, Reference: Chapter 10, P. 407, Difficulty: M

100. Relational aggression is most likely to be displayed by
   a. boys
   b. girls
   c. older children
   d. younger children

Answer: b, Reference: Chapter 10, P. 407, Difficulty: M

101. "I hate you!" and "Stay away from me!" are examples of
   a. verbal tussles
   b. hostile aggression
   c. relational aggression
   d. instrumental aggression

Answer: c, Reference: Chapter 10, P. 407, Difficulty: D

102. Studies conducted by Patterson, DeBaryshe, and Ramsey (1989), that observed the aggressive behavior of nursery school children, led them to conclude that aggressive behavior
   a. is innate
   b. is natural and necessary
   c. automatically accompanies maturation of the young
   d. is learned because it is often rewarding to the aggressor

Answer: d, Reference: Chapter 10, P. 408, Difficulty: D

103. All but which of the following have been proposed as a cause of aggression?
   a. parental models
   b. cognitive training
   c. biological maturation
   d. reward or reinforcement

Answer: b, Reference: Chapter 10, P. 408, Difficulty: E

104.   When G. R. Patterson and his colleagues watched the aggressive behavior of
        preschoolers, they found that
        a.   aggressive action was infrequent
        b.   25 percent of the aggressive acts were followed by positive consequences for
              the aggressor
        c.   75 percent of the aggressive acts were followed by positive consequences for
              the aggressor
        d.   an aggressive response to an aggressive act had no effect on the likelihood
              that the act would be repeated
Answer: c, Reference: Chapter 10, P. 408, Difficulty: M

105.   When Albert Bandura and his colleagues modeled aggressive behavior for
        preschoolers, they found that children who had seen the modeled aggression
        a.   limited their aggressive acts to those which were specifically modeled
        b.   were likely to supplement the aggressive behaviors with novel forms of their
              own
        c.   had levels of subsequent aggressive behavior equal to those of children who
              had not seen the model
        d.   were more likely to commit subsequent aggressive acts if the model had been
              a cartoon character rather than a human
Answer: b, Reference: Chapter 10, P. 409, Difficulty: M

106.   The best way to organize existing theories of aggression is to
        a.   consider aggression as separate from other social behaviors
        b.   pose biological and environmental-learning theories as opposites
        c.   consider biological and environmental-learning theories as fundamentally the
              same
        d.   understand that aggression is a complex set of behaviors that result from both
              biological and environmental interactions
Answer: d, Reference: Chapter 10, P. 411, Difficulty: E

107.   Mechanisms that limit aggression
        a.   do not exist
        b.   must be taught
        c.   are limited to humans
        d.   are widespread among animal species
Answer: d, Reference: Chapter 10, P. 411, Difficulty: E

108.   F. F. Strayer and his colleagues (1989, 1991) observed in 3- and 4-year olds, a close
        connection between aggression and
        a.   ethnicity
        b.   birth order
        c.   gender-roles
        d.   dominance hierarchies
Answer: d, Reference: Chapter 10, P. 411, Difficulty: D

109. The establishment of dominance hierarchies
    a. has no equivalent in human behavior
    b. demonstrates that aggression must be learned
    c. does not control aggression in young children
    d. provides evidence for a biological component to aggression control
Answer: d, Reference: Chapter 10, P. 411, Difficulty: D

110. Social dominance hierarchies among humans
    a. can be a means of controlling aggression
    b. take the place of internalized social rules
    c. have not been observed in nursery schools
    d. can be considered analogous to street gangs
Answer: a, Reference: Chapter 10, P. 411, Difficulty: D

111. Catharsis is
    a. only effective if the activity is physical
    b. an effective way of reducing aggression
    c. an effective way of increasing aggression
    d. not an effective way of reducing frustration responses
Answer: d, Reference: Chapter 10, P. 412, Difficulty: M

112. Mallick and McCandless found that aggressive behavior toward one member of a group who impeded group activity
    a. diminished when the boys experienced catharsis
    b. could be reduced by explaining that the boy was not feeling well
    c. was increased when the group discovered that the boy was not feeling well
    d. stopped when the group was given the opportunity to punish the boy severely with electric shocks
Answer: b, Reference: Chapter 10, P. 412, Difficulty: M

113. Punishment is least likely to suppress aggression when
    a. it is used consistently
    b. it is used occasionally
    c. it is used inconsistently
    d. the child identifies strongly with the victim
Answer: c, Reference: Chapter 10, P. 412, Difficulty: E

114. Several studies have found that parents who control their children's behavior with physical punishment
    a. have more compliant children
    b. have more aggressive children
    c. eliminate children's aggressive behaviors
    d. have children that do not differ in rate of aggressive behavior from parents who use other means of control
Answer: b, Reference: Chapter 10, P. 412, Difficulty: M

115. G. R. Patterson and his colleagues found that children labeled as overly aggressive by schools and clinics
    a.   never found themselves in coercive situations
    b.   were unaffected by parental threats of raw power
    c.   sometimes inadvertently trained their own parents to be aggressive
    d.   rarely came from homes in which parents used aggressive punishment
Answer: c, Reference: Chapter 10, P. 413, Difficulty: D

116. Kenneth Dodge found a link between physical punishment in the home and
    a.   reactive aggression in school
    b.   bullying aggression in school
    c.   instrumental aggression in school
    d.   empathic and altruistic behavior in school
Answer: a, Reference: Chapter 10, P. 414, Difficulty: M

117. According to Kenneth Dodge, aggression in children can be partly blamed on
    a.   misinterpreting social cues
    b.   innate biological tendencies
    c.   learning that aggression works
    d.   inadequate socialization and response inhibition
Answer: a, Reference: Chapter 10, P. 414, Difficulty: D

118. A selective-attention approach to controlling aggressive behavior includes
    a.   instructing the aggressor in nonviolent assertive techniques
    b.   plying the victim with attention following an aggressive attack
    c.   ignoring the victim and the aggressor during an aggressive act
    d.   plying the aggressor with attention following an aggressive act
Answer: b, Reference: Chapter 10, P. 414, Difficulty: D

119. Zahavi and Asher (1978) found that it was possible to teach 4-year-olds that aggression does not solve problems by using
    a.   modeling
    b.   punishment
    c.   explanations
    d.   reinforcement
Answer: c, Reference: Chapter 10, P. 414, Difficulty: D

120. Altruism is an example of a(n) _____ behavior.
    a.   moral
    b.   prosocial
    c.   aggressive
    d.   punishment
Answer: b, Reference: Chapter 10, P. 415, Difficulty: M

121. Which of the following is a helping behavior?
    a. altruism
    b. empathy
    c. catharsis
    d. a prosocial behavior
Answer: a, Reference: Chapter 10, P. 415, Difficulty: D

122. Because it promotes the survival of others with whom genes are shared, according to biologists, evolutionary theory explains
    a. altruism
    b. aggression
    c. identification
    d. appropriate sex-role behavior
Answer: a, Reference: Chapter 10, P. 415, Difficulty: D

123. Children's first display of empathy is likely to be
    a. laughing when another child falls down
    b. biting the mother's breast while teething
    c. feeling sympathy for a character in a story
    d. crying at the sound of another infant's cries
Answer: d, Reference: Chapter 10, P. 416, Difficulty: E

124. In discussing young babies crying at the sound of another infant's cries, Nancy Eisenberg (1992) labels this phenomenon
    a. contagious crying
    b. sympathetic tears
    c. emotional support
    d. emotional contagion
Answer: d, Reference: Chapter 10, P. 416, Difficulty: M

125. The phenomenon of infants, as young as two days old, crying at the sound of another infant's cries has been termed "emotional contagion" by
    a. Dunn
    b. Kitcher
    c. Hoffman
    d. Eisenberg
Answer: d, Reference: Chapter 10, P. 416, Difficulty: M

126. According to Martin Hoffman, all of the following are important in the development of empathy except
    a. self-awareness
    b. use of language
    c. feeling anger in response to another's pain
    d. understanding that feelings occur within a larger set of experiences
Answer: c, Reference: Chapter 10, P. 416, Difficulty: M

127. Children can respond helpfully to another person's distress by, for example, trying to put a bandage on a cut by the age of
    a.   9 months
    b.   1.5 to 2 years
    c.   4 years
    d.   7 years
Answer: b, Reference: Chapter 10, P. 417, Difficulty: M

128. The Zahn-Waxler and Radke-Yarrow studies of prosocial behavior document all of the following as early as the second year of life except
    a.   care-giving
    b.   helping eagerly
    c.   showing compassion
    d.   reluctance to help with household chores
Answer: d, Reference: Chapter 10, P. 417, Difficulty: E

129. Zahn-Waxler and Radke-Yarrow found that the likelihood of helping behavior is facilitated if the target is
    a.   a friend
    b.   a parent
    c.   a sibling
    d.   a stranger
Answer: a, Reference: Chapter 10, P. 417, Difficulty: D

130. Joan Grusec (1991) observed that the use of explicit rewards to promote prosocial behavior
    a.   did not work
    b.   has been found to create situations where children demand bigger and bigger rewards
    c.   has been found to create situations where children behave aggressively unless rewarded
    d.   has been found to create situations where children resent the behaviors they have been rewarded for
Answer: a, Reference: Chapter 10, P. 418, Difficulty: M

131. Which of the following is most effective to promote prosocial behavior
    a.   coercion
    b.   induction
    c.   explicit rewards
    d.   physical punishment
Answer: b, Reference: Chapter 10, P. 418, Difficulty: E

132. Linda Michaleson and Michael Lewis found that very young children could assess the emotions of another if the situations were
    a. sad
    b. happy
    c. simple
    d. familiar
Answer: c, Reference: Chapter 10, P. 419, Difficulty: M

133. Lisa Bridges and Wendy Grolnik found that 3 1/2-to-4 1/2-year-old children can resist temptation by
    a. active engagement
    b. cognitive self-control
    c. using a "not thinking" strategy
    d. playing with the forbidden item
Answer: a, Reference: Chapter 10, P. 420, Difficulty: M

134. A child is unlikely to be able to fake emotions until the age of
    a. 2
    b. 3
    c. 4
    d. 5
Answer: b, Reference: Chapter 10, P. 420, Difficulty: D

135. Alissa does not get the puppy she wanted but she smiles bravely and says "thank-you for the nice coat." Alissa could be as young as
    a. 2
    b. 4
    c. 6
    d. 8
Answer: b, Reference: Chapter 10, P. 420, Difficulty: D

136. Which of the following was not presented in the chapter as a component of social competence?
    a. the awareness of one's emotional state
    b. the awareness of cultural display rules
    c. the capacity to use self-regulation strategies
    d. the ability to produce an effective helping strategy
Answer: d, Reference: Chapter 10, P. 420, Difficulty: D

137. Erik Erikson is known for all of the following *except*
    a. use of psychohistories
    b. use of cross-cultural comparisons
    c. adding an important social dimension to Freud's theory
    d. adding an important biological dimension to Freud's theory
Answer: d, Reference: Chapter 10, P. 402, Box 10.2, Difficulty: E

138. Erik Erikson contends the main theme of life is the quest for
     a.   ego
     b.   identity
     c.   defense mechanisms
     d.   psychosexual success
Answer: b, Reference: Chapter 10, P. 402, Box 10.2, Difficulty: E

139. Erikson's term for the "personal picture" of yourself that you develop throughout you life is
     a.   identity
     b.   self-esteem
     c.   self-concept
     d.   personal construct
Answer: a, Reference: Chapter 10, P. 402, Box 10.2, Difficulty: M

140. The psychosocial stage of development proposed by Erikson that corresponds to Freud's phallic stage is
     a.   initiative versus guilt
     b.   intimacy versus isolation
     c.   industry versus inferiority
     d.   autonomy versus shame and doubt
Answer: a, Reference: Chapter 10, P. 403, Box 10.2, Difficulty: M

141. Which of the following is *not* one of the psychosocial stages proposed by Erik Erikson that would be experienced in adulthood
     a.   integrity versus despair
     b.   intimacy versus isolation
     c.   industry versus inferiority
     d.   generativity versus stagnation
Answer: c, Reference: Chapter 10, P. 403, Box 10.2, Difficulty: D

Essay Questions

1. Describe the relationship between personality and socialization, and how they are distinct from each other. In what ways are they interdependent? Give examples.

2. Describe Freud's theory of how young boys and girls come to acquire appropriate sex-role identification.

3. Social development is a two-sided process. Identify and define each side.

4. Explain the functions and development of the id, ego, and the superego. What are their relationships to one another and with the individual's personality?

5.   Describe how Chodorow's theory of how boys and girls arrive at appropriate sex-role identification is similar to that of Freud's theory. How does it differ?

6.   What is the evidence that sex-appropriate behaviors are shaped by the distribution of rewards and punishments in the environment? Give examples.

7.   What are the similarities between Kohlberg's cognitive sex-role identification theory and Bandura's social learning explanation? What are the differences?

8.   What evidence supports Kohlberg's theory that children's concept of sex reflects their overall cognitive development?

9.   List and describe Freud's five stages of psychosexual development.

10.   Compare and contrast identification through differentiation, affiliation, observation and imitation, and cognition.

11.   Describe the classic studies on the development of ethnic and racial identity conducted by Kenneth and Mamie Clark in the 1930's and 1950's. Discuss the results of the studies and any legal ramifications. What concerns have been raised about the interpretations made by these researchers? What interpretations have been offered by later researchers of ethnic identity?

12.   List and describe Erikson's eight stages of psychosocial development. Compare and contrast with Freud's stages of development.

13.   Describe the major changes that occur in the expression of aggression by children two to six years of age. Give examples.

14.   Describe the development of morality in young children.

15.   What is heteronomous morality? Give an example.

16.   What is autonomous morality? When does it develop?

17.   Discuss the four kinds of inhibition that young children master as identified by Maccoby.

18.   Define a dominance hierarchy and describe its function. What evidence suggests this system might apply to humans? What are the limitations of such a system among humans?

19.   Describe how certain kinds of punishment can increase the aggressive behaviors of both parents and children.

20. Compare and contrast instrumental and hostile aggression.

21. Define prosocial behavior, and describe stages which occur during its development. How can children's prosocial behavior be increased?

22. Discuss "venting" as a safe and socially acceptable means of controlling aggression. What is the current status of this concept? Explain.

23. How is cognitive training used to control aggression?

24. Describe Hoffman's four stages of empathy.

25. What is induction? What role does it play in the development of prosocial behaviors in young children?

26. Describe the use of active engagement to promote resistance to temptation.

27. Describe the stages in the development of the control of emotion in the young child.

28. How are emotional, social, and cognitive development related? Explain.

The Contexts of Early Childhood Development

Multiple-Choice Questions

1. According to Urie Bronfenbrenner, the environment of development can be thought of as
    a. a unidirectional hierarchy of achievements
    b. determined by the personality of the parents
    c. a series of concentric circles nested within one another
    d. independent of society until the child reaches adolescenceAnswer: c, Answer: b, Answer b, Reference: Chapter 11, P. 428, Difficulty: M

2. The environment that has the most direct impact on a young child's development is
    a. media
    b. school
    c. family
    d. social environment in which the child plays
    Answer: c, Reference: Chapter 11, P. 428, Difficulty: E

3. According to Robert Le Vine, which of the following are goals of parents in all cultures?
    a. survival, economic, cultural
    b. survival, political, economic
    c. survival, comfort, self-actualization
    d. survival, education, meaningfulness
    Answer: a, Reference: Chapter 11, P. 428, Difficulty: M

4.   What is the term used to describe the ideal American family, consisting of mother, father, and their children?
     a.   nuclear
     b.   extended
     c.   polygynous
     d.   multi-parent
Answer: a, Reference: Chapter 11, P. 429, Difficulty: M

5.   What is the term for the practice in which each man has more than one wife?
     a.   bigamy
     b.   polygyny
     c.   polyandry
     d.   monogamy
Answer: b, Answer: b, Reference: Chapter 11, P. 429, Difficulty: E

6.   Which family configuration is the most common on a world scale?
     a.   nuclear
     b.   polygyny
     c.   monogamy
     d.   single-parent
Answer: b, Answer: b, Reference: Chapter 11, P. 429, Difficulty: M

7.   The birth of a second child is particularly upsetting for first born children if they are
     a.   male
     b.   adopted
     c.   the opposite sex
     d.   less than four years old
Answer: d, Answer: b, Reference: Chapter 11, P. 430, Box 11.1, Difficulty: M

8.   First born children may respond to their mother's inattentiveness after the birth of a new baby by
     a.   becoming detached
     b.   being less demanding
     c.   demonstrating more positive behaviors
     d.   focusing their attention on the infant and ignoring the mother
Answer: a, Answer: b, Reference: Chapter 11, P. 430, Box 11.1, Difficulty: M

9.   Typically during the first year
     a.   siblings imitate the new baby
     b.   the new baby imitates older siblings
     c.   siblings do not interact with the new baby
     d.   there are no disruptive interactions between siblings and the new baby
Answer: a, Answer: a, Reference: Chapter 11, P. 430, Box 11.1, Difficulty: M

10.   Research has clearly demonstrated that how well siblings get along is affected by
        a.   sex of siblings
        b.   age of siblings
        c.   temperament of siblings
        d.   intellectual level of siblings
Answer: c, Reference: Chapter 11, P. 431, Box 11.1, Difficulty: M

11.   Which of the following is not a variable in sibling antagonism
        a.   parental conflict
        b.   sex of the siblings
        c.   temperaments of the siblings
        d.   differential treatment by mothers
Answer: b, Reference: Chapter 11, P. 431, Box 11.1, Difficulty: D

12.   Which of the following seems to increase sibling fighting?
        a.   parental fighting
        b.   similar treatment by mother
        c.   two children of the same sex
        d.   spacing of births close together
Answer: a, Reference: Chapter 11, P. 431, Box 11.1, Difficulty: E

13.   Several studies have found that the more parents intervene in sibling disputes the
        a.   more disputes there are
        b.   fewer disputes there are
        c.   more aggression is turned toward the parents
        d.   more children observe how to resolve differences
Answer: a, Reference: Chapter 11, P. 431, Box 11.1, Difficulty: E

14.   It has been suggested that parental intervention in sibling disputes increases the
        number of disputes because
        a.   children quarrel in order to get their parents' attention
        b.   parental intervention provides them with the opportunity to learn to resolve
                their conflicts
        c.   parents intervention provides a model for children of fighting which increases
                their tendency to fight
        d.   parents interventions occur when fights are more intense and intensity is
                related to frequency of fights
Answer: a, Reference: Chapter 11, P. 431, Box 11.1, Difficulty: D

15. Different culturally organized contexts for development
     a.   influence the way parents treat their children
     b.   produce variations in basic economic activities and family life
     c.   influence both how parents treat their children and affect variations in basic
          economic activities
     d.   have little effect on how parents treat their children more on the basic
          economic activities available
Answer: c, Reference: Chapter 11, P. 431, Difficulty: D

16. When the Whitings studied cultural contexts among six diverse cultures, they found
     that within the African Gussi culture
     a.   mothers were rarely separated from their infant children
     b.   the community had a few highly specialized occupations
     c.   children's economic contributions to their families were vital by the age of 7
     d.   children spent more time in the company of adults than did the children of
          Orchard Town
Answer: c, Reference: Chapter 11, P. 432, Difficulty: M

17. When the Whitings compared cultural contexts among six different cultures, they
     found that within the New England Orchard Town culture, children were
     a.   often asked to do chores
     b.   encouraged to think of themselves as group members
     d.   less likely to engage in prosocial behaviors than were Gussi children
     c.   very likely to be found engaged in "nurturant- responsible" behaviors
Answer: c, Reference: Chapter 11, P. 432, Difficulty: M

18. The cross-cultural study of Gusii and Orchard Town children found that children
     who were both "sociable and intimate" and "dependent-dominant" came from
     households which were
     a.   nuclear
     b.   extended
     c.   polygynous
     d.   either extended or nuclear
Answer: a, Reference: Chapter 11, P. 433, Difficulty: D

19. The Whitings studies of six cultures
     a.   showed that parents rarely try to control their children's behavior
     b.   found different child rearing practices between individuals within Kenyan
          society
     c.   concluded that the Gussi of Kenya are prosocial and that U.S. children are
          self-centered
     d.   contributed to our knowledge of how cultural differences shape children's
          personalities and behavior
Answer: d, Reference: Chapter 11, P. 434, Difficulty: M

20. Studies of child rearing have found that parenting styles vary along which of the following dimensions?
    a. control and affection
    b. control and autonomy
    c. socialization and aggression
    d. permissiveness and intimacy
Answer: a, Reference: Chapter 11, P. 434, Difficulty: D

21. Parents who are characteristically both rejecting and unresponsive and demanding and controlling are thought to be using an ___ parenting style
    a. indulgent
    b. indifferent
    c. authoritative
    d. authoritarian
Answer: d, Reference: Chapter 11, P. 434, Table 11.2, Difficulty: M

22. Parents who are demanding and controlling but also accepting and responsive are thought to be characteristic of an ___ parenting style
    a. indulgent
    b. indifferent
    c. authoritative
    d. authoritarian
Answer: c, Answer: a, Reference: Chapter 11, P. 434, Table 11.2 Difficulty: M

23. All of the following are parenting styles described by Diana Baumrind except
    a. passive
    b. permissive
    c. authoritative
    d. authoritarian
Answer: a, Reference: Chapter 11, P. 435, Difficulty: E

24. According to Diana Baumrind, authoritarian parents
    a. demand less achievement than do permissive parents
    b. favor punitive measures to control children's behavior
    c. accept more immature behavior than other types of parents
    d. are willing to listen to their children although they do not agree with them
Answer: b, Answer: b, Reference: Chapter 11, P. 435, Difficulty: M

25. According to Diana Baumrind, permissive parents
    a. are unlikely to consult children about family policies
    b. exert little explicit control over their children's behavior
    c. attempt to control children through explanation and reason
    d. demand achievement and mature behaviors from their children
Answer: b, Reference: Chapter 11, P. 435, Difficulty: E

26. Diana Baumrind found that children's behavior
     a.   is not influenced by personality
     b.   is independent of parenting style
     c.   varies in accordance with parental styles
     d.   is influenced mostly by individual differences among children
Answer: c, Reference: Chapter 11, P. 436, Difficulty: E

27. Children of authoritarian parents
     a.   tend to lack social competence
     b.   behave with spontaneity and curiosity
     c.   often take the initiative in social interactions
     d.   are more self-controlled and self-reliant than other children
Answer: a, Reference: Chapter 11, P. 436, Difficulty: M

28. Which parenting style is generally associated with better school performance and
     better social adjustment in students?
     a.   permissive
     b.   easy-going
     c.   authoritative
     d.   authoritarian
Answer: c, Reference: Chapter 11, P. 436, Difficulty: M

29. Which parenting style was associated with children's behavior in preschool that was
     characterized as immature, low in impulse control, and difficulty with accepting
     responsibility for their actions?
     a.   permissive
     b.   authoritarian
     c.   authoritative
     d.   preschool behavior was not found to be linked to parenting style
Answer: a, Reference: Chapter 11, P. 436, Difficulty: M

30. Research on the personalities of biologically unrelated children growing up in the
     same households shows that
     a.   within a family, parental styles do not vary
     b.   parental styles are the determining factor in children's personalities
     c.   parental styles may have little effect on children's behavior patterns
     d.   parental style with the oldest child sets the pattern for interactions with all
          the other children
Answer: c, Reference: Chapter 11, P. 437, Difficulty: D

31. The causal effect of parenting styles on children's development has recently been challenged by research that shows biologically
     a.   related children raised by the same parents are quite similar
     b.   related children raised by the same parents are quite different
     c.   unrelated children raised by the same parents are quite similar
     d.   unrelated children raised by the same parents are quite different
Answer: d, Reference: Chapter 11, P. 437, Difficulty: M

32. A study by Baumrind found that African American children who were raised with a(n) _____ parenting style behaved more like white middle class children who were raised with a _____ parenting style.
     a.   permissive, authoritative
     b.   permissive, authoritarian
     c.   authoritarian, authoritative
     d.   authoritative, authoritarian
Answer: c, Reference: Chapter 11, P. 437, Difficulty: D

33. According to a study by Sanford Dornbusch and his colleagues, level of authoritarian parenting practices did not predict school performance for which group of students?
     a.   white
     b.   Latino
     c.   Asian American
     d.   African American
Answer: c, Reference: Chapter 11, P. 437, Difficulty: D

34. Ruth Chao (1994) has demonstrated that when compared to European American parents, Chinese-Americans perceive the concept of authoritarian parenting
     a.   as essentially the same
     b.   different in both the control and affection dimensions
     c.   the same in the control dimension, but different in the affection dimension
     d.   the same in the affection dimension, but different in the control dimension
Answer: c, Reference: Chapter 11, P. 438, Difficulty: D

35. According to the 1993 U.S. Census Bureau approximately what percentage of U.S. children are living in single family homes
     a.   18%
     b.   27%
     c.   42%
     d.   56%
Answer: b, Reference: Chapter 11, P. 438, Difficulty: D

36.   According to data presented in the text the number of births among unmarried
       teenagers over the last 30 years has
       a.   increased slightly
       b.   decreased slightly
       c.   stayed about the same
       d.   increased dramatically
Answer: d, Reference: Chapter 11, P. 438, Difficulty: M

37.   Which of the following is *not* likely to be true of young, unwed mothers?
       a.   they are socially isolated
       b.   they vocalize more to their babies
       c.   they are likely to be poorly educated
       d.   they are less emotionally equipped to be competent parents
Answer: b, Reference: Chapter 11, P. 438, Difficulty: M

38.   A recent study by the U.S. Census Bureau (1991) reported the average income of
       single-parent families created by divorce or separation falls by approximately
       a.   18%
       b.   37%
       c.   46%
       d.   61%
Answer: b, Reference: Chapter 11, P. 439, Difficulty: D

39.   Which of the following seems to pose the greatest risk for children?
       a.   parent's divorce
       b.   parental conflict
       c.   a working mother
       d.   authoritarian parenting
Answer: b, Reference: Chapter 11, P. 440, Difficulty: E

40.   The effects of marital disharmony and of divorce seem to be
       a.   greater in girls than in boys
       b.   greater in boys than in girls
       c.   minimal for both girls and boys
       d.   about the same for boys and girls
Answer: b, Reference: Chapter 11, P. 440, Difficulty: E

41.   Children who react to their parents' divorce by blaming themselves are most likely
       to
       a.   be male
       b.   be adolescents
       c.   be preschool age
       d.   have a difficult temperament
Answer: c, Reference: Chapter 11, P. 440, Difficulty: E

42.   Children who have the best ability to cope with the stresses following their parents' divorce are most likely to
    a.   be female
    b.   be adolescents
    c.   be preschool age
    d.   have an easy temperament
Answer: b, Reference: Chapter 11, P. 440, Difficulty: E

43.   The long-term effects of divorce
    a.   do not usually have much effect on the stability of future relationships
    b.   seem to be minimized if the divorce occurs while the children are of preschool age
    c.   almost never affect a child's confidence in her adult abilities to maintain a relationship
    d.   include vivid memories of parental conflicts if the children were beyond early infancy at the time of the divorce
Answer: b, Reference: Chapter 11, P. 440, Difficulty: M

44.   Children's long term adjustment to parent remarriages are determined by all of the following except
    a.   the children's gender
    b.   gender of the new parent
    c.   age when parent remarries
    d.   duration of the new marriage
Answer: b, Reference: Chapter 11, P. 441, Difficulty: D

45.   Economic factors are
    a.   independent of family structure
    b.   independent of parental behavior
    c.   not important in determining children's behavior
    d.   an important determinant of family social structure
Answer: d, Reference: Chapter 11, P. 442, Difficulty: M

46.   Parents view obedience as
    a.   always less important than autonomy.
    b.   important only during the preschool years
    c.   the means by which their children will succeed in the world, especially if they themselves are affluent
    d.   the means by which their children will succeed in the world, especially if they themselves have little money
Answer: d, Answer: a, Reference: Chapter 11, P. 442, Difficulty: D

47.   A mother under stress is more likely to act in which of the following ways toward her children?
       a.   punitive
       b.   nurturing
       c.   permissive
       d.   authoritative
Answer: a, Reference: Chapter 11, P. 442, Difficulty: M

48.   Compared with middle-class parents, working-class parents are
       a.   less concerned about their children's futures
       b.   more concerned with their children's futures
       c.   more concerned with punctuality and obedience
       d.   more likely to emphasize the ability to work without supervision
Answer: c, Reference: Chapter 11, P. 443, Difficulty: D

49.   Which of the following is true regarding child abuse?
       a.   there are no reliable data on its prevalence
       b.   most cases of abuse are eventually reported
       c.   the large number of unfounded claims of abuse distorts reporting of incidents of child abuse
       d.   there is complete agreement on what is considered abuse in the context of parenting practices
Answer: a, Reference: Chapter 11, P. 444, Box 11.2, Difficulty: E

50.   Which children are most likely to be neglected?
       a.   defiant children
       b.   passive children
       c.   irritable children
       d.   hyperactive children
Answer: b, Reference: Chapter 11, P. 444, Box 11.2, Difficulty: M

51.   Which of the following is not a factor placing a child at greater risk for abuse?
       a.   being male
       b.   being premature
       c.   being hyperactive
       d.   being under 3 years of age
Answer: a, Reference: Chapter 11, P. 445, Box 11.2, Difficulty: E

52.   Approximately what percent of individuals abused as children grow up to become abusing parents?
       a.   10%
       b.   30%
       c.   50%
       d.   60%
Answer: b, Reference: Chapter 11, P. 445, Box 11.2, Difficulty: M

53.   Which of the following characteristics is not typical of children who have been sexually abused?

    a.   anxiety

    b.   depression

    c.   poor social skills

    d.   extremely self-controlled

Answer: d, Reference: Chapter 11, P. 446, Box 11.2, Difficulty: M

54.   Which of the following has been suggested by the text as the most effective intervention to reduce child abuse?

    a.   reduce poverty

    b.   create social networks of support for parents

    c.   provide teens with formal training for parenthood

    d.   attack several risk factors rather than just a single one

Answer: d, Reference: Chapter 11, P. 446, Box 11.2, Difficulty: E

55.   Which of the following is not true with regard to extended families?

    a.   they are more likely to be minority

    b.   they worsen the effects of poverty on the family

    c.   they provide important resources to many young children

    d.   they may include grandparents, cousins, and distant relatives

Answer: b, Reference: Chapter 11, P. 443, Difficulty: E

56.   Chase-Lansdale and others claim that extended families are most important when

    a.   a family is poor

    b.   a family relocates

    c.   parents are elderly

    d.   a child is born out of wedlock

Answer: d, Reference: Chapter 11, P. 446, Difficulty: M

57.   A recent study by Comstock and Paik (1991) found that in the average American home television is on for an average of ___ hours per day and young children watch it for ___ or more of those hours

    a.   4; 2

    b.   6; 2

    c.   8; 4

    d.   10; 6

Answer: b, Reference: Chapter 11, P. 447, Difficulty: M

58.   Meltzoff (1988) found that infants could be observed to imitate the gestures of an
      adult on an object that they had observed on television at age
      a.   6 weeks
      b.   9 months
      c.   14 months
      d.   24 months
Answer: c, Reference: Chapter 11, P. 447, Difficulty: M

59.   A recent study by John Flavell and his colleagues has found that children understand
      that images on television are pictures and not real physically present objects by age
      a.   2 years
      b.   3 years
      c.   4 years
      d.   5 years
Answer: c, Reference: Chapter 11, P. 447, Difficulty: M

60.   Once children come to understand that one thing can represent another they
      a.   no longer confuse the real with the fictitious
      b.   understand television images are just pictures
      c.   would know that when a bad guy is shot he isn't really dead
      d.   realize that actors portraying lovers do not need to like each other
Answer: b, Reference: Chapter 11, P. 448, Difficulty: M

61.   Five-year-old Stephen watches a TV program about a fireman who sets buildings on
      fire and then attempts dramatic rescues. Stephen is likely to
      a.   realize that this is a fictitious thriller
      b.   want to be a fireman when he grows up
      c.   have difficulty distinguishing between reality and fiction
      d.   recall between 75 percent and 100 percent of the content
Answer: c, Reference: Chapter 11, P. 448, Difficulty: M

62.   Which of the following is true about television?
      a.   it has little or no effect on children's text reading
      b.   it requires mental effort similar to that of reading
      c.   it is a medium in which people are portrayed realistically
      d.   it moves at a fast pace that makes it difficult to think about what is presented
Answer: d, Reference: Chapter 11, P. 449, Difficulty: D

63.   Recent research has shown that children who watch a great deal of television
      a.   read less
      b.   do better in school
      c.   have more general knowledge
      d.   show more prosocial behavior
Answer: a, Reference: Chapter 11, P. 449, Difficulty: E

64.   What ethnic group is usually stereotyped as gangsters when portrayed on television, according to Berry and Asamen (1993)?
  a.   Latin Americans
  b.   Italian Americans
  c.   Native Americans
  d.   African Americans
Answer: b, Reference: Chapter 11, P. 449, Difficulty: E

65.   According to Nancy Signorelli (1993), children's programs have
  a.   about 4 females to every male
  b.   about 4 males to every female
  c.   an equal number of males and females
  d.   generally portrayed women as strong and independent
Answer: b, Reference: Chapter 11, P. 449, Difficulty: M

66.   A recent study of Saturday morning commercial programming for children by Greenberg and Brand (1994) found that
  a.   only 3 programs featured Latin American characters
  b.   only 3 programs features African American characters
  c.   many more women are portrayed as assertive than in the 50's
  d.   males and females were represented in gender stereotypic ways
Answer: b, Reference: Chapter 11, P. 450, Difficulty: M

67.   Gorn, Boldberg, and Kanango observed that children who observed children of various ethnic groups interacting were
  a.   more likely to ignore children of different groups
  b.   less likely to play with children of different ethnic groups
  c.   more likely to play with children of different ethnic groups
  d.   more likely to act aggressively to children of different ethnic groups
Answer: c, Reference: Chapter 11, P. 450, Difficulty: M

68.   Tannis Williams observed that when a community in Canada had access to television for the first time, the behavior of the children in that community
  a.   was unaffected by the experience
  b.   showed an increase in aggression
  c.   showed an increase in imaginative play
  d.   was observed to increase in prosocial behaviors
Answer: b, Reference: Chapter 11, P. 451, Difficulty: M

69.   Evidence from recent decades of research suggests that watching television violence
    a.   only has an effect on preschool age children
    b.   has no effect on the behavior of young children
    c.   increases violent behavior in only those children "predisposed" to be violent
    d.   increases violent behavior among many viewers, not just among those "predisposed" to be violent
Answer: d, Reference: Chapter 11, P. 451, Difficulty: M

70.   Singer and Singer found that children who were aggressive in preschool and who watched television
    a.   often watched television with their parents
    b.   also had parents who controlled how the children spent their time
    c.   were permitted to stay up at night and watch whatever they chose
    d.   also had parents who often took them out of the house on excursions
Answer: c, Reference: Chapter 11, P. 451, Difficulty: M

71.   When preschool age children understand that marks on paper somehow convey information we call this knowledge
    a.   content literacy
    b.   letter awareness
    c.   emergent literacy
    d.   visual-graphic knowledge
Answer: c, Reference: Chapter 11, P. 453, Difficulty: M

72.   Existing evidence indicates that which of the following behaviors in early childhood facilitates reading once children get to school
    a.   having an older sibling
    b.   watching Sesame Street
    c.   being read to frequently
    d.   seeing others read to themselves
Answer: c, Reference: Chapter 11, P. 453, Difficulty: E

73.   Reading to 2-year-old children helps them to do better in school because
    a.   they watch less television
    b.   they spend more time with adults
    c.   the format of the reading is similar to later teacher-child interchanges
    d.   the reading lessons are used by parents to teach children to sit still and pay attention
Answer: c, Reference: Chapter 11, P. 453, Difficulty: M

74.   When adults and children read together, with the adult asking questions, adding information from outside the book, and listens to the child, this process is called
    a.   joint reading
    b.   dialogic reading
    c.   conjoint dialogue
    d.   emergent literacy
Answer: b, Reference: Chapter 11, P. 454, Difficulty: M

75.   The greatest difference between television learning and book learning is
    a.   adult control of content
    b.   the child's control of content
    c.   the child's ability to sit still and listen
    d.   the child's ability to make sense of pictures and words
Answer: a, Reference: Chapter 11, P. 454, Difficulty: M

76.   Bruno Bettelheim contends that fairy tales
    a.   misrepresent ethnic groups
    b.   are inappropriate for children
    c.   foster violence and aggression
    d.   provide solutions to children's inner conflicts
Answer: d, Reference: Chapter 11, P. 454, Difficulty: M

77.   Soviet author, Komei Chukovsky, believed that fantasy
    a.   is inappropriate for children
    b.   provides children with an escape from reality
    c.   provides a means for children to learn about reality
    d.   is independent of the social values of home and community
Answer: c, Reference: Chapter 11, P. 455, Box 11.3, Difficulty: D

78.   In 1993 more than ___ percent of U. S. mothers with children below the age of 6 years were working and their children were in some form of day care
    a.   25%
    b.   40%
    c.   60%
    d.   80%
Answer: c, Reference: Chapter 11, P. 456, Difficulty: E

79.   The most popular day care arrangement in the United States is
    a.   home day care
    b.   day care center
    c.   mixed day care
    d.   family day care
Answer: a, Reference: Chapter 11, P. 456, Difficulty: M

80.   According to 1993 statistics from the U. S. Bureau of the Census the least-used day
        care arrangement for children of working mothers is
        a.   family day-care
        b.   day-care centers
        c.   home care with a relative
        d.   home care with a babysitter
Answer: b, Reference: Chapter 11, P. 456, Difficulty: M

81.   Most family day care settings
        a.   are licensed
        b.   are unlicensed
        c.   use relatives to care for children
        d.   fail to provide home-like routines
Answer: b, Reference: Chapter 11, P. 456, Difficulty: E

82.   The most important factor in providing quality day care for 3- to 5-year-old
        children is
        a.   group size
        b.   the existence of rules
        c.   exposure to academics
        d.   the scheduling of activities
Answer: a, Reference: Chapter 11, P. 456, Difficulty: M

83.   Compared to a daycare center chosen by working-class parents, middle-class parents
        are more likely to choose a day care center which is
        a.   larger
        b.   smaller
        c.   less structured
        d.   more structured
Answer: c, Reference: Chapter 11, P. 458, Difficulty: D

84.   Most early research on day care
        a.   examined long term effects of day care
        b.   compared high and low quality day care
        c.   was conducted in university-affiliated day care centers
        d.   revealed a clear cut pattern of developmental effects of day care
Answer: c, Reference: Chapter 11, P. 458, Difficulty: M

85.   One limitation of day care research is that much of it has
        a.   ignored licensing criteria
        b.   focused only on long-term effects
        c.   involved cross-cultural comparisons
        d.   been conducted in university-affiliated centers
Answer: d, Reference: Chapter 11, P. 458, Difficulty: M

86. The intellectual development of children in day care
    a. has not been studied
    b. may be accelerated for low-income children
    c. is never as good as when children are cared for at home
    d. is normal for middle-class but not for low-income children
Answer: b, Reference: Chapter 11, P. 459, Difficulty: M

87. Compared to children who receive day care in other countries, children who receive daycare in the United States tend to be more
    a. polite
    b. dependent on adults
    c. independent of adults
    d. compliant with adults
Answer: c, Reference: Chapter 11, P. 460, Difficulty: D

88. In the United States, compared to children who do not receive day care, children receiving day care tend to be less
    a. self-sufficient
    b. independent
    c. socially knowledgeable
    d. agreeable and compliant with adults
Answer: d, Reference: Chapter 11, P. 460, Difficulty: M

89. At the age of 2 1/2, children in day care
    a. take turns
    b. generally ignore one another
    c. respond to adults rather than peers
    d. interact with each other as physical but not social objects
Answer: a, Reference: Chapter 11, P. 460, Difficulty: M

90. Children are likely to be rejected from a group which they are attempting to join if they
    a. do not ask questions
    b. ask inappropriate questions
    c. do not tell other's how they feel
    d. act as though they are already part of the group
Answer: b, Reference: Chapter 11, P. 460, Difficulty: M

91. When attempting to gain access to a group, most young children
    a. boldly enter the group
    b. will first linger on the periphery
    c. are likely to be admitted regardless of their overall popularity
    d. are accepted regardless of their understanding of the group activity
Answer: b, Reference: Chapter 11, P. 460, Difficulty: M

92.   A preschool girl who attempts to play with a group of boys
       a.   will be readily admitted if she is socially skillful
       b.   will have a difficult time being admitted to the group
       c.   will be admitted more easily than a boy attempting to play with girls
       d.   is equally as likely to be admitted to the group of boys as to a group of girls
Answer: b, Reference: Chapter 11, P. 460, Difficulty: D

93.   All of the following are likely outcomes of day care *except*
       a.   decrease in self-sufficiency
       b.   learning to become a desirable companion
       c.   increased compliance with parental wishes
       d.   behavior which conflicts with parental standards
Answer: a, Reference: Chapter 11, P. 460, Difficulty: M

94.   Nursery schools during the twentieth century developed
       a.   in response to increased childcare demands
       b.   in response to demands for better preschool nutrition
       c.   as a means of teaching middle-class children to read
       d.   as a means of promoting mastery within a sheltered environment
Answer: d, Reference: Chapter 11, P. 462, Difficulty: E

95.   In the example presented in the text Japanese preschool teachers differed from their
       American counterparts in that the Japanese teachers
       a.   thought disruptive behavior was a sign of intelligence
       b.   were far more tolerant of disruptive behavior among the children
       c.   thought smaller classrooms were needed to give children individualized
             attention
       d.   thought a larger classroom gave children different kinds of situations and
             taught them to get along in a group
Answer: d, Reference: Chapter 11, P. 462, Box 11.4, Difficulty: M

96.   For Japanese teachers "intelligence" is related to being
       a.   disobedient
       b.   well-behaved
       c.   individualistic
       d.   independent and assertive
Answer: b, Reference: Chapter 11, P. 463, Box 11.4, Difficulty: M

97.   Project Head Start
       a.   is internationally acclaimed for its success
       b.   preceded the War On Poverty by 15 years
       c.   assumed schooling was a social mechanism for success in society
       d.   was designed primarily to provide young parents with affordable day care
Answer: c, Reference: Chapter 11, P. 464, Difficulty: E

98.   The effectiveness of Project Head Start as a demonstration of the importance of preschool education
    a.   became known internationally
    b.   was equally true for both the summer and year-round programs
    c.   was minimized by all studies that looked at its long- term effects
    d.   was minimized because there was no control group against which the treatment group could be compared
Answer: d, Reference: Chapter 11, P. 464, Difficulty: D

99.   Longitudinal studies of the effectiveness of Head Start have shown that Head Start students
    a.   had lowered IQ scores when entering school
    b.   had lowered occupational aspirations while in high school
    c.   were less likely to be placed in remedial classes during high school
    d.   were no better at mathematics and reading than children who did not attend
Answer: c, Reference: Chapter 11, P. 465, Difficulty: M

100.   An extensive report prepared by Ron Haskins in 1989 on the effects of the Head Start Program suggest all of the following *except*
    a.   meaningful gains in intellectual performance
    b.   positive outcomes for later school achievement
    c.   meaningful gains in socioemotional performance
    d.   saving substantial taxpayer money that would otherwise have to be spent for special services
Answer: d, Reference: Chapter 11, P. 465, Difficulty: E

101.   Preschoolers can be viewed as similar to adults who are
    a.   poor
    b.   novices
    c.   socially retarded
    d.   mentally deprived
Answer: b, Answer: b, Reference: Chapter 11, P. 467, Difficulty: E

Essay Questions

1.   Describe how the factors in a child's life can be thought of as a "nested set of contexts." How might different levels of contexts reciprocally influence one another? Give examples.

2.   Compare and contrast the social behavior of Gussi children reared in Kenya with the social behavior of children reared in New England's Orchard Town.

3. Discuss how culture shapes the behavior of children to prepare them for life within their own societies. What evidence is there that cultural practices contribute to socialization?

4. Describe the limitations of Baumrind's study of parenting styles and children's behavior patterns. Explain.

5. Since parents contribute to their children's genotypes as well as their environments, how do we know if correlational data provided by Diana Baumrind and others indicate a causal role for parenting practices or whether the real causal agent is genetic? Use Scarr and McCartney's gene-environment interaction model to explain.

6. Describe two factors that contribute to the adoption of different parenting styles among parents of preschoolers. Cite examples and describe the research evidence.

7. Describe the three factors believed to contribute to the negative developmental effect of being raised by a young, unmarried mother. Explain each.

8. What are three of the immediate and long-term effects of divorce on a child's development? Explain.

9. Describe three possible reasons researchers have suggested for the general finding of lowered academic performance in children following a divorce. Explain.

10. How does a child's age at the time of their parents' divorce effect their adaptation to the changing family situation? Explain.

11. How do the family social structures of children whose parents hold working-class jobs differ from those whose parents hold middle-class jobs? What are the implications of these differences for research on parenting styles?

12. Describe the long-term effects of abuse and neglect on children. How can you explain these effects? Cite evidence when possible.

13. Describe the risk factors for abuse. Explain.

14. Describe the developmental consequences of child abuse in infancy. Explain.

15. What are the characteristics of children who are at risk for sexual abuse? Explain.

16. List the three strategies identified by the text for intervention into the lives of vulnerable families in order to reduce abuse. Explain.

17. What is an extended family? What important functions does it serve for many poor, minority children? Explain.

18. What techniques are used by television producers to capture children's attention? What techniques are used by television to create a story and how do they affect children's understanding of the story?

19. What are three problems associated with children's television viewing? What can parents do to improve the effects of television viewing on their children?

20. Discuss the effect of television as a model for behavior in young children. Give examples of real behaviors that have been shown to increase with viewing of television models.

21. How does the way children learn from books differ from the way they learn from television? Explain why is this is important.

22. How does a child's early experiences with books prepare her for learning literacy skills in school? Explain.

23. Describe the three types of day care most commonly used by working families, discussing their similarities and differences. Discuss three or more features that contribute to quality day care?

24. Discuss the effects of adequately staffed and equipped day care centers on the development of children's intellectual and social development. Cite research to substantiate your claims.

25. Describe Project Head Start. Explain why was it founded and what can be said about its effectiveness.

26. Discuss the assumptions of promoting social reform through early childhood education that led to the development of programs such as Project Head Start.

27. Contrast day care centers with preschools or nursery schools.

28. Even when people agree about data, they sometimes differ as to how useful it is. Using Project Head Start as an example, describe how and why people disagree in their conclusions about the importance of preschool education.

29. Cite evidence of television viewing as a positive force in the socialization of children.

30. What family dynamics affect the amount of sibling fighting?

31. How are Japanese and American views of intelligence different? What role might these views have on schooling? Explain.

32. Compare and contrast the "ideal" American and Japanese pre-school environment.

Cognitive and Biological Attainments of Middle Childhood

Multiple-Choice Questions

1. A child typically looses her first tooth at about how many years of age?
    a. 2
    b. 4
    c. 6
    d. 8
Answer: c, Reference: Chapter 12, P. 476, Difficulty: E

2. The event that signals a transition to more independence for the Ngoni of Malawi is the
    a. onset of walking
    b. loss of milk teeth
    c. beginning of puberty
    d. appearance of first words
Answer: b, Reference: Chapter 12, P. 476, Difficulty: M

3. A difference in the way the boys of the Ngoni of Malawi are treated compared to girls is that around age 6-7 they are
    a. held accountable for rude behavior
    b. expected to begin learning adult skills
    c. supposed to stop playing childish games
    d. expected to move into dormitories away from their mothers
Answer: d, Reference: Chapter 12, P. 476, Difficulty: M

4.   Which of the following accompanies the loss of baby teeth in a wide variety of
       cultures?
       a.   the development of preoperational thought
       b.   additional responsibilities imposed by adults
       c.   an increase in time spent supervised by adults
       d.   a move into dormitories away from their family
Answer: b, Reference: Chapter 12, P. 476, Difficulty: E

5.   Compared with preschoolers, the time that children in middle childhood spend with
       adults
       a.   remains constant
       b.   decreases slightly
       c.   increases markedly
       d.   decreases markedly
Answer: d, Reference: Chapter 12, P. 478, Difficulty: M

6.   Seven-year-olds such as Raymond Birch described in the text, spend one-third of
       their time in settings
       a.   such as daycare
       b.   supervised by adults
       c.   unsupervised by adults
       d.   more supervised than preschool settings
Answer: c, Reference: Chapter 12, P. 478, Difficulty: M

7.   At what age did Cornell, Heth, and Rowat (1992) find that children were able to find
       their way back across a university campus?
       a.   4 years
       b.   6 years
       c.   12 years
       d.   22 years
Answer: c, Reference: Chapter 12, P. 479, Box 12.1, Difficulty: M

8.   Cornell, Heth, and Broda (1989) found that 6-year-old children were better able to
       find their way back across a university campus when
       a.   told to glance back at their path
       b.   landmarks were pointed out to them
       c.   told they would have to lead the adult back
       d.   both told to glance back at their path and had landmarks pointed out
Answer: d, Reference: Chapter 12, P. 479, Box 12.1, Difficulty: M

9.   The number of children killed crossing the street each years is
    a.   twice the number reported for adults
    b.   four times the number reported for adults
    c.   three times the number reported for adults
    d.   the same as the number reported for adults
Answer: b, Reference: Chapter 12, P. 479, Box 12.1, Difficulty: M

10.   A study by Ampofo-Boateng and colleagues (1993) found that when children were
    asked to identify a safe route to cross the road, 11-year-old children were successful
    a.   25% of the time
    b.   50% of the time
    c.   75% of the time
    d.   almost all the time
Answer: c, Reference: Chapter 12, P. 479, Box 12.1, Difficulty: M

11.   A study by Ampofo-Boateng and colleagues (1993) found that children improved in
    their ability to identify a safe way to cross a busy street when
    a.   specifically trained to do so
    b.   they practiced independently
    c.   they observed others crossing safely
    d.   they practiced crossing with an adult observing them
Answer: a, Reference: Chapter 12, P. 479, Box 12.1, Difficulty: M

12.   During middle childhood, the average child grows about how many inches?
    a.   12
    b.   18
    c.   24
    d.   36
Answer: b, Reference: Chapter 12, P. 480, Difficulty: M

13.   During middle childhood, the average child gains about how many pounds?
    a.   20
    b.   30
    c.   40
    d.   50
Answer: d, Reference: Chapter 12, P. 480, Difficulty: M

14.   At which age will girls not be taller than boys?
    a.   4 1/2
    b.   6 1/2
    c.   8 1/2
    d.   9 1/2
Answer: d, Reference: Chapter 12, P. 480, Difficulty: D

15.   When nutrition is the same, the height of children
       a.   is the same regardless of ethnic origin
       b.   is determined by socio-cultural factors
       c.   depends, in part, on genetic background
       d.   is greater for Asian children than for African-American children
Answer: c, Reference: Chapter 12, P. 481, Difficulty: E

16.   Which of the following ethnic groups reaches adult height latest in development?
       a.   Asian
       b.   European
       d.   African American
       c.   American Caucasian
Answer: b, Reference: Chapter 12, P. 481, Difficulty: E

17.   Catch-up growth is an example of
       a.   canalization
       b.   reaction range
       c.   a socio-cultural effect
       d.   the effect of the environment
Answer: a, Reference: Chapter 12, P. 481, Difficulty: M

18.   Nigerian boys from well-off homes compared to those who were from poor homes
       were found to be
       a.   4 inches taller
       b.   12 inches taller
       c.   the same in height
       d.   only slightly taller
Answer: a, Reference: Chapter 12, P. 481, Difficulty: M

19.   Obesity in which age group is most likely to result in obesity in adulthood?
       a.   infancy
       b.   2- to 5-year-olds
       c.   3- to 9-year-olds
       d.   10- to 13-year-olds
Answer: d, Reference: Chapter 12, P. 482, Box 12.2, Difficulty: M

20.   A study by Stunkard and colleagues (1986) of Danish adoptees found a
       a.   weak correlation between adoptive parent and adopted child weight
       b.   strong correlation between adoptive parent and adopted child weight
       c.   weak correlation between biological parent and adopted child weight
       d.   strong correlation between biological parent and adopted child weight
Answer: d, Reference: Chapter 12, P. 482, Box 12.2, Difficulty: M

21.   One factor thought to contribute to obesity in children is that obese children
    a.   eat more than non-obese children
    b.   consume more calories from fat then non-obese children
    c.   have a diet higher in carbohydrates than non-obese children
    d.   consume more calories from protein than non-obese children
Answer: b, Reference: Chapter 12, P. 482, Box 12.2, Difficulty: M

22.   Successful programs for treating obesity in children
    a.   focus primarily on dieting
    b.   involve both parents and children
    c.   focus primarily on increasing activity
    d.   involve counseling efforts to provide alternative activities to eating
Answer: b, Reference: Chapter 12, P. 482, Box 12.2, Difficulty: M

23.   During middle childhood, boys are generally better than girls at
    a.   running
    b.   hopping
    c.   drawing
    d.   skipping
Answer: a, Reference: Chapter 12, P. 483, Difficulty: D

24.   During middle childhood, girls are generally better than boys at
    a.   jumping
    b.   catching
    c.   skipping
    d.   throwing
Answer: c, Reference: Chapter 12, P. 483, Difficulty: D

25.   Boys are most likely faster at running and better at throwing and catching than girls
    because
    a.   of genetic factors
    b.   boys are slightly larger
    c.   of cultural expectations
    d.   boys have more muscle mass
Answer: c, Reference: Chapter 12, P. 483, Difficulty: M

26.   All except which of the following provides evidence of biological changes in the
    brain during the onset of middle childhood?
    a.   increased melanization
    b.   changes in electrical activity
    c.   increases in the available neurotransmitters
    d.   decreases in alpha activity and increases in theta activity
Answer: d, Reference: Chapter 12, P. 483, Difficulty: D

27.   The synchronization of electrical activity of the brain is called
       a.   EEG rhymicity
       b.   EEG myelinization
       c.   EEG synchronicity
       d.   EEG coherence
Answer: d, Reference: Chapter 12, P. 483, Difficulty: M

28.   After about age 7, EEGs of children's brains show
       a.   more theta activity
       b.   more alpha activity
       c.   less alpha and theta activity
       d.   equal amounts of alpha and theta activity
Answer: b, Reference: Chapter 12, P. 483, Difficulty: D

29.   Which part of the brain coordinates planning and goal setting?
       a.   brain stem
       b.   cerebellum
       c.   hypothalamus
       d.   frontal lobes of the cortex
Answer: d, Reference: Chapter 12, P. 484, Difficulty: M

30.   All of the following represent changes seen in middle childhood except
       a.   an increase in brain size
       b.   marked increase in memory performance
       c.   increasing ability to carry out tasks independently
       d.   a shift from predominantly alpha activity to predominantly theta activity
Answer: d, Reference: Chapter 12, P. 484, Difficulty: D

31.   A study by Stauder and colleagues on conservation tasks found that
       a.   older but not younger children solved the tasks
       b.   brain activity was different in children who solved the task
       c.   brain activity was greatest immediately before children gave their responses
       d.   brain activity differed as a function of age, regardless of whether children
             could solve the task or not
Answer: b, Reference: Chapter 12, P. 484, Difficulty: D

32.   Which of the following challenges the theory that changes in brain growth causes
       specific changes in behavior?
       a.   Alpha waves begin to dominate theta waves at age 7.
       b.   Melanization spurts precede spurts in cognitive development.
       c.   People with frontal lobe damage experience difficulty maintaining goals.
       d.   Brains can become more complex as a result of being in more challenging
             situations.
Answer: d, Reference: Chapter 12, P. 484, Difficulty: D

33. According to Piaget, an operation is
    a. a qualitatively new form of remembering
    b. an abstract manipulation of formal thought
    c. a way of increasing one's own knowledge base
    d. an internalized mental action coordinated with others
Answer: d, Reference: Chapter 12, P. 485, Difficulty: E

34. Concrete operations are called "concrete" because
    a. they are not reversible
    b. they are "hard" to perform
    c. they are performed on real objects
    d. in order to perform them, children must suppress visual imagery
Answer: c, Reference: Chapter 12, P. 485, Difficulty: M

35. All of the following are characteristic of the thought processes of middle childhood, according to Piaget, except
    a. thinking that includes consideration of alternatives
    b. the ability to manipulate abstract ideas and symbols
    c. the ability to mentally retrace steps when problem solving
    d. the understanding that transformations in appearance do not change the basic properties of number, mass, and volume
Answer: b, Reference: Chapter 12, P. 485, Difficulty: D

36. Concrete operations are reflected in
    a. increased aggressive behaviors
    b. the appearance of symbolic play
    c. the ability to form groups of similar objects
    d. the ability to see things from another's point of view
Answer: d, Reference: Chapter 12, P. 485, Difficulty: M

37. When 3-year-olds attempting to master a liquid conservation task are asked if there is more liquid in the taller beaker, they
    a. focus on a single attribute
    b. try to coordinate height and width
    c. answer yes only because they cannot express what they really mean
    d. decenter if shown that the liquid will be the same when poured back into the original container
Answer: a, Reference: Chapter 12, P. 488, Difficulty: M

38.   According to Piaget's observations, most children transitional for developing liquid conservation
        a.   usually traverse this state at age 2
        b.   usually traverse this state at age 8
        c.   are still unaware that they need to consider both the height and width of the container
        d.   know that height and width are important but have difficulty keeping both in mind simultaneously
Answer: d, Reference: Chapter 12, P. 488, Difficulty: D

39.   According to Piaget, conservation of liquid first appears around the age of
        a.   3-4 years
        b.   5-6 years
        c.   7-8 years
        d.   9-10 years
Answer: c, Reference: Chapter 12, P. 488, Difficulty: M

40.   Children who understand liquid conservation know that
        a.   reversibility does not apply to liquids
        b.   it is logically necessary for the amount of liquid to remain the same
        c.   one dimension such as height cannot compensate for another such as width
        d.   that one-to-one correspondence is a property of liquids poured from one beaker to another
Answer: b, Reference: Chapter 12, P. 488, Difficulty: E

41.   A father pours a glass of milk for his daughter. The daughter wants more so the father pours the milk from a short, fat glass into a tall, thin one. The daughter is not amused and asks for a bigger glass. The daughter
        a.   is able to reason abstractly
        b.   has reached, at least, the preoperational stage
        c.   has reached, at least, the formal operational stage
        d.   has reached, at least, the concrete operational stage
Answer: d, Reference: Chapter 12, P. 488, Difficulty: D

42.   The concept of identity in the context of a conservation task refers to
        a.   the ability to reverse a mental operation
        b.   children's knowledge of their own gender
        c.   a mental operation in which children know that one dimension can compensate for another
        d.   a mental operation in which children know that changes in appearance do not change the amounts involved
Answer: d, Reference: Chapter 12, P. 488, Difficulty: M

43.   When asked to justify her statement that there is the same amount of water as before in a taller, thinner container, a child who can conserve liquid quantity and argues on the basis of compensation might say

    a.   "You didn't add or take anything away."

    b.   "This glass is taller but it's also skinnier."

    c.   "It's still the same water, so it's still the same amount."

    d.   "If you pour the water back into the first glass it will still go up to the same level."

Answer: b, Reference: Chapter 12, P. 488, Difficulty: D

44.   When children say "the liquid is higher but the glass is thinner" to explain why quantities have not changed in a conservation of liquid task, they are demonstrating the mental operation of

    a.   identity

    b.   negation

    c.   reversibility

    d.   compensation

Answer: d, Reference: Chapter 12, P. 488, Difficulty: M

45.   Piaget's concept of reversibility refers to the

    a.   mental operation of identity

    b.   understanding that one operation can negate another

    c.   ability to understand numbers in spite of physical transformation

    d.   he physical gross motor skills required for children to learn to walk backward

Answer: b, Reference: Chapter 12, P. 488, Difficulty: E

46.   Conservation of number refers to the ability to

    a.   count the number of items in two or more rows

    b.   assign number words to written number symbols and objects

    c.   recognize that the last number counted is the total number of items

    d.   recognize one-to-one correspondence between two sets of objects in spite of spatial rearrangements

Answer: d, Reference: Chapter 12, P. 488, Difficulty: M

47.   Children who do not understand the principle of conservation

    a.   can look systematically but do so very slowly

    b.   can look systematically at a display if first instructed to do so

    c.   look systematically at different parts of a display they are viewing

    d.   look as if their attention was captured by a single feature of a display

Answer: d, Reference: Chapter 12, P. 488, Difficulty: D

48.   As part of a conservation-of-number task, a child counts the same number of items in each of two rows but says that the experimenter's longer row has more. When asked why, her most likely response is
       a.   "because I can move them back"
       b.   "because the number is the same"
       c.   "because they are still the same cards"
       d.   "because this row goes all the way here"
Answer: d, Reference: Chapter 12, P. 489, Difficulty: E

49.   Gelman demonstrated that 3- and 4-year-old children can conserve if
       a.   the set size is small
       b.   other children model correct responses
       c.   different numbers are associated with a winner and a loser
       d.   they are given feedback from examiners about the accuracy of their responses
Answer: c, Reference: Chapter 12, P. 490, Difficulty: E

50.   Alternative interpretations of children's failures in conservation tasks have focused on
       a.   the difficulty of the task
       b.   the sex of the experimenter
       c.   the school experiences of the child
       d.   children's belief that adults repeat questions if the initial answer is wrong
Answer: d, Reference: Chapter 12, P. 492, Difficulty: M

51.   Which of the following provides evidence that Piaget overstated preschoolers' inability to conserve?
       a.   an experiment by Ginsburg in which cards were rearranged within rows
       b.   the failure of training to improve preschoolers' performance on conservation tasks
       c.   Siegal's study of the reasons children gave to explain other children's conservation judgments
       d.   the fact that children aged 6 or 7 never become confused when asked to make number conservation judgments
Answer: c, Reference: Chapter 12, P. 492, Difficulty: D

52.   When children organize their stamp collections they often use
       a.   a single criteria
       b.   multiple criteria
       c.   properties of identity
       d.   the concept of one-to-one correspondence
Answer: b, Reference: Chapter 12, P. 493, Difficulty: E

53. Grouping baseball cards according to league, team, and position represents a
    a. conservation of categories
    b. classification system typically used by preschoolers
    c. task that is too difficult for children in middle childhood
    d. multiple classification system as used by children in middle childhood

Answer: d, Reference: Chapter 12, P. 493, Difficulty: E

54. A common element underlying concrete operational tasks is the
    a. ability to talk about abstract ideas
    b. ability to reverse simultaneous operations
    c. ability to think simultaneously about two aspects of a thing
    d. inability of children under the age of 10 to perceive more than one dimension

Answer: c, Reference: Chapter 12, P. 493, Difficulty: M

55. Preschoolers presented with a class inclusion problem asking whether there are " more dogs or more dachshunds" in a group of animals consisting of two cats, three poodles, and five dachshunds are likely to
    a. find the problem easy because the numbers are small
    b. find the problem easy because the categories consist of animals
    c. answer "more dachshunds than dogs" when asked which category is larger
    d. answer" more dogs than dachshunds" when asked which category is larger

Answer: c, Reference: Chapter 12, P. 493, Difficulty: M

56. The ways in which of preschoolers think about class inclusion problems makes it
    a. easy for them to communicate effectively
    b. impossible for them to cluster objects into groups
    c. difficult for them to reason systematically about objects
    d. easy for them to understand relationships between parts and wholes

Answer: c, Reference: Chapter 12, P. 494, Difficulty: E

57. Studies attempting to explain the difficulty preschool children have in class inclusions problems as a problem with communication have found that asking "are there more black cows or sleeping cows" found that
    a. no children showed any improvement
    b. about half the 4- to 6-year-old children improved
    c. most 4- to 6-year-old children answered correctly
    d. most 4- to 6-year-old children answered incorrectly

Answer: d, Reference: Chapter 12, P. 493, Difficulty: E

58. The ability to understand classification is substantial by which stage?
    a. sensorimotor
    b. preoperational
    c. concrete operational
    d. formal operational

Answer: c, Reference: Chapter 12, P. 493, Difficulty: E

59.   Multiple classification enables children to
       a.   learn classification before the age of 5
       b.   limit their thinking to a single dimension
       c.   make the transition from early to middle childhood
       d.   think systematically about relationships between things
Answer: d, Reference: Chapter 12, P. 493, Difficulty: E

60.   The mature concept necessary for comprehending the balance beam problem is
       called
       a.   torque
       b.   identity
       c.   reversibility
       d.   compensation
Answer: a, Reference: Chapter 12, P. 494, Difficulty: E

61.   Which theoretical framework do the studies by Siegler on balance beam reasoning
       in children represent?
       a.   learning
       b.   constructivist
       c.   information processing
       d.   biological-maturational
Answer: c, Reference: Chapter 12, P. 495, Difficulty: E

62.   How many rules did Siegler identify that children sequentially use in their approach
       to the balance beam problem?
       a.   2
       b.   3
       c.   4
       d.   6
Answer: c, Reference: Chapter 12, P. 495, Difficulty: E

63.   Siegler found that when he tested children of various ages on the balance beam
       problem,
       a.   few of the 13–17-year-olds had mastered the concept of torque
       b.   most of the 13–17-year-olds had mastered the concept of torque
       c.   by 10 years of age most children had mastered the concept of torque
       d.   none of the children even at the oldest ages had mastered the concept of
             torque
Answer: a, Reference: Chapter 12, P. 495, Difficulty: D

64.   When 4- and 5-year-olds are shown ambiguous pictures, they are
       a.   able to interpret both alternatives immediately
       b.   unable to see multiple features until after their reasoning improves
       c.   are able to see more than one interpretation after both alternatives are
             pointed out
       d.   unable to see more than one interpretation even when both alternatives are
             pointed out to them
Answer: d, Reference: Chapter 12, P. 496, Box 12.3, Difficulty: D

65.   According to Siegler, children are the least consistent in replying to the balance
       beam problem if they have a rule for
       a.   weight only
       b.   the torque concept
       c.   weight and distance, without understanding torque
       d.   weight, with the expectation that if weights are equal distance is important
Answer: c, Reference: Chapter 12, P. 496, Difficulty: D

66.   Siegler found that his notions of rules for solving the balance beam problem allowed
       him to predict that
       a.   the number of problems solved would increase with age
       b.   in certain situations 5-year-olds would correctly answer more problems than
             17-year-olds
       c.   children with a certain rule for the balance beam problem would classify
             objects in certain specific ways
       d.   the same child could use more than one rule and her choice of rule to apply
             could vary from one trial to the next
Answer: b, Reference: Chapter 12, P. 496, Difficulty: M

67.   On a memory task for the balance beam problem Siegler found that
       a.   5-year-olds encoded distance but not weight
       b.   5-year-olds encoded weight but not distance
       c.   8-year-olds encoded distance but not weight
       d.   8-year-olds encoded weight but not distance
Answer: b, Reference: Chapter 12, P. 496, Difficulty: M

68.   Siegler gave training experiences to children on the balance beam problem and
       found that
       a.   5- but not 8-year-old children profited from training
       b.   8- but not 5-year-old children profited from training
       c.   both 5- and 8-year-old children profited from training
       d.   neither 5- nor 8-year-old children profited from training
Answer: b, Reference: Chapter 12, P. 497, Difficulty: M

69.   A study by Susan Carey (1985) found that
  a.   7-year-old children judge animal behavior on the basis of biological category
  b.   7-year-old children judge animal behavior in terms of their similarity to humans
  c.   10-year-old children judge animal behavior in terms of their similarity to humans
  d.   both 7- and 10-year-old children judge animal behavior on the basis of biological category
Answer: b, Reference: Chapter 12, P. 497, Difficulty: M

70.   A study by Frank Kiel (1992) found that when provided with a meaningful biological context for questions
  a.   4-year-old children become more accurate in judging animal behavior
  b.   4-year-old children still use similarity to humans to judge animal behavior
  c.   10-year-old children continue to use biological category to judge animal behavior
  d.   7-year-old children are transitional in whether the information assists their judgements of animal behavior
Answer: a, Reference: Chapter 12, P. 497, Difficulty: M

71.   Memory span tasks measure
  a.   STM
  b.   LTM
  c.   metamemory
  d.   sensory memory
Answer: a, Reference: Chapter 12, P. 498, Difficulty: M

72.   Robbie Case believes that improved memory performance in middle childhood is accounted for by an increase in
  a.   vocabulary
  b.   memory size
  c.   efficiency of memory
  d.   number of digits that can be remembered
Answer: c, Reference: Chapter 12, P. 498, Difficulty: M

73.   Cross cultural research comparing digit span performance of U.S. children to Chinese children 4 to 6 years of age showed that
  a.   neither group of children were capable of digit span tasks
  b.   the U.S. children were superior in digit span performance
  c.   the Chinese children were superior in digit span performance
  d.   the children from both countries were comparable in their performance
Answer: c, Reference: Chapter 12, P. 499, Difficulty: M

74. The shorter Chinese words for the digits may be the reason that Chinese 4- to 6-year-olds out-performed 4- to 6-year-olds from the United States. This provides evidence for which view of expanded memory capacity in middle childhood?
    a. a physically larger frontal lobe
    b. greater efficiency in information processing capabilities
    c. increase in ability to hold information in working memory
    d. an increase in knowledge about things children try to remember
Answer: b, Reference: Chapter 12, P. 499, Difficulty: D

75. Chi compared the memories of 10-year-old chess buffs with college-age chess novices and found that
    a. college students were more accurate in all areas
    b. college students used spatially oriented memory strategies
    c. performance for chess arrangements was the same for both groups
    d. 10-year-olds were more accurate at remembering chess arrangements
Answer: d, Reference: Chapter 12, P. 499, Difficulty: D

76. Chi and Koeske read lists of dinosaur names to a 4 1/2-year-old child and found that the best-remembered names were the ones that
    a. were most novel
    b. the child learned first
    c. were most familiar to the child
    d. were positioned at the beginning and ends of the lists
Answer: c, Reference: Chapter 12, P. 500, Difficulty: M

77. Memory strategies
    a. are rarely seen until adolescence
    b. lead to better memory performance
    c. are too complex for use by preschool age children
    d. are unplanned activities that occur spontaneously in middle childhood
Answer: b, Reference: Chapter 12, P. 500, Difficulty: M

78. Elementary memory strategies have been observed in children as young as
    a. 18 months
    b. 3 years
    c. 5 years
    d. 7 years
Answer: a, Reference: Chapter 12, P. 500, Difficulty: D

79. It does not appear that children create and use strategies for remembering until the age of
     a. 3 years
     b. 5 years
     c. 7 years
     d. 10 years
Answer: c, Reference: Chapter 12, P. 500, Difficulty: M

80. Psychologists' use of the term "rehearsal" refers to
     a. the ability to follow complex directions
     b. the role-playing games preschoolers play
     c. self-repetition of material to be remembered
     d. the way preschoolers repeatedly perform the same actions.
Answer: c, Reference: Chapter 12, P. 500, Difficulty: M

81. Psychologists have found that teaching 5-year-olds to rehearse material they are given to remember
     a. is impossible
     b. does not improve their memory performance
     c. brings their memory performance up to the level of older children
     d. is only helpful to children who are already able to rehearse on their own
Answer: c, Reference: Chapter 12, P. 501, Difficulty: E

82. The grouping of to-be-remembered items in meaningful chunks is called
     a. rehearsal
     b. clustering
     c. metamemory
     d. memory organization
Answer: d, Reference: Chapter 12, P. 501, Difficulty: E

83. Which of the following sequences of words is most representative of the way a child in middle childhood would recall words from a list?
     a. hat-bat
     b. dog-cat
     c. cat-milk
     d. milk-glass
Answer: b, Reference: Chapter 12, P. 501, Difficulty: E

84. Metamemory refers to
     a. knowledge about the process of remembering itself
     b. the ability to remember exceptionally large numbers of items
     c. memory that occurs before the onset of concrete operations
     d. a hypothesis that undermines the concept of qualitatively different memory during middle childhood
Answer: a, Reference: Chapter 12, P. 501, Difficulty: E

85.   Which of the following is true regarding the development of metamemory?
   a.   Metamemory appears late in middle childhood
   b.   Metamemory first appears in the preschool years
   c.   Even 5-year-olds have some metamemory ability
   d.   We rarely see any sign of metamemory before age 8
Answer: c, Reference: Chapter 12, P. 501, Difficulty: E

86.   Which of the following is true of metamemory?
   a.   Before the age of 8, children have no understanding of their own memory processes
   b.   When shown a set of 10 pictures, 5-year-olds know they cannot remember all of them
   c.   5- and 8-year-olds have approximately equivalent knowledge of their own memory abilities
   d.   5-year-olds have some understanding of their own memory process but not as much as 8-year-olds
Answer: d, Reference: Chapter 12, P. 501, Difficulty: E

87.   When 5-year-olds and 8-year-olds are shown a set of pictures and asked if they will be able to remember them
   a.   both the 5-year-olds and the 8-year-olds assert their ability to remember the pictures
   b.   neither the 5-year-olds nor the 8-year-olds have confidence in their ability to remember the pictures
   c.   the 5-year-olds typically assert their ability to remember all the pictures, but the 8-year-olds say that they will not
   d.   the 5-year-olds typically say they will not be able to remember all of the pictures, and the 8-year-olds say that they will
Answer: c, Reference: Chapter 12, P. 501, Difficulty: M

88.   Fabricius and Hagen found that 6- and 7-year-old children who used an organizational strategy to help them remember
   a.   used the strategy on all trials
   b.   used the strategy in another session
   c.   were aware that the strategy helped their memory
   d.   used the strategy in another session only if they were aware that it helped them
Answer: d, Reference: Chapter 12, P. 502, Difficulty: M

89.   Similar memory strategies will be used by both preschoolers and children aged 7 to
        8 years when
        a.   preschoolers are trained to play chess
        b.   familiar and simplified materials are used
        c.   children are trained in metamemory strategies
        d.   preschoolers are given unlimited time to study the materials
Answer: b, Reference: Chapter 12, P. 502, Difficulty: D

90.   Which statement is most correct regarding cognitive changes characteristic of the
        transition to middle childhood when assessed by standard procedures?
        a.   cross cultural research supports the universality of these changes
        b.   many children in non-industrialized societies do not display these changes
        c.   cross cultural research is inconclusive about the universality of these changes
        d.   children from non-industrialized societies display these changes before
                children in industrialized societies
Answer: b, Reference: Chapter 12, P. 503, Difficulty: D

91.   One source of difficulty in cross-cultural conservation studies is that
        a.   intellectual development is poor in nonindustrial societies
        b.   people being tested fail to understand what is expected of them
        c.   training can only be done by members of the same culture as those being
                tested
        d.   the justifications children from other cultures give when they understand
                conservation differs from those given American children
Answer: b, Reference: Chapter 12, P. 504, Difficulty: E

92.   The finding of Pierre Dasen and his colleagues that even when aboriginal children
        were trained, their performance on conservation tasks lagged behind the
        performance of children from Canberra,
        a.   proves that training has no benefit
        b.   suggests that aboriginal children would be ill advised to move to Canberra
        c.   proves that language is a problem for understanding conservation problems
        d.   suggests that aboriginal culture does not provide a great deal of practice
                relevant to the concept of conservation
Answer: d, Reference: Chapter 12, P. 505, Difficulty: M

93.   In attempting to understand why some cultures lag behind others in the onset of
        concrete operations, psychologists have found that
        a.   native testers sometimes deliberately mislead the children they are testing
        b.   specialized training for children is necessary if the time lag is to be eliminated
        c.   training might be unnecessary and the lags might disappear if the testers are
                from the same culture as the children they are testing
        d.   native testers are unable to follow the flexible questioning procedure
                necessary for the clinical interview technique to be successful
Answer: c, Reference: Chapter 12, P. 505, Difficulty: M

94.   A cross cultural study by Raphael Nyiti (1982) comparing performances of 10- and
      11-year-old children from different cultural groups on a conservation task, suggests
      that developmental lags may be due to
      a.   parenting style
      b.   previous training
      c.   differences in quality of school instruction
      d.   inadequate experimenter/subject communication
Answer: d, Reference: Chapter 12, P. 506, Difficulty: M

95.   Cross cultural studies of conservation have found that
      a.   the attainment of conservation appears to be universal
      b.   in the absence of specific training, conservation fails to develop
      c.   the attainment of conservation is found only among children who have
            attended school
      d.   there are some societies in which no one ever develops an understanding of
            conservation
Answer: a, Reference: Chapter 12, P. 506, Difficulty: E

96.   Which of the following most accurately summarizes the findings of cross cultural
      studies of cognitive development?
      a.   concrete operations are not universal
      b.   concrete operations appear universal but are affected by variations in task
            familiarity
      c.   the ability to perform concrete operational tasks is unaffected by variations in
            culture
      d.   only children who have been to school can successfully solve concrete
            operational problems
Answer: b, Reference: Chapter 12, P. 506, Difficulty: D

97.   Michael Cole and his colleagues studied the memory performance tribal children of
      rural Liberia on a free recall task of items in four distinct categories. They found
      a.   use of categories to aid recall
      b.   comparable performance to U.S. school children of the same age
      c.   little improvement in performance of nonschooled children after the age of
            10
      d.   no difference in memory performance compared with children in
            industrialized Liberian societies
Answer: c, Reference: Chapter 12, P. 507, Difficulty: M

98.   When Michael Cole and his colleagues presented to be remembered items in a story instead of a list in random order, nonschooled Liberian children
   a.   recalled items easily
   b.   used simple memory strategies
   d.   used categories to remember the items
   c.   were aware that longer stories would be more difficult to remember
Answer: a, Reference: Chapter 12, P. 508, Difficulty: E

99.   When familiarity of materials is accounted for in cross cultural studies of memory
   a.   categorical memory always improves
   b.   cross cultural memory differences disappear
   d.   schooling has no effect on free recall performance
   c.   specific types of remembering associated with activities in each culture becomes more apparent
Answer: d, Reference: Chapter 12, P. 508, Difficulty: D

100.   One conclusion that can be drawn from cross cultural research on middle childhood is that
   a.   culture-specific contexts are major factors in development
   b.   culture-specific contexts have little effect on children during the period of middle childhood
   d.   differences in memory performance across cultures remain large even when materials are organized in meaningful ways
   c.   differences in memory performance across cultures are minimized when the materials to be remembered are randomly constructed lists
Answer: a, Reference: Chapter 12, P. 508, Difficulty: D

101.   Which statement most accurately reflects current thinking about middle childhood?
   a.   it is a distinctive stage of development
   b.   cognitive changes that occur in middle childhood are universal
   d.   changes in adult behavior toward children entering middle childhood occur in every culture
   c.   a change in adult behavior toward children entering middle childhood only occurs in industrialized societies
Answer: c, Reference: Chapter 12, P. 508, Difficulty: D

Essay Questions

1.   Parent's expectations of children in middle childhood are different from their expectations of younger children. Describe three of the daily activities of middle childhood that exemplify these changed expectations.

2.   Describe the general patterns of growth that occur in middle childhood.

3.   Describe the biological changes that take place in the brain between the ages of 5 and 7. How might these changes account for observed behavioral changes during middle childhood? Explain.

4.   Explain the correlation between increased mental capacity and the competence with which children in middle childhood meet increased parental expectations?

5.   Cite evidence that brain growth and maturation are responsible for the changes in behavior that occur during middle childhood. Can this evidence be interpreted to mean that brain growth and maturation cause specific behavioral changes? Why or why not?

6.   What alternate explanations have been given for young children's lack of demonstration of conservation ability. Address the traditional research paradigm used to assess conservation.

7.   How does Piaget define operation? Give an example.

8.   Define conservation. Describe a task that might be used to ascertain whether a child can conserve. Explain.

9.   What is the most important criticism of Piaget's procedures in identifying conservation abilities of children? Explain.

10.   Describe the characteristics of concrete operational thought. How do these characteristics contribute to changes in children's behavior and adult expectations during middle childhood?

11.   According to Piaget, there are 3 mental operations that a child might describe which demonstrate an understanding of unchanged quantities in conservation experiments. List and briefly define each.

12.   Describe a class inclusion problem. Explain how a 5-year-old and an 8-year-old each might answer a question comparing subordinate and superordinate levels of the hierarchy.

13.   List and describe several ways that concrete operations manifest themselves as abilities in children during middle childhood.

14.   Describe Siegler's analysis of the balance beam problem. What rules do children use? How do the rules used affect errors they make on different sets of balance beam problems?

15. What memory differences has Siegler noted between 5- and 8-year-olds on the balance beam problem? How do these relate to the rules they use? How are children of these ages affected by training on the balance beam problem?

16. What four factors appear to create the differences in memory performance between early and middle childhood? Provide a brief explanation of each and how it might account for memory differences.

17. What is a "free-recall" task? How do children from different cultures differ in these tasks? Explain.

18. What did Gustav Jahoda find when he compared the abilities of Scotch and Zimbabwean children to act as shopkeepers? What are the implications of his findings? Explain.

19. Compare and contrast the results of cross cultural tests of memory with cross cultural tests of concrete operational thinking. What conclusions about universal mental processes can be made from each type of test?

20. What is metamemory? When does it appear in cognitive development?

21. How does an increased knowledge base contribute to improvements in memory? Provide an example from the work of Michelene Chi.

22. What is the relationship between metamemory and memory? Explain.

23. How does memory capacity or ability develop during middle childhood? Explain.

24. What is a memory strategy? Give an example. Describe the development of strategies during the middle childhood period.

25. Describe the strategy of memory organization. When is it likely to appear in the memory work of children?

26. Describe cross cultural differences in the acquisition of conservation. What factors are important in evaluating children from non-industrialized cultures?

27. Describe cultural differences in memory. What factors are involved in memory ability in non-industrialized cultures?

28. What makes children obese? Explain.

Schooling and Development in Middle Childhood

Multiple-Choice Questions

1. Most young Americans spend more than ___ hours being educated before entering the work force.
   a. 5,000
   b. 15,000
   c. 25,000
   d. 50,000
Answer: b, Reference: Chapter 13, P. 514, Difficulty: D

2. The deliberate teaching of children to pass on knowledge, information, and skills is called
   a. teaching
   b. education
   c. socialization
   d. a0prenticeship
Answer: b, Reference: Chapter 13, P. 515, Difficulty: E

3. The form of job preparation in which a novice spends an extended period of time working for an adult master and learning the trade on the job has historically been known as:
   a. education
   b. apprenticeship
   c. work experience
   d. on-the-job-training
Answer: b, Reference: Chapter 13, P. 516, Difficulty: E

4.   Currently in the industrial world, most children acquire proficiency in adult skills through
      a.   education
      b.   apprenticeship
      c.   work experience
      d.   on-the-job-training
Answer: a, Reference: Chapter 13, P. 516, Difficulty: E

5.   Formal education differs from informal education in all of the following except
      a.   social organization
      b.   the motives for learning
      c.   helps prepare children for adult life
      d.   the social relations of pupil and teacher
Answer: c, Reference: Chapter 13, P. 516, Difficulty: M

6.   Formal education differs from apprenticeships in which of the following areas?
      a.   apprenticeship includes explicit instruction in target skills
      b.   formal education includes explicit instruction in target skills
      c.   apprenticeship is much less closely woven into the fabric of the society than is education
      d.   formal education includes a much closer social bond between the teacher and student than typically exists between the apprentice and master
Answer: a, Reference: Chapter 13, P.516, Difficulty: E

7.   Schooling is a specialized form of child-rearing that is
      a.   universal
      b.   constant throughout history
      c.   an historically old development
      d.   specific to certain societies and historical eras
Answer: d, Reference: Chapter 13, P. 516, Difficulty: D

8.   Historically, which of the following was the first precursor of modern literacy
      a.   cuneiform writing
      b.   training of scribes
      c.   bronze implements
      d.   symbols on sheets like papyrus
Answer: a, Reference: Chapter 13, P. 517, Difficulty: M

9.   With regard to language, an important function of written symbols is that they
      a.   make it understandable
      b.   allow language to be taught to children
      c.   allow language to operate over time and space
      d.   prevent the meaning of language from changing over time
Answer: c, Reference: Chapter 13, P. 517, Difficulty: M

10. Schooling arose in response to
    a. a need to teach writing
    b. a historical need to care for children
    c. recognition of children's language learning abilities
    d. the change from hunting and gathering to subsistence farming
Answer: a, Reference: Chapter 13, P. 517, Difficulty: D

11. The earliest schools were places where young men were brought together for the purpose of
    a. learning to hunt
    b. becoming scribes
    c. learning a primitive form of medicine
    d. training for contests of physical strength
Answer: b, Reference: Chapter 13, P. 517, Difficulty: M

12. What we now consider education was once
    a. prohibited
    b. available to everyone
    c. restricted to the upper class
    d. delivered by family members
Answer: c, Reference: Chapter 13, P. 517, Difficulty: M

13. One of the problems facing modern teachers is
    a. there is more to teach than previously
    b. education is more widely available than previously
    c. students are more curious and demanding than previously
    d. reading has changed significantly and is more difficult to learn than previously
Answer: a, Reference: Chapter 13, P. 518, Difficulty: E

14. Historically the focus of education has been
    a. math and science
    b. reading and religion
    c. religion and morality
    d. reading and mathematics
Answer: d, Reference: Chapter 13, P. 519, Difficulty: E

15. Most psychologists agree that reading is a
    a. simple decoding skill
    b. skill closely related to math skills
    c. method of communication easily learned
    d. complex skill requiring the coordination of interrelated sources of information
Answer: d, Reference: Chapter 13, P. 519, Difficulty: E

16.   A writing system in which the symbols stand for words or ideas is called
       a.   syllabic
       b.   phonemic
       c.   alphabetic
       d.   ideographic
Answer: d, Reference: Chapter 13, P. 519, Difficulty: M

17.   A writing system in which the symbols stand for sound or parts of words is called
       a.   syllabic
       b.   phonemic
       c.   alphabetic
       d.   ideographic
Answer: a, Reference: Chapter 13, P. 519, Difficulty: M

18.   A writing system in which the symbols stand for sounds is called
       a.   syllabic
       b.   phonemic
       c.   alphabetic
       d.   ideographic
Answer: c, Reference: Chapter 13, P. 519, Difficulty: M

19.   The learning of the sound-letter rules is the core of the task in learning
       a.   writing
       b.   reading
       c.   meaning
       d.   language
Answer: b, Reference: Chapter 13, P. 520, Difficulty: M

20.   When children learn to decode they are learning
       a.   to read
       b.   to speak
       c.   to write the symbols of their language
       d.   correspondence between the letters of their alphabet and the sound of the
             language
Answer: d, Reference: Chapter 13, P. 520, Difficulty: M

21.   Which of the following skills is basic to leaning to read?
       a.   spelling
       b.   seeing syllables
       c.   hearing phonemes
       d.   blending phonemes
Answer: c, Reference: Chapter 13, P. 520, Difficulty: M

22. The inability to break words into their component syllables and phonemes predicts
    a. poor spelling
    b. difficulty in speaking
    c. difficulty in learning to read
    d. difficulty in learning to write
Answer: c, Reference: Chapter 13, P. 520, Difficulty: M

23. Practice speaking "pig Latin" is apparently useful in learning
    a. to read
    b. to spell
    c. the alphabet
    d. a second language
Answer: a, Reference: Chapter 13, P. 520, Difficulty: M

24. Benita Blachman's implementation of exercise in linking sounds and letters with special language analysis exercises resulted in
    a. no noticeable effects
    b. children who were above grade level in reading
    c. children who could pronounce words but could not read
    d. an improvement in reading for elementary school children
Answer: b, Reference: Chapter 13, P. 520, Difficulty: M

25. One difficulty facing children who are learning to read English is that
    a. letters are pronounced differently in different contexts
    b. the blending of phonemes sound like words but are not
    c. letters are always pronounced the same even in different situations
    d. phonemes are easier to hear and understand in isolation than when embedded in a word or sentence
Answer: a, Reference: Chapter 13, P. 521, Difficulty: M

26. Which of the following is an example of "bottom-up" processing?
    a. identifying letters
    b. understanding the meaning of an ambiguous passage
    c. using information for interpretation based on prior knowledge
    d. learning letters, then words, then phrases, then sentences, then paragraphs, etc.
Answer: d, Reference: Chapter 13, P. 521, Difficulty: D

27. Jody was able to make sense out of the sentence because she was very familiar with music. This is an example of
    a. decoding of words
    b. top-down processing
    c. bottom-up processing
    d. guessing the meaning of a word before it is decoded
Answer: b, Reference: Chapter 13, P. 521, Difficulty: D

28. All of the following statements about reading comprehension are true except
    a. the process that results in reading comprehension proceed from the "bottom up"
    b. "top down" information is needed for meaningful reading and results in reading comprehension
    c. "top down" processing integrates the reader's prior knowledge with the information from the words and phrases
    d. "Bottom up" processing means learning letters, then words, then phrases, then sentences, then paragraphs, etc

Answer: a, Reference: Chapter 13, P. 521, Difficulty: D

29. In reading, which of the following is best accomplished by "top-down" processing?
    a. identifying letters and phonemes
    b. sounding out a word phonetically
    c. understanding the meaning of an ambiguous passage
    d. careful enunciation of individual words in a sentence

Answer: c, Reference: Chapter 13, P. 521, Difficulty: M

30. When we have a well worked out script for an activity being discussed in a reading passage, we benefit from
    a. a phoneme
    b. "top down" information
    c. "bottom up" information
    d. fluid analysis of the words

Answer: b, Reference: Chapter 13, P. 524, Difficulty: M

31. If readers can decode all words in a passage, then they can understand the
    a. meaning of the passage
    b. intent of the author in writing the passage
    c. meaning of the passage by "bottom-up" processing alone
    d. meaning of the passage only if they can imagine what it is about

Answer: d, Reference: Chapter 13, P. 524, Difficulty: M

32. The transition which children experience in approximately third or fourth grade is best characterized as beginning to read
    a. syllabically
    b. phonetically
    c. for meaning
    d. word by word

Answer: c, Reference: Chapter 13, P. 524, Table 13.1, Difficulty: M

33. The term "multiple viewpoints" is used to describe a
    a. type of reading encountered in high school textbooks
    b. type of reading encountered during Jean Chall's stage 3
    c. method of reading instruction designed to teach children to decode text
    d. method of reading instruction that was popular early in the twentieth century
Answer: a, Reference: Chapter 13, P. 524, Table 13.1, Difficulty: D

34. What did Jean Chall call the stage in learning to read in which a reader is required to reconcile different opinions in order to understand the meaning of a passage?
    a. ungluing
    b. multiple viewpoints
    c. confirmation and fluency
    d. construction and reconstruction
Answer: b, Reference: Chapter 13, P. 524, Table 13.1, Difficulty: M

35. According to Jean Chall, the first stage of learning to read involves
    a. sounding out the individual letters of a word
    b. the ability to interpret events on the basis of partial signs
    c. being able to blend together the sounds that comprise a word
    d. being able to scan alphabetic print and understand what it says
Answer: b, Reference: Chapter 13, P. 525, Difficulty: M

36. According to Jean Chall, being able to recognize the logo of a fast food restaurant
    a. occurs only when children are literate
    b. might be a first step in learning to read
    c. occurs later in the process of learning to read
    d. is an example of "bottom up" processing alone
Answer: b, Reference: Chapter 13, P. 525, Difficulty: D

37. According to Jean Chall's stage theory of reading acquisition, the basic task of stage 1 is
    a. decoding
    b. "ungluing"
    c. prereading
    d. learning the letters
Answer: d, Reference: Chapter 13, P. 525, Difficulty: E

38. According to Jean Chall, children in stage 3 of learning to read
    a. use only "top-down" processing
    b. read letter by letter and word by word
    c. experience what Chall calls "ungluing"
    d. are using reading to learn something new
Answer: d, Reference: Chapter 13, P. 525, Difficulty: D

39.   When children can first think about a topic while they are reading about it they are
       in which of Chall's stages of reading?
       a.   stage 1
       b.   stage 2
       c.   stage 3
       d.   stage 4
Answer: c, Reference: Chapter 13, P. 525, Difficulty: M

40.   Researchers disagree about how to best accomplish decoding for reading. All of the
       following are beliefs about decoding except
       a.   reading means guessing at what a word means before it is decoded
       b.   decoding is best accomplished when children are drilled on sound-letter
             correspondence
       c.   children will naturally figure out decoding patterns if they learn to recognize
             enough words
       d.   step one of decoding is to learn the arbitrary set of alphabet letters and their
             correspondence to the sounds of spoken language
Answer: a, Reference: Chapter 13, P. 526, Difficulty: M

41.   According to Jean Chall, knowing when to skim, reread, or take notes occurs
       a.   when students are learning to do more than decode text
       b.   by the time readers are exposed to multiple viewpoints
       c.   during the transition from "learning to read" to reading for meaning"
       d.   during the same stage in which readers are constructing their own knowledge
Answer: d, Reference: Chapter 13, P. 525, Difficulty: D

42.   Word attack skills would be most important during which of Chall's reading
       acquisition stages
       a.   1 & 2
       b.   2 & 3
       c.   3 & 4
       d.   4 & 5
Answer: a, Reference: Chapter 13, P. 525, Difficulty: M

43.   Recent opponents to emphasizing decoding claim
       a.   decoding is not important or necessary to read
       b.   anyone can learn to read even without learning letter sounds
       c.   if a parent reads enough to a child, the child will know how to read
       d.   the narrow focus on decoding may cause some children to give up trying to
             read for meaning
Answer: d, Reference: Chapter 13, P. 526, Difficulty: E

44. A "Whole-language" curriculum for teaching reading
    a. does not teach phonics
    b. teaches reading in isolated lessons
    c. emphasizes decoding as a first step
    d. is a comprehension-based alternative to the code-emphasis-first approach

Answer: d, Reference: Chapter 13, P. 526, Difficulty: E

45. The main task in whole language curriculums is
    a. decoding
    b. top-down processing
    c. bottom-up processing
    d. maintaining children's interest in reading

Answer: d, Reference: Chapter 13, P. 526, Difficulty: E

46. When a teacher and small group of students read silently through a portion of text and then take turns leading a discussion of its meaning, this is known as
    a. reciprocal teaching
    b. integrated teaching
    c. collaborative teaching
    d. individualized teaching

Answer: a, Reference: Chapter 13, P. 526, Difficulty: E

47. Probably the main reason reciprocal teaching is effective is because
    a. every child feels important in the process
    b. teachers decide on the topics to be discussed
    c. teachers and children model the behaviors necessary for comprehension
    d. children are reinforced when they later try to teach the material to their parents

Answer: c, Reference: Chapter 13, P. 527, Difficulty: M

48. Reciprocal teaching involves all of the following except
    a. reading out loud
    b. summarizing material
    c. figuring out what the text means
    d. asking questions about the content

Answer: a, Reference: Chapter 13, P. 527, Difficulty: E

49. Reciprocal teaching is an example of
    a. transition learning
    b. concrete operations
    c. bio-social-behavioral shift
    d. a zone of proximal development

Answer: d, Reference: Chapter 13, P. 527, Difficulty: M

50.   In which of the following does a child participate in a cognitive activity before he or
        she has mastered the full set of abilities for that activity?
        a.   the horizontal dècalage
        b.   bio-social-behavioral shift
        c.   discontinuous development
        d.   zone of proximal development
Answer: d, Reference: Chapter 13, P. 527, Difficulty: M

51.   The "zone of proximal development" is an idea most associated with which of the
        following theorists?
        a.   Freud
        b.   Piaget
        c.   Vygotsky
        d.   G. Stanley Hall
Answer: c, Reference: Chapter 13, P. 527, Difficulty: E

52.   The effect of reciprocal teaching on children's reading skills is a
        a.   slowly acquired, durable increase in skills
        b.   rapidly acquired, durable increase in skills
        c.   slowly acquired, temporary increase in skills
        d.   rapidly acquired, but short-lived increase in skills
Answer: b, Reference: Chapter 13, P. 527, Difficulty: D

53.   In general, research on reading comprehension makes all of the following points
        except
        a.   decoding is irrelevant to mature reading
        b.   decoding needs to be integrated into the process of comprehension
        c.   relatively simple procedures can make a large difference in learning outcomes
        d.   reciprocal teaching is an effective means to produce marked improvement in
                reading and other school subjects
Answer: a, Reference: Chapter 13, P. 527, Difficulty: M

54.   Learning mathematics requires the acquisition and coordination of all of the
        following kinds of knowledge except
        a.   utilization
        b.   procedural
        c.   conceptual
        d.   formal operational
Answer: d, Reference: Chapter 13, P. 527, Difficulty: E

55. According to Gelman, Meck, and Merkin (1986) the knowledge that underlies a problem is
   a. utilization knowledge
   b. conceptual knowledge
   c. procedural knowledge
   d. automatized knowledge
Answer: b, Reference: Chapter 13, P. 527, Difficulty: M

56. You would know if a particular method would apply in a particular situation if you had
   a. utilization knowledge
   b. conceptual knowledge
   c. procedural knowledge
   d. automatized knowledge
Answer: a, Reference: Chapter 13, P. 527, Difficulty: D

57. Early school mathematics
   a. is limited to drill and practice
   b. is limited to learning to count, add, and subtract
   c. builds on children's prior knowledge of numbers
   d. has been virtually ignored by educational researchers
Answer: c, Reference: Chapter 13, P. 527, Difficulty: D

58. Adding a number and then subtracting the same number does not change the original number. This is known as
   a. utility
   b. inversion
   c. procedure
   d. transitive knowledge
Answer: b, Reference: Chapter 13, P. 527, Difficulty: M

59. The principle which asserts that adding a number to a given quantity and then subtracting it leaves the total unchanged is not usually understood until the age of
   a. 7 years
   b. 9 years
   c. 11 years
   d. 13 years
Answer: c, Reference: Chapter 13, P. 528, Difficulty: M

60.   Robert Siegler has suggested that children's knowledge of mathematics instruction develops in such a way that _____ is essential to master the procedures of addition, subtraction and other mathematical operations.
      a.   written ability
      b.   reading ability
      c.   finger counting
      d.   use of strategies
Answer: d, Reference: Chapter 13, P. 528, Difficulty: M

61.   The superior performance of child street vendors in Brazil on arithmetic problems involving transactions of goods the children were selling is an example of
      a.   utilization knowledge
      b.   conceptual knowledge
      c.   procedural knowledge
      d.   computational knowledge
Answer: a, Reference: Chapter 13, P. 528, Difficulty: D

62.   The use of one's body as a counting device
      a.   is a universal strategy
      b.   is a hindrance in learning to count
      c.   limits children who want to count beyond 20
      d.   is used by children from a limited number of cultures found in the Pacific Islands
Answer: a, Reference: Chapter 13, P. 528, Difficulty: E

63.   The superior performance of child street vendors in Brazil on arithmetic problems involving transactions of goods the children were selling
      a.   was specific to the market situation
      b.   involved pencil and paper calculations
      c.   was based on a general conceptual skill
      d.   was replicated by good arithmetic skills in other contexts
Answer: a, Reference: Chapter 13, P. 529, Difficulty: D

64.   What technique for teaching mathematics did Thorndike emphasize ?
      a.   place value
      b.   code emphasis
      c.   drill and practice
      d.   meaningful problems
Answer: c, Reference: Chapter 13, P. 529, Difficulty: M

65.   The advantage of drill and practice is that it
    a.   generalizes well to new materials
    b.   provides rapid and automatic learning
    c.   promotes understanding of underlying mathematical principals
    d.   teaches children to rely on past knowledge for meaningful interpretations of problems
Answer: b, Reference: Chapter 13, P. 529, Difficulty: M

66.   Modern school mathematics curricula emphasize
    a.   drill and practice
    b.   meaningful problems
    c.   recitation and rote memorization
    d.   a balance between drill, practice and the use of meaningful problems
Answer: d, Reference: Chapter 13, P. 529, Difficulty: E

67.   The purpose of instructional discourse is
    a.   finding out the answer to a question
    b.   providing curriculum stimulated information
    c.   direct instructions of concepts and procedures
    d.   the social reinforcement of appropriate behavior
Answer: b, Reference: Chapter 13, P. 532, Difficulty: E

68.   When a teacher asks a student to give an answer that the teacher already knows, the teacher is using
    a.   drill and practice
    b.   practical knowledge
    c.   instructional discourse
    d.   metacognitive discourse
Answer: c, Reference: Chapter 13, P. 532, Difficulty: M

69.   If a teacher asks a student, "What does this say?" the teacher
    a.   is providing an evaluation
    b.   is using instructional discourse
    c.   probably can not see the word
    d.   is engaging the child in conversation
Answer: b, Reference: Chapter 13, P. 532, Difficulty: M

70.   Instructional discourse often takes the form of
    a.   initiation-evaluation-reply
    b.   evaluation-initiation-reply
    c.   initiation-reply-evaluation
    d.   evaluation-reply-initiation-reply
Answer: c, Reference: Chapter 13, P. 532, Difficulty: D

71.   The language use of children who attend school
       a.   occurs in isolation from its referents
       b.   rarely requires children to learn abstract concepts
       c.   does not differ from that of children who do not attend school
       d.   is less abstract that the language of children who don't attend school
Answer: a, Reference: Chapter 13, P. 532, Difficulty: M

72.   Learning to read numbers is more complex than learning to read words because
       a.   number symbols are more concrete than letter symbols
       b.   for each number students must learn a word, a numeric symbol, and the
             corresponding abstract concept
       c.   there is no prior real-world knowledge children can bring to the classroom to
             help them learn about number
       d.   children must learn to "unglue" themselves from the early body-reference
             systems they use in learning number
Answer: b, Reference: Chapter 13, P. 533, Difficulty: D

73.   When comparing the cognitive performances of children who have attended school
       with those who have not, it is possible to
       a.   specify the role of the schooling in intelligence
       b.   evaluate the role of schooling in the workplace
       c.   specify the contributions of schooling to cognitive development
       d.   demonstrate the dependence of cognitive development on schooling
Answer: c, Reference: Chapter 13, P. 534, Difficulty: E

74.   The number of children who enter school in the U.S. not able to speak or
       understand English is about
       a.   500, 000
       b.   1,000,000
       c.   1,750,000
       d.   2,500,000
Answer: d, Reference: Chapter 13, P. 534, Box 13.3, Difficulty: E

75.   The issue of how to educate U. S. children whose native language is not English is
       made difficult because
       a.   very few schools have set up "English only" programs
       b.   there are so few non-English speaking children to study
       c.   it is not possible to set up a true experiment to study the question
       d.   the approach to teaching these children is the same all over the country so
             that there is no comparison group
Answer: c, Reference: Chapter 13, P. 534, Box 13.3, Difficulty: D

76.   According to Krashen and Biber, the best way to teach English to all children who speak another language at home is
        a.   an English-only approach
        b.   initial teaching in the native language
        c.   teaching in the native language with translation
        d.   a true bilingual approach, that is, teaching in two languages at the same time
Answer: b, Reference: Chapter 13, P. 534, Box 13.3, Difficulty: M

77.   Which of the following did Krashen and Biber not identify as a characteristic of successful programs to teach English to non-native speakers in the elementary schools?
        a.   teaching of English as a second language
        b.   a strong foundation of literacy in the first language
        c.   high-quality teaching of subject matter in the child's first language
        d.   teaching part of the day in English and part of the day in the child's first language
Answer: d, Reference: Chapter 13, P. 535, Box 13.3, Difficulty: M

78.   Current research on how first and second language learning should be sequenced favors
        a.   teaching both languages simultaneously
        b.   immersing the child in the new language
        c.   waiting until the child has completely mastered the first language before teaching the second
        d.   acquiring basic skills in a child's first language and gradually shifting instruction to the new language
Answer: d, Reference: Chapter 13, P. 535, Box 13.3, Difficulty: D

79.   The biggest problem facing schools in the U.S. with large minority populations in trying to establish bilingual programs is
        a.   finding teachers who speak a second language
        b.   exposing majority children to minority languages
        c.   coping with the linguistic variety in the classrooms
        d.   locating minority children who are currently not attending school
Answer: c, Reference: Chapter 13, P. 535, Box 13.3, Difficulty: E

80.   The school cutoff strategy
        a.   is used to limit the total number of children in any one class
        b.   is used to assess the impact of schooling with age held constant
        c.   helps to determine when a particular child is ready to attend school
        d.   is effective in determining when formal education should be terminated
Answer: b, Reference: Chapter 13, P. 536, Difficulty: E

81.   When measured by language and memory skills, schooling
       a.   contributes to general cognitive performance
       b.   actually inhibits general cognitive functioning
       c.   does not contribute to general cognitive performance
       d.   contributes to cognitive performance if the materials used for evaluation are different from those used in school
Answer: a, Reference: Chapter 13, P. 536, Difficulty: D

82.   When measured by performance on Piagetian tasks, schooling
       a.   contributes to general cognitive performance
       b.   actually inhibits general cognitive functioning
       c.   does not contribute to general cognitive performance
       d.   contributes to cognitive performance if the materials used for evaluation are different from those used in school
Answer: c, Reference: Chapter 13, P. 536, Difficulty: D

83.   The work of Bisanz (1989) that examined children's responses to a standard Piagetian test of number conservation where children were asked to add small numbers found that performance
       a.   in mental arithmetic improved largely as a function of age
       b.   in mental arithmetic improved largely as a function of schooling
       c.   on the conservation task improved largely as a function of schooling
       d.   on the conservation task and mental arithmetic improved largely as a function of schooling
Answer: b, Reference: Chapter 13, P. 536, Difficulty: D

84.   Recent research has supported Piaget's belief that the ability to conserve quantity
       a.   develops without any special instruction
       b.   develops only with some formal schooling
       c.   develops before children enter the formal education system
       d.   is not usually developed in normal children before age 10 years
Answer: a, Reference: Chapter 13, P. 536, Difficulty: M

85.   Which of the following is relatively unaffected by schooling?
       a.   fluency
       b.   memory
       c.   concrete operations
       d.   metacognitive skills
Answer: c, Reference: Chapter 13, P. 536, Difficulty: M

86. Studies comparing the concrete operational performance of children who have attended school with those who have not find that schooling
    a. always improves performance
    b. does not accelerate performance
    c. decreases children's ability to talk with unfamiliar adults
    d. increases children's familiarity with the circumstances of testing

Answer: d, Reference: Chapter 13, P. 537, Difficulty: M

87. The effect of schooling on children's lexicons is that those who have attended school are more
    a. sensitive to noncategorical organizations
    c. likely to organize their lexicons thematically
    b. likely to associate words like "duck" and "fly"
    d. likely to associate words like "duck" and "chicken"

Answer: d, Reference: Chapter 13, P. 537, Difficulty: D

88. When Sharp and his colleagues studied nonliterate Mayan farmers, they found that the farmers
    a. did not distinguish categories like "duck" and "fowl"
    c. distinguished between animal categories but not between verb categories such as "eat" and "swim"
    b. knew the categories "duck" and "fowl" but did not use the categories spontaneously in a free-association test
    d. used the categories "duck" and "fowl" in a free-association test but were unable to label them correctly when talking about their own animals

Answer: c, Reference: Chapter 13, P. 537, Difficulty: D

89. Schooling appears to sensitize children to
    a. complex social forms of a society
    b. the abstract, categorical meanings of words
    c. the varied associations that words can have
    d. an appreciation for real-life practical knowledge

Answer: b, Reference: Chapter 13, P. 537, Difficulty: M

90. Compared to American school children, memory performance in school children from other cultures
    a. is consistently higher across age groups than that of American schoolchildren
    b. is lower than that of American school children or unschooled age mates from their own villages
    c. is closer to that of American children than to the performance of non-schooled age mates from their own villages
    d. is closer to that of unschooled age mates from their own village than to the performance of American school children

Answer: c, Reference: Chapter 13, P. 537, Difficulty: M

91.   When Wagner compared memory for location among Mayan children with that skill in U.S. children, he found that
    a.   schooling led to improved memory for children in both cultures
    b.   schooling made no difference in children's memory for location
    c.   improvement in memory was not associated with increased rehearsal
    d.   schooling improved the memories of the American but not the Mayan children
Answer: a, Reference: Chapter 13, P. 537, Difficulty: D

92.   When studying memory for location among schooled and nonschooled children, Wagner found that the pattern of improvement for educated children
    a.   varied across cultures
    b.   was the same as that uneducated children
    c.   did not seem to be related to using rehearsal strategies
    d.   was the pattern expected if they were using rehearsal strategies
Answer: d, Reference: Chapter 13, P. 538, Difficulty: D

93.   When Rogoff and Wadell placed objects to be remembered in a diorama of the subjects own town, they found that
    a.   schooled children remembered only categorical items
    b.   schooling enhanced children's memory for the objects
    c.   unschooled children were much better at remembering the objects
    d.   schooled and unschooled children's memory performance was the same
Answer: d, Reference: Chapter 13, P. 538, Difficulty: E

94.   Which of the following describes the effect of schooling on memory?
    a.   Schooling has no effect on memory
    b.   Schooling increases children's overall memory capacity
    c.   Schooling appears to teach children strategies for remembering
    d.   Schooling has no effect on the ability to reflect on one's own memory
Answer: c, Reference: Chapter 13, P. 538, Difficulty: E

95.   The ability to explain the reason that one thinks in the way that her or she does is called
    a.   metacognition
    b.   lexical awareness
    c.   metalinguistic awareness
    d.   formal operational thought
Answer: a, Reference: Chapter 13, P. 538, Difficulty: E

96.   Educated Vai people from Liberia could judge grammatical correctness of phrases but were unable to explain the basis of their judgment. This can be explained by the impact of schooling on
    a.   metacognition
    b.   lexical organization
    c.   utilization knowledge
    d.   procedural knowledge
Answer: a, Reference: Chapter 13, P. 538, Difficulty: D

97.   When Scribner and Cole compared the abilities of educated and uneducated Vai people to judge the grammatical correctness of sentences, they found that
    a.   both groups did equally well
    b.   this metacognitive task was too difficult for both groups
    c.   the literate Vai were much better able to identify grammatical sentences
    d.   the illiterate Vai were much better able to identify ungrammatical sentences
Answer: a, Reference: Chapter 13, P. 538, Difficulty: D

98.   Perhaps the most important effect of schooling on development is that
    a.   schooling teaches people to respect their peers
    b.   schooling is a gateway to power and status outside school
    c.   schooling changes basic cognitive processes so that we think about the world differently
    d.   basic cognitive processes are changed to become more like those basic processes described by Piaget
Answer: b, Reference: Chapter 13, P. 539, Difficulty: D

99.   All of the following are true of intelligence except
    a.   modern tests are able to measure intelligence precisely
    b.   the meaning of intelligence varies somewhat from one culture to another
    c.   the concept of intelligence is used to explain differences in school performance
    d.   all languages have terms that describe people's abilities in ways that are collectively called "intelligence"
Answer: a, Reference: Chapter 13, P. 540, Difficulty: M

100.   Early tests for aptitude were developed to
    a.   register men for the draft
    b.   assist children in apprenticeship programs
    c.   classify employees on the basis of intelligence
    d.   determine the causes and cures for children who seemed unable to learn
Answer: d, Reference: Chapter 13, P. 541, Difficulty: E

101.   Binet and Simon developed a test designed to
    a.   measure the intellectual capacity of preschoolers
    b.   measure the intelligence of the French population
    c.   find those children who were mentally subnormal
    d.   find those children who were especially advanced in their abilities
Answer: c, Reference: Chapter 13, P. 540, Difficulty: E

102.   One of Binet and Simon's contributions was to provide a test that
    a.   is culture free
    b.   defines intelligence
    c.   identifies and measures the component skill that are present at birth in
            children
    d.   matches a progression of cognitive tasks to the ages at which most children
            can accomplish these tasks.
Answer: d, Reference: Chapter 13, P. 541, Difficulty: E

103.   All of the following were tasks Binet and Simon asked children to perform as part of
        an intelligence test except
    a.   identify missing parts of a picture
    b.   draw a picture of their feelings while in school
    c.   follow directions while keeping several components in mind at once
    d.   manipulate numbers by recalling random digits and counting backwards from
            20
Answer: b, Reference: Chapter 13, P. 541, Difficulty: M

104.   Which concept did Binet and Simon create to characterize mental subnormality?
    a.   mental age
    b.   deviation IQ
    c.   mental retardation
    d.   intelligence quotient
Answer: a, Reference: Chapter 13, P. 541, Difficulty: E

105.   Stanford psychologist, Lewis Terman, modified the Binet - Simon scales in an effort
        to
    a.   make 100 the average score
    b.   determine the origins of mental giftedness
    c.   measure the intelligence of World War I draftees
    d.   compare the performances of American and French school children
Answer: b, Reference: Chapter 13, P. 541, Difficulty: E

106.   The psychologist who developed an adult intelligence scale was
    a.   Binet
    b.   Stern
    c.   Terman
    d.   Wechsler
Answer: d, Reference: Chapter 13, P. 542, Difficulty: E

107.   Who introduced the concept of IQ?
    a.   Alfred Binet
    b.   William Stern
    c.   Lewis Terman
    d.   David Wechsler
Answer: b, Reference: Chapter 13, P. 542, Difficulty: E

108.   A child with a mental age of 9 and a chronological age of 10 would have an IQ of
    a.   90
    b.   100
    c.   109
    d.   111
Answer: a, Reference: Chapter 13, P. 542, Difficulty: D

109.   To account for the fact that mental development is more rapid early in life than later psychologists use
    a.   mental age
    b.   deviation IQ
    c.   chronological age
    d.   developmental quotient
Answer: b, Reference: Chapter 13, P. 543, Difficulty: M

110.   Intelligence tests are composed of questions that
    a.   are always culture-free
    b.   form a progression of difficulty
    c.   are selected so as to be unrelated to school performance
    d.   will be answered in the same way by all children at one age level
Answer: b, Reference: Chapter 13, P. 543, Difficulty: M

111.   Unlike other early psychologists, V.A. C. Henmon thought high intelligence scores were only associated with
    a.   success in life
    b.   social competence
    c.   school performance
    d.   the person's genetic heritage
Answer: c, Reference: Chapter 13, P. 544, Difficulty: D

112.   The man who proposed a theory of multiple intelligences including musical and
        spatial intelligence is
        a.   Louis Terman
        b.   Louis Thurstone
        c.   Howard Gardner
        d.   Robert Sternberg
Answer: c, Reference: Chapter 13, P. 544, Difficulty: E

113.   Gardner has
        a.   argued for the unity of intelligence
        b.   redefined the way IQ scores are calculated
        c.   agreed on the specific components of intelligence
        d.   attempted to identify multiple components of intelligence
Answer: d, Reference: Chapter 13, P. 544, Difficulty: M

114.   Arthur Jensen's published objections to the Head Start program argued that Head
        Start
        a.   was a program designed for teachers, not children
        b.   teachers were mostly members of minority groups
        c.   funding was inadequate because the funding level was too low to provide the
                level of intervention that the children needed
        d.   could not work because the children served did not have the genetical ability
                to perform the mental processes necessary in school
Answer: d, Reference: Chapter 13, P. 546, Difficulty: M

115.   Arthur Jensen is a proponent of which hypothesis of intelligence?
        a.   innatist
        b.   scholastic
        c.   cultural-context
        d.   environmentalist
Answer: a, Reference: Chapter 13, P. 546, Difficulty: M

116.   Currently, most scholars take a position on the variation in intelligence test scores
        that are
        a.   innatist
        b.   contextual
        c.   interactionist
        d.   environmentalist
Answer: c, Reference: Chapter 13, P. 546, Difficulty: E

117. The modern view of intelligence is best characterized by which statement?
    a. IQ is primarily a reflection of a person's genotype.
    b. IQ is primarily a reflection of a person's environment.
    c. IQ is the result of the interaction between a person's genotype and the environment.
    d. None of the above; there is little or no agreement about the roles of genes and the environment among modern psychologists.

Answer: c, Reference: Chapter 13, P. 546, Difficulty: E

118. A problem with comparisons designed to measure intellectual differences between identical and fraternal twins raised in different environments is
    a. intelligence can not be measured
    b. finding identical and fraternal twins
    c. finding a situation in which the environments are exactly comparable
    d. finding a situation in which the difference between environments is large enough to lead to a difference in outcome

Answer: d, Reference: Chapter 13, P. 547, Difficulty: D

119. Ask a !Kung child how many fingers he or she has on each hand and the child may not know. Ask an American child of the same age and he or she knows. A French child identifies Napoleon's tomb easily. An American child has no idea what it is. These examples illustrate the importance of _____ on intelligence testing.
    a. culture
    b. memory
    c. schooling
    d. reasoning

Answer: a, Reference: Chapter 13, P. 547, Difficulty: D

120. Which of the following is true of culture-free tests?
    a. They are pictorial.
    b. There are none that are generally satisfactory.
    c. They are language free and rely on graphic representations.
    d. They use written materials translated into the test-taker's native language.

Answer: b, Reference: Chapter 13, P. 548, Difficulty: E

121. To say that 25 percent of the IQ scores of native Martians is determined by genetics means that
    a. 25 percent of the total scores are attributable to genotype
    b. 25 percent of each Martian's score is attributable to genotype
    c. 25 percent of the variation in a group of scores can be attributed to genotype
    d. 75 percent of the individual scores are attributable to Martian environmental factors

Answer: c, Reference: Chapter 13, P. 548, Difficulty: D

122. While the degree of heritability of intelligence is still in dispute, a notable summary of data by Plomin (1990) estimates that _____ of the variation in test performance within population groups is controlled by genetic factors.
      a.   25%
      b.   50%
      c.   75%
      d.   90%
Answer: b, Reference: Chapter 13, P. 549, Difficulty: D

123. When the average heritability of a trait is the same within groups,
      a.   the two groups should be identical with respect to that trait
      b.   the average difference between groups must be the same as well
      c.   the average difference between groups cannot be caused by genetic factors
      d.   differences between groups may be caused by differences in the two environments
Answer: d, Reference: Chapter 13, P. 549, Difficulty: D

124. The IQ scores of African American children, adopted by white middle-class families, are
      a.   nearly identical to the national average
      b.   identical to the expected scores for the black population
      c.   used as evidence for the importance of genotype in determining IQ
      d.   nearly the same whether the children were adopted at birth or after one year of age
Answer: a, Reference: Chapter 13, P. 550, Difficulty: E

125. The Brooks-Gun and associates (1995) study of African American and White low birth weight children revealed that
      a.   age of the child and birth weight played a role in IQ
      b.   when environments were equated, IQ differences almost disappeared
      c.   all the variability in IQ could be explained by environmental differences
      d.   the white children had higher IQs no matter what the developmental environment
Answer: b, Reference: Chapter 13, P. 550, Difficulty: M

126. The classroom teaching technique which encouraged cooperation among young Hawaiian children is described in the text as being
      a.   culture sensitive
      b.   traditional teaching
      c.   a loosening of standards
      d.   an unsuccessful classroom technique
Answer: a, Reference: Chapter 13, P. 551, Difficulty: M

127. Research on Cambodian, Vietnamese, and Laotian refugee children who were relocated to the U.S. during the 1970's and 1980's suggest that the majority of these students
    a. failed to stay enrolled in U.S. schools
    b. were successful in both educational and economic endeavors
    c. did not complete schooling but were economically successful
    d. were academically successful but could not translate the accomplishment into economic success
Answer: b, Reference: Chapter 13, P. 551, Difficulty: M

128. Which of the following variables does not account for the success of refugee immigrants?
    a. parents' commitment to education
    b. parents who read to their children
    c. English literacy skills of the parents
    d. parental involvement in the completion of homework
Answer: c, Reference: Chapter 13, P. 551, Difficulty: D

129. The basic classroom teaching technique in Liberia is
    a. rote recitation
    b. lecture and testing
    c. reciprocal teaching
    d. cooperative learning
Answer: a, Reference: Chapter 13, P. 552, Box 13.4, Difficulty: M

130. Harold Steven son's study of mathematics performance in three cultures revealed that the most likely reason for the Japanese superiority over the Americans was
    a. the time on task in school
    b. the education al level of the teachers
    c. the educational level of the parents of the children
    d. Japanese schools pay their teachers more hence attract better teachers
Answer: a, Reference: Chapter 13, P. 552, Box 13.4, Difficulty: D

131. Research comparing the performance of Japanese, Taiwanese, and American classrooms has suggested a number of approaches to bring American children to the level of performance of their Asian counterparts. The most promising seems to be
    a. to assign more homework
    b. to lengthen the school year
    c. a shift to small group activities
    d. a shift to teacher-led whole group lessons
Answer: b, Reference: Chapter 13, P. 553, Box 13.4, Difficulty: D

132. Labov and Robbins compared the reading scores of school age children who were members of a peer group with those who were not. They found that the influences of a peer group
    a.   only effect students from minority groups
    b.   are minimal after the elementary school years
    c.   can have a powerful effect on general cognitive development
    d.   can have a powerful negative effect on students' academic achievements
Answer: d, Reference: Chapter 13, P. 554, Difficulty: D

133. When studying the effect of peer group participation on a school's success, William Labov and Clarence Robbins found
    a.   physical size, toughness, and fighting skill had nothing to do with group prestige
    b.   reading was a skill that was important to the group when it was used outside of school
    c.   the values of the groups they studied were incompatible with the values of the schools
    d.   the reading scores of nongroup members showed virtually no improvement as the group progressed through the grades
Answer: c, Reference: Chapter 13, P. 554, Difficulty: D

134. In a study of male peer groups in Harlem Labov and Robbins found that
    a.   reading was rarely if ever used outside of the school
    b.   all children in grades 4 to 10 were members of a gang
    c.   peer-group activity had no influence on school activity
    d.   skill with language was not a part of peer group activities
Answer: a, Reference: Chapter 13, P. 554, Difficulty: E

135. Margarita Azmitia and Marion Perlmutter (1989) found that collaborative work among school age children
    a.   is a fad which is likely to pass
    b.   is unsuitable for this age group
    c.   is interesting for students but produces negligible effects
    d.   is helpful in improving children's problem solving abilities
Answer: d, Reference: Chapter 13, P. 554, Difficulty: E

136. Which of the following was found to be true of immigrant Asian households?
    a.   the more children in the family the higher the grade point average
    b.   the more children in the family the higher the school drop out rate
    c.   the fewer number of children in the family the higher the grade point average
    d.   the fewer number of children in the family the higher the school drop out rate
Answer: a, Reference: Chapter 13, P. 554, Difficulty: M

137. After comparing secondary schools in central London Michael Rutter and his colleagues concluded that
    a. schooling has no impact on the achievements of inner-city youth
    b. successful schools are more modern and have higher paid teachers
    c. differences in schools can have a profound impact on students' academic success
    d. peer pressure is more important than the quality of schools in determining students' academic success
Answer: c, Reference: Chapter 13, P. 555, Difficulty: M

138. In a large-scale study of secondary schools in London, Michael Rutter found that successful schools were characterized by which of the following?
    a. they were more modern
    b. they had better trained teachers
    c. they expected students to master academic subjects
    d. they had teachers with better pay and better training
Answer: c, Reference: Chapter 13, P. 555, Difficulty: M

139. Pupils attain higher levels of achievement in schools when the schools
    a. emphasized academic achievement and assigned more homework
    b. recognized that school was not an important part of students' lives
    c. were willing to spend more money on bulletin boards and supplies
    d. de-emphasized the importance of academic achievement and assigned less homework
Answer: a, Reference: Chapter 13, P. 555, Difficulty: M

140. The most effective teachers
    a. are better trained and more highly paid
    b. stop their classes often in order to discipline promptly
    c. do not expect their students to work quietly and independently
    d. coordinate and manage different activities, allowing some students to work independently
Answer: d, Reference: Chapter 13, P. 555, Difficulty: M

141. Punishment _____ in the most successful classrooms, according to Michael Rutter and his colleagues.
    a. has no place
    b. should be as frequent as praise
    c. should be less frequent than praise
    d. should be more frequent than praise
Answer: c, Reference: Chapter 13, P. 555, Difficulty: E

142.   Rosenthal and Jacobsen found that children who were singled out as "bloomers"
   a.   showed no increase in IQ scores if they were Mexican- American
   b.   showed increases in IQ scores only if they were Mexican-American
   c.   had post test IQ scores an average 15 points higher than their pretest scores
   d.   did no better than their classmates who had not been identified as "bloomers"
Answer: c, Reference: Chapter 13, P. 556, Box 13.5, Difficulty: E

143.   One explanation for the failure to replicate the Rosenthal and Jacobson results is that some teachers
   a.   ignore the most capable children
   b.   give extra help to the most capable children
   c.   ignore those children from whom they expect little
   d.   focus attention on children they believe more capable
Answer: a, Reference: Chapter 13, P. 557, Box 13.4, Difficulty: E

144.   The feedback that teachers give to children is
   a.   rarely based on prior expectations
   b.   often different for boys than for girls
   c.   rarely based on the behavior of the children themselves
   d.   independent of the children's expectations of themselves
Answer: b, Reference: Chapter 13, P. 557, Box 13.4, Difficulty: E

145.   All of the following are typical of teachers' expectations except
   a.   boys are more likely to challenge classroom decorum
   b.   teachers' expectations are independent of children's behavior
   c.   elementary school girls are better behaved than their male counterparts
   d.   teachers have lower expectations for poor children than for those from middle class families
Answer: b, Reference: Chapter 13, P. 557, Box 13.4, Difficulty: M

146.   Children within a classroom setting can be viewed as
   a.   passive recipients of knowledge
   b.   victims of teachers' expectations
   c.   active participants whose behavior influences the expectations of teachers
   d.   passive recipients whose behavior has little or no influence on the expectations of teachers
Answer: c, Reference: Chapter 13, P. 557, Box 13.4, Difficulty: D

147.   Teachers are more likely to praise
   a.   boys for their social behaviors
   b.   boys for their intellectual behaviors
   c.   girls for their intellectual achievements
   d.   girls and boys equally for their social behaviors
Answer: b, Reference: Chapter 13, P. 557, Box 13.4, Difficulty: M

148. When told by a teacher that he has failed, a boy might typically
    a. stop trying
    b. believe that the teacher has correctly assessed his ability
    c. place blame elsewhere thus retaining his self-confidence
    d. blame everyone else while secretly believing the teacher has correctly assessed his ability

Answer: c, Reference: Chapter 13, P. 557, Box 13.4, Difficulty: M

Essay Questions

1. Define education and describe three forms. How does schooling relate to education?

2. What are the features of an apprenticeship? What value does it serve in the education of the individual involved?

3. State and describe the four main ways in which informal instruction in the family setting differs from apprenticeship training.

4. Why have researchers suggested that more aspects of apprenticeship be included in school curricula?

5. What is the relationship between the evolution of writing systems and the development of schools?

6. Explain the advantage and disadvantage of using a phoneme-based writing system. Compare with a syllable-based writing system.

7. Describe the two major component processes in current theories of reading. Explain each.

8. What is decoding? How does it relate to learning to read? Explain.

9. Describe the first two stages of learning to read according to Jean Chall. How would you expect difficulties in these two stages to affect a child's reading?

10. What problems do teachers encounter when teaching children to read phonetically? How do they try to get around these problems?

11. Briefly name and describe each of Chall's 6 stages of reading acquisition.

12. What is the meaning of the following statement: "children in the primary grades learn to read, while in secondary school they read to learn"? Explain.

13. What are "top down" and "bottom up" processing referring to? Explain how each operates. What is their importance in learning to read?

14. Compare and contrast the "look say" and phonetic methods of learning to read.

15. What is a whole-language curriculum? Describe the philosophy behind this approach.

16. What is reciprocal teaching and how might it improve the teaching of reading? Explain.

17. What are the key elements in reciprocal teaching? How does this approach resemble Vygotsky's notion of "zone of proximal development"? Address the effectiveness of this approach.

18. What types of knowledge has Rochel Gelman and her colleagues identified as important in learning mathematics? Describe each.

19. Learning to count, read, and use numbers involves more than just learning to recite number words. What else is involved in the process of learning these basic arithmetic skills?

20. In what ways is learning to read and write numbers different from learning to read and write words?

21. What if any evidence is there that meaningful instruction is better than the "drill and practice" method of teaching mathematics?

22. What are the characteristics of instructional discourse? Using examples, explain how instructional discourse differs from ordinary discourse.

23. What is an initiation-reply-evaluation sequence and how is it used in classroom teaching? Include at least one example in your answer.

24. What is a "school cutoff strategy"? When and for what is it used?

25. Explain the impact of school attendance on a child's lexical organization.

26. What is metacognition? How is it affected by school attendance?

27. It has been suggested that intelligence tests measure only school specific aptitudes. Assume this is true and discuss the implications for definitions of intelligence.

28. If intelligence tests measure only school specific aptitudes, what are the implications for cross-cultural comparisons? What are the implications for life outside school?

29. Briefly explain why the theories of intelligence by recent theorists such as Robert Sternberg and Howard Gardner would not support the use of early intelligence tests by Binet and Simon.

30. Compare and contrast the innatist hypothesis of intelligence and the environmentalist hypothesis of intelligence.

31. What do current scholars believe accounts for the variation in intelligence from person to person? Give reasons for your statements.

32. What evidence is there to support the position that culture-free tests are impossible? Explain.

33. Citing evidence from the study of London schools by Rutter and his colleagues, what policy recommendations would you give to the principal of an inner city high school who wishes to increase students' academic success.

34. What does the Labov and Robbins study of peer groups in Harlem tell us about the effects of peer groups on academic achievement?

35. Cross cultural research has suggested some interesting family contributions to academic achievement. Describe the findings of such contributions among Cambodian, Vietnamese and Laotian refugees.

36. Discuss how children might influence teachers' expectations and thus influence the ways their own behavior will, in turn, be shaped within the classroom.

37. What factors may be important in causing between-group and within-group differences when interpreting the intelligence test scores of different groups of people?

38. If a teacher increases her expectations of a minority pupil, we might expect an even larger increase in IQ score than would occur if a teacher increases her expectations of a white child. Discuss how and why this IQ score increase might occur.

39. Compare and contrast learning within an apprenticeship system and learning within a formal school system.

40. What evidence is there to indicate that differences in genetic endowment do not explain why children from some ethnic groups do so poorly in school?

41. Why are Japanese and Chinese students superior in mathematics performance? Explain.

42.   What is the relevance of the findings concerning the Japanese and Chinese superiority in mathematics? How might this information be used in America?

43.   Briefly describe the differences found in the instruction of classrooms in the United States, Japan, and Taiwan. How have these differences effected the performance of the students involved?

Social Development in Middle Childhood

Multiple-Choice Questions

1. During middle childhood, peer interactions are
   a. about as frequent as during early childhood
   b. more than twice as frequent as during early childhood
   c. more than four times as frequent as during early childhood
   d. more than three times as frequent as during early childhood
   Answer: b, Reference: Chapter 14, P. 564, Difficulty: M

2. The behavior of children during middle childhood acting without an adult present can be described in the following way
   a. one child is chosen to take the role of an adult
   b. one child always dominates, as if "might makes right"
   c. authority is established by negotiation, compromise, and discussion
   d. power struggles center on physical prowess, especially among boys
   Answer: c, Reference: Chapter 14, P. 565, Difficulty: D

3. During middle childhood, the person who is the source of power within a group of children
   a. is usually the physically largest child
   b. varies with the activities of the group
   c. is usually chosen by some outside adult authority
   d. tends to remain constant as long as the group remains constant
   Answer: b, Reference: Chapter 14, P. 565, Difficulty: M

4.   The time that children spend among their peers is best described as
      a.   a cause of development
      b.   an effect of development
      c.   is both a cause and effect of development
      d.   is neither a cause nor an effect of development
Answer: c, Reference: Chapter 14, P. 565, Difficulty: M

5.   About the same time children begin spending time in peer groups, most parents
      a.   limit the time children spend with friends
      b.   limit the responsibilities they give their children
      c.   recognize children's increased ability to think for themselves
      d.   recognize children's need for control by using more physical force
Answer: c, Reference: Chapter 14, P. 565, Difficulty: E

6.   Peer groups challenge children to develop all of the following except
      a.   social skills
      b.   a sense of self
      c.   cognitive skills
      d.   defense mechanisms
Answer: d, Reference: Chapter 14, P. 565, Difficulty: D

7.   Peer groups affect children's
      a.   sense of self
      b.   stability of gender constancy
      c.   ability to select a single identity
      d.   awareness of their role with their siblings
Answer: a, Reference: Chapter 14, P. 565, Difficulty: E

8.   During middle childhood, parental behavior toward children becomes more
      a.   direct
      b.   indirect
      c.   physical
      d.   controlling
Answer: b, Reference: Chapter 14, P. 566, Difficulty: E

9.   Compared with parents of young children, parents of children in middle childhood
      are more likely to
      a.   rely less on discussion and explanation
      b.   restrict the time children spend with peers
      c.   rely on physical force to control their children
      d.   rely on children's understanding of the consequences of their own actions
Answer: d, Reference: Chapter 14, P. 566, Difficulty: M

10. A child's ability to regulate social relations by herself
    a. is mostly the result of maturation
    b. develops during the game playing of middle childhood
    c. develops mostly from disciplinary techniques of parents
    d. is expressed in the role-playing games of early childhood
Answer: b, Reference: Chapter 14, P. 566, Difficulty: M

11. A noticeable difference in the game playing of children in middle childhood compared to preschool years is the
    a. playing of games based upon rules
    b. marked increase in fantasy role play
    c. marked decrease in fantasy role play
    d. following of social rules consistent with fantasy roles
Answer: a, Reference: Chapter 14, P. 566, Difficulty: E

12. Which of the following is universally true of game playing during middle childhood?
    a. games with explicit rules always appear
    b. specific rules used for games are the same
    c. uneducated children do not play rule-based games
    d. role-playing function of games remains paramount
Answer: a, Reference: Chapter 14, P. 566, Difficulty: D

13. Games are to rules as fantasy play is to
    a. rules
    b. roles
    c. culture
    d. society
Answer: b, Reference: Chapter 14, P. 566, Difficulty: D

14. A group of 4-year-olds are playing house. The pretend parents tell the pretend children that it is time for bed. The pretend children never tell the pretend parents that it is time for bed. This is an example of
    a. conservation expressed in play
    b. preschoolers lack of reversibility
    c. the egocentric nature of preschoolers
    d. the use of implicit rules in preschoolers' play
Answer: d, Reference: Chapter 14, P. 567, Difficulty: M

15. The rules of fantasy play are_____, where as the rules of games are_____
    a. implicit, explicit
    b. nonexistent, real
    c. authoritarian, libertarian
    d. imposed by adults, imposed by children
Answer: a, Reference: Chapter 14, P. 567, Difficulty: D

16.   Preschoolers gain the most satisfaction from a game when they can
        a.   win a competition in spite of the rules
        b.   break the social rules implicit in role playing
        c.   demonstrate their ability to follow explicit rules
        d.   exercise their imaginations in the company of others
Answer: d, Reference: Chapter 14, P. 567, Difficulty: M

17.   Little League baseball is important in allowing children to learn to
        a.   function independently
        b.   work as a member of a team
        c.   negotiate and resolve conflicts with others
        d.   focus on enjoying the process of playing rather than the outcome
Answer: b, Reference: Chapter 14, P. 568, Box 14.1, Difficulty: M

18.   Little League has been criticized
        a.   as too competitive
        b.   because it fails to teach cooperation
        c.   for focusing too much on skill development
        d.   for providing too many failure experiences for children
Answer: a, Reference: Chapter 14, P. 568, Box 14.1, Difficulty: M

19.   Fathers of boys who play in Little League games
        a.   spend less time with their children
        b.   are generally critical of Little League
        c.   are more likely to have played in Little League themselves
        d.   spend more time in mutually satisfying activities with their boys
Answer: d, Reference: Chapter 14, P. 568, Box 14.1, Difficulty: M

20.   Boys who play in Little League are more likely than boys who do not to
        a.   have positive self-esteem
        b.   score higher on intelligence tests
        c.   be rated as physically attractive by teachers
        d.   score higher on tests of gross and fine motor coordination
Answer: a, Reference: Chapter 14, P. 568, Box 14.1, Difficulty: M

21.   Which of the following is true of preschool play?
        a.   typical play group size is 5 to 7 children
        b.   episodes of play typically last 30 minutes
        c.   teachers are most likely to organize fantasy play
        d.   large group activities are likely to be organized by teachers
Answer: d, Reference: Chapter 14, P. 570 Difficulty: M

22. Piaget argued that the child's ability to participate in rule based games was the application of concrete operational thought to
   a. moral situations
   b. the social world
   c. the words of objects
   d. physical transformations
Answer: b, Reference: Chapter 14, P. 570, Difficulty: M

23. For Piaget, participation in rule based games allows the child to
   a. practice teamwork
   b. explore imaginative possibilities
   c. develop concrete operational reasoning
   d. balance desires against social constraints
Answer: d, Reference: Chapter 14, P. 570, Difficulty: M

24. Piaget proposed a developmental progression of children's understanding of social rules based on observations of what game?
   a. tag
   b. marbles
   c. checkers
   d. hide-and-seek
Answer: b, Reference: Chapter 14, P. 570, Difficulty: E

25. When compared to boys during middle childhood, girls play
   a. in larger groups
   b. less complex games
   c. more complex games
   d. in groups the same size as boys do
Answer: b, Reference: Chapter 14, P. 572, Box 14.2, Difficulty: D

26. When playing competitive games, girls
   a. rarely talk
   b. are more competitive than boys
   c. play less cooperatively than boys
   d. compete against a score rather than one another
Answer: d, Reference: Chapter 14, P. 572, Box 14.2, Difficulty: E

27. According to Lever, boys' games
   a. are more cooperative than girls' games
   b. are competitive only when boys are playing team sports
   c. prevent them from learning to coordinate a large number of people
   d. provide boys with the opportunity to work for collective as well as for personal goals
Answer: d, Reference: Chapter 14, P. 572, Box 14.2, Difficulty: D

28.   Team sports provide boys with the opportunity to
       a.   maintain self-control
       b.   play in smaller groups
       c.   work primarily for personal goals
       d.   compete against objective criteria rather than other boys
Answer: a, Reference: Chapter 14, P. 572, Box 14.2, Difficulty: M

29.   The most general type of social rule is called a
       a.   moral rule
       b.   group rule
       c.   social norm
       d.   social convention
Answer: a, Reference: Chapter 14, P. 573, Difficulty: D

30.   Social conventions are
       a.   particular to a single society
       b.   characteristic of small peer groups
       c.   the most general type of social rule
       d.   based on principles of justice and welfare
Answer: a, Reference: Chapter 14, P. 573, Difficulty: M

31.   During middle childhood children rank violations of social rules from most to least
       serious in which of the following orders?
       a.   personal rules, social conventions, moral rules
       b.   moral rules, personal rules, social conventions
       c.   moral rules, social conventions, personal rules
       d.   social conventions, moral rules, personal rules
Answer: c, Reference: Chapter 14, P. 574, Difficulty: D

32.   Children in middle childhood can distinguish among moral rules, social
       conventions, and personal rules at an early age but their ability to ___ continues to
       develop.
       a.   understand each type of rule
       b.   rate the relative importance of rule types
       c.   judge moral transgressions as being wrong
       d.   judge personal rules as being more important than social convention
Answer: a, Reference: Chapter 14, P. 574, Difficulty: D

33.   The majority of research on moral development in middle childhood is based on
       children's
       a.   behavior
       b.   game playing
       c.   reasoning processes
       d.   responses to written surveys
Answer: c, Reference: Chapter 14, P. 574, Difficulty: D

34. According to Piaget, children who argue that a child is bad who disobeys an adult prohibition is demonstrating
    a. the morality of constraint
    b. autonomous moral reasoning
    c. conventional moral reasoning
    d. preconventional moral reasoning
Answer: a, Reference: Chapter 14, P. 574, Difficulty: M

35. According to Piaget, children who argue that a child is bad who hits another child because that child would not like it if someone hit him is demonstrating
    a. the morality of constraint
    b. autonomous moral reasoning
    c. conventional moral reasoning
    d. preconventional moral reasoning
Answer: b, Reference: Chapter 14, P. 574, Difficulty: M

36. Children begin to recognize that rules can be changed by consensus at about the same time that they
    a. begin to spend more time with adults
    b. begin to spend less time with their peers
    c. can make judgments based on their own thinking
    d. can make judgments based on an external authority
Answer: c, Reference: Chapter 14, P. 574, Difficulty: M

37. Kohlberg's investigation of moral reasoning used
    a. story-dilemmas
    b. role-playing situations
    c. experiments that manipulated moral behavior
    d. interviews with children about their lying behavior
Answer: a, Reference: Chapter 14, P. 574, Difficulty: E

38. Moral judgments in Kohlberg's preconventional level are based on
    a. what other people think
    b. concrete operational thought
    c. direct physical consequences of an action
    d. the reciprocity of interpersonal relationships
Answer: c, Reference: Chapter 14, P. 576, Difficulty: E

39. When children begin to recognize that others have different perspectives Kohlberg refers to this as
    a. autonomous morality
    b. instrumental morality
    c. heteronomous morality
    d. moral perspective taking
Answer: b, Reference: Chapter 14, P. 576, Difficulty: D

40.   "Instrumental morality" first appears in Kohlberg's stage
       a.   1
       b.   2
       c.   3
       d.   4
Answer: b, Reference: Chapter 14, P. 576, Difficulty: M

41.   According to Kohlberg, the conventional level of moral reasoning
       a.   relies on individual self-interest
       b.   involves avoidance of punishment
       c.   relates points of view through the golden rule
       d.   coincides with the development of formal operations
Answer: c, Reference: Chapter 14, P. 576, Difficulty: D

42.   The moral reasoning of children in middle childhood rarely goes beyond Kohlberg's
       stage
       a.   1
       b.   2
       c.   3
       d.   4
Answer: c, Reference: Chapter 14, P. 576, Difficulty: M

43.   In response to the Heinz dilemma, children who indicate they would steal the drug
       because "you can't put a price on life" are
       a.   probably in stage 2 reasoning
       b.   displaying instrumental morality
       c.   reasoning on the basis of heteronomous morality
       d.   using moral reasoning associated with the "golden rule"
Answer: d, Reference: Chapter 14, P. 577, Difficulty: D

44.   William Damon's investigation of children's conceptions of positive justice examined
       how children
       a.   place blame
       b.   distribute rewards
       c.   accept responsibility for their actions
       d.   decide on appropriate punishments for transgressions
Answer: b, Reference: Chapter 14, P. 577, Difficulty: M

45.   In his study of positive justice, William Damon found that children in this group
       were most likely to believe that all participants deserved equal shares
       a.   girls
       b.   boys
       c.   4 year-olds
       d.   6 year-olds
Answer: d, Reference: Chapter 14, P. 578, Difficulty: M

46. At what age do children begin to believe that some individuals (for example those who are disadvantaged) might have a legitimate claim to more than an equal share of a group's rewards?
   a. 4
   b. 8
   c. 10
   d. 12
Answer: b, Reference: Chapter 14, P. 578, Difficulty: M

47. Decisions made by children about fairness were investigated by Thorkildsen (1989). This research indicated that
   a. all children 6 to 11 years of age have general rules about fairness that they apply in all situations
   b. both 6 and 11 year old children consider the social context of an action in making decisions about fairness
   c. eleven year old children take particular circumstances into account when judging fairness, but 6 year old children do not
   d. none of the children in the 6 to 11 year old group take the context of the circumstances into account in making decisions about fairness
Answer: b, Reference: Chapter 14, P. 579, Difficulty: D

48. William Damon based his descriptions of the levels of children's reasoning about fairness on their
   a. game playing
   b. only reasoning processes
   c. both behavior and reasoning
   d. only behavior in a laboratory task
Answer: c, Reference: Chapter 14, P. 580, Difficulty: D

49. When the children in William Damon's study of fairness were confronted with the task of distributing real candy bars, half the group
   a. expected the experimenter, the adult in authority, to make a decision
   b. took more candy than they thought they would when presented with a hypothetical situation
   c. took the same number of candy bars that they had predicted based on a hypothetical situation
   d. distributed the candy more equitably in the real situation as compared with the hypothetical situation
Answer: c, Reference: Chapter 14, P. 580, Difficulty: D

50.   At about what age do children first appear to recognize the differences between moral principles and social conventions?
    a.   5 years
    b.   7 years
    c.   12 years
    d.   18 years
Answer: a, Reference: Chapter 14, P. 581, Difficulty: M

51.   According to Elliot Turiel, social conventions
    a.   are identical in concept to moral reasoning
    b.   are in a different domain from moral reasoning
    c.   are that from which true moral reasoning grows
    d.   cannot be distinguished from moral infractions by preschoolers
Answer: b, Reference: Chapter 14, P. 581, Difficulty: D

52.   Cross-cultural studies of social conventional and moral reasoning appear to support the conclusion that
    a.   children's moral evaluations are independent of cultural norms
    b.   in some cultures, children are likely to see breaches of social convention as moral issues
    c.   American children are more sophisticated in their moral reasoning than children from other cultures
    d.   children from other cultures make the same distinctions as American children between social conventions and moral rules
Answer: b, Reference: Chapter 14, P. 582, Difficulty: D

53.   John Gottman's (1983) study of friendship that paired children of the same age who were previously strangers found all of the following as important aspects distinguishing pairs who became friendly from those that did not except
    a.   common interests
    b.   ability to resolve conflicts
    c.   good communication skills
    d.   ability to engage in collective monologues
Answer: d, Reference: Chapter 14, P. 583, Difficulty: E

54.   Weisner reports that children in non-technological societies differ from American children in that when interacting with friends they are more likely to
    a.   play
    b.   gossip
    c.   help each other with chores
    d.   help each other with school tasks
Answer: c, Reference: Chapter 14, P. 584, Difficulty: E

55. For preschoolers, the critical aspect of a friend is a
    a. sibling
    b. playmate
    c. person to gossip with
    d. person who shares their feelings
Answer: b, Reference: Chapter 14, P. 584, Difficulty: E

56. Research by Parker and Gottman (1989) has suggested that gossip
    a. rarely occurs in middle childhood
    b. is seen as a positive part of friendship conversation in middle childhood
    c. is the primary reason for termination of friendships in middle childhood
    d. tends to distort cultural norms in friendship conversations in middle childhood
Answer: b, Reference: Chapter 14, P. 584, Difficulty: E

57. Studies that ask children to nominate a "best friend" have found that from 6 to 12 years of age the percent of children reporting "best friends" of the same sex
    a. increases
    b. decreases slightly
    c. decreases dramatically
    d. remains about the same
Answer: a, Reference: Chapter 14, P. 585, Difficulty: E

58. Cazden and Michaels found that when a computer mail system was introduced into a second grade classroom, children wrote
    a. just to the teacher
    b. only to same-sexed classmates
    c. to all the children in the classroom
    d. to their friends regardless of gender
Answer: b, Reference: Chapter 14, P. 586, Box 14.3, Difficulty: M

59. Sutton-Smith and Roberts found that in societies where boys marry outside their communities,
    a. girls chase boys
    b. boys chase girls
    c. neither boys nor girls chase each other
    d. boys and girls chase each other equally
Answer: b, Reference: Chapter 14, P. 586, Box 14.3, Difficulty: D

60. Compared with girls, boys have
    a. more friends
    b. more implicit rules
    c. more intimacy with friends
    d. less explicit competition in their play
Answer: a, Reference: Chapter 14, P. 587, Difficulty: M

61.   Boys are most often socialized for
      a.   competition
      b.   cooperation
      c.   activities involving implicit rules
      d.   sensitivity to the feelings of others
Answer: a, Reference: Chapter 14, P. 588, Difficulty: E

62.   Girls are most often socialized for
      a.   competition
      b.   cooperation
      c.   activities involving explicit rules
      d.   having a greater number of friends than boys
Answer: b, Reference: Chapter 14, P. 588, Difficulty: E

63.   As more women in the United States enter the workplace the socialization
      differences between boys and girls during middle childhood
      a.   appear unaffected
      b.   have changed in the last decade
      c.   differ markedly from those in other Western nations
      d.   have disappeared at least with respect to competition
Answer: a, Reference: Chapter 14, P. 588, Difficulty: M

64.   Children's understanding of friendship parallels their understanding of
      a.   social rules
      b.   moral reasoning
      c.   interpersonal conflict
      d.   social perspective-taking
Answer: d, Reference: Chapter 14, P. 589, Difficulty: M

65.   What stage of friendship precedes friendship based on mutual likes and dislikes,
      according to Robert Selman?
      a.   momentary friendships
      b.   autonomous independent friendships
      c.   friendships based on adjustment and cooperation
      d.   friendship based on mutual intimacy and support
Answer: a, Reference: Chapter 14, P. 590, Difficulty: D

66.   According to Robert Selman, autonomous, independent friendships follow
      a.   momentary friendships
      b.   friendship based on mutual likes and dislikes
      c.   friendships based on adjustment and cooperation
      d.   friendship based on mutual intimacy and support
Answer: d, Reference: Chapter 14, P. 590, Difficulty: D

67.   According to Robert Selman, the key to developmental changes in friendship is
   a.   maturation
   b.   game playing
   c.   moral reasoning
   d.   the ability to take another's perspective
Answer: d, Reference: Chapter 14, P. 589, Difficulty: D

68.   Children who are considered bossy or hard to understand by their peers may be
   a.   surrounded by friends
   b.   intellectually precocious
   c.   skilled in perspective taking
   d.   incapable of reasoning about the meaning of friendship
Answer: b, Reference: Chapter 14, P. 591, Difficulty: M

69.   Why might intellectually precocious children as well as emotionally disturbed
        children be found together in a clinical workshop for the emotionally disturbed?
   a.   both groups have difficulty forming friendships
   b.   emotional disturbance is synonymous with intellectual precocity
   c.   emotional disturbance is a characteristic of intellectual precocity
   d.   the intellectually precocious children help those who are emotionally
          disturbed
Answer: a, Reference: Chapter 14, P. 591, Difficulty: D

70.   The term social repair mechanisms refers to
   a.   strategies used by people to reconcile differences
   b.   adults who monitor disputes between preschoolers
   c.   a type of therapy used to help emotionally disturbed children
   d.   the desire of children entering the period of formal operations to help solve
          world problems
Answer: a, Reference: Chapter 14, P. 591, Difficulty: M

71.   Why are developmental psychologists interested in studying the social status of
        children?
   a.   high status children often turn out to be geniuses
   b.   high status in childhood predicts vocational success
   c.   low status children are at risk for negative development
   d.   social status is the primary determinant in personality development
Answer: c, Reference: Chapter 14, P. 591, Difficulty: D

72.   Sociograms are used to investigate
   a.   social status
   b.   moral reasoning
   c.   social perspective taking
   d.   social repair mechanisms
Answer: a, Reference: Chapter 14, P. 591, Difficulty: E

73.   During middle childhood, a child's popularity is positively related to his or her
        a.   activity level
        b.   attractiveness
        c.   aggressiveness
        d.   socioeconomic status
Answer: b, Reference: Chapter 14, P. 592, Difficulty: E

74.   A study of popularity and social skills showed that boys who were rejected from a
        group were
        a.   quieter
        b.   those who reminded others of the rules
        c.   more likely to wander away from the group
        d.   more likely to stay with the group during an activity
Answer: c, Reference: Chapter 14, P. 594, Difficulty: E

75.   In a study of popularity within a group during middle childhood, "neglected" boys
        a.   often offended other children
        b.   rarely offended other children
        c.   were aggressive toward the other children
        d.   were more talkative and more active than the other children
Answer: b, Reference: Chapter 14, P. 594, Difficulty: M

76.   What factor is thought to be associated with both disruptive and aggressive behavior
        in peer interactions, according to Dodge and his colleagues?
        a.   low intellectual level
        b.   deficient social information processing
        c.   insecure/resistant attachment in infancy
        d.   being at the preoperational level of cognition
Answer: b, Reference: Chapter 14, P. 594, Difficulty: M

77.   Research on social rejection in elementary school suggests
        a.   high status children were often rejected as not fitting in with children at play
        b.   low status children were more likely to be ignored by a group already at play
        c.   low and high status children differ dramatically in their skill in joining a
                group already at play
        d.   both low and high status children were equally successful in gaining entry
                into a group already at play
Answer: b, Reference: Chapter 14, P. 595, Difficulty: M

78. A two-sided view of social rejection is supported by evidence of
    a. lower levels of social cognition in aggressive children
    b. parental-intervention in the play of low social status children
    c. social understanding in aggressive children equivalent to that of average children
    d. misinterpretation of aggressive children's behavior as aggressive even when it is not

Answer: d, Reference: Chapter 14, P. 595, Difficulty: D

79. A primary cause of rejection of children by their peers is
    a. shyness
    b. aggressiveness
    c. unattractiveness
    d. high intelligence

Answer: b, Reference: Chapter 14, P. 595, Difficulty: E

80. A study by Thomas Dishion (1990) that examined the relationship between social and family variables found that rejected boys were more likely to come from
    a. single parent homes
    b. middle-class environments
    c. coercive family environments
    d. households with extended families

Answer: c, Reference: Chapter 14, P. 596, Difficulty: M

81. The influence of adults within the peer groups of middle childhood
    a. is minimal
    b. controls most activities
    c. can be seen only when an adult is present
    d. can be seen in patterns of children's cooperation and conflict

Answer: d, Reference: Chapter 14, P. 596, Difficulty: D

82. With respect to children's socialization, Kibbutzim emphasize _____ , while middle-class Israeli parents emphasize _____.
    a. individual effort, cooperation
    b. cooperation, individual effort
    c. artistic effort, problem solving
    d. problem solving, artistic effort

Answer: b, Reference: Chapter 14, P. 596, Difficulty: M

83. Kibbutz children at the top of their classes are likely to feel
    a. proud
    b. ashamed
    c. competitive
    d. no different than other children

Answer: b, Reference: Chapter 14, P. 596, Difficulty: D

84.   When two groups of children are in competition, one way to unify them is to
       a.   serve them meals together
       b.   arrange for recreational activities together
       c.   get them together in pleasant social circumstances
       d.   arrange a task that requires cooperation for mutual benefit
Answer: d, Reference: Chapter 14, P. 598, Box 14.4 Difficulty: E

85.   Marida Hollos found that children from isolated farms and from towns or villages in
       Norway and Hungary performed similarly on tests of
       a.   social norms
       b.   logical operations
       c.   concrete operations
       d.   social perspective-taking
Answer: b, Reference: Chapter 14, P. 599, Difficulty: D

86.   On the basis of studies of children living in towns or on isolated farms, Marida
       Hollos concluded that peer interaction helps develop the ability to
       a.   behave morally
       b.   learn explicit rules
       c.   take another's perspective
       d.   perform logical operations
Answer: c, Reference: Chapter 14, P. 599, Difficulty: M

87.   Harry Stack Sullivan believed that children's middle childhood friendships are
       precursors of
       a.   skill in problem solving
       b.   intimate adult relationships
       c.   the ability to take another's perspective
       d.   the ability to perform logical operations
Answer: b, Reference: Chapter 14, P. 600, Difficulty: M

88.   Compared with the behavior of parents toward a 3 year old child, the behavior of
       parents towards a 9 year old child is likely to be
       a.   warmer
       b.   friendlier
       c.   more critical
       d.   more sheltering
Answer: c, Reference: Chapter 14, P. 600, Difficulty: E

89. Cross-cultural studies of parental standards and behaviors toward children in middle childhood indicate
    a. universal strategies for correcting children's misbehavior
    b. cultures are so different no general statements can be made
    c. different strategies for correcting misbehavior based on how competent children are viewed to be
    d. cross-cultural consistency about the ages parents believe children should be competent to do things

Answer: c, Reference: Chapter 14, P. 600, Difficulty: M

90. Which ethnic group expected their children to display emotional maturity and politeness earlier than the other groups according to cross-cultural studies?
    a. Japanese
    b. Lebanese
    c. American
    d. Australian

Answer: a, Reference: Chapter 14, P. 601, Difficulty: E

91. Recent research on the effects of maternal employment on children's development has demonstrated
    a. no effects at all
    b. direct positive effects
    c. direct negative effects
    d. no direct effects, either positive or negative

Answer: d, Reference: Chapter 14, P. 604, Box 14.5, Difficulty: E

92. Maternal employment has a positive effect on
    a. all boys
    b. middle-class boys
    c. middle class children with well educated mothers
    d. children of single, impoverished, poorly educated mothers

Answer: d, Reference: Chapter 14, P. 604, Box 14.5, Difficulty: D

93. A study of after-school care arrangements found that third and fifth grade children who had the highest ratings for antisocial behaviors, anxiety, and peer conflicts were cared for after school by
    a. relatives
    b. in-home child care
    c. after-school care programs
    d. unemployed single mothers

Answer: d, Reference: Chapter 14, P. 604, Box 14.5, Difficulty: E

94.   Maternal employment outside the home has been shown to
       a.   have a positive effect on boys
       b.   have an adverse effect on girls
       c.   generally have no effect on children
       d.   sometimes have an adverse effect on boys
Answer: d, Reference: Chapter 14, P. 604, Box 14.5, Difficulty: M

95.   According to 1991 U.S. Department of Labor statistics the percent of women in the
       work force with children under 3 years of age is approximately
       a.   25 %
       b.   40 %
       c.   55 %
       d.   70 %
Answer: c, Reference: Chapter 14, P. 604, Box 14.5, Difficulty: M

96.   Which ethnic group makes up the smallest percentage of women in the work force
       with children of all ages, according to 1991 U.S. Department of Labor statistics?
       a.   Asian
       b.   black
       c.   white
       d.   Hispanic
Answer: d, Reference: Chapter 14, P. 604, Box 14.5, Difficulty: M

97.   Compared with children in early childhood, following a confrontation with their
       parents, children in middle childhood are more likely to
       a.   whine
       b.   express anger
       c.   become depressed
       d.   behave aggressively
Answer: c, Reference: Chapter 14, P. 603, Difficulty: M

98.   The term coregulation refers to
       a.   cooperation among peer groups
       b.   a balance between the ego and superego
       c.   a system of rules shared among children
       d.   a system of control shared by parents and children
Answer: d, Reference: Chapter 14, P. 603 Difficulty: M

99.   With regard to social comparison, children's sensitivity to themselves in relation to
       others their own age increases significantly around the age of
       a.   6 years
       b.   8 years
       c.   10 years
       d.   12 years
Answer: b, Reference: Chapter 14, P. 606, Difficulty: E

100. Asked to define herself, a child in middle childhood is most likely to say,
    a. "I am a girl who roller skates."
    b. "I am a girl who dislikes candy."
    c. "I am a girl who gets good grades."
    d. "I am a girl who can jump rope better than Sara."
Answer: d, Reference: Chapter 14, P. 606, Difficulty: D

101. The study by Ferguson and Colleagues found that children thought that behavior reflected an underlying, stable characteristic at about age
    a. 5 years
    b. 8 years
    c. 11 years
    d. 15 years
Answer: b, Reference: Chapter 14, P. 607, Difficulty: M

102. In a study which asked children to make a self-assessment about their performance in a game of modified basketball, researchers found that 5 to 7-year-old children
    a. did not engage in social comparison
    b. reported more failure when compared to older children
    c. became upset when asked to evaluate their performance
    d. assessed their performance compared with others in their age group
Answer: a, Reference: Chapter 14, P. 608, Difficulty: M

103. In a study of self-evaluation of 4- to 7-year-old children, Harter and Pike (1984) found that children evaluated their self-worth in terms of what two broad categories
    a. physical and emotional
    b. acceptance and competence
    c. competence and intelligence
    d. intelligence and understanding
Answer: b, Reference: Chapter 14, P. 609, Difficulty: D

104. Harter found that when 8-year-old children evaluate themselves on questionnaires, their self-evaluations are
    a. not associated with parental styles
    b. not consistent with evaluations made by peers
    c. not consistent with evaluations made by teachers
    d. consistent with evaluations by both teachers and peers
Answer: d, Reference: Chapter 14, P. 610, Difficulty: D

105. Children are more likely to have high self-esteem when their parents
    a. are controlling
    b. set clearly defined limits
    c. permit children to set their own limits
    d. encourage children to be dependent on them
Answer: b, Reference: Chapter 14, P. 610, Difficulty: M

106. Research has suggested that the key to high self-esteem, transmitted in large part by the family, is some ability to
   a.   do well in sports
   b.   perform well in school
   c.   control one's own future
   d.   make friends and be popular
Answer: c, Reference: Chapter 14, P. 610, Difficulty: D

107. The social interactions of middle childhood are
   a.   independent of cultural influences
   b.   independent of parental influences
   c.   solely dependent on peer interactions
   d.   influenced by peers, culture, and parents
Answer: d, Reference: Chapter 14, P. 610, Difficulty: M

108. Middle childhood can be best characterized as
   a.   independent of biology
   b.   a universal pattern of change
   c.   a developmental stage in Western culture
   d.   unaffected by a bio-social-behavioral shift
Answer: b, Reference: Chapter 14, P. 613, Difficulty: D

Essay Questions

1. Children between the ages of 6 and 12 spend an average of 40 percent of their waking hours in the company of peers. Discuss how this time might be spent and how it contributes to children's development.

2. Describe how game playing in middle childhood differs from game playing among preschool age children. Give an example.

3. How do changes that occur during middle childhood, including those that involve peer groups, contribute to a child's developing sense of self? Explain.

4. Parents assign new responsibilities to children 6 to 7 years of age. At the same age children begin to play in a rule-governed manner. What underlying mental abilities might be common to both these events? Explain.

5. Differentiate between moral rules, social norms, and personal rules. What differences are there in how children view these distinctions? Explain.

6.   Give an example of a moral rule, a social rule, and a personal rule. Explain how each fits the definition.

7.   Describe how play contributes to the ability of children to regulate and govern their own behavior during middle childhood.

8.   Compare and contrast the social experiences of boys and girls related to the games they play. What are the apparent effects? Explain.

9.   In what two ways did Piaget consider games to be models of society?

10.   From middle childhood on, North American children can distinguish among three different kinds of rules. What are they? Explain.

11.   What are the three levels of moral judgment corresponding to the three major Piagetian stages of cognitive development proposed by Lawrence Kohlberg? Briefly describe each stage.

12.   Describe how children use rules in their games at different stages of development. Give an example of each.

13.   Compare and contrast what children do when asked a hypothetical question about fairness with what they do when confronted with a real life issue of fairness. Explain the reasons for the differences.

14.   Explain why we might find intellectually precocious, but emotionally normal children in the same clinical workshop as emotionally disturbed children.

15.   How does the ability to take the perspective of another person develop in parallel with children's friendships during middle childhood? Explain.

16.   Describe the four developmental functions of friendship identified by Willard Hartup. Explain the role of each.

17.   Explain the role of "gossip" in friendships during middle childhood.

17.   Describe the most commonly used technique to research moral reasoning among children. What information has this approach provided?

18.   Compare and contrast the friendship and socialization patterns of boys with the friendship and socialization patterns of girls.

19.   Describe the different characteristics of boys, who are likely to become (a) popular, (b) neglected, or (c) rejected within a peer group. Explain each.

20. What are social repair mechanisms? Give an example.

21. Identify the five aspects of children's social interactions that distinguish pairs of children who become friendly from those who do not. Explain each.

22. What characteristics, other than attractiveness, are associated with popular children? How do these characteristics facilitate the "standing" of a child within a group? Explain.

23. Describe the role of attractiveness in social status in middle childhood.

24. How are peer-group interactions affected by competition or cooperation? Cite evidence to support your arguments.

25. Discuss the similarities and differences between children's relationships with their parents during both early and middle childhood. Explain.

26. What are sociograms? What area of developmental psychology are they used to research? Give an example.

27. What are the main concerns of parents about their children during early and middle childhood?

28. Describe the effect of a coercive family environment on children's relationships with their peers. Explain.

29. Compare and contrast ways parents exert control over their children in early and in middle childhood. What are the most common forms of discipline for children in these two age groups?

30. How do parental expectations concerning the competency of children affect the way they react when their children misbehave?

31. If asked to prepare a report on the effects of maternal employment on children, what specific findings would you include?

32. Describe the changes in children's self concepts as they enter middle childhood.

33. Discuss how patterns of child rearing influence the self-esteem of children. Provide three parental characteristics that combine to produce high self-esteem in middle childhood.

34. Name the three specific domains of self-esteem identified by Susan Harter and others. Explain the importance of each.

35.   Explain the relationship found between parenting style and children's self-esteem.

36.   Describe the function of Little League Baseball in the development of boys in middle childhood.

37.   What can we learn about social development from Kibbutz-reared children in Israel? Explain.

38.   Describe the nature of male-female contact in middle childhood.

Biological and Social Foundations of Adolescence

Multiple-Choice Questions

1.   The eighteenth-century philosopher Jean-Jacques Rousseau thought that adolescence was
    a.   not a universal feature of development in all cultures.
    b.   a time of emotional instability caused by biological maturation
    c.   characterized by biological changes but not by any important cognitive development
    d.   a period during which the recent evolutionary history of the species was recapitulated
Answer: b, Reference: Chapter 15, P. 623, Difficulty: E

2.   According to Rousseau, young people
    a.   experience adolescence as a time of renewed commitment
    b.   recapitulate earlier stages of development during adolescence
    c.   recapitulate both earlier stages of development and human evolution
    d.   recapitulate the stages of evolution of the species during individual development
Answer: b, Reference: Chapter 15, P. 623, Difficulty: E

3.   The idea that "ontogeny recapitulates phylogeny"
      a.   has been largely confirmed by research
      b.   has influenced theories of other psychologists
      c.   was invoked by nineteenth-century scholars to explain individual development
      d.   was both used to explain individual development and influenced other theorists

Answer: d, Reference: Chapter 15, P. 623, Difficulty: M

4.   Recent research has suggested that G. Stanley Hall's insistence that the young recapitulate the entire history of the human species
      a.   has been confirmed
      b.   has been discredited
      c.   simplifies a complex concept
      d.   is only true for certain cultures

Answer: b, Reference: Chapter 15, P. 623, Difficulty: D

5.   Most adolescence researchers identify themselves with which of the following perspectives?
      a.   no single unified theory exists
      b.   biological-maturational perspective
      c.   the environmental-learning perspective
      d.   the universal-constructivist perspective

Answer: a, Reference: Chapter 15, P. 623, Difficulty: E

6.   Gesell believed that abstract thinking and self-control are achieved relatively late in development because they
      a.   are strongly influenced by biological maturation
      b.   occurred fairly late in human evolutionary history
      c.   are dependent on advanced educational experiences
      d.   develop through shaping by social interactions with peers

Answer: b, Reference: Chapter 15, P. 624, Difficulty: M

7.   The period of adolescence corresponds to which stage in Freud's theory of psychosexual development?
      a.   genital
      b.   phallic
      c.   latency
      d.   Oedipal

Answer: a, Reference: Chapter 15, P. 624, Difficulty: E

8. Margaret Mead described the Arapesh of New Guinea, who cut off the arm and leg bands of an adolescent who has just started to menstruate. The reason for this is
   a. to mark her as an adult
   b. to sever her ties to the past
   c. that they are seen as contaminated
   d. that they are not appropriate decorations for adults

Answer: b, Reference: Chapter 15, P. 624, Difficulty: M

9. According to the text the onset of menstruation is typically seen as
   a. traumatic
   b. depressing
   d. life-changing
   c. exciting and scary

Answer: d, Reference: Chapter 15, P. 624, Difficulty: M

10. In the Freudian view, emotional upheaval during adolescence results from
    a. imitation of the behavior of peers
    b. hormonal imbalance caused by biological maturation
    c. psychological imbalance caused by the reawakening of primitive instincts
    d. failure of sexual urges to reawaken at the same time that biological maturation occurs

Answer: c, Reference: Chapter 15, P. 625, Difficulty: M

11. The striking similarities between the development of dominance relations in nonhuman species and human children has lead researchers to hypothesize
    a. cross-species learned behavior
    b. a common biological mechanism
    c. a common history among species
    d. similar parenting techniques among human and nonhuman species

Answer: b, Reference: Chapter 15, P. 626, Difficulty: D

12. A number of ethological studies of nonhuman primates has shown that _____ go through the transition from adolescence to adulthood similar to humans.
    a. only males
    b. only females
    c. both males and females
    d. neither males or females

Answer: a, Reference: Chapter 15, P. 626, Difficulty: D

13.   As an environmental-learning theorist, Albert Bandura argues that
a.   imitation of adult models plays a significantly reduced role for adolescents
b.   adolescent aggression, which many think is biologically based, is a product of social reinforcement
c.   adolescents have more emotional difficulties than adults because of the hormonal upheaval of puberty
d.   principles of learning that explain behavior at earlier ages cannot account for behavior during adolescence

Answer: b, Reference: Chapter 15, P. 626, Difficulty: E

14.   Margaret Mead's study of Samoan girls going through adolescence
a.   determined that adolescence, as a separate stage, does not exist
b.   supported the idea that adolescence is a stressful time, even in preindustrial societies
c.   called into question the idea that conflict and stress are necessarily a part of adolescence
d.   demonstrated that the biological, behavioral, and social changes of adolescence are basically the same in different cultures

Answer: c, Reference: Chapter 15, P. 626, Difficulty: M

15.   Margaret Mead's study of adolescent Samoan girls forced psychologists to pay attention to which of the following factors as contributing to the characteristics of adolescence?
a.   genetic
b.   cultural
d.   cognitive
c.   biological

Answer: b, Reference: Chapter 15, P. 627, Difficulty: E

16.   Diana Baumrind found anti-social behavior and family conflict among adolescents whose parents were
a.   indulgent
b.   permissive
c.   authoritative
d.   authoritarian

Answer: d, Reference: Chapter 15, P. 627, Difficulty: M

17.   The study by Guerra and Slaby (1990) with adolescents in a state juvenile correction facility demonstrated that a training session which gave instruction in recognizing social cues, generating solutions to problems, and making good choices among alternatives produced
    a.   drastic changes in attitudes toward authority
    b.   no changes among these adolescent behaviors
    c.   marked reductions in aggression and impulsivity only in the training environment
    d.   marked reductions in aggression, impulsivity, and inflexibility both during and after the training
Answer: d, Reference: Chapter 15, P. 627, Difficulty: D

18.   The theories of Erik Erikson and Jean Piaget explain the distinctive qualities of adolescence as
    a.   being primarily the result of social learning
    b.   being due to the dramatic biological changes that occur at this time
    c.   depending heavily for their development on a society's cultural organization
    d.   deriving from the interaction of biological and social factors found in all societies
Answer: d, Reference: Chapter 15, P. 628, Difficulty: M

19.   A pattern of beliefs which, for adolescents, reconciles the ways in which they are like others with the ways in which they are different is called
    a.   identity
    b.   conflict
    c.   autonomy
    d.   formal operational thought
Answer: a, Reference: Chapter 15, P. 628, Difficulty: M

20.   According to Erik Erikson, failure to resolve the central crisis of adolescence leads to feelings of
    a.   guilt
    b.   inferiority
    c.   shame and doubt
    d.   identity confusion
Answer: d, Reference: Chapter 15, P. 628, Difficulty: D

21.   Whose theory is notable, in that it does not view adolescence as the end point of development?
    a.   Freud's
    b.   Piaget's
    c.   Erikson's
    d.   Rousseau's
Answer: c, Reference: Chapter 15, P. 628, Difficulty: E

22.   The existence and nature of adolescence depends on
        a.   culture
        b.   puberty
        c.   identity
        d.   maturation
Answer: a, Reference: Chapter 15, P. 628, Difficulty: D

23.   Compared to adolescents from the Kalahari desert who experience no delay between
        puberty and marriage, when 13 and 14 year olds in the U.S. have children they
        a.   have an easier adjustment due to extensive support systems
        b.   face greater hardships because they cannot sustain themselves or their
                children
        c.   have less of an adjustment because they usually live at home with their
                parents
        d.   face greater hardship because parents are usually unwilling to support a
                grandchild
Answer: b, Reference: Chapter 15, P. 629, Difficulty: M

24.   The hypothalamus signals the pituitary to produce greater amounts of growth
        hormone at the beginning of which of the following?
        a.   puberty
        b.   adolescence
        d.   formal operational thought
        c.   multiple perspective taking
Answer: a, Reference: Chapter 15, P. 629, Difficulty: D

25.   The hormone that controls the adolescent growth spurt is produced in the
        a.   hypothalamus
        b.   adrenal cortex
        d.   pituitary gland
        c.   ovaries and testes
Answer: c, Reference: Chapter 15, P. 629, Difficulty: M

26.   Gonadotrophic hormones
        a.   are called estrogen and testosterone
        b.   cause all body tissues to grow faster
        c.   are unrelated to reproductive capacity
        d.   stimulate the ovaries and testes to produce sex hormones
Answer: d, Reference: Chapter 15, P. 629, Difficulty: M

27.   During puberty, the level of testosterone in males increases over the level present in middle childhood by
       a.   double
       b.   three times
       c.   eight times
       d.   eighteen times
Answer: d, Reference: Chapter 15, P. 630, Difficulty: D

28.   During puberty, the level of estrogen in females increases over the level present in middle childhood by
       a.   double
       b.   three times
       c.   eight times
       d.   eighteen times
Answer: c, Reference: Chapter 15, P. 630, Difficulty: M

29.   In males, the adolescent growth spurt
       a.   occurs at about the same age for all girls
       b.   occurs, on the average, at the same time it does in males
       c.   lasts 2 to 3 years and results in as much as 6-7 inches of growth
       d.   lasts 2 to 3 years and results in as much as about 9 inches of growth
Answer: d, Reference: Chapter 15, P. 630, Difficulty: M

30.   In females, the adolescent growth spurt
       a.   occurs at about the same age for all girls
       b.   occurs, on the average, at the same time it does in males
       c.   lasts 2 to 3 years and results in as much as 6-7 inches of growth
       d.   lasts 2 to 3 years and results in about as much as 9 inches of growth
Answer: c, Reference: Chapter 15, P. 630, Difficulty: M

31.   Young people reach 98 percent of their adult height
       a.   by the end of middle childhood
       b.   by the end of the growth spurt of puberty
       c.   about the time they graduate from high school
       d.   before they show signs of developing sexual maturity
Answer: b, Reference: Chapter 15, P. 630, Difficulty: E

32.   According to Tanner, which body part has its adolescent growth spurt earliest?
       a.   legs
       b.   arms
       c.   trunk
       d.   shoulders
Answer: a, Reference: Chapter 15, P. 630, Difficulty: E

33.   During the adolescent growth spurt, the brain
        a.   does not grow appreciably
        b.   attains 90 percent of its adult weight
        c.   recapitulates its early stages of development
        d.   begins to myelinate connections between the cognitive areas
Answer: a, Reference: Chapter 15, P. 630, Difficulty: M

34.   Strength, as measured by hand grip or arm pull, is
        a.   considerably greater in boys than in girls throughout development
        b.   approximately equal in boys and girls of equal size throughout development
        c.   greater in girls than in boys of equal size before puberty, and greater in boys
                thereafter
        d.   nearly equal in boys and girls of equal size before puberty, but greater in boys
        thereafter
Answer: d, Reference: Chapter 15, P. 630, Difficulty: D

35.   Which is a correct assessment of physiological differences between males and
        females?
        a.   males are stronger, healthier, and better able to tolerate long-term stress
        b.   females have larger hearts and lower resting heart rates, and can exercise for
                longer periods
        d.   males have greater capacity for physical exercise, but females are healthier
                and tolerate stress better
        c.   there are no appreciable differences in the capacity of males and females for
                exercise and athletic performance
Answer: c, Reference: Chapter 15, P. 630, Difficulty: D

36.   Anatomical and physiological signs that outwardly differentiate males and females
        are
        a.   gonadotrophic hormones
        b.   primary sexual characteristics
        d.   ovulation and spermatogenesis
        c.   secondary sexual characteristics
Answer: d, Reference: Chapter 15, P. 631, Difficulty: E

37.   Which is a secondary sexual characteristic?
        a.   the onset of menarche
        b.   the production of sperm
        d.   the production of semen
        c.   the appearance of pubic and underarm hair
Answer: d, Reference: Chapter 15, P. 631, Difficulty: E

38.   Which if the following does not usually occur until fairly late in puberty?
    a.   the growth spurt
    b.   deepening of the voice
    c.   the appearance of pubic hair
    d.   the appearance of the breast bud
Answer: b, Reference: Chapter 15, P. 631, Difficulty: M

39.   The occurrence of the first menstrual period
    a.   is called menarche
    b.   marks the beginning of ovulation
    c.   is the first event of puberty for girls
    d.   comes at about the same age for all girls
Answer: a, Reference: Chapter 15, P. 631, Difficulty: E

40.   Ovulation usually begins
    a.   with menarche
    b.   at the beginning of puberty
    c.   12-18 months after the onset of menarche
    d.   about the same time as the appearance of breast buds
Answer: c, Reference: Chapter 15, P. 631, Difficulty: E

41.   All of the following environmental influences affect the timing of puberty except
    a.   stress
    b.   nutrition
    c.   reinforcement history
    d.   high level of physical exercise
Answer: c, Reference: Chapter 15, P. 632, Difficulty: E

42.   The timing of the events of puberty is
    a.   more similar for identical than for fraternal twins
    b.   the same, on the average, for children of all cultures
    c.   later in many societies, for boys and girls, than it was 100 years ago
    d.   related to socioeconomic status, with girls from poor families reaching
            menarche earlier than girls from affluent families
Answer: a, Reference: Chapter 15, P. 632, Difficulty: M

43.   Although there is wide individual variation, on average, the physical changes
        associated with puberty indicates that it lasts approximately
    a.   1 year
    b.   2 years
    c.   3 years
    d.   4 years
Answer: d, Reference: Chapter 15, P. 633, Difficulty: M

44.   The ritual ceremonies which express the important contributions to society the young person is supposed to make in his or her adult life are known as
a.   rites of passage
b.   adolescent resolutions
c.   pubertal behavioral shifts
d.   pubertal transition ceremonies
Answer: a, Reference: Chapter 15, P. 633, Difficulty: E

45.   Jeanne Brooks-Gunn and her colleagues research on girls' attitudes and beliefs about menstruation have found that a girl's physical symptoms experienced during menstruation are often correlated with her
a.   own expectations before menarche
b.   degree of popularity before menarche
d.   peer's physical symptoms during menstruation
c.   mother's physical symptoms during menstruation
Answer: a, Reference: Chapter 15, P. 635, Difficulty: M

46.   Which of the following were found to be more mature socially and psychologically than their peers in a study by Mary Cover Jones and Nancy Bayley (1950)?
a.   physically late-maturing girls
b.   physically late-maturing boys
d.   physically early-maturing girls
c.   physically early-maturing boys
Answer: d, Reference: Chapter 15, P. 636, Difficulty: M

47.   While the results of studies are mixed, the overall effect of early maturation for girls appears to be
a.   minimal
b.   short-lived
c.   more negative than positive
d.   more positive than negative
Answer: c, Reference: Chapter 15, P. 637, Difficulty: M

48.   Early maturing girls are more likely to say they are
a.   satisfied with their height and weight
b.   dissatisfied with their height and weight
c.   satisfied with their height but dissatisfied with their weight
d.   dissatisfied with their height but satisfied with their weight
Answer: b, Reference: Chapter 15, P. 637, Difficulty: M

49.   A criteria for anorexia nervosa is
        a.   preoccupation with food
        b.   loss of 15% body weight
        c.   binging and purging cycles
        d.   kidney failure or heart damage
Answer: b, Reference: Chapter 15, P. 637, Box 15.1 Difficulty: M

50.   The disorder characterized by binge eating is called
        a.   anorexia nervosa
        b.   bulimia nervosa
        c.   binge-purge disorder
        d.   a form of personality disorder
Answer: b, Reference: Chapter 15, P. 637, Box 15.1 Difficulty: M

51.   An eating disorder is most likely to occur in a girl who
        a.   is generally anxious
        b.   has a poor body image
        c.   has a supportive family
        d.   goes through puberty late
Answer: b, Reference: Chapter 15, P. 637, Box 15.1 Difficulty: M

52.   A longitudinal Swedish study comparing adolescent early-maturing girls to late
        maturing girls found that early-maturing girls were more likely to do all of the
        following except
        a.   achieve high grades
        b.   have a stable boyfriend
        c.   have unwanted pregnancies
        d.   have sexual experiences by mid-adolescence
Answer: a, Reference: Chapter 15, P. 638, Difficulty: E

53.   Which of the following behaviors was not found to increase in the Swedish study of
        early-maturing girls?
        a.   truancy
        b.   shoplifting
        c.   drug and alcohol use
        d.   academic achievement
Answer: d, Reference: Chapter 15, P. 638, Difficulty: E

54. Studies of the consequences of early and late maturation seem to show that
    a.   late-maturing boys tend to be less intellectually curious and more conventional than early-maturers
    b.   both early-maturing boys and girls have better emotional stability and self-control than late-maturers
    c.   early-maturing boys are less likely than late-maturers to smoke, drink, and use drugs during adolescence
    d.   late-maturing girls are initially dissatisfied with their appearance, but later in adolescence may become more satisfied than early-maturers

Answer: d, Reference: Chapter 15, P. 638, Difficulty: D

55. A recent study found that early-maturing Swedish girls
    a.   completed fewer years of schooling than other girls their age
    b.   were higher in emotional and self control than other girls their age
    d.   were more satisfied with their appearance than other girls their age
    c.   were more likely to delay having children than other girls their age

Answer: a, Reference: Chapter 15, P. 638, Difficulty: M

56. Adolescents are more likely to require their friends to_____ than children in middle childhood.
    a.   be loyal
    b.   live close by
    c.   be of the same sex
    d.   come from similar families

Answer: a, Reference: Chapter 15, P. 640, Difficulty: M

57. Self-disclosure in adolescence compared to middle childhood is
    a.   often joked about
    b.   generally about the same
    c.   often followed by lengthy discussions about the problem
    d.   met with statements of solidarity such as "I know" and "Me too"

Answer: c, Reference: Chapter 15, P. 641, Difficulty: M

58. Which of the following is true regarding the friendships of boys and girls
    a.   girls are less likely to form friendships as close as that of boys
    b.   boys are less articulate about the nature and meaning of friendship
    c.   boys want their friends to be someone they could confide in about opposite-sex relationships
    d.   girls are more likely than boys to have a group of friends to maintain independence from control by adults

Answer: b, Reference: Chapter 15, P. 642, Difficulty: E

59. Adolescent boys want friends who
    a. get good grades in school
    b. do not already have another "best friend"
    c. will support them in conflicts with authority
    d. will advise them about their relationships with girls
Answer: c, Reference: Chapter 15, P. 642, Difficulty: M

60. An adolescent "clique" consists of
    a. a loosely associated group of couples
    b. two girls or two boys who are "best friends"
    c. a group of six or seven friends, of the same sex
    d. a group of fifteen to twenty friends, of mixed sex
Answer: c, Reference: Chapter 15, P. 642, Difficulty: M

61. According to Dunphy, the size of an adolescent "clique" is about the same size as
    a. a football team
    b. a nuclear family
    c. an extended family
    d. a classroom of students
Answer: c, Reference: Chapter 15, P. 642, Difficulty: M

62. In adolescent social development, "crowds"
    a. are unrelated to cliques
    b. consist of six or seven same-sex friends
    c. are groups of fifteen to thirty friends of both sexes
    d. consist of individuals with widely varying interests and skills
Answer: c, Reference: Chapter 15, P. 642, Difficulty: M

63. According to James Coleman's work, both adolescent boys and girls, consider which of the following to be the most important characteristic of people in the "leading crowds" of their high schools?
    a. good grades
    b. good manners
    c. a good personality
    d. a nice car and nice clothes
Answer: c, Reference: Chapter 15, P. 643, Difficulty: E

64. Boys, but not girls, in a leading crowd, are valued for
    a. having good grades
    b. wearing good clothes
    c. having a good personality
    d. being physically attractive
Answer: a, Reference: Chapter 15, P. 643, Difficulty: D

65.   Research on adolescent peers groups conducted by James Coleman more than 30 years ago
       a.   has been thoroughly discredited
       b.   continues to enjoy wide acceptance among researchers who study adolescence
       c.   shares only a vague resemblance with findings of current adolescent researchers
       d.   has been found to be dated with respect to current adolescent peer group behavior

Answer: b, Reference: Chapter 15, P. 643, Difficulty: M

66.   Academic achievement was found to decrease popularity in some
       a.   elementary schools
       b.   upper class communities
       c.   Asian American communities
       d.   African-American communities

Answer: d, Reference: Chapter 15, P. 643, Difficulty: E

67.   Adolescents are most susceptible to peer pressure
       a.   during the last year of high school
       b.   at 14 or 15 years of age; then susceptibility declines
       c.   at about 12 years of age; then susceptibility declines
       d.   none of the above: they are equally susceptible at all ages

Answer: b, Reference: Chapter 15, P. 645, Difficulty: D

68.   Behaviors considered antisocial during adolescence, such as smoking, drinking, and engaging in sexual relations
       a.   are signs of personality disorders
       b.   are usually attempts to outrage adults
       c.   may be attempts to model adult behavior
       d.   are products of young people's lack of self-control

Answer: c, Reference: Chapter 15, P. 645, Difficulty: M

69.   Research on adolescent peers groups conducted by Dexter Dunphy more than 30 years ago
       a.   has been thoroughly discredited
       b.   continues to enjoy wide acceptance among researchers who study adolescence
       c.   shares only a vague resemblance with findings of current adolescent researchers
       d.   has been found to be dated with respect to current adolescent peer group behavior

Answer: b, Reference: Chapter 15, P. 645, Difficulty: M

70. Dexter Dunphy found that the first "cliques" formed by adolescents
   a. break apart into friendships of two or three
   b. allow the formation of heterosexual couples
   c. typically are mixed-sex groups of six or seven friends
   d. occasionally get together with other cliques to form "crowds"
Answer: d, Reference: Chapter 15, P. 645, Difficulty: E

71. Which of the following is part of a sequence of "scripted" activities through which adolescents learn sexual behavior typical in our culture?
   a. petting
   b. bisexuality
   c. masturbation
   d. gender conformity
Answer: a, Reference: Chapter 15, P. 645, Difficulty: M

72. Compared to adults, adolescents contract sexually transmitted diseases
   a. half as often
   b. twice as often
   c. three times as often
   d. at about the same rate
Answer: b, Reference: Chapter 15, P. 646, Box 15.2, Difficulty: M

73. Cross-cultural studies of adolescent antisocial behavior have shown that it is
   a. universal
   b. reduced when more time is spent with adults
   c. reduced when more time is spent in peer groups
   d. reduced when more time is spent caring for younger children
Answer: b, Reference: Chapter 15, P. 646, Box 15.2, Difficulty: M

74. A study by Marilyn Quadrel (1993) asking adults and adolescents to rate their risk for being in a car accident or getting pregnant found that
   a. adolescents rated themselves as less at risk than did adults
   b. adults rated themselves as less at risk than did adolescents
   c. both adults and adolescents rated themselves as less at risk than they rated others
   d. both adults and adolescents rated themselves as more at risk than they rated others
Answer: c, Reference: Chapter 15, P. 647, Box 15.2, Difficulty: M

75. Jeffrey Arnett (1992) makes the argument that risk taking in adolescence is due to
   a. biological changes
   b. peer group pressure
   c. changes in the cognitive processes that occur
   d. the availability of cultural models on television
Answer: a, Reference: Chapter 15, P. 647, Box 15.2, Difficulty: M

76.   Cynthia Lightfoot found evidence that adolescents explain their risk taking as
        a.   sensation seeking
        b.   due to peer pressure
        c.   a way of testing their limits
        d.   a way of seeking novelty for its own sake
Answer: c, Reference: Chapter 15, P. 647, Box 15.2, Difficulty: M

77.   The example of "ngweko" lovemaking among the Kikuyu of Kenya demonstrates
        that
        a.   in many cultures, bisexuality is an important aspect of learning sexual
                behavior
        b.   the script for learning sexual behavior in adolescence is nearly identical across
                cultures
        c.   the scripts according to which sexual behavior are learned may be quite
                different in different cultures
        d.   African cultures are generally less restrictive about premarital intercourse
                than are industrialized cultures
Answer: c, Reference: Chapter 15, P. 650, Box 15.2, Difficulty: D

78.   According to Kinsey and his coworkers more than 80% of the men they surveyed
        reported they had masturbated to orgasm by the age of
        a.   10 years
        b.   12 years
        c.   15 years
        d.   18 years
Answer: c, Reference: Chapter 15, P. 651, Difficulty: M

79.   The masturbatory behavior among male and female adolescents
        a.   has not been researched
        b.   is essentially the same for males and females
        c.   reinforces the males' commitment to sexual behavior
        d.   reinforces the females' commitment to sexual behavior
Answer: c Reference: Chapter 15, P. 651, Difficulty: M

80.   The socialization, masturbatory behavior, and fantasies of adolescent males and
        females seems to lead to
        a.   male and female commitment to sexuality
        b.   male and female commitment to romantic love
        c.   male commitment to sexuality and female commitment to romantic love
        d.   female commitment to sexuality and male commitment to romantic love
Answer: c, Reference: Chapter 15, P. 651, Difficulty: E

81. In one study, boys most often reported that their initial response to their first sexual experience was feeling _____ , while girls most often reported feeling _____ .
    a. relieved, mature
    b. glad, ambivalent
    c. ambivalent, sorry
    d. embarrassed, satisfied
Answer: b Reference: Chapter 15, P. 651, Difficulty: M

82. Reliable forms of contraception
    a. are often not part of adolescents' "script" for sexual activity
    b. have kept unwanted pregnancies among teenagers to a minimum
    c. are usually procured before adolescents experience sexual intercourse for the first time
    d. are the decisive factor causing the trend to earlier sexual activity that began in the 1960's
Answer: a, Reference: Chapter 15, P. 652, Difficulty: D

83. The average delay between initiation of sexual activity and the first use of prescription birth control is about
    a. 6 months
    b. 1 year
    c. 2 years
    d. 5 years
Answer: b, Reference: Chapter 15, P. 652, Difficulty: M

84. The percentage of never-married girls who were sexually active increased for all ages 15 and 19 years from 1971–1990. The greatest percent of change was among
    a. Asian females
    b. black females
    c. white females
    d. hispanic females
Answer: c Reference: Chapter 15, P. 652, Difficulty: D

85. The percentage of high school students who were sexually active who report protecting themselves against AIDS or other sexually transmitted diseases in 1992 was
    a. less than 20%
    b. less than 50%
    c. more than 50%
    d. more than 70%
Answer: b, Reference: Chapter 15, P. 652, Difficulty: M

86. During the first few months following menarche
    a.   parents allow greater autonomy to their girls
    b.   mothers and daughters become closer than ever
    c.   there is an increase in the disagreements between mothers and daughters
    d.   mothers increase their attempts to control their daughters while fathers decrease their control

Answer: c, Reference: Chapter 15, P. 652, Difficulty: D

87. The influence of puberty on family relations
    a.   is generally the same for boys and girls
    b.   depends upon the age of puberty in boys
    c.   depends upon the age of menarche in girls
    d.   is more notable in adolescent-father than adolescent-mother relationships

Answer: b, Reference: Chapter 15, P. 652, Difficulty: D

88. Which of the following family relationships is most impacted by puberty?
    a.   sibling relationships
    b.   adolescent-father relationships
    c.   adolescent-mother relationships
    d.   all family relationships are equally impacted

Answer: c, Reference: Chapter 15, P. 652, Difficulty: D

89. Which of the following has been suggested as a reason for the difference in adolescent-mother and adolescent-father relationships?
    a.   adolescents view their mothers as having lower status than their fathers
    b.   adolescents believe their fathers are more likely to grant them autonomy
    c.   adolescents have formed closer emotional relationships with their fathers
    d.   adolescents believe achieving autonomy from their mother will be easier than achieving it from their father

Answer: a, Reference: Chapter 15, P. 652, Difficulty: M

90. According to a survey of 37 countries, when compared with teens in other countries, U.S. teenagers are
    a.   less sexually active
    b.   more sexually active
    c.   more likely to become pregnant
    d.   arc less likely to become pregnant

Answer: c, Reference: Chapter 15, P. 653, Box 15.4, Difficulty: M

91.   What percent of pregnancies of girls ages 15–19 years in the United States end in
        abortion?
        a.   20%
        b.   33%
        c.   40%
        d.   60%
Answer: b, Reference: Chapter 15, P. 653, Box 15.4, Difficulty: M

92.   Teenagers who become pregnant are
        a.   less likely to keep their babies if they are African American
        b.   more likely to keep their babies than to give them up for adoption
        c.   more likely to give their baby up for adoption if they are religious
        d.   less likely to terminate their pregnancies if they are doing well in school
Answer: b, Reference: Chapter 15, P. 653, Box 15.4, Difficulty: M

93.   Pregnant teenagers are more likely to choose abortion if
        a.   they are African American
        b.   they are doing well in school
        c.   their mothers are not well educated
        d.   they have strong religious convictions
Answer: b, Reference: Chapter 15, P. 653, Box 15.4, Difficulty: E

94.   Research by psychologists on "youth culture" indicate
        a.   there is evidence of a discontinuous and self-contained "youth culture"
        b.   there is considerable disagreement between generations about most
                important issues
        c.   there is considerable continuity between the culture of adolescents and that
                of their parents
        d.   each individual's "youth culture" is shaped by prevailing social phenomenon
                which differ from one generation to the next
Answer: c, Reference: Chapter 15, P. 654, Difficulty: D

95.   During adolescence, young people report
        a.   generally feeling close to their parents
        b.   becoming closer to their fathers than to their mothers
        c.   spending far more time with their peers than with their parents
        d.   that they disagree with their parents on most important issues
Answer: a, Reference: Chapter 15, P. 654, Difficulty: D

96.   Research has shown that adolescents and their parents generally agree on which of
        the following issues?
        a.   hours of sleep
        b.   styles of dress
        c.   religious issues
        d.   issues related to sex
Answer: c, Reference: Chapter 15, P. 654, Difficulty: M

97.   Which of the following was found to be true of adolescent-parent interactions?
        a.   Fathers are approached mostly for practical advice
        b.   Adolescents talk to their mothers to validate their feelings
        c.   Adolescents have more intimate relationships with their fathers
        d.   Mothers are approached on personal matters only when special advice is
                needed
Answer: b, Reference: Chapter 15, P. 654, Difficulty: D

98.   The data on the role of parents and peers in shaping adolescent behavior points to
        a.   no evidence of a "generation gap"
        b.   strong evidence of a "generation gap"
        c.   little evidence of adolescents breaking away and establishing relationships
                outside the family
        d.   a process of individuation whereby adolescents and their parents negotiate a
                new form of independence
Answer: d, Reference: Chapter 15, P. 658, Difficulty: E

99.   While it has been estimated to be much higher in many inner-city neighborhoods,
        the school drop out rate has been conservatively estimated at
        a.   10%
        b.   25 %
        c.   38 %
        d.   50 %
Answer: a, Reference: Chapter 15, P. 658, Difficulty: D

100.   Which of the following statement is true regarding the rate of employment for Afro-
        American 15- and 16-year-olds?
        a.   it is equal to whites
        b.   it is half that of whites
        c.   it is twice that of whites
        d.   it is insignificant compared to whites
Answer: b, Reference: Chapter 15, P. 659, Difficulty: M

101.   Which of the following statements regarding teenage employment is not true?
   a.   girls work longer hours than boys
   b.   typically teenagers work longer hours during the summer
   c.   high school seniors work more hours on average than sophomores
   d.   minority and lower SES youth work longer hours than middle-class youth
Answer: a, Reference: Chapter 15, P. 659, Difficulty: E

102.   Adolescents typically work at jobs that
   a.   pay minimum wage
   b.   prepare them for future careers
   c.   result in feelings of powerlessness
   d.   offer opportunities for advancement
Answer: a, Reference: Chapter 15, P. 659, Difficulty: E

103.   Which is a disadvantage of part-time work for teenagers?
   a.   working generally lowers a teenager's self-esteem
   b.   teens rarely feel a sense of accomplishment in jobs
   c.   working many hours per week may affect school performance
   d.   teens do not earn enough money to pay for anything meaningful to them
Answer: c, Reference: Chapter 15, P. 660, Difficulty: M

104.   Recent research by Steinberg, Fegley, and Dornbusch (1993) has revealed that adolescents who work part time
   a.   earn a higher grade point average
   b.   are generally less involved in school
   c.   are also more inclined to be involved in school
   d.   do not differ significantly from their nonworking classmates
Answer: b, Reference: Chapter 15, P. 660, Difficulty: E

Essay Questions

1.   Describe the three characteristics of adolescence suggested by eighteenth-century philosopher Jean-Jacques Rousseau.

2.   What is meant by the statement that "the young recapitulate the entire history of the human species?" Who is associated with this idea and what is its current status? Explain.

3.   In Freud's view, what kinds of psychological development take place during adolescence? Explain.

4. Describe adolescence from the biological-maturation, environmental-learning, interactional, and cultural-context points of view.

5. Describe the characteristics of physical growth and development during puberty.

6. Describe the gender-related changes during puberty.

7. Name two theorists who support the biological-maturational perspective of adolescent development. Briefly describe their views of the process at work during the development of the adolescent.

8. Compare and contrast the factors associated with popularity in American boys and girls.

9. Describe how, in Dunphy's study of adolescent social interaction, teenagers' social contacts progressed from same-sex groups to couples.

10. Describe how social and cultural factors influence the ways in which adolescents learn sexual behavior.

11. What is meant by the term "youth culture"? Does research provide evidence for or against a discontinuous, self-contained "youth culture"? Explain.

12. How do males and females differ in the expectations they bring to sexuality and romantic love? What are their respective reactions to their first sexual intercourse?

13. What variables influence teenagers who decides to have and keep the child of an unplanned pregnancy? Discuss termination of pregnancy and adoption as options.

14. What features characterize relations with parents and peers during adolescence, and in what ways do these relations differ from their forms during earlier periods of development?

15. Are adolescents especially sensitive to peer pressure? What factors influence teenagers' tendency to conform, and what kinds of behaviors are most likely to result?

16. What are the most typical sources of conflict between adolescents and their parents?

17. How has the work of Margaret Mead facilitated the study of adolescents among psychologists?

18. Describe the concept of "identity". What changes take place in identity in the transition of young people to adulthood?

19. Briefly describe the sequence of appearance of secondary sexual characteristics in boys and girls. Be sure to indicate when these changes take place.

20. What is menarche? When in the pubertal period does it usually occur? How does it relate to the onset of ovulation?

21. What environmental factors are thought to influence the age of menarche? Explain.

22. What are rites of passage? Give an example.

23. Summarize the findings of studies investigating the effect of early maturation in boys and girls.

24. Describe the effect of puberty on family relations.

25. Describe the changes that occur in friendships of children as they enter adolescence.

26. How does self-disclosure in adolescence differ from that in middle childhood? Explain why this might be true..

27. What are "cliques"? How do they differ from "crowds"? How are they similar?

28. Describe some of the factors which have participated in the trend toward increasing sexual activity among unmarried people.

29. State some positive and negative aspects of teenagers working in part-time jobs.

30. What is the relationship of working in part-time jobs to education and later career success. Explain.

31. What is the nature of adolescent risk taking. Give two alternative views of this behavior.

The Psychological Achievements of Adolescence | CHAPTER 16

Multiple-Choice Questions

1.   Which of the following is characteristic of adolescents?
     a.   skepticism about adult opinions
     b.   seeking out adult models to imitate
     c.   ignoring adult models of behavior as irrelevant
     d.   both skepticism about adult opinions and seeking adult models
Answer: d, Reference: Chapter 16, P. 666, Difficulty: M

2.   All except which of the following characteristics distinguish adolescent thought from that of middle childhood?
     a.   planning ahead
     b.   focus on the here and now
     c.   thinking about possibilities
     d.   thinking through hypotheses
Answer: b, Reference: Chapter 16, P. 666, Difficulty: M

3.   The generation and testing of hypotheses is strongly characteristic of the thinking children in
     a.   late infancy
     b.   adolescence
     c.   early childhood
     d.   middle childhood
Answer: b, Reference: Chapter 16, P. 667, Difficulty: E

4. Compared to the thinking of a younger child, an adolescent's thinking is characterized by the
   a. ability to systematically generate and test hypotheses
   b. ability to generate classification systems of more than one level
   c. discovery that objects exist independently of their actions on them
   d. realization that people's identities remain constant despite changes in appearance

Answer: a Reference: Chapter 16, P. 667, Difficulty: M

5. "Metacognitive thinking" is
   a. rarely seen outside of school related tasks
   b. the ability to reason about physical objects and events
   c. the ability to think about one's own thought processes
   d. an ability that first appears in the preoperational period

Answer: c, Reference: Chapter 16, P. 667, Difficulty: E

6. All of the following are true of adolescent thinking except
   a. they think about thought
   b. they think within conventional limits
   c. they can think about possibilities and context
   d. thought processes depend heavily on the content of the problems

Answer: b Reference: Chapter 16, P. 667, Difficulty: M

7. The Piagetian stage in which problems are solved systematically by considering all possible combinations is called
   a. formal operations
   b. formal responding
   c. abstract operations
   d. concrete operations

Answer: a Reference: Chapter 16, P. 667, Difficulty: E

8. The combination-of-chemicals task, in which children discover how to mix four colorless liquids to make a yellow color, requires which type of thinking skills for its solution?
   a. preoperational
   b. formal operational
   c. concrete operational
   d. post-formal operational

Answer: b Reference: Chapter 16, P. 669, Difficulty: M

9.   Which Piagetian task requires formal operations for its solution?
      a.   conservation of liquid
      b.   classifying objects into sets according to multiple criteria
      c.   identifying which combination of chemicals produces a yellow solution
      d.   predicting how a perceptual display will appear when viewed from a different
            angle
Answer: c, Reference: Chapter 16, P. 669, Difficulty: M

10.   In Piaget's system, a structured whole
      a.   is the end result of identity formation in adolescence
      b.   is one of the characteristics of concrete operational thought
      c.   is a system of relationships that can be logically thought about
      d.   describes the way the world appears to adolescents before they are able to
            differentiate their sensory modalities
Answer: c Reference: Chapter 16, P. 670, Difficulty: M

11.   Studies on the chemical task by Inhelder and Piaget asked children to determine
      which combination of chemicals would turn yellow when another chemical was
      added. On this task seven-year old children
      a.   were unsystematic in combining chemicals
      b.   could be trained to solve the task correctly
      c.   were systematic in combining chemicals from the start of the task
      d.   could combine chemicals systematically when given prompts from the
            experimenter
Answer: a, Reference: Chapter 16, P. 670, Difficulty: E

12.   Studies on the chemical task by Inhelder and Piaget asked children to determine
      which combination of chemicals would turn yellow when another chemical was
      added. On this task adolescents
      a.   were unsystematic in combining chemicals
      b.   could be trained to solve the task correctly
      c.   were systematic in combining chemicals from the start of the task
      d.   could combine chemicals systematically only when given prompts from the
            experimenter
Answer: c, Reference: Chapter 16, P. 670, Difficulty: E

13.   The key to formal operational performance on the combination-of-chemicals task is
      to combine the four liquids
      a.   all at once
      b.   systematically
      c.   as quickly as possible
      d.   in more than one order
Answer: b, Reference: Chapter 16, P. 670, Difficulty: E

14.   The ability to solve the problem, "All cars are red. That is a car. That must be red."
       requires
       a.   deductive reasoning
       b.   hypothetical thinking
       c.   transductive reasoning
       d.   systematic manipulation of variables
Answer: a, Reference: Chapter 16, P. 671, Difficulty: M

15.   In a series of studies by Overton and his colleagues, deductive reasoning was
       observed in 6th graders
       a.   only rarely
       b.   about 30% of the time
       c.   about 55% of the time
       d.   more than 70% of the time
Answer: a, Reference: Chapter 16, P. 672, Difficulty: M

16.   In a series of studies by Overton and his colleagues, deductive reasoning was
       observed in 12th graders
       a.   only rarely
       b.   about 30% of the time
       c.   about 55% of the time
       d.   more than 70% of the time
Answer: d, Reference: Chapter 16, P. 672, Difficulty: D

17.   About what percentage of well-educated American teenagers are capable of solving
       problems like the balance-beam and the combination of chemicals problems in ways
       that are characteristic of formal operational reasoning?
       a.   10-20%
       b.   30-40%
       c.   50-60%
       d.   85-90%
Answer: b, Reference: Chapter 16, P. 672, Difficulty: M

18.   Studies by Siegler and Liebert in which 10-13 year old children were asked to find
       the combination of open and closed positions on four switches needed to make a
       model train go, revealed that with training and tutoring
       a.   all children solved the problem correctly
       b.   some of the children at both ages responded correctly
       c.   13 year old children improved but the 10 year olds did not
       d.   no improvements occurred in the ability to solve the problem either for 10-
             year olds or 13-year olds
Answer: a, Reference: Chapter 16, P. 672, Difficulty: M

19. Studies of U.S. subjects' performance on tests of formal operations have shown that
   a. many people fail to use formal operations to solve problems in the absence of specific instruction
   b. virtually all educated people 11 years of age and older routinely use formal operations in solving problems
   c. many younger adolescents perform poorly on laboratory measures; however, performance improves during late adolescence and early adulthood
   d. adolescent and adult subjects often have trouble with the laboratory measures, but consistently use formal operations in "real world" contexts such as grocery shopping

Answer: a, Reference: Chapter 16, P. 673, Difficulty: D

20. Some investigators think that girls are at a disadvantage when tested on Piagetian tasks which involve
   a. formal operations
   b. the ability to plan ahead
   c. the use of spatial abilities
   d. reasoning about hypothetical situations

Answer: c, Reference: Chapter 16, P. 673, Difficulty: M

21. A meta-analysis of sex differences from the 1970's and 1980's found
   a. similar sex differences across both decades
   b. a decline in sex differences across the decades
   c. an increase in the content areas of sex differences over time
   d. an increase in the magnitude of the sex differences over time

Answer: b, Reference: Chapter 16, P. 673, Difficulty: D

22. Sex differences found on Piagetian formal operational tasks have been attributed to
   a. male superiority in science
   b. biological differences in the sexes
   c. boys' greater interest in the content of the task
   d. girls greater interest in interpersonal relationships

Answer: c, Reference: Chapter 16, P. 674, Difficulty: E

23. Adolescents and adults are likely to apply formal operational thought to solve problems
   a. whose content is unfamiliar to them
   b. whose content they are already familiar with and interested in
   c. for which concrete operational thought alone would be adequate
   d. of familiar or unfamiliar content, that cannot be solved using concrete operations

Answer: b, Reference: Chapter 16, P. 674, Difficulty: D

24.   Cross-cultural research on the development of formal operations suggests
        a.   the formal operational stage is universal
        b.   the formal operational stage is sometimes skipped
        c.   all normal people attain the level of formal operations
        d.   people from non-technological societies rarely demonstrate formal
                operations using Piagetian methods
Answer: d, Reference: Chapter 16, P. 675, Difficulty: E

25.   Which of the following provides the greatest challenge to the concept of universality
        of formal operations?
        a.   cultural variations in formal operations
        b.   male superiority on formal operations tasks
        c.   variability in the age of onset of formal operational reasoning
        d.   significant variability in the level of logical reasoning among adults
Answer: a, Reference: Chapter 16, P. 675, Difficulty: M

26.   Piaget concluded that formal operations develop
        a.   in a few gifted individuals
        b.   more often in males than in females
        c.   universally among people from technologically advanced societies but not
                among those from preindustrial societies
        d.   in all normal people, but are applied to different problem areas that
                correspond to their interests and areas of special expertise
Answer: d, Reference: Chapter 16, P. 675, Difficulty: D

27.   Which theorists view the development of adolescent thought as the result of
        improvements in memory and the use of increasingly efficient problem-solving
        strategies?
        a.   Piagetian
        b.   biological-maturation
        c.   information-processing
        d.   environmental-learning
Answer: c, Reference: Chapter 16, P. 676, Difficulty: E

28.   Which of the following is proposed by the information processing theorists to
        explain advances in thought processes during adolescence?
        a.   horizontal dÈcalage accounts for changes during this period
        b.   adolescents discover a new relation between thought and language
        c.   acquisition of more powerful and efficient strategies to solve problems lead to
                new abilities
        d.   specialized practice in particular domains of experience leads to abstract
                thought processes
Answer: c, Reference: Chapter 16, P. 676, Difficulty: M

29.   Information-processing theories describe the characteristics of adolescent thought in which of the following ways?
  a.   during adolescence, children's problem solving reflects a qualitatively different mode of thought
  b.   adolescents solve the same kinds of problems as younger children, and solve them in the same ways, but faster
  c.   adolescents are able to solve more complex problems than younger children because of greater processing efficiency
  d.   there are no differences between the performance of adolescents and younger children on most cognitive tasks

Answer: c, Reference: Chapter 16, P. 676, Difficulty: M

30.   A study by Kuhn and her colleagues (1995) found that, when presented with a complex problem involving multiple variables, over repeated trials adults
  a.   used more sophisticated strategies while children did not
  b.   used a different mixture of logical strategies than children
  c.   refined their initial theories of relevant features while children did not
  d.   were logically consistent in making inferences about the same problem while children were not

Answer: b, Reference: Chapter 16, P. 677, Difficulty: M

31.   In language studies which examined how 9 - 12-year-old children make sense of an unfamiliar word in a series of sentences, Werner and Kaplan found that
  a.   all children treated the sentences as separate entities
  b.   9 and 10 year olds were too confused to attempt any word meanings
  c.   only 11 and 12-year-old were able to find a meaning that fit all cases
  d.   all children were able to compare possible meanings in each sentences and find a meaning that fit all cases

Answer: c, Reference: Chapter 16, P. 678, Difficulty: M

32.   The performance of 9-year-old compared to 15-year-old children on quasi-analogies such as "A bird uses   ; a fish uses " is
  a.   significantly better
  b.   significantly worse
  c.   roughly comparable
  d.   unimportant since they are not "true" analogies

Answer: c, Reference: Chapter 16, P. 678, Difficulty: D

33.   A study by Levinson and Carpenter (1974) found that for "true" analogies
  a.   9-year-olds outperform 15-year-olds
  b.   15-year-olds outperform 9-year-olds
  c.   15-year-olds still have significant trouble
  d.   the performance of 9-year-olds and 15-year-olds is similar

Answer: b, Reference: Chapter 16, P. 678, Difficulty: M

34.   Research demonstrating that adolescents find analogies easy to solve shows changes in the structure and use of which of the following are important in adolescent cognitive development?
        a.   games
        b.   morality
        c.   memory
        d.   language
Answer: d, Reference: Chapter 16, P. 678, Difficulty: E

35.   Experiments on the development of verbal concepts suggesting that new structures of word meaning begin to take shape during adolescence
        a.   demonstrate that language and thought are unrelated in adolescence
        b.   contradict the idea that a new form of logic contributes to adolescent thinking
        c.   demonstrate that these thought processes are not effectively investigated through the use of analogies
        d.   demonstrate that changes in the structure of language as well as changes in the logic of problem solving are important aspects of adolescent cognitive development
Answer: d, Reference: Chapter 16, P. 678, Difficulty: M

36.   The cultural-context perspective theorizes that formal operational thought
        a.   is applied in the same contexts in all societies
        b.   is applied in different contexts among different human groups
        c.   does not occur in enough people to be considered a feature of adolescent thought
        d.   occurs only among people whose educational experiences stimulate them to develop it
Answer: b, Reference: Chapter 16, P. 678, Difficulty: M

37.   Anthropologists have observed that South Sea islanders' system of navigation using a "star compass" and a "reference island"
        a.   is not very accurate
        b.   makes use of formal operational thought
        c.   is understood best by sailors with Western-style educations
        d.   can be learned by people whose thinking is at the preoperational level
Answer: b, Reference: Chapter 16, P. 680, Box 16.1 Difficulty: E

38. The "planning a holiday meal" activity used to investigate formal operational thought would most likely be used by a researcher who followed which of the following approaches?
     a.   Piagetian
     b.   linguistic
     c.   cultural-context
     d.   information-processing
Answer: c, Reference: Chapter 16, P. 681, Difficulty: M

39. Adults who are solving complex problems as part of everyday activities (such as planning a holiday meal)
     a.   are not able to think logically
     b.   do not need to use logical thinking skills
     c.   use formal operations in the same way as they do in Piagetian laboratory tasks
     d.   take short cuts in their reasoning, rather than considering all combinations of possibilities
Answer: d, Reference: Chapter 16, P. 682, Difficulty: M

40. Tschirgi's study of formal operational thought which asked participants to hypothesize about success or failure of ingredients in a cake, demonstrate that the kind of reasoning a person used differed depending upon
     a.   their sex
     b.   the sex of the child in the story
     c.   the expectations of the experimenter
     d.   whether the outcome of the situation was viewed as positive or negative
Answer: d, Reference: Chapter 16, P. 682, Difficulty: E

41. Evidence from information-processing and cultural-context approaches suggest
     a.   expectations about outcomes rarely influence logical thinking
     b.   formal operations are acquired equally across multiple contexts
     c.   scientists often take shortcuts in scientific reasoning based on intuition
     d.   the expectation of the experimenter can contribute to the reasoning observed on problem solving tasks
Answer: c, Reference: Chapter 16, P. 683, Difficulty: E

42. Research has shown that children think seriously about the nature of society but still do not understand political issues as young as
     a.   6 years of age
     b.   9 years of age
     c.   12 years of age
     d.   15 years of age
Answer: b, Reference: Chapter 16, P. 683, Difficulty: E

43. Research has found that a major change in children's reasoning about politics occurs about the age of
    a. 8 years
    b. 10 years
    c. 12 years
    d. 14 years
Answer: d, Reference: Chapter 16, P. 684, Difficulty: E

44. When Adelson and his colleagues asked American, British, and German adolescents how they would organize a hypothetical new society, which of the following did they find to be the most important predictor of changing views on this subject?
    a. age
    b. gender
    c. nationality
    d. social class
Answer: a, Reference: Chapter 16, P. 684, Difficulty: M

45. When Adelson and his colleagues asked adolescents to reason about law and government, they found that 15 to 16- year-olds
    a. accepted what exists as what should be
    b. considered only one aspect of a problem at a time
    c. assumed that society's current solutions are incorrect
    d. took many aspects of a problem into account and thought about what might be as well as what is
Answer: d, Reference: Chapter 16, P. 684, Difficulty: M

46. Typically 12- to 13-year-old adolescents think the best way to deal with law breaking is
    a. education
    b. rehabilitation
    c. severe punishment
    d. a combination of education and rehabilitation
Answer: c, Reference: Chapter 16, P. 685, Difficulty: M

47. Which group is most authoritarian in its views about social control (for example, crime, punishment, and retribution)?
    a. adults
    b. all are equally authoritarian
    c. young adolescents (12 to 13-year-olds, for example)
    d. middle adolescents (15 to 16-year-olds, for example)
Answer: c, Reference: Chapter 16, P. 685, Difficulty: D

48.   Young adolescents (12- to 13-year-olds) conceive of the law as
    a.   unnecessary
    b.   a way to prevent bad behavior
    c.   a set of guidelines for behavior
    d.   powerless to control people's behavior
Answer: b, Reference: Chapter 16, P. 685, Difficulty: M

49.   Which of the following is not characteristic of adolescent thinking about political processes?
    a.   it is often idealistic
    b.   it is frequently religious
    c.   it is increasingly cynical
    d.   it focuses on practical solutions
Answer: d, Reference: Chapter 16, P. 686, Difficulty: M

50.   Evidence suggests that adolescent thought on politics becomes
    a.   more rigid during adolescence
    b.   less realistic during adolescence
    c.   more cynical during adolescence
    d.   more optimistic during adolescence
Answer: c, Reference: Chapter 16, P. 686, Difficulty: M

51.   Adolescents, in reasoning about political processes
    a.   can generally see no problems with current political and legal systems
    b.   can see problems in current systems, but are not able to work out solutions
    c.   are able to suggest workable alternatives to current political and legal systems
    d.   can work out solutions to current problems but are not motivated to put them into effect
Answer: b, Reference: Chapter 16, P. 686, Difficulty: D

52.   According to Kohlberg, during adolescence the dominant mode of reasoning about moral issues is
    a.   law and order
    b.   social contract
    c.   good child morality
    d.   conventional morality
Answer: c, Reference: Chapter 16, P. 688, Difficulty: D

53.   At least some ability to engage in formal operational thought is necessary for moral reasoning at Kohlberg's Stage
    a.   1
    b.   2
    c.   4
    d.   both 3 and 4
Answer: d, Reference: Chapter 16, P. 688, Difficulty: E

54.   In Stage 4 of Kohlberg's system describing the development of moral reasoning, moral thinking is based on
        a.   principles of universal justification
        b.   appreciation of the relativity of moral values
        c.   individuals fulfilling their responsibilities to society
        d.   each person acting in his own interest and allowing others to do the same
Answer: c, Reference: Chapter 16, P. 688, Difficulty: M

55.   Recognition that existing laws may be in conflict with moral principles is characteristic of which stage of moral reasoning?
        a.   2
        b.   3
        c.   4
        d.   5
Answer: d, Reference: Chapter 16, P. 688, Difficulty: D

56.   Which of the following is true of Kohlberg's stage 5 of moral reasoning?
        a.   it involves a "political contract"
        b.   it involves universal ethical principles
        c.   it does not appear until early adulthood
        d.   it does not appear until early adolescence
Answer: c, Reference: Chapter 16, P. 688, Difficulty: M

57.   According to Kohlberg, a person who places universal moral principles above the rules of society is reasoning at Stage
        a.   3
        b.   4
        c.   5
        d.   6
Answer: d, Reference: Chapter 16, P. 688, Difficulty: M

58.   Individuals who risked their lives during World War II to help rescue Jews headed for extermination were probably motivated by ethical principles found in Kohlberg's stage
        a.   3
        b.   4
        c.   5
        d.   6
Answer: d, Reference: Chapter 16, P. 688, Difficulty: E

59.   Which has not been cited as an objection to Kohlberg's theory of moral development?
a.   moral reasoning is not reliably related to moral behavior
b.   most adolescents are not yet able to reason about hypothetical moral dilemmas
c.   it can be difficult to score interview answers to determine a person's stage of reasoning
d.   some studies have found no correspondence between cognitive development and moral reasoning

Answer: b, Reference: Chapter 16, P. 688, Difficulty: D

60.   A person's level of moral reasoning
a.   is not reliably related to behavior
b.   is completely unrelated to moral behavior
c.   accurately predicts behavior with lower levels being associated with more moral actions
d.   accurately predicts behavior, with higher levels being associated with more moral actions

Answer: a, Reference: Chapter 16, P. 691, Difficulty: D

61.   A study by Herbert Richards and his colleagues found that better classroom behavior was related to moral reasoning at which stage?
a.   2
b.   3
c.   4
d.   5

Answer: b, Reference: Chapter 16, P. 692, Difficulty: M

62.   Research on the reasoning of juvenile delinquents by Trevethan and Walker (1989) found the dominant stage of reasoning of this group to be Kohlberg's stage
a.   1
b.   2
c.   3
d.   4

Answer: b, Reference: Chapter 16, P. 692, Difficulty: M

63.   Carol Gilligan has argued that, in their moral reasoning
a.   most females are at a lower level than most males
b.   most females are at a higher level than most males
c.   females are oriented toward interpersonal relationships
d.   females are more interested than males in rules and litigation

Answer: c, Reference: Chapter 16, P. 692, Difficulty: E

64.   Carol Gilligan argued that female responses to moral dilemmas are lower on
        Kohlberg's scale than those of males because moral thinking among women is
        oriented toward
        a.   justice
        b.   altruism
        c.   independence
        d.   moral behavior
Answer: b, Reference: Chapter 16, P. 692, Difficulty: E

65.   In Carol Gilligan's view, male moral reasoning is based upon _____ and
        female moral reasoning upon _____.
        a.   logic; emotion
        b.   selfishness; altruism
        c.   biblical law; individual freedom
        d.   individual rights; a sense of responsibility for others
Answer: d, Reference: Chapter 16, P. 693, Difficulty: M

66.   Most studies show that the moral reasoning of people from preindustrial societies, as
        measured by Kohlberg's dilemmas, is
        a.   at the same level as that of people from technologically more advanced
                societies
        b.   at a lower level than that of people from technologically more advanced
                societies
        c.   at a higher level than that of people from technologically more advanced
                societies
        d.   completely different from that of people from technologically more advanced
                societies, and cannot be evaluated
Answer: b, Reference: Chapter 16, P. 694, Difficulty: E

67.   Subjects from technologically unsophisticated societies who continue to live in
        relatively small, face-to-face communities, have been found to reason up to which
        stage on Kohlberg's scheme?
        a.   1
        b.   2
        c.   3
        d.   4
Answer: c, Reference: Chapter 16, P. 694, Difficulty: M

68. Kohlberg thought that cross-cultural differences in moral reasoning could best be explained in which way?
    a. moral dilemmas are not applicable to people of other cultures
    b. people in technologically less advanced societies reason much as women do in more advanced societies
    c. only people who are brought up under a democratic political system are likely to develop higher levels of moral reasoning
    d. in some cultures, people receive less intellectual simulation and do not develop the cognitive skills which underlie higher levels of moral reasoning

Answer: d, Reference: Chapter 16, P. 694, Difficulty: M

69. The Golden Rule ("Do unto others as you would have others do unto you") corresponds to which stage in Kohlberg's system of moral reasoning?
    a. 1
    b. 2
    c. 3
    d. 4

Answer: c, Reference: Chapter 16, P. 694, Difficulty: D

70. Susan Harter (1990) has found that the self-concepts of adolescents differ from those of younger children in that adolescents
    a. include fewer core attributes
    b. have integrated a picture of themselves across a variety of contexts
    c. tailor their descriptions of themselves to correspond to the particular context in question
    d. usually describe themselves in terms of either social competence or cognitive competence

Answer: c, Reference: Chapter 16, P. 696, Difficulty: E

71. In general, research on adolescence has shown that adolescents
    a. tend to use a single description of the self
    b. usually experience an increase in self-esteem
    c. see attractiveness as less important than before
    d. become better able to resolve the contradictory selves they are in different contexts

Answer: d, Reference: Chapter 16, P. 696, Difficulty: M

72. In adolescents, high self-esteem is most associated with
    a. attractiveness
    b. peer acceptance
    c. a good personality
    d. strong religious convictions

Answer: a, Reference: Chapter 16, P. 696, Difficulty: M

73. Studies show that in the United States, self-esteem is lowest in
    a. early adulthood
    b. middle childhood
    c. early adolescence
    d. middle adolescence
Answer: c, Reference: Chapter 16, P. 697, Difficulty: M

74. According to Erikson, the fundamental task of adolescence is
    a. taking initiative
    b. developing trust
    c. identity formation
    d. becoming autonomous
Answer: c, Reference: Chapter 16, P. 697, Difficulty: M

75. According to Erikson, adolescents need to extend to the social world their feelings of
    a. trust
    b. identity
    c. intimacy
    d. autonomy
Answer: a, Reference: Chapter 16, P. 697, Difficulty: E

76. During adolescence, choosing one's own path in life establishes
    a. trust
    b. industry
    c. initiative
    d. autonomy
Answer: d, Reference: Chapter 16, P. 698, Difficulty: E

77. What percentage of males had reached a homosexual orgasm at least once in their lives according to a survey conducted by Alfred Kinsey and his colleagues in the 1950's?
    a. less than 10%
    b. about 20%
    c. over 30%
    d. over 50%
Answer: c, Reference: Chapter 16, P. 701, Box 16.2, Difficulty: M

78. According to recent surveys of adolescent sexual behavior
    a. adolescents are willing to admit their homosexuality
    b. tolerance toward homosexual orientation is declining
    c. more young people admit they are homosexuals than admit they had engaged in homosexual activity
    d. more young people admit they had engaged in homosexual activity than admit being homosexuals
Answer: d, Reference: Chapter 16, P. 701, Box 16.2, Difficulty: M

79.   There is disagreement among researchers on which of the following statements
       a.   homosexual behavior may be a way for young men to learn about sex
       b.   public declaration of homosexual identity is a necessary part of assuming
             homosexual identity
       c.   homosexual identity represents consistent and enduring self-recognition of
             the meanings that sexual orientation and sexual behavior have for oneself
       d.   homosexual orientation consists of a preponderance of sexual or erotic
             feelings, thoughts, fantasies, and behaviors involving persons of the same sex.
Answer: b, Reference: Chapter 16, P. 701, Box 16.2, Difficulty: E

80.   In identity formation, which of the following is actively pursuing his or her own
       goals?
       a.   forecloser
       b.   identity diffuser
       c.   identity achiever
       d.   moratorium chooser
Answer: c, Reference: Chapter 16, P. 700, Difficulty: D

81.   James Marcia and his colleagues have given this label to adolescents who have
       adopted their parents' patterns of identity rather than forming their own.
       a.   forecloser
       b.   identity diffuser
       c.   identity achiever
       d.   moratorium chooser
Answer: a, Reference: Chapter 16, P. 700, Difficulty: D

82.   James Marcia labeled the middle of an identity crisis the
       a.   foreclosing
       b.   moratorium
       c.   identity diffusion
       d.   identity achievement
Answer: b, Reference: Chapter 16, P. 700, Difficulty: M

83.   According to James Marcia, adolescents who have tried a variety of identities
       without being able to make a commitment to any would be classified as
       a.   foreclosure
       b.   moratorium
       c.   identity diffusion
       d.   identity achievement
Answer: c, Reference: Chapter 16, P. 700, Difficulty: M

84.   The proportion of adolescents categorized as identity achievers
      a.   increases steadily during the high school years
      b.   stays the same in young people 15 years and older
      c.   decreases sharply among college-age young people
      d.   does not increase in adolescence but increases sharply among college age people
Answer: a, Reference: Chapter 16, P. 703, Difficulty: D

85.   In the Freudian view, during adolescence, the conflicts of earlier developmental periods are
      a.   repressed
      b.   recognized
      c.   recapitulated
      d.   succumbed to
Answer: c, Reference: Chapter 16, P. 704, Difficulty: D

86.   According to Freud, one of the most important developmental tasks an adolescent faces is to learn to love
      a.   their same-sex friends
      b.   people in their families
      c.   people outside the family
      d.   their opposite-sex parents
Answer: c, Reference: Chapter 16, P. 704, Difficulty: E

87.   Adolescence is a time of special danger for personality development, according to
      a.   Jean Piaget
      b.   Anna Freud
      c.   Albert Bandura
      d.   Lawrence Kohlberg
Answer: b, Reference: Chapter 16, P. 705, Difficulty: M

88.   Freudian psychologists believe that identity formation during adolescence
      a.   follows the same pattern in males and females
      b.   is a "crisis" for females but an easier process for males
      c.   is different for males and females, with females more oriented toward relationships with others
      d.   is different for males and females, with females being more oriented toward mastery of the physical world
Answer: c, Reference: Chapter 16, P. 705, Difficulty: M

89.   Minority group adolescents who are in Phinney's first stage of ethnic identity are
        most likely to fall into which two of Marcia's categories of identity formation?
        a.   forecloser and identity diffuser
        b.   moratorium chooser and forecloser
        c.   identity diffuser and identity achiever
        d.   identity achiever and moratorium chooser
Answer: a, Reference: Chapter 16, P. 705, Difficulty: D

90.   Minority adolescents who are in Phinney's second stage of ethnic identity could
        often be characterized as
        a.   being a forecloser
        b.   being an identity diffuser
        c.   being an identity achiever
        d.   having an oppositional identity
Answer: d, Reference: Chapter 16, P. 708, Difficulty: E

91.   Cultures that value themselves primarily in relation to the social group adhere to
        a(n)
        a.   cultural construal of self
        b.   communal construal of self
        c.   independent construal of self
        d.   interdependent construal of self
Answer: d, Reference: Chapter 16, P. 708, Difficulty: M

92.   Americans typically emphasize the _____ in identity formation
        a.   universal self
        b.   relational self
        c.   collective self
        d.   autonomous self
Answer: c, Reference: Chapter 16, P. 709, Difficulty: D

93.   The most distinctive fact about identity formation in agricultural, hunter-gather
        societies is that it
        a.   is optional
        b.   is relatively painless
        c.   involves little personal choice
        d.   involves significant cognitive deliberation
Answer: c, Reference: Chapter 16, P. 710, Difficulty: E

94.   Which of the following is true about adolescence?
   a.   Adolescence has all the characteristics of a separate stage of development
   b.   Adolescence occurs in the females of all societies but is not universal as a
         stage among males
   c.   Adolescence does not appear in all cultures as a separate stage of development
         between childhood and adulthood
   d.   Adolescence is bounded by two bio-social-behavioral shifts, one at the end of
         middle childhood and one at the beginning of adulthood
Answer: c, Reference: Chapter 16, P. 710, Difficulty: M

95.   Adolescence was not generally recognized as a category defining children of a
       certain age regardless of sex until
   a.   the 18th century
   b.   the 20th century a mass basis
   c.   formal schooling was available for both sexes
   d.   psychologists began studying it as a phenomenon
Answer: c, Reference: Chapter 16, P. 711, Difficulty: M

96.   Late adolescence is generally thought to correspond to the grouping of individuals
       in modern society in
   a.   college
   b.   high school
   c.   elementary school
   d.   middle of junior high school
Answer: a, Reference: Chapter 16, P. 711, Difficulty: E

97.   In modern industrialized societies the transition to adulthood at the end of middle
       childhood is different from the transitions associated with earlier stages of
       development because
   a.   few social changes occur
   b.   few biological changes occur
   c.   few behavioral changes occur
   d.   biological, behavioral, and social changes are not as closely coordinated as
         they are in earlier transitions
Answer: d, Reference: Chapter 16, P. 711, Difficulty: E

98.   In modern industrial societies, the social changes associated with the transition to
       adulthood
   a.   often result in very early marriage
   b.   closely accompany changes in the biological and behavioral domains
   c.   are often put off and temporarily replaced with simulated adult activities
   d.   lead young people to take responsibility for themselves at earlier ages than is
         typical in preindustrial societies
Answer: c, Reference: Chapter 16, P. 712, Difficulty: M

99.   If young people's compulsory education increases further, a likely result will be
        a.   a decrease in the length of adolescence
        b.   an increase in the length of adolescence
        c.   the disappearance of adolescence as a stage
        d.   changes in the behavioral but not the social aspects of adolescence
Answer: b, Reference: Chapter 16, P. 712, Difficulty: M

Essay Questions

1.   Describe the five basic characteristics, suggested by Daniel Keating, that distinguish
        adolescent thinking from thought during middle childhood. How do these compare
        to Piaget's ideas?

2.   Explain how formal operational thought differs from the concrete operational
        thought of middle childhood. Describe how a child at each level might respond to
        one of the Piagetian tasks.

3.   In what ways might formal operations be used in everyday problem solving? What
        differences occur between "laboratory" formal operations and "everyday" formal
        operations?

4.   In normal subjects, to what extent can formal operational thought be said to be
        universal? What was Piaget's position on this question? Explain.

5.   Describe cross-cultural evidence addressing the universality of the formal operations
        stage. Explain its significance.

6.   What factors influence sex differences in the use of formal operations?

7.   What is an information processing perspective? Explain how it differs from the
        Piagetian analysis of adolescent cognition?

8.   Discuss how changes in the structure and use of language contribute to an
        adolescent's ability to solve problems.

9.   Micronesian navigators have developed a system for sailing long distances without
        compasses or other instruments. How are these navigation skills related to formal
        operational thought? Explain.

10.   How do thoughts about society in 12-year-olds differ from those of 16-year-olds?

11.   What does the development of idealism have to do with adolescence? Explain.

12.   Describe the characteristics of moral reasoning that begin to appear during adolescence.

13.   Identify the final stage (stage 6) of Kohlberg's system of moral reasoning. What ideas characterize this stage? Give an example of behavior based on Kohlberg's stage 6 reasoning.

14.   What kinds of changes occur in an adolescent's reasoning about politics and social control? What are typical adolescent views of an ideal society? Explain.

15.   How does the moral reasoning of adolescents differ from that of younger children? What forms of cognitive development are thought to underlie this development in moral reasoning? Explain.

16.   List and describe the six stages of Kohlberg's moral reasoning theory and describe the characteristics each stage. Which of Kohlberg's stages are particularly associated with adolescence? Explain.

17.   To what extent do studies show sex differences in moral reasoning? How does Carol Gilligan interpret the differences that might occur?

18.   Carol Gilligan has been highly critical of Kohlberg's description of sex differences in the development of moral reasoning. Describe the focus of this criticism.

19.   Explain the relationship between formal operational thinking and moral judgment according to Kohlberg.

20.   Is there cultural variation in moral reasoning? Explain and cite examples.

21.   What are the effects of cultural differences on moral reasoning, as measured by Kohlberg's criteria? Explain.

22.   According to Erikson, how do adolescents rework previous developmental crises involving trust, autonomy, initiative, and industry? What is the central developmental crisis of adolescence?

23.   How have studies by James Marcia and others illuminated the processes of identity formation during adolescence? Describe Marcia's four identity statuses and discuss their relation to age and family interaction.

24.   How do gender and culture affect an adolescent's path to identity formation?

25. Describe the evidence for and against defining adolescence as a separate stage of development before adulthood.

26. What social and historical factors led to adolescence appearing as a distinct period of development in modern, industrialized societies?

27. In what way is adolescence, as a stage of development, different from the stages that precede it?

28. A number of theorists (e.g., Freud and Erikson) believe there are sex differences in forming an identity. Address recent research findings in this area. Explain.

29. Describe the special problems encountered by minority youth in identity formation as discussed by Spencer and Markstrom-Adams (1990).

30. Explain the difference in cultures that adhere to an independent construal of self compared to those that adhere to an interdependent construal of self.

31. Argue either for or against the universality of adolescence as a stage of development. Cite evidence to support your views.

32. Discuss the development of self-esteem over the course of adolescence. Cite evidence.

33. Describe the central tasks of the adolescent period. Explain.

34. Describe James Marcia's views on identity formation.

35. Describe the bio-social-behavior shift that occurs during adolescence. Be sure to address both biological maturation and social changes.

36. Jon and Liz Jones report that their 15-year-old son, Jason, has become involved in an authoritarian religious cult. Having previously been quite close to his parents, Jason became estranged from them after their marital problems led to a six-month separation. Jon and Liz are concerned about Jason's latest interest, and don't understand what might account for his uncharacteristic behavior. What explanation and/or advice might you give them that would help them understand his behavior?